THE MASS: A LITURGICAL COMMENTARY

Volume Two

THE MASS
A LITURGICAL COMMENTARY

by
A. CROEGAERT
Canon of Malines
Formerly Professor of Liturgy at
the Grand Séminaire of Malines

Vol. II

THE MASS OF THE FAITHFUL

THE NEWMAN PRESS
WESTMINSTER, MARYLAND

This abridged translation of Les Rites et les Prières du saint Sacrifice de la Messe: II—La Messe des Fidèles (*H. Dessain, Malines*) *was made by*

J. HOLLAND SMITH

NIHIL OBSTAT: ANDREAS MOORE, L.C.L.
CENSOR DEPVTATVS
IMPRIMATVR: E. MORROGH BERNARD
VICARIVS GENERALIS
WESTMONASTERII: DIE XII DECEMBRIS MCMLVIII

English translation © Burns Oates & Washbourne Ltd. 1959

Printed in Great Britain

CONTENTS

Chap.		Page
1.	The Ordering of the Jewish Pasch	1
2.	The Eucharistic Liturgy of the Last Supper . . .	9
3.	The Eucharistic Sacrifice of the Mass	21
4.	Who offers the Holy Sacrifice of the Mass? . . .	29
	I. The principal offerer of the sacrifice is Christ, who offers through the ministry of priests.	
5.	Who offers the Holy Sacrifice of the Mass? . . .	39
	II. The Universal Church, the mystical body of Christ, is, with Christ, the principal offerer of each and every Mass celebrated throughout the world. She offers it through the ministry of her priests.	
6.	Who offers the Holy Sacrifice of the Mass? . . .	51
	III. In a subordinate manner, the ministers.	
	Additional note: The recruitment and systematic training of acolytes	54
7.	Who offers the Holy Sacrifice of the Mass? . . .	56
	IV. In a subordinate manner, the faithful present (*circumstantes*) and those who give the Mass offerings.	
8.	What is the Victim offered in the Sacrifice of the Mass?	65
9.	Preparation for the Eucharistic Sacrifice: Processional offering by the Faithful accompanied by the Offertory Chant (Roman elements)	72
	Preparation: The deacon (the servant, server) spreads the cloth (the corporal)	72
	Dominus vobiscum. Oremus	73
	The offertory procession	74
	The offertory chant (*Offertorium*)	79
10.	Eucharistic Bread and Wine—Church Plate: Chalices and Patens	84
	Eucharistic bread	84
	Eucharistic Wine	86
	Patens	86
	Chalices	89

v

Contents

Chap.	Page
11. PREPARATION FOR THE EUCHARISTIC SACRIFICE: THE OFFERTORY PRAYERS AND CEREMONIES (Gallican elements)	91
The offering of bread	92
The offering of wine	95
Preparation: The mixing of water and wine	95
The offering of the chalice	100
The personal oblation of the priest, ministers and faithful	102
The invocation of the sanctifying Spirit (*Epiclesis*)	102
The washing of hands	104
The prayer of oblation to the Holy Trinity	106
The true meaning of the offertory	110
12. INCENSE AT THE OFFERTORY	114
The use of incense in Jewish and Roman worship	114
The beginnings of the use of incense in the liturgy of the Mass	116
The present ceremonies of censing at the offertory	117
13. THE PRAYERS OF OBLATION: THE SECRETS (Roman)	123
Orate fratres (Gallican)	123
The secret	125
14. EUCHARISTIC THANKSGIVING: ITS ORIGINS AND SOME EARLY EXAMPLES	130
Jewish and Christian prayer in general	131
The Jewish sources of the eucharistic thanksgiving	133
The eucharistic thanksgiving: some early examples	139
The "Didache"	139
The First Epistle of St Clement of Rome to the Corinthians	142
Pliny's letter to the Emperor Trajan	145
St Justin Martyr	146
The "Traditio Apostolica" of St Hippolytus	148
The Anaphora of Der Balyzeh	151
The Strasburg Papyrus	153
The Anaphora of Serapion	154
The Apostolic Constitutions	158
The Louvain Papyrus	160
Conclusion	161
15. THE PREFACE: THE PROLOGUE TO THE EUCHARISTIC THANKSGIVING	163
Name and character of the preface	163
The preface as The beginning of the canon	164
Divisions of the preface	165
The decoration of the text of the preface in manuscripts and Missals	173

Chap.	*Page*
The preface, model for the formularies of the sacraments and sacramentals	174
16. THE SERAPHIC HYMN: THE "SANCTUS"	176
The *Sanctus* in the setting of the eucharistic thanksgiving	177
The chant and ritual attitude	179
Associated ceremonies	181
The *Vere Sanctus*: the transition between the *Sanctus* and the narrative of the institution of the Eucharist, *Qui pridie*	182
Conclusions	182
17. THE CANON	184
The names and limits of the canon	184
The nature, character and general plan of the canon	186
The origins of the text of the Roman canon	187
First traces of a Latin canon in Rome	189
The unity of the Roman canon	191
The literary peculiarities of the canon	193
The silent recitation of the canon	194
18. FROM THE BEGINNING OF THE CANON TO THE CONSECRATION	197
The *Te igitur* with the commemoration of the universal Church, the Pope, the Bishop (the prince), and of all the bishops	197
Decoration at the beginning of the canon	203
The *Memento* of named living persons and the faithful present	204
Union with the victorious members to gain their intercession	206
Hanc igitur	212
Quam oblationem: the preconsecratory epiclesis	214
19. THE CONSECRATION AND ELEVATION	216
The consecration	216
The mystery of the consecration	218
The consecration occupies a central place in the liturgical economy of the Mass	219
The elevation	220
Related ceremonies	223
Conclusion	223
20. AT THE HEART OF THE EUCHARISTIC SACRIFICE: THE ANAMNESIS	225
The Lord's command: "Do this in commemoration of me"	225
The anamnesis: the Church's response to Christ's command	226
The text	227
We offer: "*Offerimus*"	232
21. THE CANON FROM THE ANAMNESIS TO THE FINAL DOXOLOGY	234
The prayers for the acceptance of the eucharistic sacrifice:	234

Chap.	Page
Supra quae and *Supplices*	234
"*Supra quae*"	234
"*Supplices*"	236
Additional note: The epiclesis	238
The diptych *Memento etiam* of the dead	241
The diptych *Nobis quoque peccatoribus*	242
The end of the canon	246
"*Per quem . . . praestas nobis*"	246
The doxology: *Per ipsum, et cum ipso, et in ipso* . . .	247
Ceremonies	248
"*Per omnia saecula saeculorum. Amen*"	250
22. THE LORD'S PRAYER	251
The invitatory: why we dare say the Lord's Prayer . .	251
The Lord's Prayer	252
The Lord's Prayer in the Mass	252
Commentary	254
Why the Lord's Prayer is sung or said aloud at Mass .	256
The embolism upon the seventh petition: *Libera nos quaesumus, Domine*	257
Additional note: The nuptial blessing and episcopal blessings	259
23. PREPARATION FOR HOLY COMMUNION	260
From the lesser elevation to the kiss of peace . . .	260
The fraction and commixture in the ceremonial of Pontifical Mass	261
The fraction and commixture today	263
The peace	265
The immediate preparation: the prayers before communion	267
Commentary	267
24. HOLY COMMUNION	271
The place of communion in the economy of sacrifice: the eating of the divine Victim	271
The place of communion in the economy of the eucharistic sacrifice and its effects in us	273
The deep significance of Jesus Christ's "first solemn communion" at the Last Supper	273
Holy communion at the papal Mass according to *Ordo Romanus I*	275
The communion of the clergy	275
The communion of the faithful	275
The communion today	276
The priest's communion	276
The communion of the congregation of the faithful . .	277

Contents

Chap.	Page
The communion chant (*Communio*)	280
The ablutions	282
25. THANKSGIVING AFTER COMMUNION: THE POSTCOMMUNION	285
Synthesis	292
26. CONCLUDING PRAYERS AND CEREMONIES	293
The prayer over the people (*Oratio super populum*)	293
The dismissal of the faithful	295
The blessing	296
The last Gospel	298
The prayers after Mass	299
The thanksgiving: *Trium puerorum*	299
Private thanksgiving: An additional note	300
INDEX	302

Letter sent to the author on behalf of Pius XII in acknowledgement of the French edition of this book

SEGRETERIA DI STATO
DI SUA SANTITA.
No. 200386.

Dal Vaticano,
29 April, 1949.

Dear Canon Croegaert,

The Holy Father was warmly appreciative of your kind offering of the second edition of your book, *Les Rites et Prières du Saint Sacrifice de la Messe*.

You are aware of His Holiness's concern for the propagation among the faithful of an ever-deeper knowledge of the sacred liturgy—a concern manifested quite recently once more in his Encyclical *Mediator Dei*—and there is no need for me to tell you that all who, like you, work zealously and skilfully to promote this liturgical apostolate can be assured of his good wishes and encouragement.

Your book will certainly furnish valuable help to priests engaged in the sacred ministry, whose duty it is to instruct the faithful in these matters. It will make their task easier by saving them the need to consult a large number of books the substance of which you have collected together for their use.

This is to inform you that the Father of all the faithful earnestly hopes that these pages may prove very fruitful for a great number of souls. With his fatherly gratitude, and invoking upon you an abundance of divine grace, he sends you the Apostolic Blessing.

Believe me,
Yours devotedly in our Lord,
(Signed) J. B. MONTINI (*Subst.*).

I
THE ORDERING OF THE JEWISH PASCH

The institution and celebration of the first Pasch in Egypt

FROM the beginning of the nineteenth dynasty in Egypt onwards, the children of Israel groaned under the yoke of slavery. But the hour of their deliverance was at hand: Jahweh said to Moses and Aaron, " For you this month is to lead in all the months, to be the first month in the year " (Exodus 12. 1). This month, which was called *abib* (that is " ears " of corn) was later called *Nisan*.[1] A new era was about to begin for the chosen people. For Israel, Nisan signified the end of the captivity, the exodus from Egypt, the covenant made with Jahweh and the victorious march to the promised land.

The regulations for the celebration of the Pasch were ordained in detail to Moses and Aaron by Jahweh:

> Make this proclamation to the whole assembly of Israel: On the tenth day of this month, each family, each household, is to choose out a yearling for its own use. . . . It must be a male yearling lamb or a male yearling kid, that you choose, with no blemish on it. These victims must be kept ready till the fourteenth day of the month, and on the evening of that day the whole people of Israel must immolate. They must take some of the blood, and smear it on the doorway, jambs and lintel alike, of the house in which the lamb is being eaten. Their meat that night must be roasted over the fire, their bread unleavened; wild herbs must be all their seasoning . . . all must be consumed, so that nothing remains till next day; whatever is left over, you must put in the fire and burn it. And this is to be the manner of your eating it: your loins must be girt, your feet ready shod, and every man's staff in his hand;

---

[1] The latter term was current after the Babylonian captivity and is derived from *Nisannu*, the name given to the first month by the Babylonians and Assyrians.

all must be done in haste. It is the night of the Pasch, the Lord's passing by; the night on which I will pass through the land of Egypt and smite every first-born thing in the land of Egypt, man and beast alike; so I will give sentence on all the powers of Egypt, I, the Lord.

The blood on the houses that shelter you will be your badge; at the sight of the blood, I will pass you by, and there shall be no scourge of calamity for you when I smite the land of Egypt.

You are to observe this day as a memorial of the past, a day when you keep holiday in the Lord's honour, generation after generation; a rite never to be abrogated. (See Exod. 12. 1-14.)

Exodus goes on to relate that Moses " called the elders of Israel together " and passed on the Lord's command for the keeping of the paschal feast, both that year and " for ever ", telling them, " if your children ask, What is the meaning of this rite? then you shall tell them, This is the victim that marked the Lord's passing-by, when he passed by the houses of the Israelites in Egypt, smiting only the Egyptians, and leaving our houses exempt " (Exod. 12. 21 ff.).

Later, in additional prescriptions, the Lord said to Moses and Aaron: " No alien is to partake (of the Pasch). . . . All of it must be eaten under the same roof; you must not take any of the victim's flesh elsewhere, or break it up into joints " (Exod. 12. 43-6).[1]

In accordance with divine command, unleavened bread was used exclusively from the evening of the 14th Nisan until 21st Nisan and all leaven was removed from dwellings. This feature was so characteristic, that this feast came to be known as " the feast of unleavened bread ".[2]

Deuteronomy records another important rule concerning the sacrificing of the paschal lamb: " This paschal victim is not to be immolated in a city here, a city there . . . no, the Lord thy God will choose out one place to be the sanctuary of his name [that is, the temple area], and there thou wilt immolate the paschal victim

---

[1] Literally, " no bone of it shall be broken "; cf. John 19. 36.
[2] See e.g. Exod. 23. 15; 34. 18; Lev. 23. 6; Deut. 16. 16; 2 Par. 8. 13; 30. 13, 21; 35. 17; 1 Esdras 6. 22 and compare Luke 22. 1; 22. 7; Acts 13. 3; 20. 6; Mark 14. 1; Matt. 26. 17 and Mark 14. 12.

..." (Deut. 16. 5–6). The celebration of the paschal feast therefore came to be preceded by a pilgrimage to Jerusalem, the " going up " to the temple.

These commandments were faithfully observed by the whole race throughout the succeeding centuries: every year, in the month of Nisan, when the full moon shone in the heavens, the children of Israel celebrated the Pasch. The varying circumstances under which it was celebrated—especially in the desert, and during the exile—brought about certain changes, especially in the ceremonial accompanying it, but it remained the most typical of the Jewish feasts.

The ceremonies and prayers of the paschal celebration in the time of Christ

At the centre from which the Jews were dispersed throughout the world, stood the temple on mount Zion, the true sanctuary, the only place in the world at which sacrifice could be offered, which was at once the pledge of Jahweh's covenant with his chosen people and the symbol of the unity of the nation. As the Pasch approached, caravans from all parts of the world went up to the holy city and numberless crowds invaded its walls. Families, or groups of ten to twenty persons, subscribed for the communal purchase of a victim as the sacrificial lamb. So, too, Jesus, accompanied by the Twelve, went up to the city to celebrate that paschal meal in the course of which he instituted the holy Eucharist; whether on the 14th Nisan, the eve of the Pasch, as the Synoptic authors suggest or on the previous day, the 13th, in accordance with the fourth Gospel is immaterial: it is the relation between the Jewish Pasch and the supper of the Eucharist which must not be overlooked. The synoptic Gospels leave no doubt in this respect: *Ubi vis paremus tibi manducare pascha?*[1]

Furthermore, St Luke recalls that there was a duty which had to be fulfilled: " Then the day of unleavened bread came; on this day the paschal victim must be killed; and Jesus sent Peter and John . . ." (22. 7 f.). On the evening or night of the 13th Nisan the father of the family, lamp or torch in hand, looked into every corner and recess in the house to seek out every trace of leaven and remove it.

---

[1] Matt. 26. 17; Mark 14. 12; Luke 22. 8. And see the replies: Mark 14. 12–17; Matt. 26. 18–20.

This old leaven was burned at midnight. The afternoon of the 14th Nisan, from the time of the killing of the lambs till the paschal feast, was kept as a strict fast.

The ceremony of the immolation of the paschal lambs was performed at the temple after the evening sacrifice and before the offering of incense and lighting of the lamps. The priests ushered in the feast by sounding trumpets, the levites sang the Hallel Psalms (113–18) and the lambs were led into the temple. Then the priests formed two ranks, the one holding golden bowls, the other, bowls of silver. Each Israelite killed his own lamb, and the priests caught the blood in the bowls, which they passed from hand to hand down the ranks, the last priest pouring the blood as an offering on the altar. The lamb was flayed and the fat, kidneys etc., set apart to be burned on the altar. While the smoke was rising, the carcase was wrapped in the skin and given back to the offerer for the paschal meal. No one left the temple area until the ceremonies were completed.

In the course of time, the very simple ritual of the primitive Pasch had evolved into a splendid ceremony accompanied by moving and symbolic chants and prayers.[1]

The feast began when the first three stars appeared in the evening. The Jews no longer stood: under the influence of Roman surroundings they had adopted habits proper to free men—they lay on long couches, leaning their left arms on cushions. Thus, St Matthew records, Jesus lay.[2]

The paschal meal began with the *Kiddush*, the singing of praises, with which was associated the first cup, the Kiddush cup. The father of the family, holding the first ritual cup, intoned the thanksgiving: "Blessed be thou, Jahweh, our God, who hast created the fruit of the vine". There then followed the blessing in honour of the feast, which tells of God's choosing the Jewish race and bringing it up out of Egypt. The cup was passed from hand to hand and each of the guests drank from it in turn. This cup is doubtless that referred to by St Luke before his account of the consecration of the bread and chalice (the third cup): "And he said to them, I

---

[1] The texts quoted below are those used until modern times by the Jews of Germany. See Dom F. J. Moreau, *Les liturgies eucharistiques* Appendice IV: "Parties anciennes de la Pâque"; pp. 222–31 (Vromant, Brussels).

[2] Matt. 26. 20 (*discumbebat*); compare Luke 22. 14 (*discubuit*).

have longed and longed to share this paschal meal with you before my passion; I tell you, I shall not eat it again, till it finds its fulfilment in the kingdom of God. And he took a cup and blessed it, and said, Take this and share it among you; I tell you I shall not drink of the fruit of the vine again, till the kingdom of God has come" (Luke 22. 15-18). It is obvious that this does not relate to the eucharistic cup, for St Luke continues his account with the consecration of bread (v. 19) and wine (v. 20). All present then washed their hands. Jesus' washing of the disciples' feet is probably linked with this (or the following) washing of hands.

After the washings, the table was placed in the middle of the guests. It was laden with various foods: next to the paschal lamb, lay bitter herbs, unleavened bread and *charoseth*, a symbolic food composed of various fruits such as apples, figs and lemons, prepared in vinegar, seasoned with cinnamon and other spices, and of the shape and colour of brick, recalling the clay moulded under the rods of the overseers in the land of the Pharaohs.

The head of the family dipped the bitter herbs into the *charoseth*, meanwhile giving thanks to God for the fruits of the earth: "Blessed be thou, Jahweh, our God, ruler of the world, who hast created the fruits of the earth". Then he partook of it himself and gave a fragment to each person present.

The second cup—called the cup of the Hagadah ("narrative")—was then poured. The youngest of those present then asked the meaning of the paschal ceremonies and the father explained them as symbolic of Israel's slavery in Egypt and the mercy of God in the exodus, the whole story of the exodus being related by one of those present. This part of the ceremonies ended with the singing of the first part of the *Hallel* (Ps. 113-17; Vulgate 112-16) and the drinking of the second cup.

They then washed their hands again, saying, "Praised be thou, Jahweh, our God, ruler of the world, who hast sanctified us by thy commandments and hast commanded us to wash our hands." The various dishes were then served.

The father of the family now took up the three unleavened loaves and said, "Praised be thou, Jahweh, our God, ruler of the world, who hast caused bread to originate from the earth. Praised be thou, Jahweh, our God, ruler of the world, who hast sanctified us by thy commandments and hast bidden us to eat unleavened bread." In memory of the bread of sorrow eaten in Egypt, the fragments were covered with bitter herbs and dipped in the *charoseth*. It was perhaps at this moment that Jesus gave the " dipped bread " to Judas (John 13. 25-6, *intinctum panem*).

After this, there followed the paschal meal properly so called: the eating of the paschal lamb (which had been roasted on a spit) together with a thanksgiving and the third cup, the " cup of blessing ". In the course of this meal, Jesus instituted the holy Eucharist. Indeed, it was " while they were at table ",[1] that Jesus took bread, gave thanks, blessed and broke it and gave it to his disciples saying, " Take, all of you, and eat of this, for this is my body ", and having taken a cup, and given thanks, he blessed it and gave it to them saying, " Take, all of you, and drink of this, for this is my blood (the blood), of the new covenant, shed for many for the remission of sins."

It was probably this third ritual cup which our Lord consecrated. This cup was usually drunk at the end of the paschal meal and was followed by the saying of the (great) *Hallel*: it was therefore called " the cup of blessing," which is precisely the name given by St Paul to the eucharistic chalice (*calix benedictionis*—I Cor. 10. 16). Moreover, speaking of the consecration of the chalice, St Luke (22. 14) and St Paul (I Cor. 11. 25) say clearly *postquam caenavit* . . . " When supper was ended. . . ." Furthermore, St Matthew (26. 30) and St Mark (14. 26) note that after the institution of the Eucharist, a hymn—the great *Hallel*—was sung. This ended with the fourth cup, which cannot therefore have been that of the Eucharist.

The singing of the *Hallel* was a solemn act of thanksgiving. Its beginning (Ps. 113 and 114. 1-8) had already been sung. This continuation comprised Psalms 115-17 (Vulgate 113. 9—*Non nobis, Domine*—to Ps. 116) followed by the Great *Hallel*, Psalm 136 (Vulgate 135), a long, lyrical prayer of thanksgiving and a hymn of praise to God for all that he did for Israel on the night of the " passing-over ". Lastly, the fourth cup, the *Hallel*, was poured out and passed from hand to hand and a final thanksgiving betokened the end of the meal. At this point, Christ and his Apostles left the upper room: *et hymno dicto* (Hallel) *exierunt* (Matt. 26. 30; Mark 14. 26).

[1] Matt. 26. 21; cf. 26. 26 and Mark 14. 18, 22.

The paschal lamb is the antitype of Christ, who has been slain

This most imposing ceremony, which reminded the children of Israel of the wonders of their past deliverance, at the same time foretold a yet more wonderful deliverance, of which the first was but a prefiguration. As St Paul said, *Haec autem omnia in figura contingebant illis.* Through the paschal celebration shines the " passing " of the coming Messias who was to deliver his people not from earthly servitude or tyranny, but from the much more powerful slavery of sin and hell. The lamb slain with bloodshed in the temple and ritually eaten prefigured the true paschal Lamb—*Pascha nostrum immolatus est Christus:* Christ, our paschal victim, has been sacrificed for us[1]—who, through his sacrifice with bloodshed on the cross was to deliver the world, whose flesh would be true food and blood true drink, used at the eucharistic paschal meal of the new covenant. As priest and victim, Christ effected the offering of himself voluntarily:

> A victim? Yet he himself bows to the stroke,
> No word comes from him.
> Sheep led away to the slaughter-house,
> Lamb that stands dumb while it is shorn;
> No word from him.

The paschal Lamb sacrificed on the cross has delivered the world by his sacrifice and the liturgy bears witness to this deliverance. The liturgy of Good Friday is a synthesis, showing at once the harmonies and contrasts between the prefigurative Pasch and the reality. The lesson (Exod. 12. 1–11) recalls the celebration of the prefigurative rites, the Gospel, from St John, gives this significant evidence, " But when they [the soldiers] came to Jesus, and found him already dead, they did not break his legs. . . . This was so ordained to fulfil what is written, You shall not break a single bone of his ".[2] By St John's reckoning, the Lamb of God was sacrificed at the same time as the blood of the prefigurative lambs were reddening the altar in the temple with their blood. The same lesson is emphasized in the reproaches and the hymn at the veneration of the Cross.

The *Exsultet*, the *praeconium* or praise of the paschal candle on

---
[1] I Cor. 5. 7.
[2] John 19. 33, 36; see Exod. 12. 46; Numbers 9. 12.

Easter night declares, *Haec sunt enim festa paschalia, in quibus verus ille Agnus occiditur, cuius sanguine postes fidelium consecrantur:* "This is the paschal feast wherein is slain the true Lamb whose blood hallows the doorposts of the faithful."

On Easter Day and throughout the paschal season, the Church repeats St Paul's words *Pascha nostrum immolatus est Christus* in the Preface, as well as in the Alleluia and Communion verses on Easter Day; and the same truth is stressed in the Easter Sequence and the Blessing of a Lamb (*Benedictio Agni*) in the Ritual.[1]

The very paschal Lamb who was once offered with bloodshed on the cross is again offered and consumed every day, under the eucharistic accidents in the sacrifice of the Mass, which (with holy Communion, which is linked with it) comprises a daily celebration of the Pasch.

Through his priesthood, in which they share, the priests of the new covenant can daily re-offer the sacrifice of the Mass to the Father.

The prefigurative characteristics of the paschal lamb are stressed in the services of *Corpus Christi*, especially in the hymn at Matins and the sequence in the Mass:

In hac mensa novi regis,	Within our new King's banquet-hall
Novum Pascha novae legis	They meet to keep the festival
Phase vetus terminat.	That closed the ancient paschal rite:
Vetustatem novitas,	The old is by the new replaced;
Umbram fugat veritas	The substance hath the shadow chased;
Noctem lux eliminat.	And rising day dispels the night.

[1] *Rit. Rom.*, Tit. IX, cap. 3, 11.

2

THE EUCHARISTIC LITURGY OF THE LAST SUPPER

ON the first day of unleavened bread, Jesus sent Peter and John, the two most prominent Apostles, to prepare the Pasch in a large, well-furnished room (*caenaculum grande*, St Mark; *magnum*, St Luke; *stratum*, Mark and Luke); and knowing that "the time had come for his passage from this world to the Father" (John 13. 1), he said, "I have longed and longed to share this paschal meal with you before my passion" (Luke 22. 15).

Thus, Christ celebrated the supper of the Eucharist within the framework of the paschal liturgy, at the very heart of the most solemn of the Jewish feasts.

Decree of the Council of Trent

At its twenty-second session, the Council of Trent thus defined the eucharistic rite instituted at the Last Supper by Christ, the mediator of the new covenant, the eternal high priest of the order of Melchisedech:

> Thus therefore, although our God and Lord was to offer himself once to God his Father by death on the altar of the cross, that eternal redemption might be effected, yet, because his priesthood was not extinguished by death (Hebrews 7. 24), at the Last Supper, on the very night of his betrayal, in order that he might leave his beloved bride the Church, as human nature requires, a visible sacrifice which would properly represent the bloody sacrifice once made on the cross, that its memorial might remain until the end of time (I Cor. 11. 24 ff.) and that its saving power might be applied for the remission of those sins which we commit daily, declaring himself to be a priest for ever after the order of Melchisedech (Ps. 109. 4), he offered his body and blood to God his Father under the species of bread and wine (*sub speciebus pani et vini*) and gave them

under these same appearances (*symbolis*) to the Apostles, whom he then made priests of the new covenant and commanded them and their successors in the priesthood (*in sacerdotio successoribus*) to offer them in these words: Do this for a commemoration of me (Luke 22. 19; I Cor. 11. 24), and so the Catholic Church has always understood and taught (canon 2).

For having celebrated the ancient Pasch, which the multitude of the children of Israel immolated in commemoration of the exodus from Egypt (Exod. 12 and 13), he instituted the new Pasch in his own person, which was to be immolated under visible signs (*sub signis visibilibus*) by the Church through the priests (*ab Ecclesia per sacerdotes*) in memory of his passing from this world to the Father when, through pouring forth his blood, he redeemed and delivered us from the power of darkness and transferred us to his kingdom (Col. 1. 13).[1]

Christ, the high priest in the line of Melchisedech: (a) *The evidence of Scripture*

" The Lord hath sworn an oath there is no retracting, Thou art a priest for ever in the line of Melchisedech " (Ps. 109. 4). In these words, Jahweh guarantees the priesthood of Christ, the future messianic king. Although the levitical priesthood and Davidic kingship were normally separate in Israel, the coming Christ would be—as was Melchisedech—both king and priest.

The Epistle to the Hebrews hails the fulfilment in Christ of this prophecy, in addition to the text already quoted (7. 21), by bestowing on him at least five times the title priest ($\iota\epsilon\rho\epsilon\upsilon\varsigma$) or high-priest ($\alpha\rho\chi\iota\epsilon\rho\epsilon\upsilon\varsigma$) " in the line of Melchisedech ".[2] The exclusive privilege of Aaron, whose descendants were normally invested with the priesthood, is revoked. It is a change of priesthood rather than of persons: Aaron's line has given way to that of Melchisedech.

In the framework of the liturgy of the Last Supper, Christ appeared in all the majesty of his priestly dignity: he is the real priest of the new covenant, the priest of Melchisedech's line. The Council of Trent paid honours to this last title in its definition of

[1] Sessio 22, 1. Cf. *Enchiridion Symbolorum*, Denzinger-Bannwart, 938.
[2] Heb. 5. 5–6; 5. 10; 6. 19–20; 7. 11; 7. 15–17 and 7. 21.

the institution of the eucharistic rite: " declaring himself to be a priest for ever after the order of Melchisedech, he offered his body and blood to God his Father under the species of bread and wine."

(b) *Why is Christ called a " high priest in the line of Melchisedech"?*

1. *Because of the meaning of the name.* Melchisedech was the king of Salem, and his name means " king of justice " (Hebrew: *melki-sedek*). King of Salem means " king of peace ". Christ is the true king of justice and peace: through his death, he has brought us righteousness and in his blood he has confirmed us in his peace. " It was God's good pleasure . . . through him to win back all things, whether on earth or in heaven, into union with himself, making peace with him through his blood, shed on the cross" (Col. 1. 20). Christ, by beginning the reign of justice and peace through the exercise of his priestly kingship, is the true Melchisedech, King of Justice, whose antitype bore the title King of Peace.

2. *Because of the silence of Scripture as to his origins.* Scripture, which is always so careful to set out the genealogies of important historical figures, is silent with regard to the extraction and death of Melchisedech: there is " no name of father or mother, no pedigree, no date of birth or of death " (Heb. 7. 3). Bodily descent—essential to future levitical priests—is unimportant to him: his title to priesthood is personal and does not depend upon his ancestry. Christ, too, was not descended from the tribe of Levi, " Our Lord took his origin from Juda, that is certain, and Moses in speaking of this tribe, said nothing about priests " (Heb. 7. 14). In his divine nature, he has no mother; in his human nature, he is fatherless: he is a priest in a unique manner.

His priesthood is eternal because it is his " not to obey the law, with its outward observances, but in the power of an unending life " (Heb. 7. 16). Because Christ lives for ever, his priesthood is not passed on: he has no successor. He alone is the true priest of the new covenant and the priests he makes are his ministers: " That is how we ought to be regarded, as Christ's servants " (I Cor. 4. 1), working in his power and authority.

3. *Because of the pre-eminence of Melchisedech, who blessed Abraham, and the subjection of the patriarch who paid tithes to him* (cf. Heb. 7. 1-2). Melchisedech blessed him in whom all races were to be blessed and received a tenth of his spoils from him. In its common ancestor,

Abraham, the whole of the priestly tribe of Levi bowed before the priestly pre-eminence of Christ, prefigured in Melchisedech.

4. *Because of his offering of bread and wine.* Melchisedech offered bread and wine to the most high God. This point is not referred to in the Epistle to the Hebrews, but the symbol, none the less, finds full realization in the liturgy of the Last Supper. Melchisedech made an offering of bread and wine: under the same appearances, Christ offered the sacrifice of his body and blood. " Melchisedech, too, was there, the king of Salem. And he, priest as he was of the most high God, brought out bread and wine with him, and gave him (Abraham) this benediction " (Gen. 14. 18–9). Although the text does not explicitly speak of a religious offering, the expression " priest as he was . . . " (coming from the Vulgate *erat enim sacerdos Dei* . . .) links this oblation with his priesthood.

In the Ambrosian liturgy of Milan, an ancient prayer from the canon on Maundy Thursday reads: " We beseech thee, O Lord, to accept with benevolence this oblation which we offer to thee for this day of fasting of the Last Supper of the Lord. On this day, our Lord Jesus Christ, thy Son, instituted the sacrificial rite of the new covenant when he changed the bread and wine that the High Priest Melchisedech offered, prefiguring the future mystery, into the sacrament of his body and blood ".[1] The prayer *Supra quae* in the modern Roman canon recalls this same prefiguring in the words . . . *et quod tibi obtulit summus sacerdos tuus Melchisedech, sanctum sacrificium, immaculatam hostiam:* " that which thy great priest Melchisedech sacrificed to thee, a holy offering, a victim without blemish."

Commentary on the Decree of the Council of Trent [2]

On the cross, Jesus Christ offered once for all the perfect sacrifice, by which he gave glory to the Holy Trinity and saved humanity. This sacrifice was unique as the Epistle to the Hebrews teaches clearly: " What he has done (made offering for sins) he has done once for all; and the offering was himself " (Heb. 7. 27; cf. 9, 26, 28; 10. 10, 14). " In accordance with this divine will we have been sanctified by an offering made once for all, the body of Jesus

---

[1] Muratori, *De rebus liturgicis dissert.*, 10; *P.L.*, 74, 944.

[2] Certain points here summarily dealt with are given lengthier treatment in the following chapters.

Christ" (Heb. 10. 10). Offering for our sins a sacrifice that is never repeated, he sits for ever at the right hand of God (cf. 10. 12).

The sacrifice is a sacrifice with the shedding of blood: it is neither ceremony, sign nor symbol. Christ the high priest offered his physical body in its natural state nailed to the cross and his scarlet blood flowing down his limbs, offered them for love and to the glory of the Father.

It was, too, a voluntary sacrifice, freely made. *Oblatus est quia ipse voluit* (Isaias 53. 7). He delivered himself up to his passion voluntarily: "Father . . . if it pleases thee, take away this chalice from before me; only as thy will is, not as mine is" (Luke 22. 42). Before Pilate, Christ could proclaim: "Thou wouldst not have any power over me at all, if it had not been given thee from above" (John 19. 11). After all, to show yet more clearly that, with his exhausted body, his empty veins, his broken heart, it yet depended upon him whether he lived or died, that "nobody can rob him of it" but that he alone has the power to put it down or take it up again, with superhuman strength he cast to heaven his last cry, "Father, into thy hands I commend my spirit". St Thomas teaches[1] that the passion of Christ was the oblation of a sacrifice inasmuch as Christ of his own free will underwent death for love.

Finally, it was an absolute sacrifice, in that it depended on no other. The eucharistic sacrifice, the Last Supper or the Mass, on the other hand, depends on that of the cross: the Supper, because it effectively signified it by anticipation; the Mass, because it is its sacramental commemoration. Without the sacrifice of the cross in which blood was shed, there could be no eucharistic sacrifice either of the Last Supper or in the Church. The rites of the Last Supper and the Mass are real but relative sacrifices.

A visible sacrifice left to the Church. The sacrifice of the cross was isolated in time and space. Of course, the great high priest of the new covenant in it offered the homage of perfect worship to the Father, but Christ came down to institute a Church. Without Christ, the Church is inconceivable; without the Church, Christ would be incomplete. Upon this Church, there has devolved a mission of prime importance which she will fulfil until the end of time: the Church works for the Father's glory. This worship is carried out not in accordance with our personal views, but accord-

[1] *Summa. Theol.*, III, q. 48, a. 3.

ing to the pattern set by Christ himself: *per Christum*, through Christ, through the supreme, infinite and unique sacrifice of the cross, made universally and perpetually present at all times and in all places in the rite of the Eucharist.

The Church is the mystical body, the fullness of Christ, her head. As the body belongs to the head, so does the head to the body. And so, as Christ has the Church at his disposal, so also the Church has Christ in his body and blood. With Christ, she is the primary offerer of the sacrifice of the Mass.

Christ, the high priest, offers his eucharistic body and blood. In offering his body and blood to his Father under the persisting appearances of bread and wine, Christ shows himself to be a priest for ever in the line of Melchisedech. At the Supper as on the cross, Christ makes his offering personally, while at Mass he offers through the ministry of priests.

Why our Lord instituted the sacrifice of the Mass. According to the Council's decree, Christ instituted the eucharistic sacrifice for three purposes: to show forth the sacrifice of the cross until the end of time, to perpetuate its commemoration and apply its saving power.

"*Do this as a commemoration of me.*" In this one phrase Christ brought into being both the Christian priesthood and the eucharistic sacrifice.

"Do this", that is "What I have just done, you do, in your turn"—take, give thanks, consecrate, break, give . . . in these words Christ gave priestly powers to his Apostles. When he bade them consecrate, he also gave them the ability to do so: if he had not then made them priests, what he commanded would have been impossible for them. Canon 2 of the Council (Session 22) adds: "If anyone says that by these words 'Do this as a commemoration of me' Christ did not make his Apostles priests or did not ordain them that they and other priests might offer his body and blood, let him be anathema".[1]

A priest is ordained in order that he may celebrate the sacrifice of the Mass. Sacrifice is the true ministry, the true work, of the priest.

Christ, the true Paschal Lamb, is immolated without bloodshed— eucharistically—by the Church through her priests. After celebrating the old Pasch, Christ instituted the new; the immolation of his own

---

[1] Cf. Denzinger, *op. cit.*, 949.

person under visible signs by the Church through her priests.

Se ipsum—his own person: Christ himself is the true paschal lamb of our Mass, but in a eucharistic mode. The sacrifice instituted by Christ is of the sacramental order. The Church, with Christ the primary offerer of the sacrifice of the Mass, acts through special agents, the priests who are the Church's ministers. Although a priest may celebrate Mass in physical isolation, it yet emanates primarily from the whole Church.

The institution of the eucharistic sacrifice of the new and everlasting covenant according to the Scriptures

The table on pp. 16–17 shows the four scriptural accounts of the institution of the Eucharist as they appear in the Vulgate. Comparison with the text of the Missal is thereby greatly simplified.

Commentary

(a) *The introductory phrases.* Both Eastern and Western liturgies stress the close connection between the institution of the Eucharist and the passion. The introductory phrases refer either to " the day before the passion " (*qui pridie quam pateretur*) or the " night on which Jesus was betrayed " by Judas (*in qua nocte tradebatur*) or delivered himself up to death. The first of these forms is characteristic of Roman and Western liturgies. According to Dom Morin[1] the primitive Roman form probably read " *Qui pridie quam pro nostra omniumque salute pateretur:* " Who, on the day before he suffered death for us and for all men ".

In qua nocte tradebatur: " In the night in which he was betrayed " (cf. I Cor. 11. 23) is used in Eastern and Mozarabic liturgies. When Christ instituted the rite of the Eucharist, his passion had already begun: Judas' betrayal was the beginning of Jesus' passion[2] and itself formed part of it. Christ suffered a great deal mentally because of it. Even his disciples " began to be sorrowful " (Mark 14. 19), and Jesus said to them, " The Son of Man goes on his way, as the Scripture foretells of him; but woe upon that man by whom the Son of Man is to be betrayed; better for that man if he had never been born " (Mark 14. 21). It should be noticed that the

---

[1] Dom Morin, " Une particularité inaperçue du *Qui pridie* de la Messe romaine aux environs de l'an DC " (*Rev. Bénéd.* XXVII, 1910, pp. 513–5).
[2] See Matt. 26. 21–5; Mark 14. 18–21; Luke 22. 21–3.

Matthew 26	Mark 14	Luke 22	1 Corinthians 11	Missale Romanum	Roman Missal
26. Coenantibus autem eis, accepit Jesus panem	22. Et manducantibus illis, accepit Jesus panem	19. Et accepto pane	23. Dominus Jesus in qua nocte tradebatur accepit panem	Qui pridie, quam pateretur accepit panem in sanctas ac venerabiles manus suas, et elevatis oculis in caelum ad te Deum Patrem suum omnipotentem tibi gratias agens, benedixit fregit, deditque discipulis suis dicens: Accipite et manducate ex hoc omnes, Hoc est enim corpus meum.	He, on the day before he suffered death, (a) took bread into his holy and worshipful hands, and lifting up his eyes to thee, God, his almighty Father in heaven, and giving thanks to thee, he blessed it, (b) broke it, and gave it to his disciples saying: Take, all of you, and eat of this,
et benedixit ac fregit, deditque discipulis suis, et ait: Accipite et comedite,	et benedicens fregit, et dedit eis et ait: Sumite,	gratias egit et fregit, et dedit eis dicens:	24. et gratias agens fregit, et dixit: Accipite et manducate		
hoc est corpus meum.	hoc est corpus meum.	Hoc est corpus meum, quod pro vobis datur hoc facite in meam commemorationem.	hoc est corpus meum, quod pro vobis tradetur hoc facite in meam commemorationem.		for this is my body. (c)
27. Et accipiens calicem	23. Et accepto calice	20. Similiter et calicem, postquam caenavit	25. Similiter et calicem, postquam caenavit	Simili modo postquam caenatum est, accipiens et hunc praeclarum calicem in sanctas ac venerabiles manus suas: item tibi gratias agens benedixit deditque discipulis suis	In like manner, when he had supped, taking also this goodly cup d) into his holy and worshipful hands and again giving thanks to thee he blessed it, (e) and gave it to his disciples
gratias egit et dedit illis	gratias agens dedit eis et biberunt ex illo omnes				

dicens:	24. Et ait illis:	dicens:	dicens:	dicens:	saying:
Bibite ex hoc omnes.				Accipite et bibite ex eo omnes	Take, all of you, and drinko this, (f)
28. Hic est enim sanguinis meus novi testamenti,	Hic est sanguis meus novi testamenti,	Hic est calix novum testamentum in sanguine meo,	novum testamentum est in meo sanguine,	Hic est enim calix sanguinis mei, novi et aeterni testamenti,	for this is the chalice of my blood of the new and everlasting covenant, (g)
				mysterium fidei,	a mystery of faith.
qui pro multis effundetur in remissionem peccatorum.	qui pro multis effundetur.	qui pro vobis fundetur.		qui pro vobis et pro multis effundetur in remissionem peccatorum.	It shall be shed for you and many others so that sins may be forgiven.
			hoc facite, quotiescumque bibetis in meam commemorationem.	Haec quotiescumque feceretis in meam memoriam facietis.	Whenever you shall do these things, you shall do them in memory of me.

Principal characteristics of the Greek text:

(a) Only unleavened bread was used at the paschal meal. The word ἄρτος used in the four scriptural accounts for " bread " means both leavened and unleavened bread, and either was used in primitive communities in celebrating the Eucharist.

(b) Luke and Corinthians read Εὐχαριστήσας; Matt. and Mark Εὐλογήσας of the bread and Εὐχαριστήσας of the chalice. The latter term probably refers to the thanksgiving at the end of the meal.

(c) The four consecratory formulae all mean the same. Those in Corinthians and Luke are more circumstantial: τοῦτό μού ἐστιν τὸ σῶμα τὸ ὑπὲρ ὑμῶν " This is my body (given up) for you " (I Cor.); τοῦτό ἐστιν τὸ σῶμά μου τὸ ὑπὲρ ὑμῶν διδόμενον—" This is my body given for you " (Luke). Both are in the present tense. Both here add Christ's command, " Do this for a commemoration of me."

(d) This cup was probably the third, called the " cup of blessing ".

(e) As each person usually drank from his own cup, Matthew and Mark stress that Jesus passed the cup round.

(f) Matthew here adds a commandment similar to that concerning the eating of the eucharistic bread.

(g) The expressions in Mark and Matthew are very similar: Mark: τοῦτό ἐστιν τὸ αἷμά μου τῆς καινῆς διαθήκης τὸ ἐκχυννόμενον ὑπὲρ πολλῶν.—" This is my blood of the new testament shed for many ". Matthew: τοῦτο γάρ ἐστιν τὸ αἷμά μου, τὸ ὑπὲρ ὑμῶν, τὸ περὶ πολλῶν ἐκχυννόμενον εἰς ἄφεσιν ἁμαρτιῶν—" This is my blood of the new testament shed for many, to the remission of sins ".

Luke: τοῦτο τὸ ποτήριον ἡ καινὴ διαθήκη ἐν τῷ αἵματί μου, τὸ ὑπὲρ ὑμῶν ἐκχυννόμενον—" This cup is the new testament in my blood which is to be shed for you. I Corinthians: τοῦτο τὸ ποτήριον ἡ καινὴ διαθήκη ἐστιν ἐν τῷ ἐμῷ αἵματι—" This cup is the new testament in my blood ".

St Paul's formula is very short. The Greek texts of the synoptic authors speak of the outpouring of the blood as present (not, as in the Latin, in the future).

Maundy Thursday liturgy emphasizes the betrayal by Judas. Thus the collect reads, " O God, author alike of the punishment that befell Judas for his guilt . . ."; the lesson is taken from the first epistle to the Corinthians in which St Paul connects the institution of the Eucharist with Judas' betrayal very closely: *In qua nocte tradebatur, accepit panem* (I Cor. 11. 23). The Gospel is drawn from St John and mentions the traitor's crime several times (John 13. 1–15). In the canon we read on that day: *Communicantes et diem sacratissimum celebrantes, quo Dominus noster Jesus Christus pro nobis traditus est* . . . " In the unity of holy fellowship we celebrate this most sacred day on which Our Lord Jesus Christ was delivered up for us ".[1] The priestly act by which Christ offered under the accidents of bread and wine his body which was about to be crucified and his blood which was about to be poured out to the Father is bound up with the betrayal of the traitor (*traditor*), who " traded " in the Saviour's natural body and blood.

(b) *The separate consecration of the eucharistic body and blood.* By his almighty power, when Christ said the words of consecration, " This is my body " and " This is my blood ", his body was really made present as he gave it to the Father for us, under the persisting accidents of bread; and his blood was really made present as he poured it out in honour of the Father, under the continuing appearance of wine.

Christ expressly stated that his body is given " for the Apostles " (I Cor. 11), and his blood poured out " for many " (Mark 14), " for the Apostles " (Luke 22), " for the remission of sins " (Matt. 26). Given to whom? To the Father, or offered to him. The meaning of these expressions is obvious: Christ gave himself in sacrifice on their behalf.[2]

Under the separate and persisting accidents of bread and wine, Christ made present his body and blood that shall be sacrificed on Calvary. The Apostles at the Last Supper were given the sacramentally sacrificed body and blood of Christ. The words of consecration themselves both express and re-affirm the fact of Christ's priestly oblation. It is in consecrating that he makes oblation. The rite of consecration is the true oblation.

[1] Compare *The Gelasian Sacramentary* (ed. Wilson), *Item in Feria V. Missa ad vesperum;* 72–3.
[2] The preposition ὑπέρ also means " instead of ". This meaning is fully reconcilable with the meaning given above.

The Jews were cognizant of offerings made for sin and knew that blood cannot remit sins unless it is offered in sacrifice. So, too, when the Lord said that his body was given for the Apostles and his blood shed for many for the remission of sins, he was clearly speaking of a sacrifice. It is unimportant whether the participles translated " given " and " shed " (or " poured out ") are translated in the present or (as in the Vulgate account of the consecration of the blood) in the future: if they are translated in the present, the sacrificial nature of the eucharistic rite is made obvious, if as future, they emphasize the sacrificial character of the cross and the extremely close links by which the eucharistic rite is bound to it.

In consecrating bread and wine separately, Christ showed forth the separation which was to occur on the cross. Indeed, to separate the blood from the body is to kill. The sacrifice in which the blood was shed is, of course, here represented symbolically, but the Eucharist is not merely a symbol or representation: this rite is sacramental—not only tangible, but also efficacious, making that which it signifies actually present.

Christ's very body, that shall be given (offered to God) for the salvation of men, is veiled under the continuing appearance of bread; his very blood that shall be poured out in God's honour for the redemption of the world, is hidden under the accidents of wine. This actual presence of his eucharistic body and blood was absolutely necessary if Christ was to make an oblation, or offer them, in a real sense, to his Father at the Last Supper. He offered his true body and blood, not (as on the cross) in their natural state, but in a sacramental state, in a eucharistic rite signifying his death on Calvary. The priest both here and on Calvary is the same, and the victim is the same, but the mode of offering is different.

(c) *The new and eternal covenant.* The eucharistic rite of the Last Supper ushered in the new covenant (Matt. 26. 28; Mark 14. 24; Luke 22. 20; I Cor. 11. 25). St Matthew and St Mark stress the cause, the blood; St Luke and St Paul emphasize the effect, the covenant between God and ourselves. It should be noticed that the high priest of the Last Supper used the very words spoken by Moses in concluding the covenant between God and his people at the foot of Sinai: " This is the blood of the covenant ". The Epistle to the Hebrews stresses certain details which accentuate the antetypal character of Moses' sacrifice as described in Exodus 24. 6-8.

"Thus, the old covenant, too, needed blood for its inauguration. When he had finished reading the book of the provisions of the law to the assembled people, Moses took blood, the blood of calves and goats, took water and scarlet-dyed wool, and hyssop, sprinkled the book itself, and all the people, and said, This is the blood of the covenant which God has prescribed to you. The tabernacle, too, and all the requisites of worship he sprinkled in the same way with blood " (Heb. 9. 18-21).

The book and the altar represented God and, through the sprinkling the people, coming into contact with the blood of the victims poured out on the altar, came into communion with God. God and his people freely contracted a covenant in the blood of the sacrifice: it was truly the blood of the covenant.

At the Last Supper, Christ recalled the words spoken at Sinai and solemnly replaced the old covenant, which was a figure, with a new, real covenant, which, like the old, was sealed in blood, his own blood offered in sacrifice. In dying on the cross, Christ perfected the new covenant in the blood of his sacrifice and there, by his blood, he redeemed humanity.

Furthermore, as the new covenant was perfected in the blood (that is by the death) of the divine victim, it is also a testament. Humanity could only receive its inheritance of everlasting good things purchased by his blood through his death on the cross, for the clauses of a will only come into force upon the death of the testator. . . . " This is my blood, the blood of the covenant " (Matt. and Mark). " This cup is the new testament in my blood which is to be shed for you " (Luke). " This cup is the new testament in my blood " (I Cor.).

What Christ's blood, poured out on the cross, earned once for all, is continually being applied to each and every particular soul in his blood offered eucharistically in the Mass. Through the eucharistic sacrifice, the new and everlasting covenant extends ever more widely by taking into its unity multitudes dispersed through space and time. The glorious mission of the Church throughout the ages is the integration of each of her members individually into this new and everlasting covenant with the Father, thus applying the eucharistic blood of Christ to them.

3

THE EUCHARISTIC SACRIFICE OF THE MASS

THE Church prays as she believes: her liturgical prayers are the expression of her beliefs. We must therefore consider the sacrifice of the Mass in the light of (a) the church's doctrine, especially that of the Council of Trent as it is repeated in the encyclical *Mediator Dei;* (b) the sacramental teaching of St Thomas Aquinas, and (c) the formularies of the Roman Missal.

(a) *The sacrifice of the Mass in the light of the teaching of the Council of Trent*

The Council's definition concerning the sacrifice of the Mass is set out in Chapter 2. The Council also produced a group of canons on this subject, the first of which reads:

Si quis dixerit, in Missa non offerri Deo verum et proprium sacrificium, aut quod offerri non sit aliud, quam nobis Christum ad manducandum dari: A.S.	If anyone says that in the Mass a true and actual sacrifice is not offered to God, or, that to be offered is nothing else but that Christ is given to us to eat, let him be anathema.

Thus, it cannot be gainsaid that in our eucharistic rite we offer a real sacrifice to God. On the nature of this sacrifice the Council says:

Et quoniam in divino hoc sacrificio, quod in Missa peragitur, idem ille Christus continetur et incruente immolatur, qui in ara crucis semel se ipsum cruente obtulit, docet sancta Synodus, sacrificium istud vere propitiatorium esse. . . .	And because in this divine sacrifice which is celebrated in the Mass, there is contained and immolated without the shedding of blood that same Christ who once offered himself with bloodshed on the altar of the cross, the holy Synod teaches that this sacrifice is truly propitiatory. . . .

> *Una enim eademque est hostia, idem nunc offerens sacerdotum ministerio, qui se ipsum tunc in cruce obtulit, sola offerendi ratione diversa. . . .*[1]
>
> For the victim is one and the same: the same now offering by the ministry of priests who then offered himself on the cross, only the mode of offering being different . . .

The sacrifice of the Mass is the same as that of the cross: the same Christ is contained in both: in both, the victim and the priest are the same. The only difference lies in the mode of offering: the sacrifice on the cross involved bloodshed; that of the Mass is made without bloodshed. On the cross, Christ personally offered himself; at the Mass, he offers himself through the ministry of priests. In other words, the sacrifice of the Mass is a eucharistic, sacramental sacrifice, representing (or signifying) the sacrifice on the cross. But a sacrament makes present what it represents and therefore, by signifying the sacrifice of the cross, the rite of the Eucharist makes it present: the Mass, therefore, is a true sacrifice.

In the Mass, Christ offers himself through the ministry of priests —the priest does not say " This is the body of Christ " but, speaking in Christ's name, " This is my body ". " The priest," St Thomas teaches, " bears the image of Christ, in whose person and power he utters the words of consecration."[2] " Christ himself cries through the priest ' This is my body,' " says St Ambrose.[3]

The catechism of the Council of Trent popularizes this teaching thus:

> We know, therefore, that the sacrifice effected at the Mass and that which was offered on the cross are, and must be, held to be one and the same sacrifice, for there is but one and the same victim, our Lord Jesus Christ, who immolated himself once on the cross . . . the immolation of whom is renewed for ever in the Eucharist . . . and there is only one and the same priest of this sacrifice, Jesus Christ. For the ministers who offer do not act in their own names: when they consecrate his body and blood, they represent the person of Jesus Christ,

---

[1] Sess. 22, 2; Denzinger, 940.
[2] *Summa. Theol.*, III, q. 93, 1 ad 3.
[3] *De Mysteriis*, 9.

as is apparent from the words of consecration themselves, for priests do not say " This is the body of Jesus Christ " but " This is my body ", thereby putting themselves in our Lord's place, to change the substance of bread and wine into the very substance of his body and blood.[1]

The Code of Canon Law declares clearly and concisely: *In sanctissima Eucharistia sub speciebus panis et vini ipsemet Christus Dominus continetur, offertur, sumitur.* " In the most holy Eucharist, Christ the Lord himself is contained, offered and eaten " (Canon 801).

In the Encyclical *Mediator Dei* (20 November 1947), Pius XII, after recalling the teaching of the Council of Trent, explains it as follows:

> The divine wisdom has devised a way in which our Redeemer's sacrifice is marvellously shown forth by external signs symbolic of death. By the " transubstantiation " of the bread into the body of Christ and of wine into his blood both his body and blood are rendered really present; but the eucharistic species under which he is present symbolize the violent separation of his body and blood, and so a commemorative showing forth of the death which took place in reality on Calvary is repeated in each Mass, because by distinct representations Christ Jesus is signified and shown forth in the state of victim.[2]

(b) *The sacrifice of the Mass in the light of the sacramental teaching of St Thomas Aquinas*

By Christ's institution, the sacraments of the new covenant are visible signs which effect what they signify (*efficiunt quod figurant*). The redemption would, of course, be a reality without them, but they collect its grace-giving powers and direct them towards us. The sacramental sign is the measure and guarantee of the internal reality.

As a sign, the eucharistic rite is composed of two separate elements: bread and wine, over which Christ said the words of consecration separately. By this rite, Christ signified—represented

---

[1] *Catech. ad paroch.* 2, 4.
[2] *Mediator Dei*, C.T.S., sect. 74.

sacramentally—the actual separation of his body and blood as they were delivered up, offered to his Father on the cross. Now, a sacrament makes present what it signifies and therefore the eucharistic rite makes the body and blood of Christ really present, as they were offered on the cross.

When he instituted the Eucharist, Christ gave to the Father—that is, he offered his body and blood to him under the species of bread and wine (sacrifice)—and he also gave them, under the same appearances, to his Apostles as food and drink (communion). St Thomas says: " This sacrament [usual sense] is at once both sacrifice and sacrament [communion]: sacrifice, in that it is offered; and sacrament, in that it is eaten [given to us] ".[1] And again: " The Eucharist is the perfect sacrament of the Lord's passion ",[2] that is, it is the sacramental and efficacious sign of the passion and in that it signifies that passion, Christ's death (which was a sacrifice), makes the sacrifice itself present in the sacramental rite.[3]

In the rite of the Eucharist, Christ is offered as he is given: *in sacramento*, that is, under the persisting appearances of bread and wine. The sacramental rite signifies both the act of oblation (*oblatio rei*) and the thing offered (*res oblata*) on Calvary. The rite of the Eucharist, therefore, includes both the act of oblation and the victim offered on the cross, that is, the whole of the reality of the true sacrifice.

All St Thomas's teaching relating to the eucharistic sacrifice is included in the section of the *Summa* in which he expounds the sacrament of the Eucharist (IIIa, q. 73). Notice his very characteristic terminology: wherever he treats of the sacrifice, he uses the word *sacramentum*. " This sacrament has a threefold meaning. One with reference to the past, in that it is commemorative of the passion of the Lord, which is a true sacrifice, as has been said above, and in this respect it is called *sacrificium* " (IIIa, 73, 4). " This sacrament is called a sacrifice in as much as it represents the very passion of Christ" (IIIa, 73, 4 ad 3). " This sacrament is both sacrifice and sacrament: it is a sacrifice in that it is offered to God; it is a sacrament in that it is eaten " (IIIa, 74, 7).

---

[1] *Summa Theol.*, III, q. 79, a. 5.
[2] *Summa Theol.*, III, q. 73, a. 5 ad 2.
[3] *Summa Theol.*, III, q. 73, a. 4.

St. Thomas never deviates from this form of expression. Moreover, the Mass is so really a "sacrament" in his eyes that he did not hesitate to formulate the following statement about it: "This sacrament consists in the consecration of matter . . . the use the faithful make of it (communion) is not necessarily of the essence of the sacrament, but is something consequent upon this sacrament" (IIIa, 83, 4, n. 8).

St Thomas's inversion of the expressions *sacramentum* and *sacrificium* is no less noteworthy. Thus, for example, in formulating an objection, he wrote, *Sacrificium novae legis* . . . and in the answer, *Ad octavum dicendum quod licet hoc sacramentum.* . . .

When, in the sixteenth century, the Protestants denied the sacrificial nature of the holy eucharist and taught a real presence at the moment of communion only, Catholic theologians, in order to restrict the field of controversy and to work with greater clarity, directed their efforts towards the real presence, reserving the term sacrament to eucharistic communion and no longer to the sacrifice. Since that time, this has been the standard terminology.

It would be disastrous, Dom Vonier[1] points out, to think of the eucharistic sacrifice as less sacramental than the communion (or even as non-sacramental in comparison with it). For St Thomas, the eucharistic sacrifice is the most typical sacrament, but he also gives it the name sacrifice because it represents and commemorates the Lord's passion, which was a sacrifice: "In as much as in this sacrament there is represented the passion of Christ by which Christ offered himself as a victim to God, as is said in Ephesians 5, it is a sacrifice; but in as much as in this sacrament invisible grace is given under a visible appearance, it is a sacrament" (IIIa, 79, 7).

But why is the holy Eucharist also called an immolation? *Immolare* means to kill or to sacrifice. The death of the divine victim on the cross could never have been brought about if he had not freely wished to offer himself to his Father: "In relation to those who killed Christ, the passion was an evil deed, but considered in relation to Christ who suffered for love, it was a sacrifice. This is why it is said that it was Christ himself who offered this sacrifice, and not those who put him to death" (III, 48, 3 ad 3). Christ did not kill himself but he voluntarily exposed himself to

[1] *A Key to the Doctrine of the Eucharist*, p. 55.

death, thus the immolation is closely related to the free offering of the divine victim, and thus the expression *immolare* connotes the action of offering (Cf. III, 47, 4 ad 2). But, the Eucharist sacramentally represents the immolation on the cross and is therefore itself also called an immolation: "The celebration of this sacrament ... is an image representative of the passion of Christ, which is his true immolation and therefore the celebration of this sacrament is called the immolation of Christ ... it is proper to this sacrament that Christ should be immolated in its celebration" (III, 83, 1).

In a letter to Bishop Boniface, St Augustine († 430) formulated the following important statement, which influenced the whole of medieval theology: " Christ has been immolated but once in himself (*in seipso*) but none the less, he is immolated every day for the people (*in sacramento*). Consequently he who is questioned on this point does not lie if he replies ' Christ is immolated' (in the eucharistic sacrifice) ".[1] He explains that " the sacraments bear the name of the things they signify " and this is why it is said that Christ is immolated in the Eucharist, because the Eucharist is a representation of the immolation of the cross.

A representation or commemoration of the passion occurs at the consecration, in so far as Christ's body and blood are there offered to God under the separate and persisting sacramental species of bread and wine: " The representation of the Lord's passion is found at the very consecration of this sacramant, in which the body must not be consecrated without the blood ".[2] When he speaks the words of consecration over the bread and wine separately, the priest sacramentally represents Christ's body and blood as separated, but this eucharistic separation is purely of the sacramental order and in no way effects the natural body and blood of Christ thus made present, for they are henceforward inseparable because they are glorified. Yet, " the Eucharist is the perfect sacrament of the Lord's passion inasmuch as it contains the very Christ who suffered " (Q. 73, art. 5 ad 2).

St Thomas teaches that the eucharistic sacrifice is offered at the consecration itself: " This sacrament is realized (*perficitur*) in the

---

[1] *S. Augustini Opera, Epist.* 98 (*al.* 33) *Bonifacio episcopo*.
[2] *Summa Theol.*, IIIa, q. 80, art. 12 ad 3; see also q. 76, 2 ad 1; q. 83, 2 ad 2.

eucharistic consecration in which the sacrifice is offered to God" (Q. 82, art. 10 ad 1).

It is obvious from this that it is a very great abuse to interpret the ceremonies of the Mass as representations of the various stages in Christ's passion, saying, for example, that when the priest kisses the altar stone, he represents Judas betraying his divine Master or that when he washes his hands, he is the living image of Pilate delivering Christ to the Jews . . . and so on.

(c) *The sacrifice of the Mass in the light of the Roman Missal* [1]

The fact that the Eucharist is a true sacrifice is stated explicitly seven times in the *Ordo Missae*: four times in the prayers of the offertory (in the prayers *In spiritu humilitatis; Veni, sanctificator; Orate fratres* and *Suscipiat*) and three times in the canon (in the *Te igitur;* the commemoration of the living and *Supra quae*).

In addition, the *Ordo Missae* refers frequently to the act of oblation and the eucharistic oblation itself in various ways between the beginning of the offertory and the end of the canon. Although, of course, only bread and wine are present on the altar before the consecration, the Church hails through them the eucharistic body and blood even before the consecration. Notice particularly at the offertory the prayer *Suscipe* which emphasizes the effectiveness and propitiatory character of the sacrifice (*Suscipe, sancte Pater . . . hanc immaculatam hostiam, quam ego . . . offero tibi . . . pro innumerabilibus peccatis, et offensionibus, et negligentiis meis . . . ut mihi et illis proficiat ad salutem in vitam aeternam*), *Offerimus* (*Offerimus tibi, Domine, calicem salutaris . . . ut . . . pro nostra et totius mundi salute cum odore suavitatis ascendat*)—which also bears witness to the effectiveness of the eucharistic sacrifice—and *Suscipe, sancta Trinitas*.

Most of the prayers of the canon, both before and after the consecration, contain obvious references to the fact that the Eucharist is an effective rite of propitiation and a sacrifice, the words of the prayers constantly bringing our attention back to the offerings themselves either by direct reference to them by name or by the use of demonstrative and relative pronouns (*haec, quae,* etc.) referring to them.

---

[1] For further details see Ch. 4–8 (Those who offer and the offering made) and the sections on the offertory and canon.

Conclusion

St Thomas wrote, *Eucharistia est sacramentum perfectum Dominicae passionis*. Both the victim offered (*res oblata*) and the sacrificial act of oblation (*oblatio rei*) of Calvary are made present sacramentally in the eucharistic rite. The Mass is, therefore, a true sacrifice and, because Jesus poured all the love, worship and glorification of which his priestly soul was capable into the offering of his body and blood to the Father on the cross, it is, furthermore, the highest possible form of adoration.

4

WHO OFFERS THE HOLY SACRIFICE OF THE MASS?

I. THE PRINCIPAL OFFERER OF THE SACRIFICE IS CHRIST, WHO OFFERS THROUGH THE MINISTRY OF PRIESTS

BEFORE beginning upon a study of this vast and important subject, reference should be made to the doctrine of the Council of Trent regarding it. Quotations from the decrees of the Council (Sess. 22, 1 and 2) are set out on pages 9–10, 21–22.

The sacrifice of the Mass is offered:

(a) by Christ, the sovereign high priest of the new covenant, that same who offered the sacrifice of the cross (*idem offerens*). But in offering his sacrifice, Christ makes use of the instrumental ministry of a priest (*sacerdotum ministerio*), his representative.

(b) by the universal Church, the mystical body and fullness of Christ, the head, and vitally embodied in the high priest, forming one with him. But the Church offers through her ministers, the priests (*ab Ecclesia per sacerdotes immolandum*). (See Chapter 5.)

(c) The priest is assisted in his priestly ministry at the altar by lesser ministers: deacon, subdeacon, acolytes, etc. (See Chapter 6.)

(d) Certain of the faithful share particularly in the offering of the sacrifice. They include especially those actually present and those who, through their Mass-offerings (*stipendium*), have made an especially effective contribution to its celebration. (See Chapter 7.)

The primary offerer of this sacrifice is Christ who also offered that of the cross

Some account of the mystery of the priestly ordination of Christ is to be found in Volume 1, Chapter 20.

On the cross, Jesus Christ, the universal high priest (*catholicus Patris sacerdos*), offered once for all the perfect sacrifice, by which he gave glory to the majesty of the holy Trinity and saved humankind.

If Christians of all succeeding generations are actually to participate in Calvary's unique sacrifice and so through Christ, with him and in him, to render all honour and glory to the Father, the sacrifice of the cross must be made present at all times and in all places. By the institution of the sovereign high priest of the Last Supper, the sacrifice of the cross is made present without the shedding of blood —sacramentally—in the rite of the Eucharist, in the sacrifice of the Mass. In both the sacrifice of the cross and that of the Mass, it is the same priest who offers and the same victim that is offered: only the mode of offering is different. . . . *Idem nunc offerens sacerdotum ministerio, qui se ipsum tunc in cruce obtulit, sola offerendi ratione diversa.*[1] . . . " The same now offering by the ministry of priests who then offered himself on the cross, only the mode of offering being different. . . ."

In the encyclical *Mediator Dei*, Pius XII teaches: " The priest, then, is the same: Jesus Christ, whose sacred person is represented by his minister. The consecration which the minister received when he was ordained to the priesthood assimilates him to the high priest and enables him to act by the power of Christ himself and in his name. And therefore when he exercises his priestly power he, as it were, ' lends Christ his tongue and gives him the use of his hand ' ".[2]

Christ offers the sacrifice of the Mass through the ministry of priests (" sacerdotum ministerio ")

The Father accepts only worship offered through the sole priestly mediator: *per Christum*. Christ renders all honour and glory to the Father through his priesthood. Therefore, to share in Christ's worship, it is necessary first to enter into participation in his priesthood: Christ's priesthood must be extended and communicated to humanity. This extension and communication is effected in the sacraments of baptism, confirmation and order.

We must, moreover, exercise participation in Christ's priesthood worthily and devoutly. Therefore, the characters (*res et sacramentum*) signified and produced by the external sacramental rites (*sacramentum tantum*) in their turn signify and produce the grace of the sacrament (*res tantum*). " After Christ had fulfilled his terrestrial

---

[1] *Conc. Trid.*, Sess. 22, 1; Denzinger, 938.
[2] *Mediator Dei*, 73; C.T.S. London 1947.

priestly mission on Calvary ... he changed his terrestrial existence into a sacramental order. The historical Christ survives among us in the sevenfold order of his sacraments. The historical order in which he could reach personally only a very few men, has been transformed into a sacramental order in which, independently of time and space, he might be perpetually accessible to every man."[1]

The Christian priesthood is as truly a sacrament as is the Christian sacrifice—indeed, it was instituted so that the sacramental sacrifice might be offered.

In the sacrifice of the Mass, Christ himself is the victim not in his natural state but in a sacramental state, that is, under the persisting accidents of bread and wine. In the same way, he is the offerer, not in his natural state, but in a sacramental state, that is, through his priest who is moulded to his priesthood by the sacrament of order (*secundum configurationem ad Christum*).[2] Just as the eucharistic species really and substantially contain the body and blood of Christ, so the sacrament of order makes Christ's priesthood present in the priest. In the Eucharist, Christ is sacramentally the victim; in the priest, he is sacramentally the one who offers. Thus, in the eucharistic sacrifice, the priest and the victim are one in a sacramental identity, as on Calvary they were one by natural identity. "The celebration of this sacrament," St Thomas teaches, "is a representative image of the passion of Christ. ... For the same reason, the priest is a (sacramental) image of Christ, in whose person and power he utters the words of consecration. And thus, in a way, the priest and victim are the same (*Et ita quodammodo idem est sacerdos et hostia*)."[3]

At the Last Supper, after the celebration of the rite of the Eucharist, the sovereign high priest declared: *Hoc facite in meam commemorationem* ("What I have just done, do you, in your turn, in commemoration of me."). If the Apostles were to "do" what Christ had done, it is obvious that he gave them the power to do it. And indeed, according to the teaching of the Council of Trent, it was by these words that Jesus conferred the priesthood upon his Apostles: "He offered his body and blood to God his Father under

---

[1] A. Munsters, *Alter Christus*, 16, 14–15.
[2] *Summa Theol.*, III, q. 64, a. 5 ad 1.
[3] *Summa Theol.*, IIIa, q. 83, a. 1 ad 2 et 3.

the species of bread and wine and gave them under these same appearances to the Apostles, whom he then made priests of the new covenant and commanded them and their successors in the priesthood to offer them in these words: Do this for a commemoration of me, and so the Catholic Church has always understood and taught."[1] And Canon 2 adds: "If anyone says that by these words 'Do this for a commemoration of me' Christ did not make his Apostles priests, or did not ordain that they themselves and other priests should offer his body and blood: let him be anathema." In this single commandment, Christ both instituted the priesthood and initiated the sacrifice (the liturgy). The priesthood and the liturgy could not be more closely connected.[2]

Sacerdotem oportet offerre. The priest's principal function is to offer the holy sacrifice, and the power to do so is conferred upon him by the bishop by the imposition of hands and the consecratory preface.[3]

At the tradition of the chalice and paten, the bishop says, "Receive the power to offer the sacrifice to God and to celebrate Masses, as well for the living as for the dead. In the name of the Lord."

Furthermore, the Council of Trent adds, "To the Apostles and their successors in the priesthood, there has been confided the power to consecrate, offer and administer his body and blood" (Sess. 23. 1).

Christ acts through the priestly character of his minister. There is a very close bond between Christ and the priest: *Sacerdos alter Christus.* According to the teaching of the Council of Trent the sacrament of order—like those of baptism and confirmation—imparts a character and, according to the teaching of St Thomas, it is in this character that priestly power resides: this character distinguishes the priest from the layman for ever.[4]

The mysterious character stamped upon the soul is—as the terms *sigillum* and *signaculum* used of it suggest—somewhat like a seal. The impress reproduces the image of the seal. This sacrament

---

[1] *Conc. Trid.*, Sess. 22, 1; Denzinger 938.
[2] The mutual dependence of the sacrifice and priesthood was emphasized by the Council of Trent—see Sess. 23, 1 in Denzinger, 957.
[3] *Constit. Apostolica: De sacris Ordinibus diaconatus, presbyteratus et episcopatus* (30 November 1947).
[4] *Conc. Trid.*, Sess. 7, canon 9 (Denziger, 852); Sess. 23, can. 4. (Denziger, 964).

imprints the character of Christ. By this character, the ordinand is marked with Christ's seal: he bears the image of Christ within him: he is moulded to Christ. But Christ is the Anointed One, the sovereign high priest, and thus the character of this sacrament is a spiritual anointing, an interior consecration. Through the priestly character, Christ makes his ministers true participants in his priestly power and confers upon them the ability to offer his sacrifice. Hallowed by this mysterious and indelible character, the priest's soul is permanently fitted to be the living instrument through which Christ may effectively exercise his priestly power.

On the other hand, by virtue of his priestly character, the priest acts under the influence of Christ and the actions he freely performs are Christ's actions. Whenever the priest acts in virtue of his priestly character, he makes present the priestly working of Christ himself. When he consecrates the Blessed Sacrament, he does not say " This is the body of Christ " but " This is my body ". When he pronounces absolution, he likewise speaks in Christ's name: *Ego te absolvo:* " I absolve thee ". In treating of the priest's power of order, St Thomas always writes *agere in persona Christi; conficere in persona Christi; in persona Christi operari; in persona Christi cujus vicem gerit per ordinis potestatem,* etc.[1]

There is, certainly, a great difference between Christ's sacramental assumption of the priest's soul and the assumption of Christ's human nature by the Word. Christ's assumption of the soul of the priest by the sacramental character does not alter the priest's personality nor change its essence but is merely added to it accidentally. Despite this difference the analogy still has substance. When the priest says " This is my body " or " I absolve thee ", Christ takes over his activity and fills it with divine power: the priest's personality is effaced before Christ's own. His words are the words of Christ. The priesthood of our priests adds nothing to Christ's priesthood for their priesthood is dependent upon Christ's and draws all its efficacy from it. But although he is Christ's instrument, the priest acts quite freely: his initiative is unimpaired. If he does not go up to the altar, take bread and wine and say the eucharistic prayer, the inflowing of Christ will not be used, the sacrifice will not be celebrated *hic et nunc.* If, on the other hand, he says the ritual words and performs the sacred action, then straightway

[1] *Summa Theol.* IIIa, q. 22, a. 4; q. 82, a. 1 and 7 ad 3.

Christ will act in him; using the lips and ministering hands of his priests, the one Priest makes the unique sacrifice of the cross present without the shedding of blood to all generations of Christians.

Through the sacramental priestly character, the sovereign high priest signifies and thus makes present his priesthood in all times and places. Through this character, he exercises his priestly influence, makes operative all the consecratory prayers spoken by his ministers. Thus, in the sacrifice of the Mass, Christ's act of oblation is indirect and potential whilst that of his priest is immediate and actual. Priests offer the sacrifice not in their own names or power, but in the name, person and power of Christ himself, and Christ remains the primary offerer of the Mass. Just as our priestly power is instrumental in relation to Christ's, so our act of oblation is dependent on his. Neither the decree of the Council of Trent nor the conciliar catechism suggests that there is a direct and renewed offering of Christ in the sacrifice of the Mass.

The holiness of this offering

It is obvious that both what is offered in the holy sacrifice (the eucharistic body and blood of Christ) and the act of oblation, in so far as this emanates from Christ, bestow a most sacred character and sovereign worth upon the Mass, making it very acceptable to God and worthy of his pleasure. These two fundamental elements do not depend upon the subjective disposition of the minister. The Council of Trent teaches: " And this is that pure oblation which no unworthiness or iniquity in those who offer can defile."[1]

There is no suggestion, however, that a priest celebrating the holy sacrifice unworthily does not burden his conscience with a great act of sacrilege. The offering of the sacrifice of the Mass demands holiness in priests: " It is for the priests of the Lord to offer their God incense and consecrated loaves: they are men set apart for God, and must never bring reproach upon his name. Alleluia ".[2]

Moulded to Christ and made partakers of his everlasting priesthood, being " new Christs " through their sacramental character, priests owe it to the eminence of their dignity to share as fully

---

[1] *Conc. Trid.*, Sess. 22, 1; Denzinger, 939.
[2] Offertory, Mass of Corpus Christi.

as possible in the fullness of grace: in the holiness of him whom they represent. The sublime nature of their office imposes on them the obligation to be perfect.

Numerous ecclesiastical sources stress the need for this holiness.[1] Thus, the Council of Trent:

> What care must be given to ensure that the holy sacrifice of the Mass is celebrated with all due religious care and reverence may easily be perceived when it is reflected that in the holy writings he who performs God's work negligently is called cursed (Jer. 48. 10). If then, of necessity, we recognize that no work can be performed by Christians, which is more holy or divine than this tremendous mystery, in which this life-giving victim by whom we have been reconciled to God the Father is immolated by priests daily on the altar, it would appear to be sufficiently clear that all application and diligence must be given to ensure its performance with the maximum inward purity of heart and exterior devotion and piety.[2]

Such exhortations to holiness take on their full significance in the setting of the ordination ceremonies. In a preliminary allocution, the bishop reveals to the ordinands the absolute necessity of holiness to them in their office. Not only holiness, but also " heavenly wisdom, upright ways and long-standing practice of justice " are prerequisites in those candidates who dare to proceed to the priesthood. They must obey God's commandments, and be honest and mature both in sacred learning and conduct. They must know that the ministers of Christ's Church must be perfect both in words and works. And because the essential basis of perfection is charity, " they must be founded in the twofold love of God and their neighbour ". They are then reminded of the mortification of passions and lusts, of the asceticism required of them. The bishop concludes by exhorting the ordinands to make their teaching a " spiritual remedy " and the " odour of their lives sweet " to Christ's Church " so that both by your words and your example you may edify the house, that is, the family of God ".

After the blessing at the Mass, as the bishop takes leave of these

---

[1] See S. *Congregatio de Seminariis et Studiorum Universitatibus*. *Enchiridion Clericorum*. *Documenta Ecclesiae sacrorum alumnis instituendis* (Herder, Rome, 1937).

[2] *Decretum de observandis et evitandis in celebratione missarum* (E. Ehses, *Concilium Tridentinum*, vol. 8; *Actorum*, 5a, pp. 962–3; Freiburg 1919).

new priests, he addresses this last admonition to them: "Beloved brethren, think carefully upon the order you have received and upon the burden placed upon your shoulders; apply yourselves to living sacredly and religiously and so as to please almighty God."

With regard to priestly holiness, St Thomas himself taught that "those who receive the sacrament of order are thereby set at the head of the faithful: they must also be leaders by merit of their sanctity".[1] The reason for this, he adds, is that "in order to exercise the ministry of the order fittingly there is required not merely some degree of virtue, but rather virtue to a pre-eminent degree". Elsewhere he writes: "Each order makes him who receives it a leader in divine matters. . . . Holiness of life is therefore necessarily required by precept (*necessitate praecepti*) for orders."[2]

When comparing the priest with a religious as such, St Thomas does not hesitate to affirm that the former's holiness should exceed that of the latter. The monk is not the model for the priest: the priest is the model for the monk. "The monastic order (*monasticus ordo*)", Denys wrote, "must follow the priestly orders (*sacerdotales ordines*) and in imitating them, ascend to divine things."[3]

The religious life is a school of perfection in which the professed train themselves in the perfection of charity by discarding everything that opposes its full scope. Order, on the other hand, raises the Christian over his brethren and invests him with divine functions. Although he does not belong to a canonical "state of perfection", the priest, because of his priestly dignity, and the sublime nature of divine functions, must have attained the perfection at which the religious (as such) must aim.

The indelible character of priesthood draws down into the soul of the priest both sacramental grace and an unceasing flow of actual graces in order that he may exercise his priestly office in a holy manner. This grace is the main effect of the sacrament of order, as the decrees of the Councils make plain. When treating of the sacrament of order, the decree *pro Armenis* of the Council of Florence (1438–45) declares: *Effectus est augmentum gratiae, ut quis sit idoneus minister*:[4] "There is brought about an increase of grace,

---

[1] *Summa Theol.*, IIIa suppl., q. 35, a. 1 ad 3.
[2] *Ibid.*, q. 36, a. 1.
[3] *Summa Theol.*, IIa, IIae, q. 184, a. 8.
[4] Denzinger, *Enchiridion*, 701.

that a man may be a worthy minister ". The Council of Trent adds, " *Cum . . . perspicuum sit per sacram ordinationem . . . gratiam conferri* ".[1]

Through grace, the priest accomplishes in holiness that which, through the sacramental character, he performs validly. " The works of God are perfect," St Thomas writes. " If God confers a power upon a creature, he at the same time gives him whatever is necessary for the fitting exercise of that power." And therefore, " when they receive the order, they [the ordinands] receive a most plenteous gift of grace which makes them capable of the greatest works ".[2]

The character of priesthood, ineffaceably imprinted upon the soul, is an everflowing source of actual grace for the priest—grace fitting him to exercise his priesthood worthily. Furthermore, in that it moulds Christ's minister so deeply, the priestly character is also the basis and pledge of his union with Christ. Aided by faith and prayer, under the stimulus provided by the character, sacramental grace accomplishes its task, transforming him into a " new Christ ", until, as St Paul's example teaches, " he is alive, or rather not he; it is Christ that lives in him " (Cf. Gal. 2. 20). Thus, the best sacramental means by which the priest may " fan the flame of that special grace which God kindled in thee, when my hands were laid upon thee " (II Tim. 1. 6), is by esteeming the priestly character at its true worth and employing it in worthy celebration of the sacrifice of the Mass " the source of all holiness ". At no other time is the priest so truly a priest.

With the grace of the sacrament, priestly charity, the virtues and gifts of the Holy Ghost and, above all, the virtue of religion and gift of piety grow strongly. The principal result of the grace of ordination is the power of true devotion and piety. " Devotion " (*devotio*), St Thomas teaches, " is derived from *devoveo* (meaning to dedicate to a God) and therefore those who dedicate themselves to God are called ' devotees ' (*devoti*). From this it may be seen that devotion is but the will to give oneself promptly to matters pertaining to the service of God." [3]

---

[1] *Ibid.*, 959; Sess. 23, III.
[2] *Summa Theol.*, III, q. 35, a. 1.
[3] *Summa Theol.*, IIa, IIae, q. 82, a. 1.

So anxious is the Church with regard to the personal devotion of her priests that references to the need for this virtue abound in ecclesiastical documents.

In his well-known encyclical *Ad catholici sacerdotii fastigium* (20 December 1935), Pius XI reminded his readers that "although all Christian virtues should flourish in a priest's soul", certain virtues are especially fitting and, as it were, proper to him, of which the chief is "piety in accordance with the Apostle's exhortation to his beloved Timothy (I Tim. 4. 8)." The Pope reminded priests that "if 'holiness is all availing' it avails above all for the proper execution of the priestly ministry".[1]

The principal form taken by the exercise of the virtue of religion by the priest is worthy celebration according to the instructions of the rubrics. What is worthy celebration?

The way in which we should give glory to the Father is not left to our whims but has been laid down once for all by his wisdom: glory is to be given *per Christum*. Christ has ordered the adoration of the Father by the Church in a definite pattern—through the sacrifice of the Mass and the sacraments, the rites and ceremonies of which have been defined in every detail by the Church. Therefore, the principal form of piety throughout the Church's public ministry lies in respect for and religious observation of the rubrics and dignified and devout recitation of the liturgical prayers.

The personal holiness of the priest, the instrument of Christ and minister of the Church, has a definite effect on the celebration of a Mass and reacts positively on its power to give glory and to sanctify. Indeed, there must be a difference between a Mass celebrated by St John or the holy Curé of Ars and one celebrated by a minister who, although in a state of grace, is lacking in fervour.

The holier the priest is, the holier—and therefore the more pleasing to and more fully accepted by God—will be the oblation (the act of oblation) of the Mass in so far as this originates in him; and so much the more also will his sacrifice give glory to God and the richer it will be in fruits and graces. Therefore, from the point of view of the efficacy of the Mass, it is important that the priest should be ever more holy.

---

[1] Pius XII's apostolic exhortation *Menti nostrae* (23 September 1950), on the occasion of the golden jubilee of his priesthood and his posthumous address (19 October 1958) intended for the seminarists of Puglie, should also be read.

5

WHO OFFERS THE HOLY SACRIFICE OF THE MASS?

II. THE UNIVERSAL CHURCH, THE MYSTICAL BODY OF CHRIST, IS, WITH CHRIST, THE PRINCIPAL OFFERER OF EACH AND EVERY MASS CELEBRATED THROUGHOUT THE WORLD. SHE OFFERS IT THROUGH THE MINISTRY OF HER PRIESTS

It is self-evident that only Christ makes use of Christ. Only the great high priest can give his body and blood. How then can we use his body and blood to give them, offer them, to the Father? St Paul's reply is exhaustive: " The Church is the mystical body of Christ." Pope Pius XII's encyclical *Mystici Corporis Christi* is devoted to this great mystery.

The Church shares in the life of her head; she and Christ are one mystery; they occupy the same place in the divine plan; she, with him, is alpha and omega, the beginning and the end of all things. Being but a single mystery with him, the Church with him forms the perfect priest, and hence, making one with him, she has at her disposal the body and blood of Christ. The head belongs to the body as the body does to the head.

The Council of Trent teaches clearly that Christ left his sacrifice to his Church: *ut dilectae sponsae suae Ecclesiae . . . relinqueret sacrificium*.[1] The Catechism of the Council of Trent is equally explicit: " First they teach that the Eucharist was instituted by Christ for two purposes: the one, that it might be a heavenly food to our souls by which we might guard and preserve the life of the spirit; and the other, that the Church might have a perpetual sacrifice."[2] The Church, then—in the priestly power of Christ, who sustains her—is with him the principal offerer of the sacrifice. The Mass is truly her sacrifice: Jesus' sacrifice belongs to the Church.

---

[1] *Conc. Trid.*, Sess. 22, 1; Denzinger, 938. Cf. *Mediator Dei*.
[2] *Catech. ex decr. Concil. Trid. ad paroch.*, 2, 4, 70.

The eucharistic sacrifice is made up of two parts: the offering, that is, the body of Christ, which nineteen centuries ago was nailed to the cross, and the blood of Christ, which was poured forth on Calvary, this body and blood being made present under the persisting accidents of bread and wine (*res oblata*); and secondly, the oblation of the offering, that is, the historical act, Christ's offering to the Father his body and blood on the cross (*oblatio rei*). The things offered, the eucharistic body and blood, are not in themselves a sacrifice: they are but its matter. The act of oblation on the cross is also necessary. The Church has taken this act to herself and associated herself with it by active participation in it. Through, in and with Christ her head, she offers her sacrifice, the eucharistic body and blood of Christ—which are hers to use—to the Father, and whoever belongs to the Church and is baptized, " plunged " into membership of her, can offer with her.

St Thomas teaches concisely: " This victim is perpetual and was once offered by Christ in such a way that it might be offered every day by his members ".[1]

It is, then, the Church which offers the sacrifice through the delegated, ministerial priesthood of her priests.

The well-known Greek *Paradosis* of St Hippolytus (*c.* 200) prays after the consecration: " We, remembering therefore his death and resurrection, offer the bread and cup to thee, giving thee thanks that thou hast found us worthy to stand before thee and minister. And, we beseech thee, send down thy Holy Spirit upon the oblation of holy Church and, gathering it into one, grant to all the saints who communicate, that they may be filled with the Holy Ghost . . ."

In the prayer *Hanc igitur* in the canon of the Roman liturgy, we beseech the Father to accept this offering made by us his servants and his " whole household ": *Hanc igitur oblationem servitutis nostrae sed et cunctae familiae tuae.* . . . This text shows quite clearly that the sacrifice is offered by the whole of God's family. The Church's consciousness of her role as offerer is also clearly shown in the Secrets. That for the Epiphany, for example, reads: " Look favourably, Lord, upon thy Church's gifts . . ."; and that for the feast of St Peter's Chair at Rome: " Let the intercession of the

[1] *In IV Sent.* Dist. XXI, expos. textus.

blessed Apostle Peter second the prayers and offerings of thy Church, we beg thee, Lord . . ."

Similar prayers are to be found in ancient liturgies. Thus, on the second Sunday in Lent the Gelasian Sacramentary reads: " Favourably accept the oblation of thy Church, O Lord," and " Sanctify the gifts of thy Church . . ." and the *Missale Gothicum* (seventh-eighth centuries) on the Tuesday after Easter: " Receive, O Lord, these gifts offered in thy name, which the Church universal has gained through the blood of Christ, and offers to thee in the resurrection of thy Son, victorious in glory . . ."

The Roman Mass contains other evidence besides that of the *Hanc igitur*. The first prayer after the consecration reads: " We thy servants, Lord, and with us, all thy holy people, offer to thy sovereign majesty . . ." and before the communion the priest prays " Lord Jesus Christ . . . look not upon my sins, but upon the Church's faith. . . ."

The prayers of the Mass are collective in form and thus are always in the plural: *oremus* (we pray), *offerimus* (we offer), *gratias agamus* (we give thanks). There are only a few exceptions to this rule: for example, the prayer after the communion, *Corpus tuum, Domine*—and these are all of relatively late date. Thus, Innocent III († 1216) teaches: " Though one man makes the offering, we say ' we offer ' because the priest offers the sacrifice not only in his own name but also in that of the whole Church."[1] The same collective characteristics are to be found in the private recitation of the Office.

Many might be tempted to suppose that high Mass is an amplification of the more primitive low Mass. But the reverse is true. Low Mass is a reduced form of high Mass and, even in private celebrations, the collective character has always been preserved. The priest at low Mass assumes the role of the deacon, subdeacon and, sometimes, acolyte. There must, however, be someone to make the responses and to represent the faithful. The Code of Canon Law decrees that " A priest may not celebrate Mass without a minister (*sine ministro*) who serves him and answers him " (Canon 813, 1). The acolyte serves by virtue of his order—he is an acolyte. He makes the responses not by virtue of his order but by virtue of his baptism, as the spokesman of the whole Christian body. The

[1] *De Sacr. Alt. Myst.*, 5, 2; *P.L.*, 271, 888.

Code also lays down that a woman may not serve Mass, but if no man is present to perform the office she may make the responses from outside the sanctuary (Canon 813, 2). Celebration without a server is forbidden under pain of mortal sin, except for important reasons, e.g. in order to consecrate the Viaticum for a dying person or to celebrate so that people may attend Mass on Sundays or holydays of obligation.

Christ is mankind's universal priest, and his priesthood must be extended and communicated to humanity. This extension and communication is brought about in the Church through the sacramental characters of baptism, confirmation and the sacrament of order. Being vitally incorporated into the unique priest by baptism, we share in his anointing: we are his anointed, his consecrated ones, *Christiani*. Throughout the centuries, the Church, through her ministers, extends Christ's anointing by the individual anointing of her new members. We who share in Christ's priestly power must exercise it worthily. This is why the characters (*res et sacramentum*) signified and produced by the external and sacramental rites (*sacramentum tantum*) in their turn signify and produce the grace of the sacraments (*res tantum*).

Participation in Christ's priesthood is infused into our souls by the character of baptism. What is this character? As its name —*sigillum, signaculum*—indicates, the mystical character imprinted upon the soul is analogous to a seal. The fathers of the Church often compared this sacramental impression to the image stamped on coins. This seal imprints a likeness, and because a sacrament is involved, this likeness is holy.

What impression or character, then, does baptism imprint upon the soul? It impresses the character of Christ, and through it, Christians bear the image or likeness of Christ, that is, they are moulded to Christ. And, as Christ is the Anointed, the great High Priest, the character of baptism is a spiritual anointing and interior consecration, making the baptized soul a " new Christ ".

The Church anoints her children, just as she anoints her priests and kings. Immediately after the baptismal washing, the priest consecrates the baptized person with chrism, conferring upon him a royal and priestly anointing. Thus Christ makes each soul Christian by means of the baptismal character, making it a true participant in his priestly power: henceforward it will be able to offer the victim of the sacrifice, to offer genuine and official worship —the liturgy of the Church. Thus, through the sacramental character we enter into the outward religion of God and his Church. Through the characters, we have the power to share in the sovereign high priest's worship, to glorify the Father through Christ, in Christ and with Christ.

St Thomas teaches these same truths. The role of the sacraments is the preparation of the soul for divine worship.[1] This worship emanates from Christ's priesthood and therefore, through the sacraments we enter into participation in the priesthood of Christ:[2] they confer true powers.[3] " Therefore the baptized person and the priest are both really though *differently* endowed with power which authorizes them to take part in ' Christian ' worship . . . they are both instruments of Christ and are both assimilated to him and fitted for religious activity. . . . Both priests and faithful are truly all these things, and these things differentiate them radically from justified but unbaptized pagans. . . . According to St Thomas, participation in Christ's worship involves two activities, giving and receiving."[4] Sacramental characters make us participants in Christ's worship either as agents, making validly present the sovereign high priest's priestly activity, or to transmit it to others (character of the sacrament of order) or as recipients, sharing validly in the worship and validly receiving the sacraments (character of baptism and confirmation). The character of the sacrament of order makes us participants in Christ's priesthood to give the sacraments. It confers the power to celebrate the eucharistic sacrifice. The baptismal character passively ordains us to worship, and allows us to receive the fruits of the Mass and other sacraments.[5] St Thomas, of course, stresses chiefly the passive power conferred by the baptismal character, yet he recognizes in it also power to act. Baptism makes us participants in ecclesiastical unity, able to take part in the activity of the Church: *Per baptismum aggregatur homo congregationi fidelium;*[6] *Ad actus fidelium nullus ante*

---

[1] Canon Thils, *Le pouvoir cultuel du baptisé* in *Ephem. théol Lov.*, 1938, pp. 685-9.
[2] *Summa Theol.*, III, q. 62, a. 5.
[3] *Ibid*, IIIa, q. 63, a. 5.
[4] *Ibid*, IIIa, q. 63, a. 2.
[5] *Ibid*, III, q. 63, a. 3c and III, q. 63, a. 6.
[6] *Ibid*, III, q. 67, a. 2.

baptismum admittitur;[1] *Baptismus est principium omnium spiritualium actuum.*[2] "Although primarily baptism bestows the ability to receive the effects of worship, we must not lose sight of the fact that the baptized person has the right to participate actively in eucharistic worship and that he is the minister of the sacrament of marriage."[3] By virtue of the character of his baptism, the Christian may take an active part in official prayers and unite himself to the offering that the priest makes in the name of the Church.

Participation in the priesthood of Christ does not make a Christian a mediator, nor does it confer upon him the power to consecrate bread and wine; priests alone are made mediators between God and men, to offer the sacrifice in the name of and on behalf of the Church. Both faithful and priests offer—but in different ways. The faithful offer in their own name and with the Church. Priests offer as mediators on behalf of the Church.

The expressions *sacerdos* and *sacerdotium* are therefore reserved to priests consecrated by the sacrament of order. Only the priesthood has the right to perform the Church's rites of glorification and sanctification; only the faithful have the power and the right to participate effectively in them and to receive their divine effects.

We are "a royal priesthood, a consecrated nation", as St Peter told the baptized (I Peter 2. 9). St John echoed his words, "He has proved his love for us by washing us clean from our sins in his own blood, and made us a royal race of priests to serve God, his Father; glory and power be his through endless ages. Amen" (Apoc. 1. 6).

The Fathers, too, constantly proclaim the participation of the faithful in the priestly power of Christ. "If we bear the name 'Christians,'" wrote Theophilus of Antioch (186), "it is because we have received the anointing with divine oil, which is the Holy Ghost."[4] "The priesthood of the laity is baptism," said St Jerome († 420).[5] "We call all Christians 'priests' (*sacerdotes*) because they are members of one priest," St Augustine teaches.[6]

---

[1] *Summa Theol.*, III, q. 70, a. 1.
[2] *In IV Sent.*, dist. 3, q. 1, a. 1; q. 4, ad 1.
[3] Thils, *art cit.*
[4] *Ad Autolycum*, 1, 12; *P. G.*, 6, 1041.
[5] *In Hom.* 3 in II Cor.; *P.G.*, 61, 417, and *Dial. contra Lucif.*, 4; *P.L.*, 23, 158.
[6] *De Civ. Dei*, 20, 10; *P.L.*, 41, 676.

Tertullian in Africa (243), St Cyril of Jerusalem (386), St Ambrose of Milan (397), St Augustine of Hippo (430), St Leo of Rome (461), St Maximus of Turin (465), St Isidore of Seville (636), St Ildephonsus of Toledo (667) revealed the grandeur of their office to the faithful in commentaries on the anointing with chrism. Thus, for instance, St. Cyprian († 258) teaches that it is through anointing that the baptized become God's anointed and receive the grace of Christ.[1]

St Cyril of Jerusalem speaks similarly: " As the bread of the Eucharist after the invocation of the Holy Ghost is no longer common bread, but the very body of Christ, so likewise holy oil after its consecration is no longer merely common oil, but the gift of Christ. The presence of the divine in it has made it that which brings the Holy Ghost. Therefore, when the body receives visible unction from it, the soul is sanctified by the Holy Ghost . . . and thus . . . you receive the name of Christians, and the name is verified in you by the grace of regeneration."[2]

St Augustine of Hippo writes: " We may very well call all those who have received anointing with chrism ' Christs ': together they form a body which, taken with its head, make only one Christ."[3]

" The Church of God is, of course, essentially hierarchical," said St Leo the Great of Rome, " but nonetheless St Peter's words are equally valid: he spoke of the royal priesthood of all the faithful (I Peter 2. 5–9). Thus, outside that service which is proper to our ministry, all Christians may think of themselves as participants in the royal nation and the priestly office, for the sign of the cross makes all those who are regenerated in Christ, kings, the anointing of the Holy Ghost consecrates them priests."[4]

The liturgy often echoes these teachings. Thus, the well-known anaphora in the *Apostolic Constitutions* prays: " Wherefore we offer to thee (the eucharistic sacrifice) for these people, that thou wouldst show them forth to the praise of thy Christ as a royal priesthood, a holy nation."

Today, too, at the consecration of the holy oils on Maundy Thursday the bishop implores God to hallow the balm that " it

---
[1] *Ep.* 70-2.
[2] *Catech. Myst.*, 3, 1-5; *P.G.*, 33, 1088-92.
[3] *De Civ. Dei*, 1, 17, 4, 9; *P.L.*, 41, 532.
[4] *Sermo* 4, 1; *P.L.*, 54, 148-9.

may become a priestly unction enriching us with grace," and later, that " it may be the everlasting chrism of priestly anointing and a salve worthy to trace the sign of the cross. . . ." The consecratory preface reads: " We beseech thee, therefore, holy Lord, Father almighty, everlasting God, through the same Christ, thy Son our Lord, to sanctify this oil, thy creature, by thy blessing and to fill it with the power of the Holy Ghost . . . this chrism by which thou hast consecrated priests, kings, prophets and martyrs. . . ."

In his Encyclical *Miserentissimus* (8 May 1928) on the Sacred Heart of Jesus,[1] Pius XI teaches: " Participation in the office of this mysterious priesthood, of satisfaction and sacrifice, has not been given merely to those whom our pontiff, Christ Jesus, uses as ministers of the unblemished offering which must be offered to God in every place from East to West, but also to the whole Christian people, which the prince of the Apostles fittingly calls ' a chosen people, a royal priesthood'. . . ."

Today, Christians who are truly aware of the majesty of their consecration in baptism are rare, but our name—Christians—should draw our attention to our royal and priestly anointing, and consideration of this should stimulate us to perform the activities related to it, for this participation in Christ's priestly power is conferred upon us in order that it may be used. Now, the power and rights bestowed by baptism are exercised in active participation in the holy sacrifice of the Mass, recitation of the Office and frequent recourse to the sacraments: in short, in liturgical worship in all its forms.

The Church offers through her priests (" per sacerdotes ")

The sacrifice is offered by the universal Church. But there immediately arises the question, "How does she offer her oblation?" The Council of Trent replies: " He instituted the new Pasch in his own person, which was to be immolated under visible signs by the Church through the priests. . . ." When the Council later refused to condemn private Masses, it declared that these Masses " are celebrated by the public minister of the Church, not for himself alone but for all the faithful who belong to the body of Christ."[2] The priest, then, by virtue of the sacramental character of

---

[1] *Acta Apost. Sedis*, 20, pp. 171–2.
[2] Sess. 22, 6; Denzinger, 944.

order is the representative of the whole mystical body in the offering of the eucharistic sacrifice, acting not only *in persona Christi* (in the person of Christ, representing him) but also *in persona totius Ecclesiae* (in the person of the whole Church, of which he is the minister).[1] Thus, in his Encyclical on the mystical body of Christ, Pius XII teaches: " The sacred ministers represent not only our Saviour, but also the whole of the mystical body and each one of the faithful. . . ."

The ordination liturgy makes it clear from the outset that priests are public ministers and the representatives of the Church. The first sentence shows that it is the Church who asks the bishop to proceed to the ordination: " Most reverend father, holy Church, our mother, requests that you confer on these deacons here present, ordination to the office of priesthood." It is no less noteworthy that the first allocution spoken by the pontiff is addressed, not to the ordinands, but to the community for whose service they are to be ordained. In former times the name of the candidate and the title or church to which he was to be appointed were both always proclaimed at the beginning of the ordination and priests were ordained only to definite titles, to which they were thenceforward bound. In the discourse that he addresses to the ordinands, the bishop constantly emphasizes their " ecclesiastical " character. " Ministers of the Church ought to be perfect in faith and works. . . . May the odour of your lives delight the Church of Christ. . . . That by an unblemished blessing they may change bread and wine into the body and blood of thy Son, in the service of thy people. . . . May the blessing of God almighty, the Father, the Son and the Holy Ghost, come down upon you, that you may be blessed in the priestly order and offer expiatory victims for the sins and offences of the people."

Priests are ordained according to the needs of the Church. The ordinand is free to accept or refuse ordination to the priesthood, but if he accepts he is " set apart for public service ": his intellect, strength, health, and time are all assumed into his ordination and placed at the service of the " ecclesial " community. The significant name " ecclesiastics " is currently given to priests. The close bond between the Church and her priests is shown very

---

[1] *Summa Theol.*, III, q. 82, a. 6,

clearly in many ancient inscriptions. " Aurelius Kapiton, a new priest of the Catholic Church," reads an epitaph dating probably from the year 262–3, discovered at Philippi. *Presbyter de catholica* is engraved on some tombstones in the catacombs. *Catholicae Ecclesiae presbyter:* " I am a priest of the Catholic Church ", proudly answered the venerable Pionius, who sealed his confession of faith with his blood at Smyrna in 250.

The holier the Church the holier will be her offering, and consequently (in so far as it is offered by her) the greater will be the glory given by the Mass and the richer its saving fruits.

In considering the offering of the sacrifice, it is necessary to distinguish between the thing offered (the body and blood of Christ, which are infinitely pleasing in themselves)—this does not concern us here—and the offering of this object, the act by which we offer it to God.

The holier this act of oblation, the more pleasing it is to God, the more fruitful in graces it will be. The holier the Church, the priests and the faithful, the more pleasing their respective acts of oblation (for this act is performed by each of them) will be to God. Let us consider the Church particularly. The Church is holy, but the degree of the Church's holiness varies. The closer the Church draws in her daily offering, through the fervour of her members, to the perfection of the priesthood of Christ himself, the more truly her sacrifice will ascend in a sweet-smelling savour before God and the richer it will be in spiritual fruits. The holiness of the Church depends to some degree on the holiness of those who compose it.

It is therefore important that in the Church militant (which offers the eucharistic sacrifice) there should be many great saints, for a Christian soul in sanctifying itself is also increasing the Church's holiness and contributing to the making of the oblation of each and every Mass more pleasing to God and more fruitful for the whole Church. The smallest act of renunciation on the part of the most humble child of the Church Catholic has an immediate influence on every Mass celebrated throughout the world. Indeed, the presence at the head of the Church militant of our Lady Immaculate, whose holiness eclipses that of all the angels and saints, confers upon the Church's offering of these sacrifices incomparable greatness, value and power of intercession.

Thus, the Bride of Christ, conscious of the deficiencies of her adoration in the face of the incomparable greatness of the victim she offers and anxious to make her act of oblation as glorifying and therefore as pleasing and fruitful as possible, devotes herself to appearing completely holy before God by availing herself of the merits and intercession of her glorified members. Many of the secrets of the Mass bear witness to this:

The Church relies:

Upon Christ: "We pray thee, Lord, holy Father, almighty and eternal God, that Jesus Christ, thy Son, our Lord . . . may himself make our offering acceptable to thee . . .";

Upon our Lady : " Hallow our sacrificial offerings, we pray thee, Lord, and at the saving intercession of God's blessed Mother, Mary, grant that those offerings may further our salvation " (Our Lady of Mount Carmel, 16 July);

Upon the Apostles: May the prayer of thy Apostles accompany the offerings we present for consecration, Lord, to thee. Grant that we may thereby obtain pardon and protection . . ." (Feast of SS. Peter and Paul, 29 June; cf. St James, 25 July; St Andrew, 30 November; St Paul, 30 June)

Upon the martyrs: " Lord, may the godly prayers of thy saints not fail to make our gifts acceptable to thee, and to obtain for us thy lasting mercy . . ." (Holy Innocents, 28 December; cf. St Venantius, 18 May);

Upon all the saints.

Conclusion: Eucharistic life, or the ceaseless offering of sacrifice throughout the world

Malachias' prophecy is being fulfilled: " No corner of the world from the sun's rise to sun's setting, where the renown of me is not heard among the Gentiles, where sacrifice is not done, and pure offering made in my honour; so revered is my name, says the Lord of hosts . . ." (Mal. 1. 11). Three hundred thousand priests of all nations, tribes and tongues now ceaselessly renew the same sacrifice from one end of the world to the other. " Jesus immolates himself continually on the altar," said Mother Mary of Jesus, Foundress of the Daughters of the Sacred Heart of Jesus († 1884). " He offers himself, but he wants to be offered by us . . . But we must not only offer Jesus, we must also immolate ourselves, let ourselves be sacrificed continually with him . . .[1]

In the light of these facts, it will be realized that it is of the greatest importance that the faithful should be made increasingly aware of: (a) the organic structure of the Church and their position as members vitally incorporated in their head; (b) the very important role of the Church, the mystical body and fullness of the head, which really has at her disposition the body and blood of Christ; (c) the importance of the word Catholic in relation to their personal sanctification as members of the Church, a sanctification which contributes towards making the Church's oblation more pleasing; and (d) the value of associating themselves in intention with all the Masses offered throughout the world: " Holy Father, through Christ the everlasting high priest, in him and with him, I offer thee all the Masses celebrated upon the earth throughout the coming day (night). I offer them to thee to thy greater glory and for the greater sanctification of thy Church, especially for our holy Father, the Pope, for our bishop, priests, seminarists and religious men and women, for the spreading abroad of your kingdom by your missionaries, the conversion of sinners, the comfort of the afflicted, the help of the dying, the relief of the souls in purgatory and in reparation for my countless sins. . . ."

[1] L. Laplace, *La Mère Marie de Jésus*, pp. 198-9 (Casterman, Tournai).

6

WHO OFFERS THE HOLY SACRIFICE OF THE MASS?

III. IN A SUBORDINATE MANNER, THE MINISTERS

The ministerial hierarchy

ALL liturgical worship is centred on the altar where the eucharistic sacrifice is celebrated, and it is in relation to the altar that the various positions of the ministers are determined according to their hierarchical status.

The priest is commissioned to offer the sacrifice of the Mass.

In the allocutions addressed by the bishop to the various classes of ordinands, the Roman Pontifical defines the functions devolving upon each of the orders. These texts were taken from a letter attributed to St Isidore of Seville († 636) in which these offices are described exhaustively.[1] Regarding priests, this document says: " It pertains to priests to effect the sacrament of the body and blood of the Lord upon the Lord's altar, to say prayers and to bless the people." Both priest and altar are hallowed for the eucharistic sacrifice.

The deacon, as his name suggests, is a servant. He is ordained to serve the priest at the altar: " The deacon must serve the altar, baptize and preach." [2] The letter attributed to St Isidore describes his duties thus: " It pertains to the deacons to assist priests and to serve them in all possible ways in everything concerning Christ's holy institutions: that is, in baptism, chrismation and in the paten and chalice; he must bring the offerings and place them upon the altar, arrange and dress the Lord's table, carry the cross, and proclaim the Gospel and Epistle. For as it was prescribed for lectors to proclaim the Old Testament, so deacons are commanded to proclaim the New. To him belongs the duty of praying and reciting

---

[1] *Epistola de gradibus; P.L.*, 83, 895.
[2] *Pontif. Rom.: De Ordinatione Diaconi.*

the names; he it is who gives the warning to give ear to God; he exhorts loudly and proclaims the peace." As the priest's immediate servant, the deacon, when he is not performing his duties, stands on the step behind the priest.

The deacon is assisted by 'followers' (*acolythi*); at their head is the subdeacon who alone may ascend the steps of the altar if his duties require him to do so. At other times he remains below, before the steps of the altar in the service of the principal servant, the deacon. Indeed, at the subdiaconal ordination the bishop explicitly declares "the subdeacon must prepare water for the service of the altar, serve the deacon, wash the altar-cloths and corporals and proffer to the deacon the chalice and paten to be used in the sacrifice".[1]

These are the sacred ministers—those invested with major orders.

Acolytes are appointed to a subordinate office: "The acolyte must carry the candle, light the lamps of the church and minister the wine and water for the Eucharist . . ." Their service is indirect and is performed through the deacon or subdeacon; they serve neither at the altar nor the communion rail. They stand by the credence—the serving-table—leaving it only when their services are called upon and returning to it immediately.

The lector[2] stands at the ambo for the lesson from the Old Testament or the Epistles: "The lector must . . . chant the lessons . . . Wherefore, when you read, stand in a raised place in the church."[3] The ambo stands at some distance from the altar but within the rail (*cancelli*) of the *schola cantorum*.

The door-keeper (*ostiarius*) is the most distant from the altar. "The door-keepers must ring the bells (*cymbalum et campanam*), open the church and the sacristy and open the book for him who preaches.[4]

The laity's place is in the nave and the strictness with which in former times they were forbidden admission to the sanctuary or presbyterium is well known. St Ambrose forbade the Emperor Theodosius to enter the sanctuary at Milan: "Only priests, O Emperor, have access to the inner places, to all others these places are closed and forbidden." Liturgical discipline has remained

---

[1] *Pontif. Rom.: De Ordinatione Subdiaconi.*
[2] The exorcist does not perform his offices at the altar.
[3] *Pontif. Rom.: De ordinatione Lectorum.*
[4] *Pontif. Rom,: De ordinatione Ostiariorum; cf.* S. Isidorus Hispalensis, *op. cit.*

faithful to this discipline and the *Ceremonial of Bishops* forbids the admission of lay persons to the choir or presbyterium.[1]

The Sacred Congregation of Rites has reiterated these decrees several times: neither magistrates, nobles or lay persons generally may occupy places in the choir or presbyterium.[2] Furthermore, according to the *Ritual*, the catafalque is to be set up not in the choir but in the middle of the church.[3]

In his article *Utrum sint septem ordines*, St Thomas points out how the ministers are distinguished from one another by their relation to the Eucharist.[4] The power of order relates either to the consecration of the Eucharist itself or to a ministry relating to the eucharistic sacrifice. The priest alone is the minister of the consecration of the Eucharist. The other ministers serve either in relation to the sacrament itself or the preparation of those who receive it.

The holiness of the ministers

Since (according to the Roman Pontifical) priests "must be perfect in faith and works, that is, fixed in the virtue of the twin love of God and their neighbour," it is obvious that the lower ministers must approach this perfection ever more closely; and this is made apparent in the texts of the various ordinations themselves. The main theme of all the exhortations addressed to ordinands is, "Apply yourselves to receiving worthily the power which is conferred upon you and then to exercising it in holiness". Then they each set out in detail the virtues of which the practice will lead the door-keeper, lector, acolyte, subdeacon and deacon respectively to perfection in their estate and a worthy exercising of their order.

We have already noticed the insistence with which many ecclesiastical documents stress the importance of religion as a priestly virtue. It follows that the lower ministers must apply themselves to it particularly. This appears with striking clarity in the ceremony of the tonsure which precedes the various ordinations and by which the cleric bids farewell to the world, its pleasures and its vanities,

[1] *Caer. Ep.*, I, 13, 13.
[2] S.C.R., *Decret.* 96 ad 6; 157; 175; 275; 1258 ad 2; 1288.
[3] *Rit. Rom*, Tit. VII, 3, 4.
[4] *Summa Theol.*, Suppl., III, q. 37, a. 2.

for the love of Christ, to cling henceforth to God alone " as his part in the inheritance and cup " in life's feast: *Dominus pars haereditatis meae et calicis mei* . . . And just as the Lord becomes the lot (κληρος whence is derived *clerus*) of the cleric (*clericus*) so also does the latter become God's portion and consecrates himself entirely to him. At the beginning of this ceremony the bishop requires his " dearly beloved brethren " to pray that our Lord Jesus Christ will give to the ordinands " the Holy Ghost who everlastingly guards in them the virtue of religion and defends their hearts from the snares of the world . . ."

Moreover, the timely performance of rites according to the prescriptions of the rubrics and decrees is for every minister not only his duty but also the chief and official form in which he practises religion. The more the deacon, subdeacon and acolytes are interiorly endowed with faith, respect, love and devotion, the more careful will they be to perform worthily the external and ritual duties entrusted to them. For each ordinand the *probatio religionis* is furnished primarily by worthy and punctual execution of his ritual duties—*exhibitio operis*.

ADDITIONAL NOTE: THE RECRUITMENT AND SYSTEMATIC TRAINING OF ACOLYTES

We have already pointed out how strictly the Church insists upon a server being present at Mass as the spokesman for the whole Christian community.

It is important that young people should have a high regard for the privilege and honour falling to them in serving Mass. The fulfilling of this function really belongs to those who are duly ordained to it. The Council of Trent stresses this point; speaking of the orders from deacon to door-keeper, it said, " The holy council, burning with the desire to restore this ancient custom, decrees that henceforth these offices shall be performed only by those who have received the said orders. It urges in the name of the Lord each and every prelate of a church, and commands them, to restore these offices . . . If clerics cannot be found to perform the functions of the four minor orders, lay persons may replace them, and these shall wear the tonsure and clerical dress in church." [1]
When there are no ordained acolytes, adult laymen may be called

---

[1] *De Reformatione*, Sess. 23, 18.

upon, and if there are no adults, boys may be employed. Catechism lessons and instructions or sermons relating to the sacrament of order are the most natural occasions for the enlightening of the faithful upon this subject. With regard to the recruiting of servers, notice Pius XII's words in the Encyclical *Mediator Dei:* " To this end [the union of the priest and his congregation in the oblation of the eucharistic sacrifice through the active participation in it of all] it will be very useful to select carefully a number of good and well-instructed boys from every class of the community, who will come forward of their own free will to serve regularly and reverently at the altar—an office which their parents, even those of the higher and more cultured class, ought to hold in great esteem."

Careful and serious training ought to precede the performance of these sacred duties, but in practice a young boy is often sent to the altar without the least previous instruction with a server who is more or less broken in to the job, who will instruct him neither well nor badly and will mumble the prayers with him. And so worship's " Holy of Holies ", the holy sacrifice of the Mass, is brought down to the level of a training ground for beginners. This, most certainly, is the best way to snuff out straightway the last traces of respect and devotion to the sacrifice in the minds of young people. A young man should be admitted to the service of the altar only if, after serious and methodical training in eucharistic devotion and ritual duties, he has proved at a practical examination that he is capable of performing them worthily.

All who wear the cassock—whether they have received the tonsure or not—must, according to the rubrics of the Missal, put on a surplice to serve Mass.[1]

" Properly instructed," writes Pius XII in his Encyclical *Mediator Dei,* " and encouraged under the watchful eye of the priest to fulfil their office reverently, regularly and punctually, these boys may well prove a source of candidates for the priesthood. Moreover, this scheme will help to avoid the unfortunate situation which occurs sometimes even in Catholic countries, in which the priest cannot find anyone to serve his Mass."

[1] *Rit. serv. in celebr. Missae,* 2.

7

WHO OFFERS THE HOLY SACRIFICE OF THE MASS?

IV. IN A SUBORDINATE MANNER, THE FAITHFUL PRESENT (*CIRCUMSTANTES*) AND THOSE WHO GIVE THE MASS OFFERINGS

THE active participation of the faithful in the offering of the eucharistic sacrifice is the exercising of the power and rights conferred upon them in their baptism (Chapter 5). Indeed, the faithful are co-offerers; the sacrifice is theirs. *Orate, fratres, ut meum ac vestrum sacrificium acceptabile fiat* . . .

The solemn rite of offering is the right and duty of each of the faithful as the Fathers and Councils constantly remind us. The whole congregation—including women—are expected to take part in the offertory. Among the most beautiful of the eulogies which St Augustine uttered in memory of his mother Monica in his *Confessions* is this: " She passed no day without making her offering at thy altar."[1] The offertory is an essential ceremony, inseparably linked with the celebration of the holy mysteries.

The Fathers, the liturgy and the Councils all bear witness to the fact that all the faithful are offerers. In about the year 150, St Justin wrote, " When our prayer is ended, bread and wine and water are brought up . . ."[2] Although the Apologist does not mention the congregation here, it seems certain that it was they who proffered these oblations. Tertullian († 243) wrote, " She prays for his [i.e. her dead husband's] soul, and beseeches refreshment for him . . . she makes an offering on the anniversary of his death."[3] After the massacre of the Thessalonians, St Ambrose († 397) deprived Theodosius of the right to offer at the altar: " Thou shalt offer when

---

[1] *Aurelii Augustini Confessiones*, 5, 9, 17.
[2] *Apologia* 67.
[3] *De Monogamia*, 10; P.L., 2, 942.

thou hast recovered the power to sacrifice, when thy offering will be pleasing to God ".[1]

The faithful make their offering of bread and wine so that the eucharistic victim may be offered in their name and be accepted as coming from them.

The prayers at the offertory in the Order of the Mass were originally prayers said by the faithful when they brought forward their offerings. Many liturgical texts bear witness to the congregation's part in the offering. The Memento of the living in the canon of the Mass makes explicit mention of those who offer " the sacrifice of praise ". Walafrid Strabo (849) explains that " the making of these oblations makes one truly the author of the sacrifice because they are to be transubstantiated into the body and blood of our victim, who is the true gift, the only gift, offered to God by the Church. It is not without reason that we say in the canon *qui tibi offerunt* (who offer to thee) and not *qui tibi obtulerunt* (who have offered to thee). It is for us to understand that we must continue to offer until the offerings are come to that end for which they have been offered."

Normally, those who offer will be present at the sacrifice because it is their sacrifice. They may not be there physically, but even in their absence they are truly those who offer. The ancient text of the canon reads simply *qui tibi offerunt* but the Middle Ages distinguished between the physical presence or absence of those who offered with the superfluous distinction *pro quibus tibi offerimus vel qui tibi offerunt* (" On their behalf we offer or they offer for themselves . . ."). Many secret prayers still recall this offering by the faithful, for example, ". . . accept the offerings we have dedicated to thee . . . (first Sunday after Pentecost); " Accept our offerings and relent, we beseech thee, Lord . . ." (fourth Sunday after Pentecost; compare the seventh Sunday). The Roman Pontifical is very interesting in this respect, in the rite for the consecration of an altar. Thus, for example, in the prayer after the anointing of the altar with the oil of catechumens and chrism, we pray that the Holy Ghost " may descend upon this altar to sanctify there our

---

[1] *Ep.* 51, 15; *P.L.*, 16, 1163. Cf. St Cyprian, *De opere et eleemosyna*, 15; St Augustine, *Ep.* 3, 8; St Caesarius of Arles, *In append. ad sermones S. Augustini*, sermo 265, 2; St Gregory the Great, *Dial.*, 1, 4, 57 and *Hom.* 38 *in Evan.*, 8.

gifts and those of thy people . . ." and that " our Lord will vouchsafe to bless and consecrate this stone . . . that it may receive the oblations and sacrifices of his people . . .."

The offering of the faithful is mentioned with especial emphasis in our Mass in the *Hanc igitur* before the consecration and in the first prayer, the anamnesis *Unde et memores*, after the consecration. " And so, Lord, we thy servants, and with us thy whole household, make this peace-offering which we entreat thee to accept " (*Hanc igitur*); ". . . we thy servants, Lord, and with us all thy holy people, offer to thy sovereign majesty " (*Unde et memores*).

Councils have legislated with regard to this matter and the strictness with which the Fathers regulated the offerings made by the faithful is worthy of careful note. In early times the faithful offered, besides bread and wine, firstfruits and harvests in the form of ears of corn and bunches of grapes and other offerings such as lamp oil, milk and honey, etc. The mixing together of all these offerings on the same altar gave rise to serious abuses and therefore the Council of Hippo (393) and the third Council of Carthage (418) laid it down that " nothing may be offered except bread and wine mixed with water, for the sacrament of the body and blood of Christ." An exception was made on Holy Saturday, when the neophytes offered bread and honey. The important Council of Mâcon in Gaul declared that " We decide that every Sunday all those present, both men and women, shall bring forth their offerings of bread and wine." [1]

Other sources of later date until the late Middle Ages (Innocent III, Sicard of Cremona, etc.) bear witness to this discipline. But such sharing in the offering on the part of the faithful was more than a duty—it was also a privilege. Many Councils from Nicaea (325) to London (1268) mention the withdrawal of this privilege as a very grave ecclesiastical penalty. But in the fourteenth and fifteenth centuries this liturgical custom began to decline.

In his well-known Encyclical on the mystical Body, Pius XII teaches quite clearly that the faithful as well as the priests offer the holy sacrifice: " The faithful, being united to the priest by their common vows and prayers, offer to the eternal Father by the hands

---

[1] Mansi, *Amplis. Conc.*, col. 9, 951; Héfele-Leclerc, *Histoire des Conciles*, 3, 1, pp. 208-9; can. 4.

of that same priest (*per ejusdem sacerdotis manus aeterno Patri porrigunt*) . . . the unblemished Lamb who is brought down on to the altar by the voice of the priest alone . . ." In his Encyclical on the liturgy, *Mediator Dei*, Pius XII enlarges upon his teaching thus:

> The priest acts in the name of the people precisely and only because he represents the person of our Lord Jesus Christ, considered as head of all the members and offering himself for them; that the priest, therefore, approaches the altar as Christ's minister, lower than Christ, but higher than the people; that the people, on the other hand, because it in no way represents the person of the divine Redeemer and is not mediator between itself and God, can in no way possess the priestly right. [Then he adds:] Yet it must be said that the Faithful do also offer the divine victim, though in a different way. The fact is clear enough from the statements of some of our predecessors and of some doctors of the Church.

" Not only do priests offer," wrote Pope Innocent III, " but all the faithful offer too; what is performed in a special way by the ministry of the priests is done in a general way by the desire of the faithful."

From this it follows that one can truly say that the Universal Church offers through Christ the oblation of the victim.

The priest acts *in persona Christi et in persona totius ecclesiae*, and he alone offers in the fullest sense of the word. By the consecration, he makes Christ present and offers him to his Father. In the act of consecration the faithful have no part but because the priest acts in the name of all the faithful, he represents *a fortiori* those who are about the altar (*circumstantes*) where he celebrates. Therefore, he also celebrates *in persona fidelium adstantium* and through him and with him they offer the eucharistic victim to God. Their act of oblation is real but it is entirely dependent upon the priest's oblation. By active participation in the priest's prayers and ceremonies they join their act of oblation to his.

> But when the people are said to offer with the priest [Pius XII teaches in *Mediator Dei*] this does not mean that all the members of the Church, like the priest himself, perform the visible liturgical rite; this is done only by the minister divinely

appointed for the purpose. No, they are said to offer with him inasmuch as they unite their sentiments of praise, entreaty, expiation, and thanksgiving with the sentiments or intentions of the priest, indeed with those of the high priest himself, in order that in the very oblation of the victim those sentiments may be presented to God the Father also by the priest's external rite. The external rite of sacrifice must of its very nature be a sign of internal worship; and what is signified by the sacrifice of the new law is that supreme homage by which Christ, the principal offerer, and with him and through him all his mystical members, pay due honour and veneration to God.

Those who by their Mass offerings (" stipendium ") cause the eucharistic sacrifice to be celebrated

The Israelite who desired to offer a sacrifice gave his lamb as his offering to the priest who offered it directly to the Lord on his behalf. Thus, he gave his gift, not to the priest, but to God and the sacrifice was really his offering and remained, as it were, his property until it was transferred to God by oblation. When the faithful give bread, wine (or the *stipendium* which replaces them), they offer the essential matter of the eucharistic sacrifice; and although after consecration by the priest the offerings are transubstantiated into the body and blood of Christ, the offerings nonetheless remain those of the faithful. For about ten centuries, the faithful brought bread and wine to the altar in person. The whole congregation took part in the offertory. " Hearing Mass " and " offering bread " were the same thing. He who did not offer was not supposed to join in the sacrifice. Like the children of Israel, Christians have gifts to offer to God. Ritually and sacerdotally, priests offer the sacrifice to God on behalf of the faithful. But the priest, St Augustine said, must have received what he offers from those on whose behalf he offers it.[1]

For practical reasons, the faithful gradually came to substitute money or material goods for offerings of bread and wine. St Epiphanius quotes the case of a Jew who had been baptized in secret on his deathbed by the bishop of Tiberias and instructed in the sacred mysteries of the Eucharist. The ceremony being over, he gave the bishop a great quantity of gold, saying, " Offer for me! "[2]

[1] *Trin.*, 4, 14.
[2] St Epiphanius († 403), *Haeres.* 30. 4–6.

By the tenth century such cases were common and in the twelfth century Honorius of Autun wrote, "In former times, it is said, people offered flour for the eucharistic bread and as all those who offered were present at the Mass, the prayer (*omnium circumstantium qui tibi offerunt* . . .) bore its full significance. But when the number of communicants dropped, flour was superfluous; it was therefore agreed that this should be replaced by *denarii* "[1]. In another place he said, "The laity offer sacrifice, these of gold, those of silver, others of other substances."[2] Thus bread and money had become interchangeable and men "offered" and "sacrificed" gold and silver as they offered bread and wine. The money given by the faithful to the priest for the celebration of a Mass is in no sense a fee and even less is it the price of the eucharistic sacrifice. It constitutes an object for oblation equivalent to bread and wine and consequently is intended not for the priest but for God.[3] So understood, these monetary offerings are as noble as the old offerings of bread and wine.

From this may be deduced the profound meaning of pecuniary oblations. Bread sustains life and life is dependent upon bread. In offering bread, Christians offered their lives, offered themselves. Today, too, the offering of money having replaced the offering of bread, when the faithful offer their monetary oblation for the sacrifice, they offer their own lives, they offer themselves.

Fr de la Taille concludes:

> The ancient view [that money offered is equivalent to bread] had three great advantages: (1) It heightens the dignity of the priest, by making him the stipendiary, not of the faithful, but of God. (2) It magnifies the role of the faithful by bringing them back to their natural state—that of a holy and priestly race, qualified by baptism to offer to God the gifts and sacrifices to be consecrated to him by the ministry of the priest invested with Jesus Christ's priesthood; and (3) it ennobles the financial transactions connected with Masses which otherwise run the risk of giving scope for the horrible expressions so common in our times: "What does a Mass cost?" "What is the price of a Mass?" "I will buy you a Mass."[4]

[1] *Gemma animae*, 1, 66; P.L., 172, 256.
[2] *Ibid.*, 1, 27; P.L., 172, 553.
[3] Cf. L. Eisenhofer, *Handbuch der liturgik*, 2, 133-4 (Herder, Freiburg im Breisgau).
[4] "*Les offrandes de Messes*": *Esquisse de la mystère de la foi*, pp. 111-251 (Beauchesne; Paris).

The more holy the congregation present is, and the more devout and active its participation, the more, too, it will on its part reinforce the glorifying and sanctifying power of the Mass

"But the time is coming, nay, has already come, when true worshippers will worship the Father in spirit and in truth; such men as these the Father claims for his worshippers" (John 4. 23). So our Lord spoke to the Samaritan woman. The sacramental character of baptism by which the faithful are enabled to participate in Christ's offering, also brings to them the grace to make their oblation worthily. A Christian is, in reality, a living temple of the Holy Ghost and a holy member of the mystical body of Christ—that is, a saint. Both St Peter and St Paul frequently honour Christians with the name *Sancti* in their Epistles. Thus St Paul wrote to the Corinthians: "From Paul . . . to the church of God which is at Corinth and to all the saints in the whole of Achaia; grace . . ." (II Cor. 1. 1).[1] St Peter wrote: "No, it is a holy God who has called you, and you too must be holy in all the ordering of your lives; You must be holy, the Scripture says, because I am holy." (I Peter 1. 15–6; cf. I Peter 2. 9).

In the anamnesis—the first prayer, *Unde et memores*—after the consecration, the Church gives full prominence to the holiness of all her members present: ". . . . we thy servants, Lord, and with us all thy holy people, offer . . ."

The Church's concern for the holiness of her members is attested by the liturgy of the Mass itself: in, for example, the sacramental of purification—the *Asperges* before the principal Mass on Sundays —and the very frequent references to contrition in the Order of the Mass.

The rite of baptism is no less insistent upon the purity that the regenerated ought to preserve throughout their lives: "Take this white garment, and see that you carry it without stain before the judgement seat of our Lord Jesus Christ, that you may have eternal life."[2]

The extreme penalty imposed by the Church is exclusion from the Mass. The *Pontifical* still contains a solemn rite of Ash Wednesday *De expulsione publice poenitentium ab Ecclesia in feria*

---

[1] Cf. Rom. 1. 7; I Cor. 1. 2; Eph. 1. 1 and 1. 4.
[2] *Rit. Rom.* II, 2. 24; cf. *ibid.*, 25.

quarta cinerum which today has fallen into disuse but which the Council of Trent wished to restore.[1]

At the hour of Terce public penitents used to go to the cathedral church to receive their penance and would then wait before the threshold until after Sext (or None) when they re-entered the church and knelt before the pontiff, who imposed ashes upon them saying, *Memento homo quia pulvis es et in pulverem reverteris: age poenitentiam, ut habeas vitam aeternam.* A canon then sprinkled them with holy water. Our modern rite of blessing and imposition of ashes is the extension to all the faithful of this, the first ceremony of the expulsion of penitents; the whole congregation now does public penance. In the old rite of expulsion the pontiff then blesses hair-shirts, sprinkles them with holy water and puts them over the penitents' heads. Then follow the great prayers: the bishop intones an antiphon and prostrates himself upon the faldstool whilst the seven penitential psalms and the litany of the saints are sung. Finally, the bishop leads the penitents from the church and after he has exhorted them to prayer, fasting, pilgrimages and alms-giving so that they may be worthy to re-enter the church on Maundy Thursday for the ceremony of reconciliation, the doors are closed upon them and Mass celebrated.

This Gallican ceremony was embodied in the Roman liturgy in about 1290 in the *Pontifical* of Durandus of Mende. There is one interesting relic of it in our present liturgy: the custom of veiling crosses at Passiontide. The whole congregation cannot be driven from the church, and therefore, because the whole congregation came to recognize its unworthiness to appear before God, the altar and celebration of Mass (*sancta sanctorum*) were veiled throughout Lent by means of the *velum quadragesimale* which hung between the altar and the choir in cathedral, collegiate and abbey churches and between the altar and the faithful in the nave (that is, at the entrance to the chancel) in ordinary churches, thus, as it were, making the whole church into a penitent's porch.

It will be realized that the considerable size of this veil[2] made its use very difficult. Therefore, towards the end of the medieval period its use was gradually restricted: in some churches it was hung

---

[1] Sess. 24, 8.
[2] That at Gurk, for example, was approximately 26 ft. 10 ins. square.

up only on Passion Sunday. The use of the veil was restricted not only with regard to time, but also with regard to size: gradually, the vast veil which hid the altar and all the ornaments of the church was replaced by veils of a smaller size which were more practical for covering the crosses and statues.

It must not be forgotten that the Church is a body not of souls, but of men who are composed of both body and soul. Therefore, it is important that the members of the congregation should play, with faith, attention and devotion, an intimate and effective part in the offering of the collective, external and visible offering which is the rite of the sacrifice of the Mass. Faith, charity and true religion are virtues which are exercised in action and shown and proved by ritual acts. It is important, therefore, that the faithful should be properly instructed and trained in the highest possible degree of intelligent, devout and active participation in the Mass. " Christ is indeed a priest," Pius XII teaches, " but he is a priest for us, not for himself, because he presents to his eternal Father religious longings and sentiments in the name of the whole human race." The holier the congregation is, the holier is its participation in the offering of the Mass, and therefore the more that Mass—in so far as it comes from them—gives glory to the holy Trinity and the richer it is in the fruits of salvation.

8

WHAT IS THE VICTIM OFFERED IN THE SACRIFICE OF THE MASS?

(a) *The body and blood of Christ under the continuing accidents of bread and wine*

JESUS Christ, St Paul teaches, is the victim of the sacrifice of our redemption:[1] " Christ has been sacrificed for us, our paschal victim " (I Cor. 5. 7).

But, according to the teaching of the Council of Trent, the victim of the sacrifice of the cross is also that of the Mass.

> He offered his body and blood to God, his Father, under the species of bread and wine and gave them under these same appearances to the Apostles whom he then made priests of the new covenant and commanded them and their successors in the priesthood to offer them by these words: " Do this for a commemoration of me.
> ... he instituted the new Pasch in his own person, which was to be immolated under visible signs[2] ...
> The victim is one and the same: the same now offering by the ministry of priests who then offered himself on the cross, only the mode of offering being different.[3]

Note that the persisting accidents of bread and wine are essential to Christ's eucharistic state. In the ritual order of sacrifice, there is only one victim at Mass, Jesus Christ himself. Declaring that we have nothing to offer to God except Jesus Christ and the infinite merits of his death, Bossuet wrote, " We offer Jesus Christ to God as our sole victim and sole propitiation through his blood." [4]

On the cross, in absolute isolation, Jesus personally offered himself as a victim to his Father's majesty. His Church did not yet

---
[1] Eph. 5. 2; 5. 25; Gal. 1. 4; I Tim. 2. 5-6; II Cor. 5. 14; Phil. 2. 8; Eph. 1. 7.
[2] Sess. 22, 1.
[3] Sess. 22, 2.
[4] *Exposition de la doctrine de l'Eglise catholique.*

exist and although he died as the "new Adam", as the head of his mystical body, it is only potentially that the Church was then contained in Christ and it is only in the course of centuries that her members have come in their successive generations to be actually united to the Lamb who represents them all and truly takes them up as his members in his oblation.

(b) *Holy Church, the mystical body of Christ, is included in the oblation of its head*

In his encyclical *Miserentissimus*[1] on the common duty of reparation to the Sacred Heart of Jesus, Pius XI emphasized the doctrine of the sacrifice of the members made in union with their head: "Through this mystical communion of saints, the Catholic faith teaches us, men and nations are not only united to one another but also to him who is the head, Christ. It is through him that the whole body . . . grows and becomes perfect in charity." Pius XII enlarges upon this teaching in *De mystico Jesu Christi corpore* (28 June 1943).

The whole Church, being the fullness of the first priest, who is also the sacrificial victim, is a victim together with him. Where the head is, there too is the body. In the sacrifice of the Mass, Christ includes his Church in his offering to the Father. Speaking of the ceremony of mixing water with wine at the offertory, St Cyprian thus expounds the mystery of the union of the Church with its head in the offering of the eucharistic sacrifice. The noble element, wine, represents the blood of Christ; water represents the faithful. The wine and the water are so intimately mingled in the chalice that they are henceforward inseparable. So is the Church inseparably united to Christ in his oblation to the Father. To consecrate the wine alone would be to offer Christ without us. To consecrate water alone would be to offer us without Christ, and as Christ and the Church are indivisibly offered in the Mass, it is important to mix a little water with the wine.

St Augustine's teaching was similar. "We are become his body," he told his neophytes one Easter Monday, "and by his mercy we are what we receive." He then went on to compare neophytes who have passed through the exercises of the catechumenate to the growth and harvesting of corn and grapes and the making of

[1] 8 May 1928; *Act. Apost. Sedis*, 1928, p. 172.

bread and wine; many grains making one loaf and many grapes making the wine for the chalice.

Ancient liturgies vividly reflect St Augustine's teaching. Thus the Anaphora of St Serapion, bishop of Thmuis in Egypt (dating from the year 350-6), reads: "As this bread was scattered over the mountains and being gathered together has become one, so also gather together thy holy Church from every nation and land, and every town, district and house, making it one living and catholic Church." [1]

Compare the *Apostolic Constitutions* (Syria: fourth century): "Almighty Lord, eternal God, as this wheat was scattered abroad and after being gathered together has made one bread, so gather together thy Church from the ends of the world into thy Kingdom." [2] The secret for Corpus Christi, which was composed by St Thomas, expresses St Augustine's profound teaching in prayer: "Lord, be gracious to thy Church we pray thee, and grant her those gifts of unity and peace of which our offerings here are the symbol . . ." In his *Summa Theologica* he taught with regard to the effect produced by the Eucharist: "Bread and wine are a fitting matter for the eucharistic sacrament inasmuch as its effects operate upon the whole Church, which indeed is built up of the diversity of the faithful as bread is made from numerous grains and wine from many grapes." [3]

The Council of Trent confirmed this teaching: the Eucharist is not only the symbol but also the sacrament of unity: "He willed that this sacrament should be the symbol of the unity of this body of which he himself is the head and to which he willed that we should be very closely united as members, through bonds of faith, hope and charity, so that we all might confess the same doctrine and so that there might not be divisions among us." [4]

(c) *The priest and his ministers, victims with Christ*

What we have said above with regard to the passive oblation of all the members with their head applies especially to priests who, in every Mass, are both offerer and offering with Christ.

At their ordination the bishop exhorts new priests: "Know

[1] F. Funk, *Didascalia*, etc., vol. 2, p. 174.
[2] F. Funk, *Constitutiones Apostolorum*, 7, 25, 3.
[3] III, q. 74, a. 1; III, q. 79, a. 1. See further, Leo XIII, Encyclical *Mirae caritatis*.
[4] Sess. 23, 2.

what it is you do, imitate what you effect, so that in celebrating the mystery of the death of the Lord, you mortify in your members all vices and lusts." The priest accomplishes this "sacrifice" of himself in celebrating the death of Jesus. Many secrets illustrate this teaching—for example, "Lord Jesus Christ, burn up our hearts in the heavenly sacrificial fire and bring out of them sweet fragrance: thou who didst enable blessed Alphonsus Mary to celebrate this rite and thereby present himself as a holy offering to thee" (St Alphonsus Mary Liguori, 2 August).

The priest's active and passive oblation in the sacrifice of the Mass was illustrated in some medieval Missals in a miniature decorating the introit for the first Sunday in Advent, *Ad te levavi animam meam:* "I lift up my soul unto thee . . ." The artist shows the priest lifting up his soul in the shape of a child, to God, in his two hands. To show that it is the priest's own soul that he is offering to God—that he is offering himself—the miniaturists took care to reproduce in the small figure the portrait of the priest himself.

The same principles apply with regard to other ministers. The order for the ordination of acolytes is particularly instructive in this respect: "For, indeed, you will offer wine and water worthily in the divine sacrifice if you yourselves are offered in sacrifice to God by a chaste life and good works." This is, of course, also true of the deacons and subdeacons who are directly and indirectly concerned in the oblation. "We must always remember," wrote Pius XI in his Encyclical *Miserentissimus,* "that all expiatory power flows down from Christ's unique sacrifice with the shedding of blood which is ceaselessly renewed without bloodshed on our altars . . . there must, therefore, be joined to the august eucharistic sacrifice the immolation of the ministers and others of the faithful so that they offer themselves as 'a living sacrifice, consecrated to God and worthy of his acceptance' (Rom. 12. 1)."

(d) *The faithful who are present and those who make Mass-offerings* ("*stipendium*")

After all that has been said above, it is unnecessary to prove that the faithful present are offerers of the Mass in an especial degree. The symbolism of the rites and prayers quoted above with respect to the passive oblation of the faithful in general applies primarily to them. They offer bread, and in offering it offer themselves *hostia pro hostia*, victims with Christ. The material offerings which represent the faithful on the altar are to play their part in the formation of the victim of the Mass: the eucharistic Christ under the species of bread and wine. After the consecration there will be present on the altar (under the appearances of bread and wine) Christ—Christ, that is, under those who offer, Christ under his faithful, under us ourselves, Christ under the unblemished garb of the living victim, bearing his Church along with him in his oblation, the Church offered to the Father and giving all honour and glory to the Holy Trinity in, through and with Christ.

The prayers of the offertory are particularly expressive of this offering of ourselves in the sacrifice of Christ. Notice particularly the prayer *In spiritu humilitatis:* "Humbled in spirit and contrite of heart, may we find favour with thee, Lord, and may our sacrifice be so offered in thy sight this day that it may please thee, Lord our God"; and the secrets, especially that for Monday after Pentecost: "In thy goodness hallow these gifts, we pray thee, Lord; accept the spiritual sacrifice we offer up; and work upon us until we too become an eternal offering to thee . . ."; and that for Trinity Sunday: "Hallow, we pray thee, Lord our God, by our invocation of thy holy name, this sacrificial offering, and work upon us until we too become an eternal offering to thee . . ."

The co-offering of ourselves with Christ in the sacrifice of the Mass is expressed especially eloquently in the construction of the Christian altar itself.[1] Relics of the martyrs—those who have been "sacrificed"—have to be enclosed in the altar sepulchre.

St Albert the Great († 1280) illustrated this doctrine in his treatise *De sacrificio Missae*.[2] With regard to the *Dominus vobiscum* he taught: "The Lord is with you when he takes you up as offerings with himself." Of the priest's *Oremus* he says: "Lofty and mighty prayer is necessary that the people being incorporated into God might be offered . . ." If the people are to be offered to God, their souls must first be uplifted to him so that the congregation may be made a sacrifice worthy of God. The exterior oblation is a sign of interior offering; just as a man through the tribute he offers

---

[1] See vol. I, Chap. I.
[2] Tract 3.1, 2, 3. Cf. *Opera omnia*, Vives, vol. 38, pp. 75-84.

to his Lord recognizes that he has dominion over him. When the priest says, " May my sacrifice and yours . . .", he lets it be understood that those who offer are offered as well as the offerings on the altar.

How do we offer ourselves?

The lamb offered by the Israelite was a visible sign of his inward desire to give himself, consecrate himself and offer himself to his creator. He laid his hands upon his victim, so, in some degree, transferring his personality to it that it might represent him before God; by sacrificing it, he offered and immolated himself. But the immolation and offering of the victim was valuable in the eyes of God only in so far as the adoration symbolized by the sacrificial victim was a reality within the worshipper himself. If the offerer did not quicken his external action by the spirit of adoration, contrition, humility and self-sacrifice, his sacrifice was reduced to an empty symbol, devoid of any spiritual content and hateful in the eyes of God.

We, too, true Israelites of the new covenant, offer a lamb, the Lamb of God who was once offered on the cross. Christ's own sacrifice, once offered, being perfect and infinite, needs no renewal. But we, too, must worship and, as the only worship pleasing to the Father is that offered through Christ, the unique sacrifice of the Lamb is renewed and made present sacramentally for us so that our interior adoration and offering of ourselves may be ritually symbolized before the Father's majesty, so that we may be represented in an external and eucharistic oblation. For this reason it is important that the love and adoration expressed in the sacramental offering of the Lamb should be matched as closely as possible by the love and adoration with which we offer ourselves in his sacrifice.

The real meaning of this offering of ourselves by ourselves is revealed very clearly in the allocution (quoted above) that the pontiff addresses to the candidates upon whom he is about to confer the power to celebrate Mass: " Know what it is you do, imitate what you effect, so that in celebrating the mystery of the death of the Lord, you mortify in your members all vices and lusts." Renunciation of ourselves and our evil desires in order to do his work is the crucifixion, the offering of ourselves, required of us. " Those who belong to Christ," St Paul teaches, "have crucified nature, with all its passions, all its impulses" (Gal. 5. 24). In his encyclical *Mediator Dei*, Pius XII teaches, "He is likewise victim; but victim for us, since he substitutes himself for guilty mankind. Now the Apostle's exhortation, 'Yours is to be the same mind as Jesus Christ showed' (Phil. 2. 5), requires all Christians, so far as human power allows, to produce in themselves the sentiments that Christ had when he was offering himself in sacrifice; sentiments of humility, adoration, praise and thanksgiving to the divine majesty. It requires them also to become victims, as it were; cultivating a spirit of self-denial, according to the precepts of the Gospel, willingly doing works of penance, detesting and expiating their sins; it requires us all, in a word, to die mystically with Christ on the cross, so that we may say with the same Apostle, 'With Christ I hang upon the cross' (Gal. 2. 19)." Later he writes, "But if the oblation, whereby the faithful in this sacrifice offer the divine victim to the heavenly Father, is to produce its full effect, they must do something further: they must also offer themselves as victims."

And this immolation is not restricted to the liturgical sacrifice. The Prince of the Apostles, precisely because we are built upon Christ, like living stones, would have us be a "holy priesthood, and offer spiritual sacrifices acceptable to God through Jesus Christ"; and St Paul makes no discrimination of time when he exhorts Christians "to offer up your bodies as a living sacrifice, consecrated to God and worthy of his acceptance: the worship due from you as rational creatures" (Rom. 12. 1).

We have already spoken of the active offering by the faithful of all the Masses celebrated throughout the world. In the light of what has been said here, it will be seen that Christians may make their vital incorporation into the Church more real every day and as victims incorporated into the victim who is continually offered may increasingly sanctify themselves by flight from sin and the occasions of sin, by renunciation of self, by the loving fulfilment of the precepts of God and the Church and by the development of the spirit of renunciation and sacrifice. It is possible for Christians, too, to offer their sacrifices with the offering of the sacrifice of their head and thus to offer themselves as victims with Christ.

9

PREPARATION FOR THE EUCHARISTIC SACRIFICE: PROCESSIONAL OFFERING BY THE FAITHFUL ACCOMPANIED BY THE OFFERTORY CHANT (Roman Elements)

BETWEEN the *Credo* and the preface of the sacrifice of the Mass there is a group of prayers called the offertory. Of these, two belong to the traditional Roman rite which goes back to the seventh century: (a) the offertory procession, the ceremony of offering bread and wine (*oblatio*), described by St Justin (*c.* 150) with the chant—the offertory, *offertorium*—which accompanies the procession; and (b) the "secret" prayer, said by the priest over the *oblata*, bread and wine, which also formed part of the ancient liturgy and was then connected with the preface as an introductory prayer.

Other ceremonies and prayers have been inserted between these two; these are mostly of Gallican origin and were incorporated into the Mass only during the Middle Ages (see chapter 11).

PREPARATION: THE DEACON (THE SERVANT, SERVER) SPREADS THE CLOTH (THE CORPORAL)

It is fitting that before offering the sacrifice of the Mass and partaking of the eucharistic meal, the altar table should be made ready. The deacon therefore first places the sacred linen cloth—the corporal—on the table. According to the *Ritual*,[1] the corporal is used *ad consecrandum super illud corpus et sanguinem Dei et Domini nostri Jesu Christi*, therefore, during the creed, after *et incarnatus est*, etc., the deacon rises and carries the corporal in the burse in both hands to the middle of the altar, where he spreads it out.[2]

The corporal is the oldest of the altar cloths. It is difficult to tell exactly when it was introduced. The distinction between cloths used to cover the altar permanently and those used at the offertory

---

[1] *Rit. Rom.*, IX, 9, 5. *Benedictio pallae et corporalis (oratio prima).*
[2] *Rit. serv.*, 6, 7. If there is no creed, the subdeacon takes the burse with the chalice.

was established by the eighth century. In his allocution to sub-deacons at their ordination, the bishop distinguishes between these two kinds of cloth: "The cloths which cover the altar must be washed in a separate vessel from that in which the corporals are washed."[1] Now this admonition is to be found in the *Missale Francorum* which dates from the eighth century. Moreover, in former times the corporal was as long as the altar and would cover it completely and therefore, according to some *Ordines Romani*, the deacon placed one end of the corporal at one end of the altar and, with the help of another minister, spread it completely over the altar.[2]

According to *Ordo VI* (German, ninth–tenth century), the corporal covered the altar as the shroud (*sindon*) covered the Lord's body and this is why it must be made of linen. Nowadays still, on Good Friday, a corporal is spread on the altar by the deacon before he brings the blessed sacrament from the place where it was reserved on Maundy Thursday.

The corporal was formerly used not only as a cloth under the eucharistic body and blood of Christ, but also to cover it, and the present form for the blessing of a corporal, which was taken almost literally from the Gelasian Sacramentary (eighth century), still refers to this.

In former times, the corporal was folded back over the chalice. For greater convenience, the upper part was later cut off and thus the pall came into being. Thus what is in appearance the lower surface of the pall and is in direct contact with the bowl of the chalice and is regarded as a lining is, liturgically, the front, the pall proper, and should be made of linen. What is apparently the upper—the visible—surface, is actually the back. From this it will be seen that an ideal pall is made without a lining, but of sufficiently stiff linen—such as damask—and decorated with eucharistic symbols. The form of blessing for a corporal is still used today for the hallowing of a pall.[3]

"DOMINUS VOBISCUM." "OREMUS"

According to the old Roman rite, before going on to the offering, the priest turns to the faithful and says *Dominus vobiscum* . . .

[1] *Pont. Rom.: De ordinatione subdiaconi.*
[2] *Ordo Rom.* V (eighth century); *P.L.*, 78, 943.
[3] *Rit. Rom.*, IX, 9, 5: *Benedictio pallae et corporalis.*

Oremus; yet no prayer follows this invitatory. Mgr Duchesne[1] considers that something has disappeared at this point and he identifies it as the *orationes sollemnes,* " the solemn collects ", which have survived on Good Friday as the bidding prayers for the Church, the Pope, the clergy and people, rulers of states, catechumens, those in affliction and danger, heretics and schismatics, the Jews, and pagans.

These collects occur, too, at this point in all non-Roman liturgies (and even in the Romano-Irish Stowe Missal—ninth century). These prayers, which unfold like a litany, were replaced by Pope Gelasius' introduction of the *Deprecatio* or litany with its petition *Kyrie eleison.*[2]

THE OFFERTORY PROCESSION

For about the first ten centuries, to be present at the holy mysteries involved playing an active and material part in the offertory by ritual and communal offering of the material substances used in the sacrifice: bread and wine were brought up to the altar by the faithful. The faithful, who had been marked with the holy character of baptism and made partakers, in an especial way, of Christ's priestly power and commissioned to participate in the Church's genuine, official worship, the sacrifice of the Mass, in a word, the liturgy, used to exercise the mandate, power and rights of their regeneration, and therefore they would co-offer. The whole congregation, without exception, used to take part in the offertory.

" Hearing Mass " was transformed for the faithful by such truly active and ritual participation in it. " Hearing Mass " and " offering bread " were one and the same thing. He who did not offer was not thought to have joined in the bishop's or priest's sacrifice—the sacrifice which is also the faithful's. The axiom of the Jewish law: " Thou shalt present thyself before me, not empty handed " (Exod. 23. 15; Deut. 16. 16) had the force of law to the Christian. Availability of the indispensable elements of the Church's sacrifice was assured by the faithful through their offerings.

We shall examine below the historical, canonical and ascetic

---

[1] *Origines du culte chrétien,* 1920, pp. 182–3. Eng. trans., *The Origin of Christian Worship* (London).
[2] Cf. Vol. 1, Chap. 17.

Preparation for Eucharistic Sacrifice 75

importance of the active participation of the faithful in the offertory ceremony. Let us consider here the ceremonial organization of this collective offering.

Ordines Romani I–VI seem obviously to delight in the detailed description of the rite of oblation. *Ordo I*, which describes the eighth-century papal Mass, contains valuable information on this point. As soon as the altar was made ready, the pope came down from his chair (*cathedra*) and went to the rail (*cancelli*) which separated the clergy from the people. He went first to the men's side (the south side, the *senatorium*) where he received the offerings of the aristocracy in order of precedence. Each man offered a flask of wine (*amula*) and a loaf. The pope handed each flask to the archdeacon who emptied it into the large chalice (*calix major*) carried by a subdeacon. When this chalice was full, the archdeacon emptied it into a larger vessel (*scyphus*) carried by an acolyte. Notice that nowhere is it said that this *scyphus* was placed on the altar or consecrated. It will be seen that the deacon's ministry is closely related to the element wine; the same applies at the communion—it is he who distributes the precious blood.

The pope also received the bread and, through the deacon of the district, passed it to the subdeacon who placed it in a cloth (*sindon*) held by two acolytes. So that the pope should not be wearied, as soon as the nobles had completed their offerings, an assistant bishop took his place to accept the offerings of the faithful. The pope then went to the " side of the matrons " (*nobilissimae matronae*) and received their offerings, too. Plebeian women followed. The pope immediately returned to the *cathedra* and washed his hands. The archdeacon then went to the altar and set out the offerings (*componit altare*), the district subdeacon gave him the loaves offered by the congregation and he placed on the altar as much as was necessary for the communion of the people.[1]

Into an empty chalice placed upon the altar, the archdeacon emptied first the flask of wine offered personally by the pope (*amulam pontificis*) and then the flasks which were the deacons' personal offerings. Then from the subdeacon he received water (*fontem*) and poured the required quantity of it into the chalice. Finally, the pope rose from his *cathedra* and came down to the altar and took the loaves (*oblatae*) offered by the deacons and the two

---

[1] The remainder was later distributed as " blessed bread ".

loaves which he himself was accustomed to offer, and placed them upon the altar. Thus, all—pope, clergy, faithful, both men and women—shared in the oblation. The offerings set out on the altar were truly representative of the various classes of people. The whole ceremony was symbolic and represented the unity of the Church in the unity of the sacrifice. " And one bread makes us the one body, though we are many in numbers, the same bread is shared by all," St Paul teaches (I Cor. 10. 17). Truly, the whole Church offers and is offered in the holy sacrifice.

Many secrets still perpetuate the memory of this great mass of offerings today: thus the secret for the feast of St John the Baptist (24 June) reads: " We heap up gifts upon thy altars, Lord. . . ."; and that from the Mass for the common of Abbots: " May the offerings we lay upon thy sacred altars, Lord, through the pleadings of thy holy abbot N. be of help to our salvation . . ."

Ordo I mentions that at the end of these ceremonies, the pope, who was standing at the altar facing the people, signalled the *Schola* to stop singing the offertory chant.

Nowadays, after the celebrant has sung *Oremus* the deacon comes to the epistle side and the subdeacon goes to the credence where he puts on the humeral veil. Then he takes the chalice—on which lies the paten, host, and pall—in his left hand, and covers them with the right-hand end of the veil, upon which he rests his other hand, and so goes up to the altar where he sets them down.[1]

The description of the offertory according to *Ordo Romanus I* is completed by another source: the ninth-century *Ordo of St Amand*, published by Mgr Duchesne.[2] According to this *Ordo* the ceremonies continued thus: during the canon the acolytes were ranged behind the deacons, each wore a cloth on his hands, some carried linen bags (*saccula*), others carried chalices (*scyphi*) of wine. *Ordo Romanus I* later recounts that at the beginning of the canon an acolyte came forward wearing a linen cloth like a scarf round his neck, by means of which he was carrying the paten before his breast. Because this linen cloth passed round his neck, the weight of the paten was borne by this minister's shoulders and he thus supported this vessel more easily. This part of the acolytes' duties later devolved upon the subdeacon. Towards the year 1300 this

[1] Cf. *Rit. Serv. in celebr. Miss.*, 7, 9.
[2] Duchesne, *Op. cit.*, Appendix.

minister used for this purpose the linen cloth with which the offerings of bread had been covered when they were carried to the altar. The modern humeral veil originated in this linen cloth. When unleavened bread in the form of thin hosts replaced leavened bread, the large offertory-trays, very heavy patens, naturally were also reduced in size, but despite this evolution the traditional use of the veil continued although, in fact, this had lost its practical usefulness, and came increasingly to be thought of as a vestment. Nevertheless, even today, the prescriptions of the liturgy concerning it are inspired by its utilitarian origins and maintain a very clear distinction between the humeral veil and vestments properly so-called. Thus, (a) the subdeacon never wears the humeral veil in Masses of the dead, which in former times constituted a liturgy *privata*—that is, without the offertory procession of the faithful; (b) even today, the humeral veil is not a vestment properly so-called (like the chasuble, stole, maniple, etc.) and therefore should not be blessed, as are these latter; (c) the subdeacon puts on the humeral veil only when he is about to use it, and where he is—that is, at the credence (he puts on the tunicle, maniple and other vestments before the ceremony and in the sacristy); he takes it off as soon as its use is over—that is, when it is time to put down the paten, just before the end of the Lord's Prayer and at the place where he stands at that time (at the left-hand corner of the altar). The priest and his assistants take off their vestments only at the end of the celebration, either in the sacristy or—in some cases and in part—at the bench (*scamnum*). (d) The humeral veil, like the ancient linen cloth, must be very supple. Moreover, according to the *Ceremonial of Bishops*, before Mass it must be laid over all the articles—chalice, cruets, etc.—placed on the credence. (e) The subdeacon never uses the humeral veil and chalice veil together.

The chalice veil is of greatly reduced size and serves to cover the empty chalice after the communion; the subdeacon does not cover the chalice with the humeral veil when carrying it back to the credence. The chalice veil, too, is not a vestment and therefore should not be blessed. This small veil, which was unknown to antiquity and the Middle Ages, should also be very supple. It may be decorated with a cross. It was assimilated to the other vestments in the sixteenth century and was made of silk of the same colour as they.

The ancient offertory procession still survives in some countries on certain occasions. At funeral Masses, after the celebrant has read the offertory (*offertorium*) the faithful with candles in their hands make their way to the altar; they " are going to the offertory." They kiss the offering-dish, the paten, to show that they want peacefully and lovingly to share in the priest's oblation; then they make a pecuniary " oblation " which replaces the ancient oblation of natural products. According to the description of the holy sacrifice by St Justin († 167)—who, doubtless, was describing the Roman liturgy—the kiss of peace then occurred before the offering of bread and wine by the faithful, during the " prayers of the faithful ". The *Apostolic Constitutions* (fourth century) also refer to it here and it is probable that before the time of Pope Innocent I († 417) the kiss of peace occurred at this point.

At ordinary Masses, too, when the celebrant has read the offertory, a collection-plate is offered to the faithful so that they may place in it an offering in the form of money; this money replaces the old offering of bread and wine by the faithful and it is therefore important that they should be made truly to understand the ceremony they are performing. Our life is bound up with our bread. The man who gives away his bread, gives his life, gives his living, gives himself. When they brought their bread and wine to the altar, the faithful were not only making an offering, but were offering themselves in anticipation with Christ. Despite new methods, the ceremony and profound significance of the oblation still survive. When they offer their money today, the faithful are still offering themselves.

The *Roman Pontifical* is rich in rites of consecration embodied in the celebration of Mass and accompanied by ceremonies of oblation. Thus, in the rite for the consecration of bishops, when the consecrator has read the offertory he goes to a faldstool placed before the altar. The newly-consecrated bishop appears before him and offers two candles, two loaves and two small kegs of wine. The same ceremony occurs at the blessing of an abbot.

A lighted candle is offered by the ordinand at the conferring of the tonsure and at each of the ordinations from door-keeper to priesthood. The same ceremony occurs in the rite for the consecration of virgins. An abbess offers two candles in the course of her blessing.

In the rite for the sacring and coronation of kings, after the reading of the Offertory, the king who has been anointed makes an offering of gold. The same ceremony occurs at the sacring and coronation of queens.

The papal Mass of canonization today is still accompanied by an imposing offertory procession composed of cardinals, dignitaries, members of the nobility, *ceremoniarii*, etc. They approach the papal throne and immediately the first group offers firstly two large candles, one of which weighs sixty pounds and bears the likeness of the new saint, and then two doves in a golden cage. The second group offers the pope two loaves wrapped in gold and silver, stamped with the sovereign pontiff's arms, and two turtle doves in a golden cage. The third group offers two small kegs of wine, plated with gold and silver respectively, with a cage of small birds.

The offering of birds seems to perpetuate the primitive oblation of food for the meal which used to conclude the ceremony. Thus, at the canonization of Blessed Bridget in 1390, Benedict IX was given an offering not only of gold to the value of a hundred ducats, but also of twenty-four capons, with the same number of pullets and pigeons, for the banquet.

Similarly, at the canonization of Blessed Nicholas of Tolentino in 1446, Eugene IV was offered, among other things, pheasants, chickens, geese, quails, turtle-doves, etc.

As has been said above, the *stipendium* or financial contribution that the believer commits to the priest for the celebration of the Mass for a special intention is not a payment made to the minister, but a monetary oblation which, under modern circumstances, replaces the material *oblata* of bread and wine. Despite the developed form of his action, the believer most certainly makes an act of oblation; he is offering his sacrifice.

THE OFFERTORY CHANT (*OFFERTORIUM*)

To some extent, the very nature of things demanded that the offertory procession should be accompanied by a processional chant—the offertory (*offertorium*). Mgr Duchesne concludes that it was embodied in the liturgy at Carthage at the time of St Augustine (c. 397).[1]

This innovation excited bitter criticism from a certain Hilary—so bitter that the holy Doctor wrote an apology *Contra Hilarium* (c. 397) to justify " the custom which was then introduced at Carthage of singing hymns from the psalms at the altar either before the oblation or during the distribution to the people of what had been offered."

At the ancient liturgical assemblies where instruction was given in the form of reading in alternation with prayer, the sections which were sung were often not without a close connexion with the various lessons to which they corresponded as complements or commentaries, in a very skilful and always free way. Indeed, there are no compositions of more touching delicacy, spontaneous tenderness and, sometimes, also, simpler familiarity than these Offertory chants. Nowhere, we believe, has the Church more clearly disclosed her knowledge of prayer and her influence over the mind of her Bridegroom. She can adapt the text of the Offertory to the Gospel lesson, join it to it, sometimes almost incorporate it into it, with consummate artistry, which however betrays neither studied refinement nor strain. We do not believe that outside the masterpieces of Greek tragedy, where the chorus freely interrupts, and unites itself closely to, the plot of the action, we could find anything more moving and touching than these sung prayers in the Missal. The intense life and profound unity which exist in the liturgical action of the Mass will never be sufficiently often demonstrated to those of the faithful who are instructed and have a lofty concern for beauty.[2]

The text of the offertory is usually taken from the psalter and this was clearly the primitive custom. In the proper of the season there are only fourteen offertories taken from other parts of the Scriptures: from Exodus, Leviticus, Isaias, Zacharias, Daniel, Job, Tobias, Esther, St Matthew and Acts. Occasionally, the text is an ecclesiastical composition (e.g. Votive Masses of our Lady.) In the ancient Antiphonaries, these chants are a skilfully formed collection.

[1] *Op. cit.*, p. 184.
[2] Dom E. Flicoteaux, *Louange et oblation* in *La Vie Spirituelle*, Feb. 1923, pp. 498, 500.

Preparation for Eucharistic Sacrifice 81

The offertory was originally composed of an antiphon and a psalm; the antiphon is repeated as a refrain after each verse. Thus, for example, in the *Antiphonarium Gregorianum*, largely the work of St Gregory († 604), the offertory for Easter Sunday is taken from Psalm 75, *Notus in Judaea Deus*. Verses 9–10 (which have been preserved in the Missal), *Terra tremuit et quievit, dum resurgeret in judicio Deus, alleluia* ("The earth trembles and is silent when God rises up to execute his sentence, alleluia."), were used as the antiphon; then verses 1, 2 and 3 of the psalm followed, each in alternation with the antiphon. For the first Sunday in Advent, it provides an antiphon and two verses. The Romano-Gallican *Ordo Romanus II* (tenth century) records, *Tunc canitur offertorium cum versibus*.[1]

Vestiges of this usage survive in the offertories for the sixteenth to the twenty-third Sundays after Pentecost. Thus the last of these consists of the antiphon *De profundis clamavi ad te, Domine* ("Out of the depths I cry to thee, O Lord") (Ps. 129. 1), the verse, *Domine, exaudi orationem meam* ("Master, listen to my prayer") (Ps. 129. 2), the antiphon, *De profundis clamavi ad te, Domine* (Ps. 129. 1). Similarly, in Masses of the dead, in which the offertory procession still survives, the Offertory *Domine Jesu Christe* (Lord Jesus Christ) is quite fully developed and, although it is not a biblical composition, has a comparable refrain, *Quam olim Abrahae . . .* ("Which thou of old didst promise to Abraham" . . .).

The Instruction of the S. Congregation of Rites (9 September, 1958) has restored the former practice by which, according to circumstances, several verses of the psalm may be sung with repetition of the antiphon after each verse or pair of verses until the time comes for concluding the psalm, with *Gloria Patri* followed by the final repetition of the antiphon.[2]

As the singing of the offertory was stopped when the offertory procession ended, the usual final doxology *Gloria Patri* is lacking. When its purpose ceases an organ atrophies: so, too, the offertory was reduced in length. In *Ordo I* (eighth century) the psalm is already reduced to one or two verses. Since the eleventh or twelfth century shortening of the act of oblation has brought about another reduction in the chant, limiting it to the antiphon

---

[1] *Ordo. Rom. II*, 9; *P.L.*, 78, 972.
[2] The same arrangement holds good for the introit cf. Vol. I, pp. 102 ff.) and the communion.

alone, as it is today. From this point of view, it is of the greatest interest to reconstruct the offertory in its primitive completeness, by rejoining to the antiphon the psalm which formerly followed it.

For its theme this chant sometimes alludes to the ceremony of offering or to the elements bread and wine: thus, at the Epiphany: *Reges Tharsis et insulae munera offerent* (Ps. 71. 10): " Gifts shall flow in from the lords of Tharsis and the islanders ". On the Wednesday after Easter: *Portas caeli aperuit Dominus: et pluit illis manna ut ederent: panem caeli dedit eis, panem Angelorum manducavit homo, Alleluia* (Ps. 77. 23-5): " The Lord threw open the doors of heaven and rained down manna for them to eat: the bread of heaven was his gift to them: man should eat the food of angels, alleluia ". At Pentectost: . . . *a templo tuo, quod est in Jerusalem, tibi offerent reges munera. Alleluia* (Ps. 67. 29-30): " in thy temple at Jerusalem kings shall offer gifts before thee, alleluia ": and on Corpus Christi, *Sacerdotes Domini incensum et panes offerunt Deo* (Lev. 21. 6): " It is for the priests of the Lord to offer their God incense and consecrated loaves."

But many offertories relate to the feast of the day and demonstrate its teaching. Thus on the feast of the Sacred Heart of Jesus: *Improperium exspectavit Cor meum et miseriam, et sustinui qui simul mecum contristaretur et non fuit; consolantem me quaesivi et non inveni* (" Naught else but shame and misery does my heart forbode; I look round for pity where pity is none, for comfort where there is no comfort to be found ") (Ps. 68. 21). This Mass has a second offertory for the paschal season.

On the feast of Christ the King: *Postula a me et dabo tibi Gentes haereditatem tuam, et possessionem tuam terminos terrae* (" Ask thy will of me, and thou shalt have the nations for thy patrimony; the very ends of the world for thy domain ") (Ps. 2. 8), and on the feast of the Annunciation: *Ave Maria, gratia plena: Dominus tecum: benedicta tu in mulieribus, et benedictus fructus ventris tui* (" Hail, Mary, full of grace: the Lord is with thee: blessed art thou among women, and blessed is the fruit of thy womb ") (Luke 1. 28, 42).

In some Masses there is a close connection between the Gospel and the offertory. Thus, for instance, in the Mass for Ember Wednesday in Lent (Station at St Mary Major), the Gospel from St Matthew records the incident of the coming of Mary and the brethren (cousins) of Jesus at Capharnaum, anxious to see him. " Then he stretched out his hand towards his disciples, and said, Here are my mother and my brethren! If anyone does the will of my Father who is in heaven, he is my brother, and sister, and mother " (Matt. 12. 49–50). The offertory is closely connected with this passage. To do the Father's will is primarily to fulfil the commandments. Therefore, the *schola* (like the chorus in a Greek tragedy) sings: *Meditabor in mandatis tuis, quae dilexi valde: et levabo manus meas ad mandata tua, quae dilexi* (Ps. 118. 47–8) (" Fain would I have all my study in the law I love: flung wide my arms to greet the law that I love ").

This connection does not, however, always appear so clearly. Indeed, many psalms were chosen as offertories because of the characteristic references proper to certain verses and when, later, these psalms used as offertory chants were shortened, the verses were eliminated. Therefore, in order to understand the choice of such an offertory, it is often necessary first to reconstruct the text of the psalm in its entirety.

Notice, too, that the general style of many offertories is that of joy, praise and thanksgiving: to give, to offer joyfully—is this not to offer twice over? *Jubilate, Benedic, Laudate, Cantate, Gloriabuntur, Mirabilis Deus.*

10
EUCHARISTIC BREAD AND WINE.—CHURCH PLATE: CHALICES AND PATENS

EUCHARISTIC BREAD

If Christ celebrated the Last Supper on the day of unleavened bread itself, it is obvious that he must have used unleavened bread; but if, on the other hand, he anticipated the legal feast on Maundy Thursday, he may have used leavened bread. This is an apparently insoluble problem, but its importance must not be overestimated. Bread—leavened or unleavened—is still bread and is therefore suitable for the eucharistic rite.

Following their Master's example, the Apostles used ordinary bread such as was available to them. Romans used to make (among other kinds) small household loaves bearing two crossed incisions (*panes decussati*); in these it was possible to see an image of the cross and it may be that, for this reason, the early Christians gave some preference to these loaves in the celebration of the holy Eucharist.

It was entirely natural that there should gradually arise the practice of making special bread for the holy sacrifice. The mosaics of Ravenna perpetuated the memory of eucharistic loaves in the form of *coronae*, that is, a spiral crown encircling a small disc marked with a cross or of a flower with four petals; St Gregory († 604) also speaks of these *oblationum coronae* or loaves of oblation. The bread used for the oblation is called *oblatio* or *oblata* in the *Ordines Romani*. Because it was to clothe the eucharistic victim with its accidents it was later called *hostia*. In Amalarius (ninth century), the word host (*hostia*) is—most fittingly—used of both the bread and the wine of the Mass, but in the Mass of Flacius Illyricus (ninth century) and in the writings of John of Avranche († 1079) and Innocent III († 1216) this term is kept for the bread alone.

Neither the Apostles nor subsequent ecclesiastical authors ever concerned themselves with the distinction between leavened and unleavened bread. Obviously, the oblation made by the faithful was leavened. Nevertheless, according to the testimony of St Bede the Venerable († 735), preference had gradually come to be given to unleavened bread from the seventh century onwards. This practice was brought to Rome from north of the Alps but was not accepted there until the ninth century. It is mentioned by Rhabanus Maurus († 856) and after that time references to it are frequent. By about the eleventh century the use of unleavened bread had completely supplanted that of leavened bread in the West. This slow substitution had a marked effect on the traditional ceremony of the faithful's offering and, moreover, thin, light unleavened hosts of ever-smaller size made the subsequent fraction of the eucharistic bread for the communion of the faithful practically superfluous. Thus by the eleventh century liturgical uses were quite distinct: unleavened bread in the West, leavened bread in the East. Yet there had never arisen the least dispute regarding the lawfulness of these uses: the Councils had never discussed them, and even Photius—who sought quarrels with the Latins on many points—never raised this question. It was Michael Cerularius (eleventh century) who first attacked the Western Church on this point and it was only after a long period of dissension that the Council of Florence (1439) declared both customs completely legitimate, unleavened bread for the West, leavened in the East.

The Code of Canon Law expressly decrees, " In the celebration of Mass, the priest must use leavened or unleavened bread in accordance with his own rite, wheresoever he celebrates Mass " (Canon 816).

The making of unleavened hosts was commonly entrusted to clerics but there is evidence that princes and queens held it an honour to be allowed to prepare them. St Wenceslas, Duke of Bohemia († 923), with his own hands sowed the corn, harvested, threshed and ground the grain and prepared the finest paste from the flour and from it baked the bread for the altar. In many medieval monasteries special ceremonies accompanied the preparation of hosts and until the Revolution in France many priests there still prepared hosts for the Mass with their own hands.

Medieval hosts were circular in shape and were usually of the size of a coin. Christ on the cross, the Lamb of God, the cross, the christological monograms are the traditional forms taken by decorations on the host.[1]

Today, the liturgical revival has influenced the decoration of the host and several new designs are to be found. Certain inscriptions are particularly suitable, for example: *Hoc est enim corpus meum;*[2] *Si quis manducaverit ex hoc pane, vivet in aeternum;*[3] *Ego sum resurrectio et vita;*[4] etc.

EUCHARISTIC WINE

Christ probably used red wine at the Last Supper. In Christian antiquity and the Middle Ages, preference was given to red wine because of the symbolism of its colour; thus, for example, the Council of Benevento and the decrees of the Synod of Cambrai (1374) prescribe the use of red wine. Yet it seems certain that, in the thirteenth century, white wine was used in the Rhineland: the Council of Cologne (1280) ordered priests to make certain that it was wine and not water that was given them for the chalice, by smelling it. Besides, red wine may easily stain altar cloths and therefore the use of white wine finally spread to the whole of the West. In eastern rites, on the other hand, red wine is still used.

Like the bread, the wine of the eucharist used to be especially prepared. St Wenceslas, Duke of Bohemia, gathered the grapes for the wine for the Mass with his own hands. St Otto, Bishop of Bamberg († 1139) cultivated vineyards reserved for this purpose. In many medieval monasteries certain terraces were reserved exclusively for the growing of vines to provide wine for the Eucharist.

PATENS

The paten, as its name *patena* or *patina* shows, is a dish or plate. The first bishops, like Christ at the Last Supper, used in the eucharistic rite the plates in use in their own times and localities. These were of various shapes and materials, sometimes round or oval,

---

[1] The Sacred Congregation of Rites has published no decree imposing universally the representation of Christ crucified on hosts; according to a decree of 26 April 1834 custom may be followed.
[2] Matt. 26. 26; Mark 14. 22; Luke 22. 19; I Cor. 11. 24.
[3] John 6. 52.
[4] John 11. 25.

sometimes square, hexagonal or octagonal, with wider or narrower rims. According to the *Liber Pontificalis* priests used glass patens (*patenas vitreas*) at pontifical Mass in the time of Pope Zephyrinus († 217). But this same source speaks also of many patens worthy of note either for their intrinsic value or for their size and weight. Thus Urban I († 230) ordered twenty-five silver patens to be made, and according to the biography of St Silvester I (314–35), he gave to the basilica built by the priest Equitius, a golden paten weighing twenty pounds,[1] and similar patens were frequently made before the ninth century both in Rome and elsewhere. They were of this large size so that the people might place their bread offerings upon them and so that they might be used for the fraction and distribution of communion to the faithful on important feast-days. Smaller patens were used at ordinary celebrations of the Mass. Gradually, respect for the eucharistic bread led to the replacing of other materials by gold and silver.

The fall in the number of communions and the introduction, in about the eleventh century, of small unleavened hosts (which made the fraction before communion of the faithful unnecessary) gradually brought about a reduction in the size of patens from over twelve inches in diameter to about six inches.

In 1596 there appeared the Roman Pontifical which prescribed that *Calix et patena sint aurei vel argentei, non aerei ut aurichalcei, vitrei vel lignei:* " The chalice and paten shall be of gold or silver, not of bronze, brass, glass or wood." Pewter may be used if need be—e.g. in times of persecution. According to the Missal, a silver paten must be plated with gold on the upper surface,[2] and this decree is confirmed by the Code of Canon Law.[3]

In former times patens were often richly decorated and from the time of Constantine onwards were often set with precious stones, but since the sixteenth century the inner surface has usually been left quite smooth to facilitate the removal of the smallest fragments of the Eucharist and this seems the most suitable arrangement. The decoration of the lower surface seems to be useless, for it is never visible.

---

[1] *Liber pontif.*, 1. 170.
[2] *Rit. serv. in celebr. Miss.*, 1, 1; *De defect. in Missa*, 10, 1.
[3] *Codex Jur. Can.*, 1305.

Many inscriptions have been cut on patens, relating to the transubstantiation of bread into the body of Christ, the real presence of Christ in the sacred host, the renewing of the sacrifice of the cross without the shedding of blood, etc., but the most strongly recommended is the engraving of a small cross on the edge of a paten, which shows the celebrant which is the front edge (these first appeared in the thirteenth century).

According to the ancient Roman liturgy, the chalice and paten were believed to have been consecrated once they had been used for the sacrifice of the Mass and Hadrian's Sacramentary (c. 790) contains no reference to the consecration of the chalice. In Gaul, however, a form of consecration is to be found in the eighth-century *Missale Francorum* and in Alcuin's *Supplement*. This passed into the Roman liturgy through the Gelasian Sacramentary and is now of obligation for both chalice and paten.[1]

In this rite, the bishop calls upon the faithful to pray that " the blessing of the divine grace may consecrate and hallow this paten upon which will be broken the body of our Lord Jesus Christ who suffered all the passion of the Cross for our salvation ". Notice that this prayer refers to the eucharistic ceremony of the fraction; according to *Ordo I*, the fraction of the consecrated bread in former times used to take place over the paten, but, in the modern rite, the fraction is performed not over the paten but over the chalice. When he has taken off his mitre, the bishop says a consecratory prayer which refers to Jahweh's commandment to Moses, " . . . anoint the tabernacle that bears record of me, and the ark where that record lies; the table with its appurtenances, the lamp-stand . . . the altar used for incense and that used for burning sacrifice and all the instruments belonging to it. All these thou shalt sanctify, and they shall be all holiness" (Exod. 30. 26-9). The bishop prays the Lord to bless, hallow and consecrate the paten for the administration of the eucharist (*in administrationem Eucharistiae*). According to *Ordo Romanus VI* (eleventh century), priests used the patens for the distribution of communion to the faithful.

The bishop then puts on his mitre and, with chrism, traces a cross from one rim of the paten to the other. Then he extends the anointing over the whole surface, while saying the formula of

---

[1] See *Rit. serv. in celebr. Miss.*, I, 1; Canons 1296, 1305; *Rit. Rom.*, Addenda: *De Patenae et Calicis consecratione*.

consecration. Lastly, after a final prayer, he sprinkles the paten with holy water.

CHALICES

The Apostles and their successors used for the holy mysteries the vessels commonly found in Roman households. Despite their infinitely varied shape, these form two chief groups—the wide, shallow cup and the tall goblet, either with or without two handles and mounted upon a foot. Between the second and the eighteenth centuries, chalices based on these two patterns were produced with an infinite variety of size, shape and decoration, but in the nineteenth century art was industrialized and a period of decadence began, until finally, in a decree dated 30 June 1922, the Sacred Congregation of Rites declared that local ordinaries were to take care that chalices did not depart from the normal shape on account of spilling the sacred species and causing scandal.[1]

During Christian antiquity and the early Middle Ages all kinds of materials were used to make chalices, but gradually synodical and episcopal decrees prohibited some materials (such as glass, horn, wood, etc.) and recommended and imposed others (such as the precious metals) and from these prescriptions modern Canon Law has arisen. "The chalice must be of gold or silver, or have at least a silver bowl gilded on the inner surface . . . and must be consecrated by a bishop".[2] Pewter is permitted under exceptional circumstances. The stem and foot of the chalice may be made from some other suitable metal, and another solid substance may be used with this metal for decorative effect.

With regard to shape, it is important to consider the following points:

(a) The basic part of a chalice is the bowl; every other part must be subordinate to it and it should be, preferably, wide and shallow, for the chalice is primarily a drinking-cup.

(b) The chalice must also be easy to handle because the celebrant may not separate his thumb and index finger between the consecration and the ablution. According to the rubrics, the chalice must have a node. This should be placed, not immediately below

---

[1] *Ordinarius loci curet ne calices a formis traditionalibus differant ob periculum effundendi sacras species et excitandi admirationem.*

[2] *Rit. Serv.*, I, I.

the bowl, but some distance from it, so the celebrant may hold the chalice by the node, in conformity with the rubrics: *Juxta nodum infra cuppam*.[1]

(c) The chalice must stand firmly upon the altar: the foot should be at least equal in diameter to the bowl.

Many forms of decoration have been used on chalices, especially symbols of Christ (the Lamb, Pelican, Eagle, Phoenix and the Lion), as well as actual representations of Christ himself and the mysteries of our Saviour's life. The Evangelists, Apostles, Old Testament figures and the saints have also been depicted upon chalices. Since the thirteenth century, a small cross has been engraved on the foot of many chalices. This is not a sign of the consecration of this vessel, but marks the front. It is not compulsory, but is very useful. Inscriptions for chalices may be taken from the Scriptures or from the *Ordinarium Missae*, from the Masses and Offices of Maundy Thursday, Corpus Christi, the Precious Blood, etc.—for example, *Hic calix novum Testamentum est in meo Sanguine* (I Cor. 11. 25); *Hic est enim calix Sanguinis mei* (*Missale Romanum*), etc.

According to the Missal, and canon law,[2] the chalice must be consecrated before being used in the sacrifice of the Mass. The rite of consecration is to be found in the Roman Pontifical in conjunction with that of the paten, under the single heading *De patenae et calicis consecratione*. In an invitatory, the bishop urges the faithful to pray that God will vouchsafe to hallow the chalice; then, having taken off his mitre, he says a prayer in which he admits that neither skill nor precious stones nor metals can make the chalice worthy to receive Christ's blood: " May thy blessing hallow this that neither art nor the nature of metal can make worthy of thine altars." When he has said this prayer, the bishop replaces his mitre and traces a cross on the inside of the bowl from one rim to another with chrism. Then he extends the anointing over the whole of the inner surface, whilst he says the consecratory prayer. After taking off his mitre again, he says a final prayer and sprinkles the chalice with holy water.[3]

---

[1] *Rit. serv. in celeb. Miss.*, 8, 7.
[2] *Missale Rom. Rit. serv. in celeb. Miss.*, 1, 1; Canon 1296.
[3] Canon 1305 defines the causes of desecration of both paten and chalice.

11
PREPARATION FOR THE EUCHARISTIC SACRIFICE: THE OFFERTORY PRAYERS AND CEREMONIES (Gallican Elements)

UNTIL the ninth century, the offertory rite was limited to the offertory procession of the clergy and people who personally brought to the altar their individual offerings (*oblata*). It was in keeping with the genius of the Gallican liturgy that it enhanced significant or symbolic rites by embellishing them with declaratory formulas. Thus where the severity and realism of the Roman rite was content to express the act of offering by the physical placing of the *oblata* on the altar, the Gallican liturgy had recourse to ritual gestures and descriptive formulas, such as the elevation of the paten and host and of the chalice, signs of the cross, and prayers accompanying the ceremonies. Let us consider this a little more closely.

In Gaul, when they offered bread and wine, the faithful repeated certain private prayers of oblation, which were usually variable in form, and evocative of sentiments of faith, repentance, humility and piety, and through them they entered into the heart of the meaning of their actions, became more fully aware of their role as co-offerers of the holy sacrifice and expressed the intentions for which they were offering the Mass with the celebrant. Notice, for example, the prayer for the offering of bread, *Suscipe, sancte Pater*. This dates from the ninth century and is to be found in the prayer-book of Charles the Bald under the title *Oratio quando offertis ad Missam pro propriis peccatis et pro animabus propinquorum vel amicorum*. It will be noticed how markedly this title stresses the intention of the act of oblation.

How and why were these most expressive Gallican rites and prayers incorporated into the sober and traditional Roman rite? Under the influence of the Carolingian reform, and after the substitution of unleavened for leavened bread, the rite of oblation of bread and wine by the faithful began to disappear. On the other hand, private Masses—without the offertory procession—began to increase in number. In these latter, the priest alone offered, that is, he alone proffered bread and wine, but he did it in the name of persons not present and in their stead. Therefore these prayers of oblation—to which men were strongly attached—passed from the lips of the faithful to those of the priest. Moreover, the ritual economy of private Masses reacted upon high Masses: the rites and prayers of oblation were finally incorporated into them.

The present prayers and ceremonies of the offertory are made up as follows: (1) The offering of bread (*Suscipe, sancte Pater*); (2) The offering of wine: (a) The preparation: the mixing of water and wine (*Deus, qui humanae*), (b) The offering (*Offerimus*); (3) The offering of priest and faithful (*In spiritu humilitatis*); (4) The invocation of the divine Sanctifier (*Veni, Sanctificator*); (5) The washing of hands (*Lavabo*); (6) The offering to the Holy Trinity (*Suscipe, sancta Trinitas*).

1. THE OFFERING OF BREAD

From the deacon the priest takes the paten on which rests the host and elevates it for the offering of the bread. The act of offering, of presenting, is expressed well by elevation. The expression *offero* is involved in his gesture. The elevation of the paten and host dates from the twelfth century. The priest also raises his eyes towards the cross for a moment and then allows them to fall once more on to the host. Then he says:

Suscipe, sancte Pater, omnipotens aeterne Deus, hanc immaculatam hostiam, quam ego indignus famulus tuus offero tibi Deo meo vivo, et vero, pro innumerabilibus peccatis et offensionibus et negligentiis meis, et pro omnibus circumstantibus, sed et pro omnibus fidelibus christianis vivis atque defunctis: ut mihi et illis proficiat ad salutem in vitam aeternam. Amen.	Holy Father, almighty, everlasting God, accept this unblemished sacrificial offering, which I, thy unworthy servant, make to thee, my living and true God, for my countless sins, offences and neglects, and on behalf of all who are present here; likewise for all believing Christians, living and dead. Accept it for their good and mine, so that, it may save us and bring us to everlasting life. Amen.

According to *Ordo Romanus I* (eighth century), the whole of the ceremony of the offering of bread consists in placing the bread upon the altar.

In a slightly later source relating to monastic custom—the *Breviarium ecclesiastici ordinis*[1]—which dates from the end of the eighth century or the beginning of the ninth century, the rite is enlarged thus: "The priest approaches the altar, takes his own offering in his hands, which he holds up and lifts up his eyes to heaven and prays to God. Then he places his oblation on the altar. And he does likewise for the offering of the wine." This provides the oldest description of the rite of the offering of bread by the priest as it takes place today. But the *Breviarium* does not mention the priest's prayer accompanying this ceremony.

Lastly, the priest raises one or more hosts, not in his hands, but on the paten, and directs his gaze towards heaven for a moment before straightway redirecting it downwards towards the host whilst praying. The prayer *Suscipe, sancte Pater*, dating, as we have said, from the ninth century, in the eleventh century appeared as a liturgical prayer to be said by the priest at the offering of bread.

The priest then lowers the host and paten again and with them makes the sign of the cross over the corporal. Finally, he slides the host on to the corporal.

The raising of the eyes. The account of the Last Supper does not mention that Christ lifted up his eyes when he took bread. Jesus was wont to do this when he was about to perform some particularly solemn action—for instance, at the raising of Lazarus and the multiplication of the loaves. So it was that raising the eyes was introduced and became a permanent part of the offertory ceremonies: (a) before the offering of the bread (*Suscipe, sancte Pater*); (b) at the offering of the chalice (*Offerimus*); (c) at the invocation of the Holy Ghost (*Veni, Sanctificator*); (d) before the prayer of oblation (*Suscipe, sancta Trinitas*) and (e) also before the consecration (. . . *et elevatis oculis in caelum . . . omnipotentem*). The priest has scarcely raised his eyes to the cross before he lowers them again to the host, in awareness of his profound unworthiness (*ego indignus famulus tuus*). Moreover, the whole of this prayer is an

---

[1] *Ordo XVII* in Andrieu: *Les Ordines Romani du haut moyen âge*, I, p. 12.

expression of humility and contrition: the text calls forth a suitable ritual attitude.

Bread and wine is placed upon the altar with a view to the consecration. It is then, at the consecration, that they will form the matter of the sacrifice. Apart from the consecration, their presence on the altar is meaningless. From this it will be seen that by desire the Church anticipates coming events and through the physical bread by anticipation, is already contemplating the sacred body of Christ, the unblemished victim (*hanc immaculatam hostiam*) whom she will proffer to the Father in the rite of consecration.

The Mass is truly a propitiatory sacrifice: that is, it makes God favourable, clement, and merciful, to forgive us our failures, our sins, and so reconciles us with him. What the Council of Trent was later (in the sixteenth century) to define, is already expressed here in the form of prayer. " The Holy Council teaches that this sacrifice (of the Mass) is truly propitiatory and that through it, if we approach God with a sincere heart and direct faith, with fear and respect, as contrite and penitent, we obtain mercy and receive the help of grace in due season. For, being appeased by this oblation, the Lord, in granting us grace and the gift of contrition, will remit our crimes and sins, even the greatest." [1]

" If anyone says that the sacrifice of the Mass is merely (a sacrifice) of praise and thanksgiving or a simple commemoration of a sacrifice accomplished upon the cross and not a propitiatory (sacrifice) . . . let him be anathema." [2]

By his sacrifice with bloodshed upon the cross, Christ earned reconciliation with his Father, remission of penalties and satisfaction for sins for all mankind. In the eucharistic sacrifice, the sacrifice of the cross is made present with all the power to propitiate and satisfy embodied in it by Christ. And we, sinners, direct all this same power to propitiate to the heart of the Father, upon which it acts with a sovereign efficacy. It appeases (*placare*) his offended majesty, makes it propitious and inclines it to have mercy upon us: that is, it bestows grace upon us. This ascending and descending motion of the propitiatory power of the Mass is outlined in a striking summary in the secret for the thirteenth Sunday after Pentecost: " Look favourably, Lord, upon thy people and upon thy people's

[1] Sess. 22, 2; Denzinger, 940.   [2] Sess. 22, 3; Denzinger, 950.

Offertory Prayers and Ceremonies

gifts. Let this offering move thy compassion, persuading thee to grant us pardon and an answer to our prayers."

That for the Saturday of the fifth week of Lent asks with especial insistence: "Accept our offerings, and relent, we beseech thee, Lord. Though our wills resist thee, press them graciously into thy service."

The priest then takes up the paten and host again, and with them makes the sign of the cross over the corporal. A Roman eleventh-twelfth century manuscript says: *Tunc (sacerdos) ordinat oblationem super corporale in modum crucis dicens: In spiritu humilitatis*, etc.

When he used to have several oblata of bread, the priest would arrange them on the corporal in the form of a cross. When it came about that there was only one host, the ceremony evolved into the making of the sign of the cross. At high Mass, after the ceremony of the offertory, the subdeacon again takes the paten and holds it before him, lifted up and covered with a humeral veil, until the Lord's Prayer.[1] According to *Ordo I*, an acolyte used to stand forward at the beginning of the canon wearing a veil which passed around his neck, with the help of which he held up the paten chest-high. This duty later devolved upon the subdeacon at the offertory. At low Mass, the priest slides the host onto the corporal and puts down the paten, concealing it a little way beneath it (*aliquantulum subtus corporale*).[2]

2. THE OFFERING OF WINE

(a) PREPARATION: THE MIXING OF WATER AND WINE

The deacon pours wine into the chalice and then the subdeacon proffers a cruet of water to the priest, who blesses it; then the subdeacon, in his turn, pours a little water into the chalice.[3] This ceremony of mixing water and wine goes back to the earliest times and is a custom of all liturgies. St Justin († 167), in his famous *Apology* to Antoninus Pius (138–61), the senate and the people of Rome, mentions this ceremony twice in his two descriptions of the celebration of Mass: "Then there is brought up to him who presides over the assembly of the brethren, bread and a cup of wine mingled with water. He takes them and praises and glorifies the Father

---

[1] *Rit. Serv.*, 7, 9.   *Rit. serv.*, 7, 3.   [3] *Rit. serv.* 7. 9.

of the universe through the name of the Son and the Holy Ghost "[1]; and again: " Then we all rise and pray together aloud. Then, as we have already said, when the prayer is ended, bread and wine and water are brought. He who presides sends up to heaven prayers and thanksgiving as much as he is able ".[2]

In the liturgy of St Basil the Great we read: " Likewise after the supper, taking the chalice of wine furnished by the vine, he mixed water with it, gave thanks, etc. . . . ." The third Council of Carthage (397) decreed: " In the sacrament of the Lord, nothing shall be offered except what the Lord has given: that is, bread and wine mixed with water, etc." Similarly, much later, the Council of Florence (1431–47) thought this rite so important that it devoted an especial commentary to it and made its adoption a condition of reunion for the Armenians.[3] A century later, the Council of Trent (1559–65) was to insist:

" Then the holy Council warns that the Church obliges priests to mix water with the wine to be offered in the chalice, both because Christ our Lord is believed to have done so and because water flowed from his side together with blood: it is this mystery which is commemorated by this mixing; and as the waters in St John's Apocalypse symbolize the nations, so there is here represented the union of the faithful people itself with Christ its head." [4]

The Council brings forward three arguments: (a) the commemoration of the rite of the Last Supper: the Jews were accustomed to dilute their wine with water, and Christ would have conformed with this custom. Moreover, many ancient liturgies bear witness that Christ performed this ceremony (e.g. the liturgies of SS. James, Mark, Basil and John Chrysostom). (b) The representation of the blood and water which flowed from Christ's side: wherefore, when performing this ceremony, the Carthusians say: *De latere Christi exivit sanguis et aqua. In nomine Patris et Filii et Spiritus Sancti.* (c) The symbol of the union of Christ and his Church: this is the traditional teaching which dates back to the earliest times —to St Cyprian († 258) of Carthage and even St Irenaeus († 202) of Lyons[5] and St Ignatius († 117) of Antioch.[6] St Cyprian teaches very significantly:

[1] *Apol.*, 65, 3.   [2] *Apol.*, 67, 5.   [3] *Decretum pro Armenis*, Denzinger, 698.
[4] *Sess.* 22, 7; Denzinger, 945.   [5] *Adv. Haer.*, 5, 1.   [6] *Eph.* 5. 1.

For because Christ who bore our sins, bore us all, we see that the water represents the people, but the wine signifies the blood of Christ. When the water is mixed with the wine in the chalice, the people is united to Christ and the believing nation is joined and united to him in whom it has believed. This mingling and union of water and wine in the Lord's chalice is effected in such a way that the elements can no longer be separated from one another. So also nothing can separate the Church, that is, the people formed into the Church and persevering faithfully and firmly in its faith, from Christ . . .

Thus one cannot in sanctifying the chalice offer the water alone, as one cannot offer the wine alone, for if anyone offered the wine alone, the blood of Christ would be made present without us; if, on the other hand, there was water only, the people would be present without Christ. When, on the other hand, the two are mixed and intermingled in an intimate union, then the spiritual and celestial sacrament is brought into being.[1]

His teaching was perpetuated throughout the Middle Ages. Rhabanus Maurus († 856) declared: "Neither of these elements ought to be offered in this sacrifice without the other: neither the wine without the water nor the water without the wine, because we ourselves must abide in Christ and Christ must abide in us".[2]

And St Thomas repeated: "When water is mixed with wine in the chalice, the people is united to Christ".[3] In other words the ceremony of mixing is necessary to the full symbolic value of the offering of the chalice. To offer the wine alone is to offer Christ without us. To offer the water alone, would be to offer us without Christ. And as in the holy sacrifice Christ our head bears us along with him as his members in his oblation, a little water must be mixed with the wine. Such is the traditional teaching.

The faithful are not merely co-offerers, they are truly co-offered with Christ. Every morning, when they take part in the offering of the Mass, they pour into the chalice of Christ's "sacrifice" —in the form of a little drop of water lost in the wine in the cup— the sum of the "sacrifices" which their faithfulness to his law

---

[1] *Epist.*, 63, 13; *P.L.*, 4, 383-4.
[2] Rhabanus Maurus, *De cleric. instit.*, 31; *P.L.*, 107, 320.
[3] *Summa Theol.*, III, q. 74, a. 6.

demands of each of them in the course of the day. From this we may see the deep ascetical significance of this ceremony.

In conclusion, we may quote the following very instructive and concise lines, in which Cardinal Mercier refers to this symbolism:

" I am the little drop of water absorbed by the wine of the Mass, and the wine of the Mass becomes the blood of the Man-God. And the Man-God is substantially united to the Holy Trinity. The little drop of water is swept into the main-stream of the life of the Holy Trinity. Shall I ever be pure enough, limpid enough, as the little drop of water destined to take part in the sacrifice of the Mass?"

According to the oldest Roman *Ordines*, it was the deacon who used to pour the wine and water into the chalice.[1] The admixture of water used formerly to be performed without either ceremony or prayer. But *Ordo I* (eighth century) adds: *infundit faciens crucem in calice:*[2] " He pours the water into the chalice in the form of a cross."

When, in the twelfth century, private Masses had increased in frequency, at low Mass the priest himself performed the deacon's (and subdeacon's) duties. On the other hand, only the priest then communicated in both species. Smaller chalices had therefore replaced the chalices formerly used for administration. The priest now consecrated only sufficient wine for his own communion and therefore the small quantity of water had been reduced to a few drops, which could not be poured out in the form of a cross. The deacon's traditional ceremony was therefore transformed into the making of the sign of the cross over the water by the celebrant. In turn, this practice reacted upon high Mass—in which the celebrant (and not the deacon) blesses the water with the sign of the cross. The change spread even further, notably into pontifical Mass[3] and Mass celebrated in the presence of a pontiff.[4] In this last, the subdeacon turns to the bishop and genuflects, and the bishop bestows his blessing upon the water from the throne. The priest does not bless the water in Masses of the dead; not because the blessing has been omitted here, but because this originally private (*privata*)

---

[1] It was only later that this ministry passed to the subdeacon.
[2] *Ordo Rom. I*, 1, 14.
[3] *Caer. Ep.*, 2, 8, 62.
[4] *Ibid.*, 2, 9, 6.

Offertory Prayers and Ceremonies

liturgy has remained faithful to the old ceremonial, that is, that of the pre-Carolingian era, when the deacon poured water into the chalice without ceremony (and not in the form of a cross).

The prayer

Deus, qui humanae substantiae dignitatem mirabiliter condidisti, et mirabilius reformasti: da nobis per huius aquae et vini mysterium, eius divinitatis esse consortes, qui humanitatis nostrae fieri dignatus est particeps, Jesus Christus, Filius tuus, Dominus noster: Qui tecum vivit et regnat in unitate Spiritus sancti Deus: per omnia saecula saeculorum. Amen.

O God, by whom the dignity of human nature was wondrously established and yet more wondrously restored, grant that through the sacramental use of this water and wine we may have fellowship in the Godhead of him who deigned to share our manhood, Jesus Christ, thy Son, our Lord, who is God, living and reigning with thee in the unity of the Holy Spirit, for ever and ever. Amen.

This magnificent prayer is an old Roman secret for the Nativity and is to be found in the Leonine (sixth century), Gelasian (c. 700) and Gregorian (eighth century) sacramentaries.[1] In about the eleventh century it was adapted by the interpolation *per huius aquae et vini mysterium* to its new purpose. It is a masterpiece of eurhythmy and doctrinal synthesis in patrician style. It opens with an ascending meditation upon the wonders of the first creation and the yet greater marvels of the second: redemption: *Deus, qui humanae substantiae mirabiliter condidisti, et mirabilius reformasti*. It is easy to enlarge upon the character of the mysteries recalled by this prayer and illustrated by the ceremony.

Qui propter nos homines et propter nostram salutem descendit de caelis (Credo) . . . "It is for us men, and for our salvation, that the Word came down from the heavens." It was for our redemption that he deigned to vest himself in our humanity (*qui humanitatis nostrae fieri dignatus est particeps Jesus Christus, Filius tuus, Dominus noster* . . .). The mystery of his incarnation, his priestly ordination, his sacring, lies in this: the incarnate Word is the God-man, between God and men, the priestly Mediator between God and ourselves, the living bridge which alone links us with the Father,

[1] *Sacrament. Leon.*, 159; *Gelasianum*, 5; *Gregorianum*, 13.

the Pontiff, the Priest, the Anointed, the Christ, he who is hallowed for ever. This union of the two natures in the singleness of his person is symbolized by the union of the noble substance, wine, and the common substance, water. This ritual mixing is so significant that the Armenian Monophysites (who saw only one nature in Christ) refused to perform it. Their custom was formally condemned by the second Council of Trullo (692).

Christ the redeemer, who was ordained priest in his very incarnation, has offered the sacrifice with bloodshed once for all, by dying for us upon the cross. It was then that, at a thrust from a lance, there flowed forth blood and water. Our ceremony recalls this new mystery: the wine represents the blood, the water represents the other substance.

On the cross, Christ earned grace—that is, the divine life—for us. At the Mass, in which the ceremony of admixture is performed, *per huius aquae et vini mysterium*, he applies the grace there won to us and makes us evermore " partakers of the divine nature " (*eius divinitatis esse consortes*).

(b) THE OFFERING OF THE CHALICE

When the chalice has been made ready, the deacon gives it to the priest. He touches the foot of the chalice or supports the celebrant's arm while he is holding up the chalice, and with him says the prayer of oblation, *Offerimus*.[1]

Offerimus tibi, Domine, calicem salutaris, tuam deprecantes clementiam: ut in conspectu divinae majestatis tuae pro nostra et totius mundi salute cum odore suavitatis ascendat. Amen.	We offer thee, Lord, the chalice of salvation, entreating thy mercy that our offering may ascend with a sweet fragrance in the presence of thy divine majesty for our salvation and for that of all the world. Amen.

This order of events has resulted from a fairly typical ritual evolution. As we know, the deacon is the traditional minister of the element wine: he it was who used to make the oblation of the chalice and communicate the faithful in the precious blood. Thus, in the time of St Cyprian († 258), it was the deacon who gave the chalice to the faithful.[2] In the *Apostolic Constitutions* (fourth

---

[1] *Rit. serv. in celebr. Missae*, 7, 9.   [2] *De lapsis*, 25: ed. Hartel, 1, 225.

century) he fulfils the same duties,[1] and this liturgical tradition is confirmed by the earliest *Ordines Romani* (eighth–ninth centuries).[2] Thus, according to *Ordo Romanus I* (eighth century): "After the pope has placed the offerings of bread upon the altar, the archdeacon (that is, the chief of the deacons) 'elevates' the chalice, taking it from the hands of the district subdeacon and places it upon the altar on the right of the pontiff's offering of bread, and wraps the cloth of oblation around the handles of the chalice."[3] When the Roman liturgy took root in Gaul, of necessity, it came under the influence of its new surroundings. The poetic and descriptive genius of the Franks adapted itself badly to the extreme sobriety inherent in some Roman ceremonies. They filled out the rite with paraphrases and declaratory formulas, accompanied by graphic gestures: the prayer *Offerimus* is one of these [4] (as in *Suscipe*, etc.). According to the Missal of Flacius Illyricus (1030) which was probably produced for a church in Westphalia, the deacon used to perform the offering of the chalice and to recite the prayer. Durandus of Mende († 1296) in his *Rationale* explains that the deacon is the principal offerer of the chalice and that the priest joins him without, however, himself performing this rite. Lastly—towards the fifteenth century—the deacon's role as principal passed to the celebrant. He it was who henceforward offered the chalice and the deacon associated himself with him only in a secondary manner (by touching the foot of the chalice or the celebrant's sleeve): it was thus that Burchard († 1506) described this rite in the Papal Mass.[5] When, therefore, the deacon today lends his support in the offering of the chalice, this is not because of the great weight of ancient chalices as some liturgists suppose—for besides, the deacon performed this ceremony alone—but by virtue of the inherent tradition that this rite was formerly proper to the deacon.

Here, too, the Church contemplates by anticipation the eucharistic blood to which the wine is going to lend the vesture of its accidents.

[1] Book 8, 13.
[2] *P.L.*, 78, 947, 978, 982.
[3] *Ordo Rom. I*, ed. Stapper (Munster, 1933). The same arrangements were made in the *Ordo* of St Amand (ed. Duchesne).
[4] E.g. in sacramentaries from an abbey near Limoges (eleventh century); from Albi (eleventh century); and from an abbey near Narbonne (twelfth century); from Girona (twelfth century), etc.
[5] *S. Caerem. S. Ecclesiae*, Venetiis, 1632, p. 131.

3. THE PERSONAL OBLATION OF THE PRIEST, MINISTERS AND FAITHFUL

Bowing slightly, the priest prays:

In spiritu humilitatis, et in animo contrito suscipiamur a te, Domine: et sic fiat sacrificium nostrum in conspectu tuo hodie, ut placeat tibi, Domine Deus.	Humbled in spirit and contrite of heart, may we find favour with thee, Lord, and may our sacrifice be so offered in thy sight this day that it may please thee, Lord our God.

This prayer may be read in the Sacramentary of Amiens (second half of the ninth century) and is an excerpt from a prayer which begins: *Hanc oblationem quaesumus, omnipotens Deus, placatus accipe* . . .

The term *humilitatis* (*humus* = earth) brings in its train the bowing of the body. The Church puts on the lips of her priest the magnificent prayer of the three young men in the furnace at Babylon: being unable to offer God the lawful sacrifices, they offered themselves with contrite hearts and humble minds: " But, O Lord, accept us still, hearts that are crushed, spirits bowed down by adversity; look kindly on the sacrifice we offer thee this day, as it had been burnt-sacrifice of rams and bullocks, thousands of fattened lambs; who ever trusted in thee, and was disappointed?" (Dan. 3. 39–40)

The whole of the emphasis of this prayer is on " May we find favour with thee, Lord." The oblations—the bread and wine—indeed represent those who offer themselves: bread is the substance which supports life. He who gives away his bread, gives his life. Thus, in offering their bread, the priest and the faithful offer their lives, they offer themselves alive. They not only offer: they are also offered. This prayer concludes the offering of bread and wine.

4. THE INVOCATION OF THE SANCTIFYING SPIRIT (EPICLESIS)

Veni, sanctificator omnipotens aeterne Deus: et bene✠dic hoc sacrificium tuo sancto nomini praeparatum.	Come, thou sanctifier, almighty, everlasting God, and bless these sacrificial gifts, prepared for the glory of thy holy name.

The invocation and blessing *Veni, Sanctificator* dates from the ninth century and occurs in *Ordo Romanus VI* (tenth century) in a greatly expanded form, in Germany and France. According to the text, this prayer is addressed to God considered in the unity of his nature: him to whom the forefathers of the Old Testament offered their sacrifices. This is obvious in a thirteenth-century Roman Missal: *Veni, sanctificator omnipotens aeterne Deus, et benedic hoc sacrificium ab indignis manibus tuo nomini praeparatum, et descende invisibiliter in hanc hostiam qui visibiliter in patrum hostias descendisti.* Moses and Solomon invoked the Lord and fire from heaven came down upon their sacrifices (Cf. II Mach. 2. 10). In the Mozarabic liturgy this prayer is addressed to the Holy Ghost: *Veni, sancte Spiritus sanctificator, sanctifica hoc sacrificium de manibus meis praeparatum.* Sanctificator means " he who consecrates ". This invocation is addressed to the Holy Ghost. The priest beseeches him to pour forth upon this oblation the highest blessing which it may receive: that is, eucharistic consecration. It will therefore be understood why this invocation is addressed to the Holy Ghost. The miracle of love which constitutes the consecration is not without analogies to the incarnation of the Word. The liturgy links the mysteries of the incarnation and the eucharist on many occasions. Thus, at Corpus Christi, the Church sings the preface for Christmas and ends its hymns *Jesu, tibi sit gloria, qui natus es de Virgine*. Now, while they are produced by the one and indivisible divine power of the three Persons as works of love, the incarnation and the consecration are attributed particularly to the Holy Ghost, the consubstantial love which proceeds from the Father and the Son. Thus, we sing in the creed: *Et incarnatus est de Spiritu Sancto ex Maria virgine: et homo factus est*. The Gregorian Sacramentary declares magnificently on the feast of the Annunciation: *Altari tuo, Domine, superposita munera Spiritus Sanctus assumat, qui hodie beatae Mariae viscera splendoribus suae virtutis replevit.* Similarly in the prayer in preparation for the celebration of Mass, which an authoritative critic has restored to John of Fécamps († 1078), the priest prays on Friday: " the unseen, all-embracing majesty of thy Holy Spirit may descend . . . turning these offerings of ours into the body and blood (of Christ) ".

This is clearly a typical example of the epiclesis.

The oldest form of our prayer is simple: *Veni, Domine sancti-*

ficator omnipotens, et benedic hoc sacrificium praeparatum tibi. Amen. (Stowe Missal, Ireland, ninth century.)

In the eleventh century in Italy, this prayer said explicitly: *Veni, Spiritus sanctificator omnium, benedic et sanctifica hoc sacrificium coadunatum tibique ab immundis manibus praeparatum* (*Ordo XVI*, St Peter's, Rome, Ebner). A contemporary southern Italian text reads: *Et descende in hanc hostiam invisibiliter sicut in patrum hostias visibiliter descendisti* (*Ordo VII* and *XV*).

The formula here takes on several of the characteristics of a true epiclesis. Moreover, other prayers at this point ask explicitly: *Sanctifica, quaesumus, Domine, Deus, hanc oblationem ut nobis Unigeniti corpus et sanguis fiat* (Ebner I, II, III, etc.).[1]

It is therefore with justice that several liturgists judge our prayer *Veni, Sanctificator* to be an epiclesis, an invocation of the Holy Ghost for consecration. The Church holds our gaze constantly fixed upon the central rite of consecration. All the preparatory ceremonies of the offertory take their meaning through and for the consecration. The true offering of the holy sacrifice is accomplished only in the consecration. All that is here called " offering " relating to the bread and wine is but a preparation for that consecratory oblation and takes its name from it: *Et benedic hoc sacrificium tuo sancto nomini praeparatum.*

5. THE WASHING OF HANDS

The priest then goes to the epistle side, where he washes his hands: that is, " the fingers of consecration ", the two thumbs and index fingers at low Mass, the hands themselves at high Mass (because of the censings). Meanwhile, he says the apt Psalm 25, verses 12–16.

Psalmus	Psalm
Lavabo inter innocentes manus meas: et circumdabo altare tuum, Domine:	With the pure in heart I will wash my hands clean, and take my place among them at thy altar, Lord,

[1] These quotations are drawn from Dom B. Capelle, *Le sens de la messe* in *Les Quest lit. et par.*, 1942, XXVI, pp. 72–3.

Offertory Prayers and Ceremonies

Psalmus	Psalm
Ut audiam vocem laudis, et enarrem universa mirabilia tua.	Listening there to the sound of thy praises, telling the story of all thy wonderful deeds.
Domine, dilexi decorem domus tuae, et locum habitationis gloriae tuae.	How well, Lord, I love thy house in its beauty, the place where thy own glory dwells!
Ne perdas cum impiis, Deus, animam meam, et cum viris sanguinum vitam meam:	Lord, never count this soul for lost with the wicked, this life among the blood-thirsty:
In quorum manibus iniquitates sunt, dextera eorum repleta est muneribus.	Hands ever stained with guilt, palms ever itching for a bribe!
Ego autem in innocentia mea ingressus sum: redime me, et miserere me.	Be it mine to guide my steps clear of wrong: deliver me in thy mercy.
Pes meus stetit in directo: in ecclesias benedicam te, Domine.	My feet are set on firm ground: where thy people gather, Lord, I will join in blessing thy name.
Gloria Patri . . .	Glory be to the Father . . .

By handling the oblations and the thurible, the priest has soiled his hands. As the canon may not be interrupted and the time of the consecration draws near, it is fitting that he should cleanse them. According to the Roman *Ordo I*, the pope washed his hands after he had received the offerings and returned to his throne. This ceremony was customary until *Ordo VI* (ninth century); *Ordo XIV* identifies two separate washings: the first before the offertory, when the pope left his *cathedra*, the other after the censings. The *Ordo* records, however, that this twofold washing was inspired by an exaggerated concern for the proprieties and that it was commonly omitted at Rome. The *Ceremonial of Bishops* still provides for a twofold washing of hands today: the first at the throne after the Gospel or *Credo* and before the offertory; the other at the altar after the offertory and censings. In former times this purely utilitarian ceremony was performed without a prayer. In the Middle Ages it was accompanied by various formulas, of which the Psalm of Innocence (Ps. 25. 6-12) is one of the most appropriate.

6. THE PRAYER OF OBLATION TO THE HOLY TRINITY

Suscipe, sancta Trinitas, hanc oblationem, quam tibi offerimus ob memoriam passionis, resurrectionis et ascensionis Jesu Christi Domini nostri, et in honorem beatae Mariae semper virginis, et beati Joannis Baptistae, et sanctorum apostolorum Petri et Pauli, et istorum, et omnium sanctorum: ut illis proficiat ad honorem, nobis autem ad salutem: et illi pro nobis intercedere dignentur in caelis, quorum memoriam agimus in terris. Per eundem Christum Dominum nostrum. Amen.

Holy Trinity, accept the offering we here make to thee in memory of the passion, resurrection and ascension of our Lord Jesus Christ; in honour, too, of blessed Mary, ever virgin, of blessed John the Baptist, of the holy Apostles Peter and Paul, of these saints [whose relics are here], and of all the saints. To them let it bring honour, to us salvation; and may they whom we are commemorating on earth deign to plead for us in heaven: through the same Christ our Lord. Amen.

    This prayer, too, is of Gallican origin. With a few variant readings it is to be found in the Sacramentary of Amiens (second half of the ninth century) where it is followed by four others, all beginning in the same way. It appears among the prayers *Post Nomina* (read after the announcing of the names of those who were to be especially commemorated in the holy sacrifice) and *Ad Pacem* (said at the Kiss of Peace) of the old Gallican liturgy and probably sprang from them.

    From the north of France, it spread rapidly to the rest of the country, and also beyond the borders, most notably to Echternach, Murbach, Basle, Monza, Como, Venice, Verona, Lucca, Arezzo, Rome and perhaps even to Monte Cassino. In the well-known Mass of Flacius Illyricus (*c.* 1030) this prayer is followed by twelve others beginning *Suscipe, sancta Trinitas,* yet, it appears that it was only in the thirteenth century that—with some adaptation—it was incorporated into the Roman liturgy. The present order of the prayers of oblation, which was fixed by St Pius V's Missal, appeared in full for the first time in a twelfth-thirteenth century *Ordo Missae* from Benevento, which was in use in Rome in the thirteenth century. *Ordo XIV* also gives our present prayers of oblation in full and in their present order.

The Mass is offered to the Holy Trinity. The Church meditates in anticipation, through the elements of bread and wine, upon Christ's body and blood, for which they furnish the indispensable clothing of their accidents. . . . *Ob memoriam passionis, resurrectionis et ascensionis J. C. D. N.* . . . As we shall see with regard to the first prayer after the consecration, the anamnesis, the Mass is the memorial of our Saviour's passion, resurrection and ascension. The Church here acclaims these mysteries beforehand. We shall comment upon these venerable mysteries in connection with the anamnesis and therefore shall return to them in that chapter.

. . . *et in honorem.* . . The holy sacrifice is offered to God alone; nevertheless, it may be offered to him in honour of a saint (*in honorem*, formerly *in honore*), that is, to give thanks to the Lord for the victory granted to his servant. Indeed, the Council of Trent, quoting this same prayer, declares: " And although the Church has sometimes been wont to celebrate Masses in honour and commemoration of the saints, yet, it teaches that the sacrifice is not offered to them, but to God alone who has rewarded them. Thus it comes about that the priest is not accustomed to say ' I offer the sacrifice to thee, Peter or Paul,' but in giving thanks to God for their victories, he implores their patronage that they, whose memory is commemorated upon earth, may vouchsafe to intercede for us in heaven." [1]

Thus, then, we thank God himself for a wondrous fund of graces which his beneficence has brought into being in the souls of the saints. Great honour is given to the saints when we give glory to God for the gifts which he has bestowed upon them. This grateful recognition moves them greatly and disposes them, for their part, to intercede for us.

Reference used to be made at this point to saints especially dear to Christians: references which would vary from place to place according to local usage: (a) the blessed Virgin Mary, who was so closely associated with the sacrifice with the shedding of

---

[1] Sess. 22, 3; Denzinger, 941. *Si quis dixerit, imposturam esse, Missas celebrare in honorem Sanctorum et pro illorum intercessione apud Deum obtinenda, sicut Ecclesia intendit:* A.S. (Sess. 22, 5; Denzinger, 952.)

blood which is made present in our Mass; (b) St John the Baptist, who once pointed out the Lamb of God who by his sacrifice of blood would blot out the sins of the world; here at the offertory, he proclaims the coming of the same Lamb whose eucharistic blood will henceforward make actual to those present the remission of sins won upon the cross; (c) the reference to St John the Baptist, the patron of the archbasilica of the Lateran and of the holy Apostles Peter and Paul, patrons of the eternal city, is of Roman origin; (d) as for the most concise term *et istorum* ("and these") this is further explained by the French form: " and of all those whose feast is celebrated today, and whose names and relics are preserved here (in the altar)".

(*offerimus*) . . . *ut* . . . *et illi pro nobis intercedere dignentur in caelis quorum memoriam agimus in terris. Per eundem Christum Dominum nostrum.* We offer the sacrifice in order that " the saints whom we are commemorating on earth may deign to plead for us in heaven ". And we ask " through the same Christ our Lord ". At first sight this prayer appears strange, in that:

(a) We ask through Christ that the saints may pray for us. Is then Christ's mediation insufficient?

(b) We speak to God that the saints may intercede for us. Is not this a vicious circle?

(*a*) Far from being insufficient, Christ's supreme mediation is so signal that it is from it that the saints take their power of intercession. The superabundant mediation of Christ is the very source from which the mediation of the saints is derived. " There are in heaven," Bossuet says, " intercessors who pray with us: but they themselves are heard only through Jesus Christ, the chief intercessor and mediator, through whom all draw near, both angels and men, both the saints who reign there, and those who yet struggle." [1]

The main purpose of this sacrifice is to unite all Christians—and especially the most holy—to God, that together they may render to him acknowledgement of their servitude. By this association of Christ's glorified members in the fundamental mediation of the high priest for his militant members, this cohesion, this unity of the Church which finds its paramount expression and consecration in the Eucharist, is affirmed and strengthened.

[1] *Explication de quelques difficultés sur la Messe*, n. 39.

(b) This prayer does not create a vicious circle: listen once again to Bossuet:

> Notice that it is through Jesus Christ that we ask God, not only for the outcome of the saints' prayers, but also for the inspiration and will to make them. Those who have evilly mocked you so greatly about the canon will perhaps be ignorant enough and foolish enough to do so even more violently with regard to the roundabout way by which we address ourselves to God asking that he may inspire the saints to pray for us; as though it would not be quicker to ask God directly for what we want than that he should ask himself through the saints. But according to these worldly arguments we should abandon all prayer; for does not God know our needs? Does he not know what we want when we pray to him, and is it not he himself who inspires our prayers? . . . But if it is replied that, nevertheless, God wills men to pray to him and that they should pray to him for others and that they should ask others to pray for them; because although we should pray neither that our prayers should be granted nor that they may be known, it is good for us to pray in all these ways and by so doing we become better: this is then no longer a vicious circle but rather a sincere exercising of that charity honoured constantly by God, when he inspires or grants these prayers. And because he would establish perfect brotherhood between all those whom he would make happy, either in heaven or on earth, he inspires not only the faithful, but also the holy angels and men who are in heaven, with the longing to pray for us; for it is a perfection in holy men who are our fellows that they should concern themselves with our salvation and a different perfection in the holy angels who are not, that they should love and reverence in us the nature to which the Son of God has chosen to unite himself personally. We can, therefore, beseech God to inspire in them these prayers which bring honour to him, because we can ask of him all the means that it pleases him to employ to manifest his glory: but we must ask through Jesus Christ, through whom alone must come to us all good things.[1]

In this prayer, the Church declares that the Mass is a true sacrifice of supplication and petition.

[1] *Ibid.*

7. THE TRUE MEANING OF THE OFFERTORY

By means of the offertory, the matter of the sacrifice, bread and wine, is withdrawn from profane use and devoted to God with a view to the eucharistic oblation. The offertory, therefore, forms a ritual preparation for the eucharistic sacrifice, separate from it and subordinate to it. It is, nevertheless, inspired by the eucharistic oblation and, in anticipation, proclaims its nature, ends and fruits.

The offertory, then, is in no sense the eucharistic offering of the sacrifice: it is not even its beginning. As we later prove, the true offering of the Mass consists in the consecration itself. There are made present by the consecration not only the thing offered (*res oblata*), that is, the body of Christ which was once nailed to the cross, and his blood which was then poured forth, but also the act of oblation (*oblatio rei*) through which the sovereign high priest of the new covenant submitted himself, with bloodshed, to his Father for the greater glory of the Holy Trinity and the salvation of mankind.

Yet this priestly consecration is only possible if the faithful first give their bread and wine to the priest. Let us not forget that the Mass is a sacrifice of a sacramental, eucharistic kind; that what is offered is indubitably the body and blood of Christ, but under the persisting accidents of bread and wine. The species of bread and wine are essential to our divine victim's eucharistic state. The body and blood of Christ offered in our Mass originate in the transubstantiation of bread and wine and keep their accidents. The faithful, then, bring their bread and wine to the altar and give them to the priest in readiness for the consecration which is shortly to follow. Without this consecration, the presence of these *oblata* on the altar would be meaningless. Consequently, the bread and wine are offered at the altar "for the consecration".

Medieval commentators likened the Canon of the Mass to the "Holy of Holies" through which only the high priest might pass. Thus the offertory is the sanctuary which adjoins it, stands before it and gives access to it, while yet being separate from it. When the terrestrial gifts of bread and wine are ceremonially placed on the altar, which receives them in God's stead, they are removed from common use, lose their profane character and become the things of God: *Deo dicata:* consecrated to God, they are hallowed, made holy things. *Munera dicata* is one of the most typical of the terms used in the secrets. By dedicating the matter of the sacrifice to God (*dedicatio materiae*) the priest prepares for its physical hallowing (*sacratio* or *sanctificatio*) which is brought about by the transubstantiation of bread and wine into the body and blood of Christ. *Sacrare, sanctificare*, usually signify the action of sanctification. We have already quoted the prayer from the rite for the dedication of churches, which is particularly characteristic in this respect: *ut quicumque tibi in hoc altari sacranda* (to consecrate) *libamina* (the offerings) *devotus obtulerit vel sacrata* (consecrated gifts) *susceperit* (communion).[1]

Many secrets pray similarly: *Munera tibi, Domine, oblata sanctifica* ... (Monday, the first week in Lent); *Propitius, Domine, quaesumus, haec dona sanctifica* (Monday in the octave of Pentecost), etc.

Suarez rightly teaches that the offertory consists in *quaedam dedicatio materiae sacrificandae per futuram consecrationem*.[2] The Church also treats a host which has been offered (but not consecrated) with especial respect: it may not be returned to the general store, but must be consumed by the celebrant after the ablutions.[3]

The holy Eucharist, the unblemished victim, the cup of salvation, the divine sacrifice of adoration and thanksgiving, the sacrifice of intercession "for our innumerable sins, offences and neglects", the sacrifice of intercession "for the salvation of us and the whole world" is the end to which the Church and her children who offer reach out with their whole souls, that they anticipate by desire, already contemplating the heavenly or eucharistic oblation beyond the physical reality of the bread and wine of their earthly offering.

While yet remaining separate from the eucharistic oblation, and subordinate to it, as its official preparation, the prayers and ceremonies of the offertory move in the sphere of influence of the consecratory oblation with which they are imbued and which has inspired them. So bottomless, indeed, is the profundity of the mystery of consecration, so simple its rite, that the Church feels the need to state and enlarge upon its meaning in the later prayers

---

[1] *Pont. Rom.: De ecclesiae dedicatione.*
[2] Examples quoted by Batiffol, *Leçons sur la Messe*, p. 162.
[3] *Missale Romanum. De defectibus* 10. 9.

of the canon, especially in the anamnesis, in which she solemnly expounds her act of oblation: *Offerimus praeclari majestati tuae de tuis donis, ac datis, hostiam puram, hostiam sanctam, hostiam immaculatam, Panem sanctum vitae aeternae, et calicem salutis perpetuae.*

But yet the consecration, the eucharistic oblation, is already in being. So that it acts in anticipation in the rites and prayers of the offertory—where, in every way, it declares the nature of its sacrifice, defines its ends and enumerates its fruits.

Suscipe, sancte Pater . . . hanc immaculatam hostiam . . .

pro innumerabilibus peccatis, et offensionibus, et negligentiis meis . . .

Offerimus tibi, Domine, calicem salutaris . . . ut in conspectu divinae majestatis tuae, pro nostra et totius mundi salute cum odore suavitatis ascendat.

The rich variety of the prayers of oblation—the secrets—attest the same truths.

It thus becomes clear that the offertory which precedes the canon is in no way the act of oblation of the eucharistic sacrifice or even its beginning. The "lesser canon" in contrast to the "great canon", as spoken of by some liturgists, is absolutely unknown to the liturgy. The offertory is not a complete, independent rite: it constitutes the ceremonial preparation for the consecration (*. . . et benedic hoc sacrificium tuo sancto nomini praeparatum . . .*) to which it is organically linked and subordinated.

To the question: "For what ends is the sacrifice of the Mass offered?" the catechism replies: (a) to give supreme honour to God (the Mass is a sacrifice of adoration); (b) to thank him for all his benefits (the sacrifice of thanksgiving); (c) to obtain forgiveness for our sins and remission of the penalties owing to them (sacrifice of propitiation); (d) to obtain other graces and blessings (sacrifice of supplication, petition).

The prayers of oblation express these admirably:

(a) *The Mass is a sacrifice of adoration:* "Holy Father, almighty, everlasting God, accept this unblemished sacrificial offering, which I, thy unworthy servant, make to thee" (Offering of the bread.).

"We offer thee, Lord, the chalice of salvation, entreating thy mercy that our offering may ascend with a sweet fragrance in the presence of thy divine majesty . . ." (Offering of the chalice).

" . . . May we find favour with thee, Lord, and may our

Offertory Prayers and Ceremonies

sacrifice be so offered in thy sight this day, that it may please thee . . ."

" Holy Trinity, accept the offering we here make to thee . . ."

(b) *The Mass is a sacrifice of thanksgiving:*

" With the pure in heart, I will wash my hands clean and take my place among them at thy altar, Lord, listening there to the sound of thy praises . . ." (*Lavabo*).

(c) *The Mass is a sacrifice of propitiation* (making God propitious, clement, merciful, to forgive us our failings, our sins, and thus reconciling sinners to him):

" . . . which I, thy unworthy servant, make to thee, my living and true God, for my countless sins, offences and neglects . . ."

" Humbled in spirit and contrite of heart, may we find favour with thee, Lord . . ."

The *Lavabo*.

(d) *The Mass is a sacrifice of supplication, of petition*, that is, it obtains (*impetrare*) new graces for us:

" Holy Father, almighty, everlasting God, accept this offering . . . which I . . . make to thee . . . on behalf of all who are present here; likewise for all believing Christians, living and dead. Accept it for their good and mine, so that it may save us and bring us to everlasting life."

" Grant that through the sacramental use of this water and wine we may have fellowship in the Godhead of him who deigned to share our manhood, Jesus Christ . . ."

" . . . entreating thy mercy that our offering may ascend with a sweet fragrance in the presence of thy divine majesty, for our salvation and that of the whole world . . . (Offering of the chalice)."

" To them (the saints) let it bring honour, to us salvation; and may they whom we are commemorating on earth deign to plead for us in heaven " (Prayer to the Holy Trinity).

Thus the single concept of the eucharist oblation runs through the Order of the Mass from the beginning of the offertory to the end of the canon.

12

INCENSE AT THE OFFERTORY

THE smoke of incense arises many times in the course of the Mass. The priest twice encircles the altar with its odour, at the introit and the offertory. The Gospel book, the offerings, the altar cross, the relics, the celebrant, the ministers, the clergy and the faithful are all censed in turn; incense arises towards the consecrated host and chalice at the elevation: the solemn ceremony of censing indubitably contributes to the augmentation of the majesty of the celebration.

We consider in turn, then: (1) the use of incense in Jewish and Roman worship; (2) the beginnings of the use of incense in the liturgy of the Mass; and (3) our present ceremonies of censing and their significance.

1. THE USE OF INCENSE IN JEWISH AND ROMAN WORSHIP

Incense is a resinous gum extracted by incising from the sap of a tree (Boswellia) native to Arabia and Abyssinia. When scattered upon glowing charcoal, it burns away giving off fumes diffusing characteristic aromatic odour. In the sacrifices of antiquity, the use of incense was so important that the name *thus* then given to it was itself taken from the verb θύειν, meaning " to sacrifice ". This is not, however, surprising, for incense, being burned by fire and giving off its odour which ascends into the heavens, is a very natural symbol of our nothingness before God, of our interior adoration and of the prayer that arises from a heart enkindled by love.

The smoke of incense, therefore, arose ceaselessly before Jahweh: the preparation and ritual use of incense are described minutely in the Pentateuch. The Lord commanded Moses to build an altar of incense, covered with pure gold and placed in the sanctuary between the seven-branched candlestick and the loaves of proposition.[1] Incense was to be burned there continually upon burning coals

[1] Exod. 30. 7-8.

taken from the altar of sacrifice. Twice a day, at nine in the morning and three in the afternoon, priests would offer incense with other aromatic substances, upon the altar of incense. It was at the hour of the offering of incense that the angel of the Lord appeared to Zacharias at the right hand of the altar of incense to announce to him the coming birth of John the Baptist.[1] The Levites alone were permitted to prepare and store incense, the use of which was restricted to bloodless sacrifices offered in honour of God alone.

Every week, a priest would replenish with incense the two golden bowls which surmounted the heaps of the loaves of proposition in the sanctuary. When the loaves were renewed on the following Sabbath, the incense was burned on the altar of burnt offerings, and the two bowls were filled anew.

Yearly, on the day of the atonement, the high priest entered the holy of holies, carrying a burning censer and a handful of incense. There, beyond the veil, he cast the incense on the fire, so that a cloud of smoke shrouded the shrine of propitiation, that he might not himself die before Jahweh.[2]

Among the Romans, the use of incense was held in great favour. Every month, they offered it to the gods who guarded the household (*lar familiaris*). Incense smoke, moreover, arose everywhere in the temples in honour of the gods. The altar of burnt offerings was set up in the open air near the entrance to the temple. Within, there stood one or more smaller altars (*arula, foculus, craticula*) for incense offerings, which were spread on burning embers or burnt in earthen or metallic vessels (*turibulum*). Burning incense before the gods was one of the chief acts of worship and was a formal profession of paganism, of devotion to the gods, an act which marked the ineradicable difference between pagans and Christians. During the persecutions, Christians were brought before these altars and called upon to burn incense. St Cyprian stigmatized those who so denied Christ in the Decian persecution with the name *turificati*, " those who have burned incense ";[3] and later Prudentius († 405) called the renegades *turifer grex*, " the flock who offer incense ". We can understand the revulsion with which the use of incense under such conditions filled the primitive Church. Yet the custom of burning incense in suitable vessels was soon introduced into the Constantinian basilicas.

[1] Luke 1. 10. [2] Lev. 16. 12–4. [3] *Epist.* 52.

2. THE BEGINNINGS OF THE USE OF INCENSE IN THE LITURGY OF THE MASS

We have already noticed in connection with the introit and Gospel how the honours commonly paid to Roman officials finally passed to ecclesiastical dignitaries, the pope and bishops. As the judges of ancient Rome, the bishops walked preceded by ministers carrying lighted candles. For fear lest these should be extinguished on the way, another assistant walked at the head of the procession carrying a brazier. Gradually, this brazier came to be supplied with aromatic substances and was transformed into a perfume-burner: that is, a censer. To ensure that this container should continue to burn, it was necessary to swing it about, and so that this might be done more easily, it was fitted with chains and became the Roman *turibulum*, which by evolution became the modern thurible. These honours, which were of Roman origin, passed into the Gallican liturgy at an early date.

Our present ceremonies, which so greatly enhance the majesty of the celebration of Mass, were unknown in the ancient Roman liturgy. They came into being in Gaul, and are derived from the ceremonial at the consecration of altars.[1] They clearly recall the offering of incense upon the altar under the old covenant. The bishop used to make an offering of incense on the altar and cense it by enveloping it with perfumed smoke on all sides. Later, the bishop confined himself to beginning this ceremony and it was continued by a priest who—as he does today—swung the thurible and swathed the altar in smoke until the bishop reached the solemn anointings. This same ceremonial is still in use today.

In *Ordo II* (Romano-Gallican, ninth century) this characteristic ceremony at the dedication of altars can be seen entering the liturgy of the Mass and being extended to persons: during the *Credo*, an acolyte went to the various altars to cense them: then the incense was carried to the clergy and people (literally: " to the noses of men, and from the hand, the smoke was carried to the mouth ").[2] After the offertory, the incense was placed on the altar.[3]

According to *Ordo V* (ninth–tenth century) one acolyte censed the altar, then the bishop, priests, deacons and clergy, and another

---
[1] *Sacramentarium Gelasianum*, ed. Wilson, Oxford.
[2] *P.L.*, 78, 972.
[3] *Ordo II*, 9; *P.L.*, 78, 972–3.

the people, during the *Credo*.[1] There was at this time, however, still no suggestion of censing the oblations.[2]

Ordo VI (Germanic, tenth–eleventh century), however, stresses the censing of the oblations: after the *oblata* had been placed on the altar, the bishop blessed them and said the *Veni, Sanctificator;* he then took incense, placed it in the thurible and offered it at the altar.[3]

From the eleventh century onwards, there arose the custom of censing at the introit, and from the twelfth century onwards it became general in the Roman liturgy at the introit, Gospel and offertory. Censing at the elevation, however, dates only from the fourteenth century. The *Ordines* knew no form of prayer for the imposition or blessing of incense, nor for use during censing: the censing of the altar was carried out in silence—as it is today—after the introit. The second censing of the altar has been accompanied by appropriate prayers since the eleventh century. The Roman *Ordo XIV* (1311) exhibits the whole modern selection of prayers.

3. THE PRESENT CEREMONIES OF CENSING AT THE OFFERTORY

Incense is not merely symbolic: by the Church's blessing, it is raised to the dignity of a sacramental, a true protection against the snares of the devil. The bishop shows this in the ceremony for the consecration of altars, when he solemnly blesses the grains of incense to be burned on the five crosses of waxen thread:

" Be pleased to bless and sanctify this creature, incense, that all listlessness, all weaknesses and all snares of the enemy may flee when they sense its odour, and be set far from thy (human) creation which thou hast redeemed by the precious blood of thy Son, that it may never be wounded by the bite of the evil serpent."

Moreover, the Church uses blessed incense as she uses holy water: to counteract the influence of the devil—for instance, at the blessing of candles (2 February) and the blessing of palms, etc. It is for this reason that, before beginning the consecration of the altar, the bishop envelops it completely in the purifying smoke and then swings the thurible crosswise over the centre and each of the four corners of the altar. Similarly, at Mass, the crosswise censing of

---
[1] Mabillon, *Musaeum Italic.*, p. 47.   [2] *Ordo V*, 7; *P.L.*, 78, 987
[3] *Ordo VI*, 10; *P.L.*, 78, 993.

the bread and chalice is a ceremony of purification and sanctification, and concern for the same end is involved in the censing of the clergy and people. Indeed, is it not when we are performing the holiest functions that we most need divine help? The censing of the Blessed Sacrament, on the other hand, is a direct act of adoration (like the elevation): the incense is not then blessed.

The form of blessing is normally simple: *Ab illo benedicaris in cuius honore cremaberis. Amen.* "May this be blessed by him in whose honour it will be burned. Amen." But here, at the offertory, the form is more solemn:

| *Per intercessionem beati Michaelis Archangeli, stantis a dextris altaris incensi, et omnium electorum suorum, incensum istud dignentur Dominus bene ✠ dicere, et in odorem suavitatis accipere. Per Christum Dominum nostrum. Amen.* | At the intercession of blessed Michael the archangel, who stands at the right hand of the altar of incense, and of all his elect, may the Lord deign to bless ✠ this incense and to accept its fragrant sweetness: through Christ our Lord. Amen. |

Eleventh- and twelfth-century Missals here mention not St Michael, but St Gabriel—and rightly, for the angel who appeared to Zachary at the right of the altar of incense was Gabriel. But in the Middle Ages there was fervent devotion to St Michael, who was identified with the unnamed angel who, in the Apocalypse, stands, thurible in hand, by the golden altar: "Then was there another angel that came and took his stand at the altar, with a censer of gold; and incense was given him in plenty, so that he could make an offering on the golden altar before the throne, out of the prayers said by all the saints. So from the angel's hand, the smoke of the incense went up in God's presence, kindled by the saints' prayer (Apoc. 8. 3-4). This is, in addition, the text of the offertory on the feast of St Michael (29 September). Thus it came about that the name St Gabriel was replaced by St Michael in this prayer. This usage was confirmed by a decree of the Sacred Congregation of Rites dated 25 September 1705.

The censing of the oblations. The priest censes the host and chalice cross-wise three times, then he encircles them in fragrance, censing them three times in a circle. Meanwhile he says:

Incense at the Offertory

Incensum istud a te benedictum, ascendat ad te, Domine, et descendat super nos misericordia tua.

With thy own blessing, Lord, let this incense rise to thee, and bring down upon us thy mercy.

The censing of the cross, relics and altar. After the proper reverence, he censes the cross with three double swings (*ductus*) (1, 2, 3), then he repeats the reverence. Next, without leaving the middle of the altar, he censes individually with one double swing, the reliquaries placed between the candlesticks, both those on the Gospel side (*a, b*) and then (after the proper reverence) those on the Epistle side (*c, d*). Then, without another reverence, the celebrant

proceeds to the censing of the altar. He first censes the altar, swinging the censer from the centre towards the three candlesticks until he reaches the Epistle corner (4, 5, 6); here he lowers his hand, and censes the side of the altar first near the ground, then near the top (7, 8). Then, raising his hand, he censes the top of the altar progressively towards the centre, swinging the censer three times (9, 10, 11) and, after the necessary reverence, he goes towards the Gospel side, giving three more swings towards the back of the *mensa* (12, 13, 14). Then he censes the side face on the Gospel side with two further swings (15, 16), first below and then above, and without moving from that point, he raises the censer to cense the front of the top of the altar (17, 18, 19). Lowering his hand he next censes the front of the altar three times whilst walking from the Gospel corner to the centre (20, 21, 22). Finally, after the required reverence, he continues to the Epistle side, and censes the other half of the front of the altar with three more swings (23, 24, 25).

Meanwhile, he says the following prayer, which is taken from Psalm 140, verses 2-4, recalling the sacrifice of incense offered in the sanctuary each morning and evening at the time of the lighting of the lamps:

Dirigatur, Domine, oratio mea, sicut incensum, in conspectu tuo: elavatio manuum mearum sacrificium vespertinum. Pone, Domine, custodiam ori meo, et ostium circumstantiae labiis meis: ut non declinet cor meum in verba malitiae ad excusandas excusationes in peccatis.	Welcome as incense-smoke let my prayer rise up before thee, Lord; when I lift up my hands, be it as acceptable as the evening sacrifice. Lord, set a guard on my mouth, a barrier to fence in my lips, lest my heart turn to thoughts of evil, to cover sin with smooth names.

The censing of the celebrant, his assistants, the clergy and people. At the Epistle corner, the celebrant halts and gives the thurible to the deacon, saying:

Accendat in nobis Dominus ignem sui amoris, et flammam aeternae caritatis. Amen.	May the Lord kindle within us the fire of his love, and the flame of undying charity. Amen.

Here is a truly exalted and lyrical prayer: the incense of prayer arises as a sweet-smelling fragrance to God, from a heart enkindled by love.

The deacon straightway censes the celebrant with three double swings. The censing of the choir, ministers and people then follows according to the rules of the Ceremonial.

The symbolism of censing. When commenting upon the offering of incense made by the Magi to Christ, the Fathers of the Church emphasize that it symbolized their adoration. Therefore, the Church pays the homage of *latria* to the Blessed Sacrament by her ceremonies of censing; and this is a direct worship of adoration (*cultus latriae directus*). But the Church also pays the homage of worship to Christ indirectly, by granting the honour of censing to objects which represent him. When she censes the altar, cross and Gospel book, the Church sees and worships not stones, wood and parchment, but Christ himself as represented by these objects (*cultus latriae indirectus*): the altar, cross and Gospel book are images of Christ.

If these inanimate objects are in truth endowed with this symbolic significance, then *a fortiori* the faithful—who are vitally incorporated into Christ by their baptism and made like to him by the sacramental character, being the living extension of his person—represent their divine head. Besides, are not the faithful (in a state of grace) temples of the Holy Trinity? Is not a Christian—according to the old definition—composed of a body, a soul and the Holy Ghost? By a yet stronger claim, the sacred ministers, and above all the priest, the "new Christ", who shares in his priestly power and acts in his name, are his representatives. Through their persons, the Church reaches out to and adores Christ and God. Therefore, the Church extends the honour of censing to the whole of Christ's congregation, from the priest to the least of the faithful.

Similarly, in her funeral rites, the Church censes our corpses out of respect for the Holy Ghost, whose host they were and for whose divine sacramental operations they were the channel.

Note: The historical symbolism of our rites is sometimes very complex. In stressing the element of worship in the censings, we in no wise suggest that this is their only aspect. Censing is often also a sacramental.

Prayer, as St Thomas teaches, is the lifting-up of the mind towards God: *ascensus intellectus (mentis) in Deum*.[1] Such a prayer springs from a heart enkindled by love: incense arises in ethereal smoke: *Dirigatur, Domine, oratio mea sicut incensum*. St John sanctions this symbolic meaning in his Apocalypse, in the vision of the twenty-four elders prostrate before the Lamb, "each bearing a harp, and having golden bowls full of incense, the prayers of the saints" (Apoc. 5. 8). Because of their exquisite fragrance, the symbolism linked with the fumes of incense grew ever richer: it is through good works proceeding from charity that, as St Paul says, "we are Christ's incense offered to God" (II Cor. 2. 15). As the homage of our incense mounts up to God, the divine mercy

---

[1] *Summa Theol.* IIa, IIae, q. 83, a. 17.

descends to us in return (*Incensum istud a te benedictum ascendat ad te, Domine, et descendat super nos misericordia tua*). When they spread over the priest, ministers and faithful, when they envelop the whole congregation in their cloud, the fumes of incense unite the whole Christian community in prayer, as in the merciful favours of God.

As has been pointed out above, censing is also a sacramental, intended to counteract the devil's powers over the altar, offerings, sacred ministers and faithful during the celebration of the paramount act of worship. The censing of the body at funerals is also inspired principally by this same preoccupation. Nowadays still, at the blessing of a new cemetery, in accordance with the Pontifical the bishop, before censing the cross, prays: " Mercifully grant to the bodies of thy servants and handmaidens that enter into this cemetery, a place of rest and protection against the attacks of all evil spirits ". The Ritual, in the blessing of gold, incense and myrrh on the feast of the Epiphany, prays for the faithful " that they may be withdrawn from all sickness of body and soul . . . and that, joyful, healthy and safe, they may serve thee in thy Church."

Thus we see what sublime truths shine through the ritual censings to him who is willing to consider the organization of their ceremonial and their symbolic meaning. As members of Christ, living temples of the Holy Trinity, it is important that Christian congregations should properly esteem this signal rite and should rise to their feet in a body to receive with requisite respect the honour and sacramental of censing.

13

THE PRAYERS OF OBLATION:
THE SECRETS (Roman)

ACCORDING to the *Ordo Missae* there next follows (1) a bidding (*Orate Fratres*—Gallican); (2) a prayer over the offerings (*super oblata*), called the secret (Roman); and (3) the preface.

Despite differences of provenance and date this triad constitutes—materially at least—a liturgical unit which is to be found in many blessings and consecrations.

Therefore, the secret, which concludes the offertory, seems also to introduce the preface. Let us consider this more closely.

1. *ORATE FRATRES* (Gallican)

According to the Ordo Missae, the priest kisses the altar and says in a subdued voice (*voce paululum elevata*):

Orate, fratres: ut meum ac vestrum sacrificium acceptabile fiat apud Deum Patrem omnipotentem.	Pray, brethren, that my sacrifice and yours may find acceptance with God the Father almighty.

The acolyte or the congregation (*minister, seu circumstantes respondent*) replies:

Suscipiat Dominus sacrificium de manibus tuis ad laudem et gloriam nominis sui, ad utilitatem quoque nostram, totiusque Ecclesiae suae sanctae.	May the Lord accept the sacrifice at your hands, to the praise and glory of his name, for our welfare also, and that of all his holy Church.

And the priest says in an undertone: *Amen.*

Once again, dialogue Mass is explicitly approved by the rubrics.

Why do the rubrics decree that this bidding is to be spoken to the faithful in a subdued voice? It is possible that this rubrical decree may be explained by the fact that this passage is a late medieval insertion which cut across the already extant offertory chant—hence the necessity of a vocal compromise. Obviously, if this rite had been primitive, it would have been sung or spoken aloud at low Mass. A similar bidding is to be found in the Sacramentary of Amiens (second half of the ninth century).

The Roman liturgy was as innocent of this invitatory as of the other prayers of the offertory which we have quoted. Rome, moreover, would never have said *Orate*, but *Oremus*.

Under Gallican influence, Roman *Ordines II* and *VI* (ninth and tenth centuries) have *Orate, Orate pro me*, doubtless as the beginning for longer formulas. Originally, the expression *fratres* was addressed to members of the clergy, to exhort them to commend their offering to the Lord. Later, when the custom of bringing the oblations to the altar had fallen into desuetude, this bidding was interpreted as though addressed to all the faithful; many forms therefore add *sorores*. Some are even completely devoid of any notion of offering: for instance, *Orate, fratres, pro me, peccatore, ut auferat Deus spiritum elationis et superbiae a me* ("Brethren, pray for me, a sinner, that the Lord take from me the spirit of arrogance and pride").[1] Many sources, such as the *Breviarium ecclesiastici ordinis* (end of the eighth, beginning of the ninth century), *Ordo II*, etc., do not mention a response (compare the Good Friday rite). Innocent III († 1216), who quoted the *Orate*, mentions no response and the Dominican rite still contains only the bidding today. The Sacramentary of Amiens (second half of the ninth century), however, quotes a response: *Sit Dominus in corde tuo et in labiis tuis, et recipiat sacrificium sibi acceptum de ore tuo et de manibus tuis pro nostrorum omnium salute*.

There are many different forms of response to this invitatory. According to the *Horae* of Charles the Bald (*c*. 870), the congregation replied using the angels's words to Mary: *Spiritus sanctus superveniat in te, et virtus Altissimi obumbret te. Memor sit sacrificii tui et holocaustum tuum pingue fiat*. Indeed, the divine operation, the consecration, which is a supreme work of love, is attributed especially to the Holy Ghost. Our present response *Suscipiat*, which dates from the eleventh century, is not Roman. A great variety of similar formulas are to be found before the thirteenth century.

---

[1] This example is to be found in the *Breviarium ecclesiastici ordinis*.

2. THE SECRET

The secret as an offertory prayer, concluding the offering of bread and wine.—This prayer has no title in the Leonine Sacramentary (*c.* 600); in the Gelasian (seventh-eighth centuries) it is called *secreta;* in the Gregorian (eighth century) it bears the endorsement *super oblata:* Prayer over the offerings. This title corresponds exactly to the contents of these forms, which speak primarily of the offerings considered either in their material aspect, as bread and wine, gathered in from the faithful, or by anticipation as that which they are to become by consecration, the body and blood of Christ, offered to the Father under the continuing appearances of bread and wine. With regard to the gathering together of these offerings, see, for example, the secret for the feast of St John the Baptist (24 June); the secret for the Mass of the Common of Abbots, and the secret for the Epiphany which points a moving contrast between the terrestrial offerings of the Magi and the offering of the body and blood of Christ seen already through the offerings of bread and wine.

Thus, by their contents, the secrets constitute a prelude to the canon; but this must be considered more fully later.

The secrets often beg, in exchange for the offerings, the graces appropriate to the character of the celebration. Thus, for example, the secret for the Thursday of Passion Week refers to food, the subject of the Lenten fast: " O Lord our God, who hast commanded and preferred that these material things, created by thee for the support of our frail nature, should also be dedicated as offerings to thy name, grant that they may not only help us in this present life, but prove a pledge of immortality."

In this respect the secret of the midnight Mass of Christmas is a precious pearl: " Accept, Lord, this day's festal offering, and in thy gracious bounty grant that through this interchange of sacred gifts, we may grow to be like him in whom our nature is made one with thine."

On the Ember Saturday in Lent, the secret is linked with the fast: " Let our fast be sanctified, Lord, by these sacrificial gifts so that our acts of penance may inwardly effect that which they outwardly proclaim."

At Pentecost, it beseeches the purifying and illuminating activity of the Holy Ghost: "Hallow our proffered gifts, we beg thee, Lord, and cleanse our hearts by the light of thy Holy Spirit."

The secret—like the collect[1]—is usually addressed to the Father through Jesus Christ, the high priest. Exceptions to this rule are unknown in the Leonine (*c.* 600) and Gelasian (*c.* 700) Sacramentaries; in the Gregorian (eighth century) there are some secrets addressed to Christ as God and ending *Qui vivis et regnas*. . . . Even today, few secrets diverge from the true liturgical tradition. The following figures were drawn up by Jungmann[2] on the Roman Missal in 1924, and have been corrected by the author to May 1945.

	Collects	Secrets	Post-communions	Outside the Mass	TOTAL
Proper of Season (Sundays and ferias)	7 (7)[3]	—	2 (2)	1	10 (9)
Proper of Seasons (Feasts)	2	—	3	—	5
Proper of Saints[4]	23 (4)	7	15	2	47 (4)
Votive Masses	1	1	3	—	5
Masses for the Dead	1 (1)	—	2 (2)	1 (1)	4 (4)
	34 (12)	8	25 (4)	4 (1)	71 (17)

The total number of collects, secrets and postcommunions rises to seventy-one; but among these there are only eight secrets. These are found, not in the traditional liturgy of the Proper of the Season, but in the Proper of the Saints, and especially in recent Masses and in one votive Mass: that of Christ the eternal High Priest. They all end *Qui vivis*. The oldest of these secrets is that on the 13 June for St Antony of Padua, which was inserted in the general calendar of the Roman rite by Sixtus V († 1590). Even

---

[1] See Vol. 1, Chap. 20.
[2] *Die Stellung Christi im liturgischen Gebet* (Aschendorff, Munster, 1925).
[3] The figures in parentheses indicate the number of these same prayers formerly addressed to the Father (in the Leonine and Gelasian Sacramentaries) and ending *Per Dominum N.J.C.* (See Jungmann, *op. cit.*, p. 103).
[4] The Mass of Christ the King employs *Qui tecum vivit* three times.

here the thought tends towards the Father: "Lord, may the present offering bring salvation to thy people, for whose sake thou didst deign to sacrifice thyself, a living victim to thy Father: thou who art God, living and reigning with the selfsame God the Father and the Holy Spirit for ever."

The other six belong to Masses with a place in the general calendar of the Roman rite only since the eighteenth century: that is, the Seven Sorrows of the Blessed Virgin Mary (Friday after Passion Sunday), St Paul of the Cross († 1775), 28 April; St Alphonsus Ligouri († 1787), 2 August; the Solemnity of St Joseph (Pius IX), Wednesday of the second week of Eastertide;[1] St Francis Caracciolo († 1608), 4 June (The last two make no reference to the offertory); and St Gabriel of the Sorrowing Virgin (27 or 28 of February).

The secret as a prayer introducing the preface.—The prayer which immediately precedes the canon bears the name *secreta* in the Gelasian Sacramentary (seventh-eighth century). Many liturgists[2] think that this term means "silent prayer". It is, indeed, said in an undertone: "it is called the secret because it is said secretly", Amalarius teaches.[3] But *secretus* means not "silently" but "secret", "mysterious." Besides, the secret was formerly said aloud and the corresponding prayer—the *oratio super oblatum*—in the Ambrosian rite is still said aloud today.

Others, such as Bossuet, Molien, etc., think that *secreta* is another form of *secretio* (from *secernere*, to separate) and designates either the prayer said at the separation of the catechumens from the faithful, or that said over the bread and wine as "set apart" as offerings: *oratio ad secretam*. But this does not explain the shortened form *secreta*.

By enlarging the field of his inquiries, one authoritative liturgist, J. Brinktrine,[4] has provided a very plausible explanation of this term.

In the Mass, the secret is closely connected with the preface.

---

[1] The new Mass of St Joseph the Worker, appointed for May 1, which supersedes that referred to in the text, does not exhibit this peculiarity.
[2] E.g. Amalarius († 850), Lebrun, Dom Martène, Mgr Duchesne, Verwilst, etc.
[3] *P.L.*, 161, 984.
[4] "Zur Deutung des Wortes *secreta*" in *Eph. lit.*, 1930, pp. 291-5 (Rome).

Now, many blessings and consecrations in the Pontifical and Missal, but not part of the Mass, also include a preface: for example, the ordination of priests and deacons, the consecration of bishops, the sacring of kings and queens, the blessing of abbots and abbesses, the consecration of virgins, the dedication of churches and altars, in the Pontifical, and the blessing of palms, of the paschal candle and of baptismal fonts in the Missal. But comparison of these prefaces with those of the Mass shows that in fourteen cases out of sixteen they are preceded by an introductory prayer analogous to the secret in the Mass. Furthermore, in many cases, this prayer is itself preceded by an invitatory analogous to *Orate fratres*, for example, *Oremus, Oremus fratres carissimi* (thirteen out of sixteen). The rubrics of the Missal themselves also clearly seem to dissociate the secret completely from the offertory, as though it belonged to a different section: " then is made the offering with the prayers, as in the Order of Mass. When the offering has been made, the secret prayers (*orationes secretae*) are said." [1]

The real meaning of *secreta* is, therefore, secret, mystery—and indeed, in the Gallican liturgy, a prayer in the canon after the consecration is called either *post secreta* or *post mysterium* indifferently. The greatest mystery, the " holy mysteries ", is the consecration: the consecration of wine, moreover, is called the *mysterium fidei*, the surpassing " mystery of faith ". In addition, the Spanish Mozarabic liturgy calls the whole canon *secreta* (mystery).[2] In the twelfth century, in his famous treatise on the Mass, Pope Innocent III called the canon *secreta* throughout: *In secreta recolitur memoria passionis:* " The commemoration of the passion is celebrated in the canon ".[3] Durandus of Mende († 1296) headed his chapter on the canon, *De secreta vel canone Missae*, and records that *Canon autem Missae . . . et secreta vocatur:* " The canon of the Mass is also called the secret." [4] We know that the preface once formed part of the canon: thus in the Gelasian Sacramentary (seventh–eighth century) we read as a heading before the preface, *Incipit Canon Actionis*.[5] From this it appears that the name *secreta*,

[1] *Rubr. Gen. Miss.*, 12, 1.
[2] Dom Férotin, *Liber Mozarabicus Sacramentorum*, 24 (1912).
[3] *De sacra altaris mysterio, Libri sex.*, Bk. 3, 2; *P.L.*, 217, 840.
[4] *Rationale*, 4, 35, 1. *Secreta dicitur, quasi nobis occulta, quia humana ratione nequaquam tantum mysterium plenarie capere potest, ad quod significandum, merito secreta voce celebratur . . . (Ibid.*, 2).
[5] Ed. Wilson; Oxford, p. 234.

referring to the canon, was extended to cover the prayer introducing it. The expression was therefore a neuter plural meaning " the holy mysteries ". When its original meaning had dropped out of sight, it was interpreted as a feminine singular adjective qualifying *oratio* (understood); and thus, by an entirely natural evolutionary process, liturgists speak of *de secreta, in secreta,* etc.

14

EUCHARISTIC THANKSGIVING: ITS ORIGINS AND SOME EARLY EXAMPLES

WE have already referred—in our outline of the ceremonies of Pasch—to the thanksgivings sung by the children of Israel.[1] The Christian thanksgiving, the holy Eucharist, which was instituted in the very heart of this moving ceremony, has retained the stamp of its origins.

Nothing is more revealing than to re-read the venerable anaphoras of the first centuries: their relationship to the Jewish paschal liturgy is undeniable; yet they differ from it greatly. But not only the Jewish paschal thanksgiving, but also the forms of grace customarily said daily before or after a meal by devout Israelites (which were always said by the head of the family at the paschal meal) have influenced the formation of the anaphora. Moreover, the Apostles and earliest converts from Judaism were commonly faithful to the synagogues. In addition, even in Apostolic times, the celebration of the eucharistic mysteries used to conclude the ritual observation of the Sabbath of the synagogue, towards dawn on Sunday. It was therefore natural that the rites of the synagogue should, to a certain degree, influence the composition of the Christian thanksgiving. When giving glory, following Jewish traditions, to the divine omnipotence for the wonders of creation and the yet greater benefits which providence had poured out upon Israel—the deliverance from Egyptian slavery and the covenant made on Sinai—the early pastors had only to follow the path thereby indicated and to give thanks for the miracle which perfected all others: the incarnation of the Son of God and the redemption of the world by Christ in the blood of the new and everlasting covenant—redemption in the fullest sense, involving together with the Saviour's "blessed passion", his resurrection, his ascension to the Father's right hand

[1] Chap. 1 above.

and the sending of the Holy Ghost. But we must add at once that this christological thanksgiving also always included a commemoration of the institution of the holy mysteries of the Eucharist by the high priest of the new covenant with the effective words of consecration by which, by Christ's command and example, they are effected. Like the stone in a ring, the consecration lies at the centre of the eucharistic anaphora.

Thus, Christological thanksgiving was grafted on to and blossomed upon the ancient stock of Jewish thanksgiving. "Do not think that I have come to set aside the law and the prophets; I have come not to set them aside, but to bring them to perfection" (Matt. 5. 17).

Real as this influence of Jewish thanksgivings on the Christian anaphoras may be, it must yet be understood that in some ancient Eucharists, the themes of creation and the precursory miracles of the old covenant may be reduced to a minimum or even completely lacking. Christ, the Gift of gifts at the heart of creation, the very Fulfilment of promises to the Jews, the ultimate Reality eclipsing all prefigurations, is the principal subject of eucharistic thanksgiving.

Jewish thanksgivings must, therefore, be compared not with the Roman Canon as we have it in the Missal today, but with the oldest eucharistic anaphoras.

We shall therefore consider here:

(1) Jewish and Christian prayer in general;

(2) some typical Jewish thanksgivings, especially those of the paschal meal and the common graces at meals;

(3) the text of the most important ancient Christian anaphoras in chronological order, emphasizing their especial characteristics and the ultimate Jewish influences the impress of which they bear.

In the course of the analytical study of the prayers of the Roman Canon, we shall have to refer to these sources.

1. JEWISH AND CHRISTIAN PRAYER IN GENERAL

In a noteworthy study of Jewish and Christian prayer, Fr. Lebreton writes:

> In its habitual orientation, Christian prayer resembles Jewish prayer, to which, moreover, it is linked by so many other characteristics: a Catholic is in no sense a Marcionite: he

worships the God of the prophets and recognizes and venerates his inspiration in the books of the Old Testament. The oldest Christian prayers—those which we read in the Gospels and apostolic writings—are full of biblical reminiscences; all exegetes have pointed out these characteristics in the *Magnificat*, in the *Benedictus* and even in the Lord's Prayer. And not only the sacred books of the Jews, but also their liturgical formulas set their imprint upon these hymns and prayers. The writings of the earliest Fathers, too, frequently manifest the same influence: the great prayer (59–61) of St Clement (96–8)[1] recalls the Jewish prayer of the eighteen benedictions in many ways, and in this same letter (34) there is already to be found, in a clearly liturgical context, the *Sanctus, Sanctus, Sanctus* taken from Isaias 6. 3. The prayers of the *Didache* (90)[2] form a marked contrast with those to be read in St Clement: in the Roman letter, prayer is solemn, full, majestic—as it was always to be in the Roman liturgy; in the short Syrian book, there is an intensity of life, a pulsation in which one recognizes the tones of the prophets; one characteristic is, however, common to both these very different fragments: their kinship with Jewish prayers: it is very marked in Clement, but it is no less there in the *Didache* . . .

The Church was never to seek to efface this marked impress of Jewish tradition on Christian prayer: she is conscious of being the true Israel; all that there was of the divine in the Jewish past belonged to her; she acknowledges in the Law, the preparation and symbol of what she is, and in the prophets, the distant vision of what she possesses; her prayer in the psalms; all this is her heritage, and she uses it freely, as controlling it, as did Jesus himself in the Gospel.

But as she is the first among created things, older than the prophets, than Moses, than the patriarchs, she is also the bride of Christ, youthful like him and able to rejuvenate and transmute all that she touches. She loves to repeat Jewish prayers, the prayers of her cradle, but she gives them a new significance. She prays to God almighty—but as her Father: this is a profound change, of which Christians are fully aware . . .

Furthermore, the Church loves to call upon this almighty

---

[1] See below, pp. 142–4.   [2] See below, pp. 139–42.

Eucharistic Thanksgiving

Father, relying upon the intercession of Christ: the Son of God is the mediator through whom all good things come to us; he is at the same time the high priest through whom all prayer must be offered.[1]

This form of prayer—addressed to the Father and depending upon the intercession of the Son—is, from the outset, characteristic of Christian prayer and distinguishes it from Jewish prayer.

Thus Christians who were born in Judaism or passed through it, loved to repeat in the bosom of the Church prayers similar in many respects to those which the synagogue had taught them to love; but the new faith, which had transformed their lives, also transformed their prayers: it climbed higher, nearer to God, who had become their Father, borne there by the beloved Son who was made their high priest.[2]

It is valuable to consider Christian worship in Apostolic times in its wholeness. In it one sees the essential characteristics which belong to the first days of Christianity after the Lord's ascension: the Christian prays to the heavenly Father, as Jesus taught him to pray, and he prays through the intercession of the Son, the high priest of our religion, the Saviour of those who believe in him. This orientation of Christian worship is especially apparent in the principal act of the liturgy, the eucharistic sacrifice: this sacrifice is offered to God the Father, and the Son is its priest and its victim. Liturgical prayer as a whole also obeys this same law: the Church offers her praise, thanksgivings and petitions to the Father, and she loves to offer them through the ministry of Jesus Christ, our Lord . . .[3]

2. THE JEWISH SOURCES OF THE EUCHARISTIC THANKSGIVING

We have already described the imposing ritual of the Jewish paschal celebration which formed the setting for the celebration of

---

[1] Cf. e.g. *Didache*, 9, 2–5; *Epistle of St Clement*, 59, 2; 61, 3; St Ignatius, *Epistle to the Ephesians*, 4, 12, etc.
[2] J. Lebreton, *Histoire du Dogme de la Trinité*, vol. 2, pp. 177–81.
[3] *Ibid.*, pp. 75–6.

the eucharistic sacrifice itself. The institution at the Last Supper left an ineradicable memory upon the deeply moved minds of the Apostles. So, when they in their turn celebrated the Holy Eucharist, they were very careful to conform to the Master's example in every respect. Like him, therefore, they intoned their thanksgivings and it was in the midst of thanksgiving that they consecrated the Eucharist.

It is indisputable that the Jewish paschal thanksgiving, the *Hallel*, exerted an influence upon eucharistic thanksgiving. Liturgists have therefore sought to define the nature and limits of this influence, and in order to do this it is necessary to bring together the *Hallel* and—not our modern Roman canon but—the oldest anaphoras. For this purpose Dr Bickell's study *Messe und Pascha* (Mainz, 1872), translated and edited by Skene as *The Lord's Supper and Paschal Ritual* (Edinburgh, 1891) is still valuable. In his work of comparison, the author assumes it established that the liturgy of the *Constitutions of the Apostles*[1] (Bks. 2 and 8), despite numerous retouchings, additions and variations introduced into the text before the end of the fourth century, is in the main the most ancient form of the canon of the Mass and that nearest to Apostolic times.[2]

There is, obviously, no question of identity of expression in the two texts.

According to Bickell, Christ would have consecrated the fourth cup.

The main heads of his arguments—without following him into details—are as follows:

Jewish Pasch	*Mass* (the Clementine canon of the *Apostolic Constitutions*)
The Fourth Cup	Offertory
Mixing of water and wine	Mixing of water and wine
Washing of hands	Washing of hands

[1] The *Apostolic Constitutions:* a compilation made in the fourth century by a Syrian author who used older materials. He attributed his work to the Apostles and its transmission to St Clement (see below p. 158).

[2] This liturgy cannot be considered to be a primitive and universal type. Few prayers had been given a fixed form before this time. It is a late redaction containing some early sections. There is in it an example of a primitive form; see *Didascalia et Constitutiones Apostolorum*, Bk. 8, Chap. 12, 5–38 (Funk, vol. 1, Paderborn).

Eucharistic Thanksgiving

Jewish Pasch	*Mass* (the Clementine canon of the *Apostolic Constitutions*)
Second part of the *Hallel*: Psalms 116–117, *Confitemini Domino*. *Dicat nunc domus Aaron.*	Preface: corresponds to this part of the *Hallel: Sursum corda. Habemus ad Dominum. Gratias agamus . . . Dignum et justum est. Sanctus. Benedictus qui venit in nomine Domini.*
Verse 26. *Benedictus qui venit in nomine Domini.* Great *Hallel*, Psalm 135, *Confitemini Domino, quoniam bonus.* God must be praised for all he has done for Israel *Confitemini Domino, quoniam bonus, Confitemini Deo deorum . . . Confitemini Domino dominorum.*	The primitive canon, which found inspiration in the same ideas
Verse 4 of the same psalm: *Qui facit mirabilia solus* (The thought of creation is passed over)	All liturgies except the Roman contain some link with the *Sanctus* by some similar idea (*Vere Sanctus, vere benedictus . . .*)
Verses 5–9: Praise for creation	The same thought occurs in the Clementine canon.
Verses 9 ff: God's benefits continued: the promised land, the defeat of the Egyptians, miracles in the desert Verse 24: *Et redemit nos ab inimicis nostris*	Same idea: the canon adds to God's favours to Israel, those after the fall of man, redemption, etc.
Verses 25–6. *Qui dat escam omni carni.*	The canon summarizes this series shortly, but adds the life of Christ, his passion, etc.
	The author suggests that it was at this point that our Lord performed the consecration. He would then have completed the recitation of the psalm. The canon of the Mass goes on to paraphrase the offering of the body and blood of Christ.

Jewish Pasch	Mass (the Clementine canon of the *Apostolic Constitutions*)
Verse 26. *Confitemini Deo caeli . . . Confitemini Domino dominorum quonian in aeternum misericordia eius.*	The Clementine intercession ends with these same verses (25–6) which correspond to the end of the canon: *Est tibi, Deo Patri . . . omnis honor et gloria.*
At the end of the Psalm, the people answered *Amen*	At the end of the canon, the congregation replies *Amen*.

In the view of some authoritative liturgists—Dom Cabrol, for example—the relationship between the Jewish Pasch and the primitive canon appears incontestable. Yet it is important to notice that none of the psalms said at the pasch is found in the canon of the Mass. The oldest canons do not even refer to the Jewish pasch. As the majority of the new recruits to Christianity were Jewish converts, it was necessary to be circumspect.

Dom Leclercq very rightly observes:

> Bickell tells us that, from Apostolic times, these psalms and prayers were replaced by prayers inspired by them. This fact would indicate sufficiently clearly the desire to point out to the faithful, most of whom came from Judaism, that the Old Law had come to an end and had made way for the New. But the former character of the pasch—its ceremonies and prayers—could not be preserved even by relating it to the Last Supper, without exposing some converts to the danger of losing sight of the true meaning of the Mass. The necessity of a reaction against Jewish rites has left a recognizable mark upon many writings of that period, beginning with the Epistle to the Hebrews and the Epistle called " of St Barnabas ".[1]

All that can be definitely concluded from these comparisons is that the prayers of the Christian canon which replaced the traditional Jewish prayers and psalms, drew a large part of their inspiration from them.

But the paschal feast was unique of its kind and took place only once a year, but the eucharistic rite had to be constantly repeated.

---

[1] Art. *Messe* in *Dict d'archéol. chrét et de lit.*, 11, 531-2.

The Apostles, being anxious to conform as faithfully as possible to their Master's institution, therefore frequently celebrated the Eucharist in close relationship to the Jewish meal. The first Epistle to the Corinthians perpetuates the memory of this custom. It is, of course, very difficult to say precisely to what extent and until what moment the celebration of the Eucharist was accompanied by a meal.[1] But it is beyond doubt that the customary Jewish blessings either before or after the meal, influenced the formation of the eucharistic thanksgiving.[2]

The following are two examples of this type of blessing: At the beginning of the meal, before the breaking of the bread, there is said: "Blessed be thou, the Eternal, our God, King of the world, who hast made bread to come forth from the earth!" And this is the blessing over the wine: "Blessed be thou, the Eternal, our God, King of the world, Creator of the fruit of the vine!"

The beginning of the solemn blessing after a Jewish meal has a dialogue structure and rhythmic pattern, like our prefaces. It gives thanks to God and commemorates his bounties: these are also characteristic elements of Christian "eucharists".

He who presides begins: "Let us say the blessing at table."

Those present: "The name of the Eternal be praised from now henceforward for ever."

He who presides: "Let us praise our God who feeds us."

Those present: "Praised be our God who feeds us and whose goodness preserves us."

He who presides repeats this praise and adds: "Praised be he and his holy name."

The first thanksgiving for food follows:

"Praised be thou, O Eternal, our God, King of the world, who in his goodness nourisheth the whole earth with benevolence, love and mercy. He giveth food for all flesh, for his mercy endureth for ever. Through his great goodness, we have never lacked food and we shall never lack food because of his great name, for he feedeth and upholdeth all things, doeth good to all and prepareth food for all his creatures that he hath made. Praised be thou, O Eternal, who feedeth all things."

---

[1] We shall not here consider the relationship between the Eucharist and the second-century Agape properly so called. On this subject, see among others, Dom H. Leclercq, *art. cit.*; 11. 520–2.

[2] This influence is recognized by able liturgists such as O. Casel and A. Baumstark.

This is followed by a second thanksgiving commemorating the land of promise:

"We give glory to thee, O Eternal, our God, because thou hast given as an heritage to our fathers an enchanting possession and far-reaching land and because thou, O Eternal, our God, hast brought us out of the land of Egypt and delivered us from the house of bondage. (We glorify thee) for thy covenant with which thou hast marked our bodies, for thy doctrine in which thou hast instructed us, for thy laws which thou hast taught us and for the life, benevolence, joy of the food with which thou hast continually fed us and upholdest us each day and hour."

The early Christians found in these prayers, full of biblical reminiscences and prefigurations, precious material for an introduction to the celebration of the eucharistic mysteries.

Later, we shall quote the text of two ancient thanksgivings from the *Didache* ("The teaching of the Apostles") dating from about the year 90.[1] The relationship is striking.

As we shall see, their "eucharistic" or sacramental character has been contested and many critics, such as Baumstark, think that they were linked with the Agape, the common meal which was followed by the celebration of the Eucharist.

But even if indirect, the influence of these prayers upon the anaphora was no less real. "The thanksgiving after the common meal," he notes, "formed the introduction to the sacramental celebration and it was itself the starting point of the evolution of the texts of the anaphoras. . . .

"Like Christian prayer, Jewish prayer of thanksgiving is preceded by an invitatory; and our Roman form *Gratias agamus Domino Deo nostro* is but a literal translation of that prescribed by the Mischna for use when less than a hundred persons participate in a common meal."[2]

Baumstark stresses the influence exerted upon the development of the Christian anaphora by a Jewish euchological prototype proper to the worship of the temple in post-exilic times and used as a morning prayer. This prayer connects Isaias' trisagion (6. 3)

---

[1] pp. 139–42.
[2] *Liturgie comparée*, 2nd ed., p. 51; Eng. trans. *Comparative Liturgy*, revised by Bernard Botte, O.S.B., translated by F. L. Cross (London, 1958), p. 47.

with a review of the story of the patriarchs and the people of Israel. The first part of this is found with all its fullness of expression in the anaphora of the eighth book of the *Apostolic Constitutions*.[1]

As for the quotation from Isaias, its first use in Christian literature occurs in a work inspired—according to the writer—not by the eucharistic liturgy, but by the meetings organized on Sunday mornings which replaced the Jewish services on the Sabbath: St Clément's Epistle to the Corinthians (96-8).

> It is, then, obvious [Baumstark concluded] that the type of prayer of which the *Jôzêr* of the synagogue rite is the modern example, was also in use in primitive Christian, non-eucharistic services. And it was at these services that a Christian voice was to be heard singing the biblical trisagion for the first time. It was when the difficulties which faced St Paul in II Corinthians compelled the separation of the eucharist from the Agape-service that it was joined to the service for Sunday morning which until that time had been aliturgical, consisting only of lessons and prayers for the instruction and edification of the faithful. It will have been at that time that the derivatives from the ancient Jewish thanksgiving after a meal and the old prayer of the synagogue from which is descended the modern *Jôzêr* were fused together. Here is the starting point of the whole process of evolution of eastern anaphoras and their western descendants.[2]

3. THE EUCHARISTIC THANKSGIVING: SOME EARLY EXAMPLES

(a) THE "DIDACHE" (90)

The *Didache* or "Teaching of the Twelve Apostles" is, after the New Testament, the oldest Christian writing which has come down to us. Of Syriac origin and written in Greek, it dates apparently from the year 90. The text was discovered at Constantinople by Mgr Bryennios in 1883. This document several times mentions thanksgiving: principally in chapter 14, then also in chapters 9 and 10.

---

[1] Baumstark, *op. cit.*, pp. 54-6. English trans., p. 50.
[2] *Liturgie comparée*, 2nd. ed., p. 55. English trans, 50-1.

Text

[Chapter 14] (1) Come together on the Lord's own day, break bread and give thanks (εὐχαριστήσατε) having first confessed your sins, that your sacrifice may be pure.

(2) He who has a dispute with his neighbour must not join with you before he has been reconciled, for fear lest your sacrifice be profaned.

(3) For the Lord hath said: "No corner of the world from the sun's rise to the sun's setting, where the renown of me is not heard among the Gentiles, where sacrifice is not done, and pure offering made in my honour; so revered is my name, says the Lord of hosts, there among the Gentiles."

[Chapters 9 and 10] Chapter 9: (1) As for the eucharist (εὐχαριστίας), give thanks (εὐχαριστήσατε) thus (2): first, for the cup:

We give thanks to thee, (εὐχαριστοῦμεν) O our Father,
for the holy vine of David thy servant,
that thou hast taught us to know
through Jesus, thy Servant,
Glory be to thee, through the ages!

(3) Then for the broken bread:

We give thanks to thee (εὐχαριστοῦμεν), O our Father,
  for life and knowledge,
  that thou hast taught us to know through Jesus, thy servant,
Glory be to thee through the ages!

(4) As this broken bread, once scattered abroad over the mountains, has been gathered together to become one whole, so let thy Church be gathered together from the ends of the earth into thy kingdom, for to thee is the glory and the power through Jesus Christ for ever!

(5) Let no one eat or drink of thy eucharist, if he be not baptized in the name of the Lord, for it was with regard to this that the Lord said: "You must not give that which is holy to dogs."

[Chapter 10] (1) After you are filled, give thanks thus: (εὐχαριστήσατε): (2) "We give thanks (εὐχαριστοῦμεν) to thee, O holy Father,

for thy holy name that thou hast enshrined in our hearts,
for the knowledge, faith and immortality that thou hast
revealed to us through Jesus, thy servant,
   Glory be to thee for ever!"

(3) Almighty Master, thou hast "created the whole world" to the honour of thy name, thou hast given food and drink to men to possess it, so that they give thanks ($εὐχαριστήσωσιν$) to thee; but to us thou hast given a spiritual food and drink and eternal life through thy servant.

(4) Above all, we give thanks ($εὐχαριστοῦμεν$) to thee because thou art mighty. Glory be to thee for ever! (5) Remember, Lord, to deliver thy Church from all evil and to make it perfect in thy love. May this sanctified Church be gathered together from the four winds into thy kingdom which thou hast prepared, for to thee is the power and the glory for ever! (6) May grace come, and this world pass away! "Hosanna to the God of David"! If any is holy, let him come! If any is not, let him do penance! The Lord cometh! ... Amen.

(7) Let the prophets give thanks as much as they will.

Commentary

These lyrical thanksgivings, which are each divided as chants into three strophes continually interrupted by doxologies, faithfully re-echo the old Jewish blessings at table.

The first (chapter 9) is strikingly similar to the Jewish blessing over broken bread and wine.[1] The second (chapter 10) is clearly in the tradition of the solemn blessing at table after a meal. Verse (3) recalls the thanksgiving for food.[2]

The wine is blessed before the bread: this order is unique in Christian literature. There is no reference to the Last Supper.

But despite its close links with Judaism, this thanksgiving is clearly Christian—indeed, together with its doxologies it is addressed solely to the Father: our Father (9. 2, 3); holy Father (10. 2). These evangelical terms are found nowhere else. Furthermore, this thanksgiving ascends "through Christ" (9. 3), the mediator, the sovereign high priest. This thanksgiving attains new and heavenly realities through the Jewish material of its images, forms of words

---

[1] p. 137.   [2] pp. 137–8.

and prefigurations—it attains too the bread of eternal life and the chalice of eternal salvation. Supra-terrestrial light and life, as spoken of in the Gospel of St John,[1] shine through this anaphora.

Finally, the *Didache* states explicitly that eucharistic thanksgiving was improvised by the prophets.[2] This evidence is confirmed by the later witness of St Justin († 167) and the Apostolic Tradition of St Hippolytus († 235).

The usual pattern of thanksgiving is already present here in outline: thanks is given for creation and gifts in the natural order (10. 3) and for grace given through Christ (10. 3; 9. 2, 3). There is even a twofold thanksgiving and a twofold prayer of petition. The final " Hosanna to the God of David " in its usual place recalls the *Sanctus*. Notice, too, the fraction (9. 3) and the almost exclusive use of the term eucharist (thanksgiving).

The whole of the Lord's Prayer is reproduced immediately before the section quoted (8. 3). Finally, notice the several doxologies—at 9. 3 and 4; 10. 2, 4 and 5.

(b) THE FIRST EPISTLE OF ST. CLEMENT OF ROME TO THE CORINTHIANS (96–98)

The great prayer which we read here is one of the treasures of Christian literature. Although it is not strictly speaking a liturgical prayer, it provides a fine example of the style of solemn prayer, such as was then voiced by the leaders of Christian communities, who, while yet respecting traditional form, allowed some degree of freedom to their personal inspiration (Cf. St Justin, *Apology*, 1, 67, 5).

Text

> (59) Thou hast opened the eyes of our hearts, that they may know thee, O thou the only Most High, even to the highest heaven, the holy one who rests in the midst of the saints, who bringest down the insolence of the proud, who leadest astray the reckonings of the nations, who exaltest the humble and bringest down the great; thou who enrichest and makest poor, and who savest and givest life.

---

[1] These prayers recall the following passages in St John: 15. 15; 16. 26; 17. 6; 11. 26; 1. 14, 6. 69; 17. 3; 20. 31; 6. 27, 35, 51–8, 63; 17. 15; 17. 23; I John 2. 5; 4. 12; 17. 17, 19.

[2] Τοῖς δὲ προφήταις ἐπιτρέπετε εὐχαριστεῖν ὅσα θέλουσιν (x.7).

Eucharistic Thanksgiving   143

O unique benefactor of souls and God of all flesh, thou who gazest upon the depths, scrutator of the works of men, help of men in peril and " their saviour in despair "; creator and overseer [bishop] of all souls! Thou who multipliest the peoples upon the earth and hast chosen from the midst of them those who love thee, through Jesus Christ, thy beloved Son, through whom thou hast taught, hallowed and honoured us. We beseech thee, O Master, be thou our help and upholder.

Be thou the salvation of us who are oppressed, have pity upon the lowly, raise up those who are fallen, show thyself to those who are in need, heal the sick, set on the right way those among thy people who have strayed, fill those who are hungry, deliver our prisoners, raise up those who languish, console the spiritless, that "all nations may know that thou alone art God" that Jesus Christ is thy Son, and that "we may be thy people and the sheep of thy pastures."

(60) O thou who through thy works hast manifested the undying ordering of the world, thou, O Lord, who hast created the earth, thou who remainest faithful unto all generations, just in thy judgements, wonderful in thy strength and grandeur, wise in creation, careful to strengthen thy created things, good in things visible, faithful towards those who put their trust in thee, merciful and compassionate, remit unto us our faults and unrighteousness, our falls and our wanderings, reckon not up the sins of thy servants and handmaidens, but cleanse us with thy truth and direct us so that we walk in holiness of heart and do that which is good and acceptable in thy sight and in the sight of our princes. Yea, O Lord, let thy face shine upon us that [we may enjoy] our goods in peace, to protect us with thy mighty hand, to deliver us from all sin by thy most strong arm, to save us from those who unjustly hate us. Grant concord and peace, to us and to all the dwellers upon earth as thou hast granted it to our fathers when they called holily upon thee in faith and truth, make us subject to thy most powerful and excellent name, to our princes and to all those who govern us upon earth.

(61) (1) It is thou, O Master, who hast given them [i.e. princes] the royal power, through thy magnificent and indescribable might, so that, knowing the glory and honour that

thou hast dispensed to them, we may be subject to them and not gainsay thy will. Grant them, O Lord, health, peace, concord and stability that they may exercise the overlordship thou hast remitted to them without hindrance.

(2) For it is thou, O Master, heavenly king of the ages, who givest to the sons of men glory, honour and power over the things of the earth. Guide, O Lord, their councils to follow what is good, what is " pleasant in thy sight " so that in exercising with mercy, in peace and without ire, the power that thou hast given them, they may find thee favourably disposed.

(3) Thou alone hast the power to do these things and to obtain for us yet greater blessings. We give thanks to thee through the high priest and patron of our souls, Jesus Christ, through whom to thee be glory and greatness, now and from generation to generation for ever. Amen.[1]

In chapter 34 (6–7), he urges Christians to sing the *Sanctus*.

Commentary

" What is certain," writes Dom Leclercq, " is that this fragment is not ' a copy of a time-hallowed formula ', it is not an excerpt from an otherwise non-existent Apostolic Missal. This brilliant improvisation contains no reference to the sacrament of Christ's body and blood, but, it can be said without exaggeration, is imbued with, woven from, biblical quotations and contains the characteristic themes of the preface and intercession which was later to figure in the liturgies." [2]

Baumstark perceives here the echo of the prayer of the primitive Christian services arranged on Sunday mornings to replace the Jewish services of the Sabbath. Fr Lebreton writes:

> One cannot read this prayer without emotion; written in the worst days of Domitian, it is yet so peaceful, so submissive, so full of humility and trust. It bows down before princes and intercedes for them, seeing in them only the repositories of that sovereign power it venerates. And, above all these

---

[1] *The Epistle to the Corinthians* in a modern translation will be found in *Ancient Christian Writers* series, Vol. 1 (Westminster, n.d., 1946), pp. 9–49.
[2] Dom H. Leclercq, *art. cit.*

miseries here below, eyes are fixed upon God most high and most holy from whom all good things come; the Christian adores this vast greatness, he contemplates it in the creation and government of the world, in the merciful solicitude with which God has guided " our fathers " and, above all, in that wondrous calling which has brought the elect out of darkness into light, out of ignorance into the knowledge of the glory of the divine name, through the beloved Son, Jesus Christ.

In this act of praise, this thanksgiving in which can be sensed such reserved and profound emotion, Catholic prayer is already to be heard in the form which it will always preserve: biblical, traditional, respecting and loving the past and at the same time throbbing with new joys and hopes.

The prayers of the *Teaching of the Apostles* (chapters 9 and 10) are also addressed to God the Father, they too are full of reminiscences of the past, of biblical or Judaic phrases, and yet at the same time they too are imbued with Christian joyfulness.

But together with these common characteristics, how great are the differences! We have already indicated the profoundly dissimilar general characteristics of these two documents: on the one side, the hieratic majesty of the Roman liturgy; on the other, the frenzied enthusiasm of prophets.[1]

(c) PLINY'S LETTER TO THE EMPEROR TRAJAN (*c.* 111-13)

Leaving aside St Ignatius of Antioch († 107)—whose Epistles none the less contain much useful material—we can pass on directly to Pliny's Letter, a celebrated piece of evidence, in fact the only non-Christian evidence for the Eucharist we possess.

Pliny the Younger, the governor of Bythinia, asked the Emperor Trajan (*c.* 111-13) for instructions regarding the course to be followed with regard to Christians and said of their assemblies:

> All [my informants] have adored your likeness and the statues of the gods, and cursed Christ. They swore that all their crime or error [as Christians] consists in this: they [the Christians] are in the habit of coming together on a fixed day (*stato die*) before daybreak (*ante lucem*) and singing in alternation (*secum invicem*) a hymn to Christ as to God; they bind

[1] J. Lebreton, *Histoire du dogme de la Trinité*, vol. 2, p. 192.

themselves by an oath (*sacramento*) to commit no crime, neither robbery nor theft nor adultery, and not to break their word, and not to refuse to surrender a trust. When they have done these things, they part, but only in order to come together again to take food but of an ordinary and innocent kind. They say that they [the apostate sources of this information] ceased to do these things after my edict, by which I forbade private gatherings (*hetaerias*) in accordance with your commands.

(d) ST. JUSTIN MARTYR († 167)

In his first Apology, which he addressed to Antoninus Pius (138–61), his adopted sons and the Senate and people of Rome, St Justin Martyr takes up the defence of Christianity and describes the liturgy of the mysterious Christian assemblies, which were charged with illegality and greatly misrepresented by pagans. As he had lived in Rome over a long period, he possibly described the liturgy of the Eternal City itself. He quotes no prayers:

Text

(65) As for us, having washed [baptized] him who believes and is joining us, we lead him into the place where are assembled those whom we call brethren. We offer fervent prayers together for ourselves, for him who is enlightened [i.e. baptized], and for all others, wherever they may be, that with knowledge of the truth, they may obtain the grace to practise virtue, keep the commandments and thus merit eternal salvation. (2) When the prayers are ended, we give one another the kiss of peace. (3) Then there is brought up to him who presides at the assembly of the brethren bread and a cup of wine mingled with water.

He takes them and praises and glorifies the Father of the universe through the name of the Son and the Holy Ghost, then he makes a long "eucharist" for all the blessings that we have received from him. When he has completed the prayers and eucharist, all the people present utter the exclamation: "Amen". (4) Amen is a Hebrew word which means "so be it". (5) When he who presides has made the eucharist and all the people have replied, the ministers we call deacons distribute to all present the consecrated bread, wine and water and bear it to those absent.

(66) (1) We call this food Eucharist, and no one can partake of it, if he believes not in the truth of our teaching and has not received the washing for remission of sins and regeneration and lives not according to Christ's precepts. (2) For we do not partake of this food as of common bread and drink. For just as, in the power of God, Jesus Christ our saviour has taken flesh and blood for our salvation, so also this food consecrated by prayer made up from the words of Christ, which by digestion should nourish our blood and flesh, is the flesh and blood of the incarnate Jesus: such is our teaching.

(3) The Apostles in their memoirs, which we call Gospels, recount that Jesus gave them these instructions: He took bread and, having given thanks, he said to them: "Do this in commemoration of me: this is my body". And likewise he took the cup and, having given thanks, said to them, "This is my blood". And he gave them to each of them. (4) Evil spirits have copied this institution in the Mithras mysteries: there bread and a cup of water are proffered in the ceremonies of initiation and certain prayers—which either are or may be known to you—are said.

(67) (1) After these things, we next renew the memory of these things among us. Those who are wealthy come to the aid of those who have need, and we give help to one another. (2) In all our offerings, we bless the creator of the universe through his Son Jesus Christ and the Holy Ghost. (3) On the day which is called the day of the sun, all—from the towns and the country—come together in one place: the memoirs of the Apostles and the writings of the prophets are read for as long as time allows. (4) When the reader has finished, he who presides speaks a discourse to warn and to urge the imitation of these noble teachings. (5) Next, we all rise and pray together aloud. Then, as we have already said, when the prayer is ended, bread and wine and water are brought and he who presides sends up to heaven prayers and eucharists as much as he is able, and all the people respond with the cry, Amen. Then follows the distribution and sharing of the consecrated things to all and their share is sent to those who are absent by the hand of the deacons.

Commentary

The structure of this liturgy is thus:

(1) Bread and wine mingled with water are brought up to the altar, where the bishop receives them (65. 3; 67. 5); (2) the bishop makes a long thanksgiving (eucharist, 65. 3), "as much as he is able" (67. 5), which included prayers (67. 5). He improvises his thanksgiving within a given framework, following an accepted theme, but himself determining the choice of words and the length of the composition. (3) Commemoration was made of the passion of the Lord (66. 3–4). (4) The congregation concluded the prayer by saying Amen (65. 3; 67. 5). (5) Communion was given in both kinds and deacons took communion to those who were absent (65. 5; 67. 5).[1]

References in other fathers and authors of this period corroborate St Justin's description. Like the *Didache* (90), St Justin twice attests that "he who presides" improvised his thanksgiving (65. 3)[2] (67. 5).[3]

(e) THE "TRADITIO APOSTOLICA" OF ST HIPPOLYTUS (218–35)

The writer was a Roman priest whose learning was encyclopaedic and who, after leading a schism and opposing Popes St Zephyrinus (203–27) and St Callistus (221–7), was reconciled with Pope Pontian (233–8) and died in exile in 235.

This is a source of paramount importance, for it is a genuine Roman anaphora. The original Greek has been lost (Ἀποστολικη παράδοσις) but the primitive text has been preserved in Ethiopic,[4] Coptic and Arabic[5] translations.

Hauler discovered an ancient Latin version at Verona in 1900,[6] and this discovery caused a sensation for this is the oldest known Latin canon.

[1] Cp. Dom H. Leclercq, *art. cit.*
[2] 65.3: και ευχαρίστιαν ὑπέρ τοῦ κατηξιῶσθαι τούτων παραὐτοῦ ἐπι πολύ ποιεῖαι
[3] 67.5: εὐχαριστίας ὅση δύναμις αὐτώ αναπέμπει
[4] Erroneously entitled *Constitutiones Ecclesiae Aethiopicae*.
[5] Erroneously entitled *Constitutiones Ecclesiae Aegyptiacae*. It was Dom Connolly who first proved that the original text of the *Traditio* is preserved in three translations: Dom R. H. Connolly, "The so-called Egyptian Church Order and Derived Documents" in *Texts and Studies*, vol. 8 (Cambridge, 1916).
[6] E. Hauler, *Didascaliae Apostolorum fragmenta Veronensia latina. Accedunt canonum quae dicuntur Apostolorum et Egyptiorum reliquiae* (Lipsiae, 1900), pp. 106–7. Dom Cagin (*L'Eucharistia*) wrongly considered that this anaphora dated from apostolic times.

Text

Dominus vobiscum.
Et cum spiritu tuo.
Sursum corda.
Habemus ad Dominum.

Gratias agamus Domino Deo nostro
Dignum et justum est.
Gratias tibi referimus, Deus, per dilectum puerum tuum Jesum Christum quem ultimis temporibus misisti nobis Salvatorem et Redemptorem et Angelum voluntatis tuae. Qui est Verbum tuum inseparabile per quem omnia fecisti et beneplacitum tibi fuit; misisti de caelo in matricem Virginis, quique in utero habitus incarnatus est et Filius tibi ostensus est ex Spiritu Sancto et Virgine natus, qui voluntatem tuam complens et populum sanctum tibi adquirens extendit manus cum pateretur ut a passione liberaret eos qui in te crediderunt: qui, cumque traderetur voluntariae passioni, ut mortem solvat, et vincula diaboli dirumpat, et infernum calcet, et justos inluminet et terminum figat, et resurrectionem manifestet,

Bishop: The Lord be with you.
All: And with you.
Bishop: Lift up your hearts.
All: We lift our hearts to the Lord.
Bishop: Let us give thanks to the Lord our God.
All: That is right and just.
Bishop: We give thanks to thee, O God, through thy beloved Son, Jesus Christ, whom thou hast sent to us in these last days as Saviour and Redeemer, the Messenger of thy will. Who is thy Word inseparable from thee through whom thou hast made all and in whom thou wast well-pleased; whom thou hast sent from heaven into the bosom of a Virgin and was borne in her womb and was incarnate there, and shown forth as thy Son born of the Holy Ghost and the Virgin, who to fulfil thy will and to gain a holy people for thee extended his hands in suffering that he might deliver from suffering those who believe in thee: who when he gave himself up voluntarily to suffering to abolish death, break the bonds of the devil, tread down hell, enlighten the just, establish the (new) ordinance and manifest the resurrection,
(*Institution*)

accipiens panem, gratias tibi agens dixit: Accipite, manducate: Hoc est corpus meum quod pro vobis confringetur.

Similiter et calicem dicens: Hic est sanguis meus qui pro vobis effunditur. Quando hoc facitis meam commemorationem facitis.

Memores igitur mortis et resurrectionis ejus offerimus tibi panem et calicem, gratias tibi agentes, qui nos dignos habuisti adstare coram te et tibi ministrare.

Et petimus ut mittas Spiritum tuum sanctum in oblationem Sanctae Ecclesiae, in unum congregans des omnibus qui percipiunt sanctis, in repletionem Spiritus sancti ad confirmationem fidei in veritate, ut te laudemus et glorificemus per puerum tuum Jesum Christum,

per quem tibi gloria et honor, Patri et Filio cum Sancto Spiritu, in sancta Ecclesia, et nunc et in saecula saeculorum. Amen.

taking bread and giving thanks to thee said: Take, eat. This is my body which is broken for you.

Likewise also the chalice saying: This is my blood which is shed for you. When you do these things, you make commemoration of me.
(*Anamnesis*)

We, therefore, remembering his death and resurrection, we offer the bread and chalice to thee, giving thanks to thee that thou hast found us worthy to stand before thee and minister.
(*Epiclesis*)

And we beseech thee to send thy Holy Spirit upon the oblation of holy Church, gathering together in one all the saints who communicate, in the fullness of the Holy Spirit to confirm their faith in truth that we may praise and give glory to thee through thy Child Jesus Christ,
(*Doxology*)

through whom be glory to thee, Father, to the Son and to the Holy Ghost in the holy Church both now and for ever. Amen.

Commentary

This anaphora, which is uninterrupted from the beginning of the preface to the final doxology, corresponds in form to primitive eucharists. The bishop presided and consecrated; the priests concelebrated with him. This anaphora is suggested to the bishop and is in no wise an invariable pattern received from the Apostles themselves.

The thanksgiving is addressed to the Father; but it ascends through the Son, the incarnate Word, whose mission in this world it expounds. This account leads naturally into the recital of the institution. Notice especially the absence of the *Sanctus*.

The anamnesis and priestly oblation are expressed with a gravity which emphasizes its majesty. In the same tradition, the Roman canon was later to comment upon and paraphrase what is here said in a short paragraph.

The epiclesis ends with a doxology which forms an organic part of it.

Hippolytus later continues:

Episcopus autem gratias agat secundum ea quae supra diximus. Attamen, non necesse est eadem verba eum proferre, quae supra diximus, ut diligentur meditetur in eis, gratias agens Deo, sed secundum facultatem unusquisque oret. Si quidem convenienter et oratione honorabili orare potest, bonum est; si vero aliter orat et orationem modice profert, nemo eum impediat; modo integre oret in orthodoxia.[1] The bishop, then, was definitely not bound to give thanks according to the literal wording of the *Paradosis*. If he was able to improvise in a fitting manner, he was permitted to do so, as long as he remained faithful to orthodoxy.

(f) THE ANAPHORA OF DER BALYZEH (FOURTH CENTURY)[2]

Fragments of papyrus were found in Upper Egypt at Der Balyzeh, not far from Asswan, in the ruins of a Coptic monastery sacked a thousand years ago. These fragments were taken to the Bodleian Library in Oxford. In them Mr. W. E. Crum recognized liturgical texts in elegant seventh- or eighth-century script, and especially the fragment of a eucharistic thanksgiving, the text of which differs from that of previously published anaphoras. This fragment reads:

Text
> O Master of the Cherubim, almighty, heavenly bishop, all virtuous Lord!

[1] Cap. 4; Funk 105
[2] See Dom P. de Puniet, *Fragments inédits d'une liturgie égyptienne écrits sur papyrus* in the *Report of the nineteenth Eucharistic Congress held at Westminster 9-13 September 1908*, pp. 367-408 (London, 1909).

O God, Father of our Lord Jesus Christ, thou who hast caused all to pass from not-being to being, the universe, thou who fillest all, being alone uncircumscribed . . . (*two lines lost*)

(*Sanctus*) . . . Around about thee stand the seraphim who each have six wings, two to hide their faces, two to hide their feet, two with which to fly: all ceaselessly acclaiming thee. With all those who acclaim thee, receive our acclamation also, who say to thee: Holy, holy, holy, Lord of hosts. Heaven and earth are full of thy glory.

Fill us with thy glory.

(*Epiclesis*) And deign to send down thy Holy Spirit upon these creatures. And make the bread the body of our Lord and Saviour Jesus Christ, and the chalice the blood of the new covenant.

(*Institution*) For our Lord Jesus Christ himself, on the night he was betrayed, took bread, broke it and having given thanks, gave it to his disciples and Apostles, saying: Take, eat of it all of you, this is my body given for you for the remission of sins. Likewise, after the meal, having taken the chalice and given thanks and drunk, he gave it to them, saying, Take, drink of it all of you, this is my blood poured out for you for the remission of sins. Every time you eat the bread and drink the chalice, you show forth my death, you proclaim my resurrection.

(*Anamnesis*) We show forth thy death, we proclaim thy resurrection; and we beseech thee . . . of thy gift, for the might of the Holy Ghost, for the strengthening and growth of faith, for hope of eternal life to come, through our Lord Jesus Christ.

(*Doxology*) Through whom to thee, Father, is the glory with the Holy Ghost for ever.

Commentary

Notice that this preface also leads into the *Sanctus;* the absence of *Benedictus qui venit* is a common characteristic of Eastern liturgies. The last words of the trisagion—*plena est gloria tua*—here introduce the epiclesis, which itself is particularly noteworthy because it occurs before the consecration (whereas in Eastern liturgies it is

Eucharistic Thanksgiving

invariably placed afterwards), and on account of its very clear references to transubstantiation. The anamnesis states very clearly that the Mass is the commemoration not only of the death but also of the resurrection of Christ.

(g) THE STRASBURG PAPYRUS (FOURTH CENTURY)[1]

In 1928, M. Andrieu and P. Collomp published the fragments of an anaphora preserved on papyrus in the library of the University of Strasburg. Careful examination reveals that it is part of an intercessory prayer recited in the liturgy called that of St Mark, by the priest and deacon between the beginning of the anaphora and the *Sanctus*. This section probably dates back to the liturgy in use in the time of St Athanasius (295-373). This discovery was yet more remarkable as the oldest known documentary sources of the liturgy of St Mark date only from the twelfth century.

Text

> ... to praise thee, day and night. Thou who hast created heaven and all that is in it and the earth and what is found thereon, the seas and the rivers and all that they contain; thou who hast made man in thine image and likeness and hast created all things through thy wisdom, thy true light, thy Son, our Lord and Saviour Jesus Christ, through whom and with whom we give thanks to thee with the Holy Ghost and offer thee this spiritual sacrifice, this ministry without bloodshed that all nations from the rising of the sun to its setting, from the north to the south, offer to thee because thy name is great among the nations and in every place incense is offered to thy holy name, a pure victim, sacrifice and offering.
>
> We pray and beseech thee, remember thy holy Church of all thy nations and flocks. Give unto all our hearts that peace which cometh from heaven, but grant unto us also the peace of this life. [Keep in peace] the prince of this world; [grant that he may nourish in his heart thoughts] of peace towards us and thy holy name; [keep in perfect peace] the leader ... of the army, the princes and the senate.

---

[1] M. Andrieu and P. Collomp, *Fragments sur papyrus de l'anaphore de S. Marc* in *Rev. des sciences relig.*, 8, pp. 489-515 (Strasburg, 1928). F. E. Brightman, *Liturgies Eastern and Western: I—Eastern Liturgies*, pp. 115-43, 144-88 (Oxford, 1896).

[Grant unto us fruits for seed-time and] harvest . . . because of the poor among thy people, the widow and the orphan, the guest and the stranger, of us all who hope in thee and call upon thy name.

Grant rest unto the souls of those who have fallen asleep. Remember those whose memorial we make this day, whose names we announce and those whose names we do not announce; [remember also] above all our holy fathers and bishops who profess the true faith and grant them a share and inheritance with the glorious community of thy holy prophets, Apostles, martyrs . . . grant them now . . . through our Lord and Saviour through whom be glory unto thee for ever.

(h) THE ANAPHORA OF SERAPION († 358)[1]

Serapion was the bishop of Thmuis in Egypt and was the contemporary and friend of St Anthony († 356) and St Athanasius († 373). A Greek Euchologion containing a widely known anaphora is adorned with his name. This " Sacramentary of Serapion " survives in a Greek manuscript (eleventh century) preserved at Mount Athos. When this document was published in 1894 by Dmitrijewski, and in 1898 by Wobbermin, it caused a sensation: it was adjudged to be an example of the greatest importance of one of the oldest of Egyptian liturgies, but gradually the critical studies of Baumstark, Dom Capelle and others and the discovery of new sources revealed its composite nature. Having completed a new critical examination of the anaphora, Dom Capelle concluded:

> That the anaphora of Serapion shows numerous archaic characteristics and certain indications of the employment of sources made precious by their antiquity is undeniable, but this inheritance from the past has been inserted by the bishop into a composition entirely his own. Although the main outlines of Egyptian anaphoras are still apparent here, their structure is so audaciously changed—even in the case of the oldest prayers —that the value of the collection as evidence of the liturgies of Egypt is thereby considerably reduced. Old compositions

---

[1] L. Duchesne, *Origines du culte chrétien*, pp. 76–81 (Fontemoing, Paris, 1920). English trans. from 3rd French edn., *Christian Worship, its Origin and Evolution*, pp. 76–9 (London, 1902).

were admitted or retained by the editor only after revision in accordance with his personal criteria.[1]

It must therefore be used with caution, but is nevertheless of considerable interest.

Text

It is right and fitting to praise thee, to hymn thee, to glorify thee, O uncreated Father of the only-begotten Son Jesus Christ. We praise thee, uncreated God, who art unknowable, ineffable, incomprehensible to all created being. We praise thee, thou who art known by the only-begotten Son and by him art revealed, interpreted and made known to all created nature. We praise thee, thou who knowest the Son and revealest his glories to the saints, thou who art known by thy only-begotten Word and by him manifested and explained to the saints. We praise thee, invisible Father who givest immortality. Thou art the fount of life, the source of light, the source of all grace and truth. Lover of men, lover of the poor, thou who reconcilest thyself to all and drawest all to thee by the coming of thy beloved Son, we pray thee thereby, make us living men; give us the spirit of illumination, so that we may know thee, the true [God] and he whom thou hast sent, Jesus Christ. Give us the Holy Ghost, that we may speak and tell of thy ineffable mysteries. May the Lord Jesus and the Holy Ghost speak in us, and give honour to thee through us. For thou art he who soarest above all commandment, all might, all power and domination, and every name that is named not only in this world, but also in the world that is to come.

(*Sanctus*) In thy train are thousands of thousands and myriads of myriads of angels, archangels, thrones, principalities, powers and dominations; near thee stand the two most honourable seraphim with six wings, with two of which they cover their faces, with two they cover their feet, and with two they fly, proclaiming that thou art holy. Receive our proclamations of thy holiness with theirs: Holy, holy, holy is the Lord

---

[1] Dom B. Capelle, *L'Anaphore de Sérapion, Essai d'exégèse* (Muséon, t. 59, 1-4, Mélanges Lefort, p. 438).

Sabaoth. Heaven and earth are full of thy glory. The heaven is full and the earth is full of thy glory.

(*Epiclesis*) Lord of powers, fill then this sacrifice with thy power and participation.

(*Interpolation*) For we have offered this living sacrifice, this unbloody offering, to thee; to thee have we offered this bread which is the likeness of the body of thy Only-begotten. This bread is the likeness of the holy body.

(*Institution, Anamnesis*) For the Lord Jesus Christ, on the night on which he was betrayed, took bread, broke it and gave it to his disciples, saying: Take and eat, this is my body, being broken for you for remission of sins. Wherefore, portraying his death, we have offered this bread and pray through this sacrifice. Be reconciled with us, be merciful, O God of truth. And as [the materials for] this bread was [were] scattered abroad over the mountains and being gathered together are become one, so gather together thy Church from all nations and countries, towns, villages and households and make it one living and universal Church. We have offered too this chalice, the likeness of the blood, because the Lord Jesus Christ, taking a chalice after the supper, said to his disciples: Take, drink, this is the new covenant, that is, my blood poured out for you in remission of sins. Wherefore we have offered the chalice, producing the likeness of blood.

(*Epiclesis*) O God of truth, let thy holy Word come down upon this bread that the bread may become the body of the Word, and upon this chalice, that the chalice may become the blood of truth. And grant that all those who partake thereof, may receive a lifegiving medicine, which may heal all sickness in them and strengthen them in all advancement and virtue, that it be not for their condemnation. O God of truth, let it result in neither sorrow nor dishonour for them. For we invoke thee, O Uncreated, through thy Only-begotten in the Holy Ghost. May mercy be upon this people, that it may be held worthy of advancement; may angels be sent to it to help it to triumph over evil and establish the Church.

(*Diptychs*) We pray to thee also for all the dead of whom commemoration is made together with proclamation of their names. Sanctify these souls, for thou hast known them all.

Sanctify all those who are fallen asleep in the Lord; add them to the number of thy holy powers; give them a place and abode in thy kingdom. Receive also this people's thanksgiving, bless those who make offerings and thanksgivings; give to this whole people health, soundness, contentment and all the blessings of both soul and body, through thine only-begotten Son.

(*Doxology*) Jesus Christ, in the Holy Ghost, as it was, is and will be unto generations of generations and for ever world without end. Amen.

Commentary

Like every preface, this anaphora begins with *Vere dignum*, but its originality sets it apart from the outset. None of the typical themes used in prefaces are to be found here—the work of creation, of providence or the redemption of Christ. It is addressed to the uncreated Father of the only Son Jesus Christ who is the *Logos* through whom we know the Father. We praise the Father through the Son and Holy Ghost. But after the clause " For thou art he that soarest above all commandment . . .", which links the preface to the *Sanctus*, the prayer is usual in form.

To the *Sanctus*—which speaks of fullness (of glory), as do those of other Egyptian liturgies—there is attached a rather broad pre-consecratory epiclesis[1] which asks: " Lord of Powers, fill then this sacrifice with thy power and participation."

There then follows a most unusual interpolation which clearly breaks the continuity between the epiclesis and the account of the institution: " For we have offered this living sacrifice. . . . This bread is the likeness of the holy body ". Notice that there are here two references to the oblation in the past tense, and that three more are made in the same tense in the text of the institution-anamnesis which follows; this is a somewhat arbitrary literary construction proper to Serapion who probably adapted a source expressing the oblation in the present (compare, for example, the Strasburg papyrus).

As regards the consecration, here the author has boldly adopted a most unusual construction, dividing that of the wine from that of the bread by incorporating in the latter a quite brief anamnesis

---

[1] In the Der Balyzeh anaphora and the Lefort papyrus at Louvain, this epiclesis formally requests the consecration of the bread and wine.

followed by a petitionary prayer inspired by *Didache* 9. 4, which, however, envisages this gathering together from an eschatological standpoint, whereas this asks that all may be gathered together in the Church militant here and now.

Notice that the epiclesis is addressed not to the Holy Ghost but to the Word.

(i) THE APOSTOLIC CONSTITUTIONS (FOURTH CENTURY)[1]

This is a Greek anthology, made by a Syrian (from Antioch or thereabouts), dating from the fourth century and comprising eight books, of which the first six reproduce the very ancient *Didascalia*, with interpolations.

The compiler has added the outline of a liturgy to book two.

Book seven is the *Didache* with interpolations.

Book eight contains a complete and now well-known liturgy. Modern liturgists have brought all their critical faculties to bear upon this very important source: from the numerous studies of which it has been the subject it seems that it may be concluded that it consists to a large degree of primitive liturgical material. But to maintain therefore that this is the primitive liturgy would be to go too far.

The thanksgiving, which is a beautiful lyrical composition, unfolds as one of those " long eucharists " of which St Justin speaks; it is pregnant with the doctrine and evidence of the devotion of early times.

The following are a few typical sentences from the anaphora.[2]

Text

> (6) *Vere dignum et iustum est, ante omnia laudare te verum Deum, ante creaturas existentem, ex quo omnis paternitas in caelo et in terra nominatur* . . . [the text speaks of the Father, then of the Son through whom all was created] (7) . . . *qui omnia ex nihilo in rerum naturam protulisti per unigenitum Filium tuum, ipsum vero ante omnia saecula genuisti voluntate et potentia et bonitate absque intermedio, Filium unigenitum, Verbum, Deum,*

---

[1] J. Quasten, *Monumenta eucharistica et liturgica vetustissima*, Pars IV, pp. 211–27 (Hanstein, Bonn, 1936).

[2] The text is that printed by F X. Funk, *op. cit.*, 8, 12.

Eucharistic Thanksgiving

sapientiam viventem, Primogenitum omnis creaturae, Angelum magni concilii tui, Pontificem tuum . . . [Sections 8–26 treat of the creation through the Son, of the things in both heaven and earth, and of the providence of God active on behalf of the Jews. This section ends with a reference to the dividing of Jordan, and leads into the *Sanctus*].

. . . (26) *Jordanem dirupisti, fluvios Ethan siccasti, muros prostravisti absque machinis et absque manu humana.* (27) *Pro omnibus tibi gloria, Domine omnipotens. Te adorant innumerabiles copiae angelorum, archangelorum, thronorum, dominationum, principatuum, potestatum, virtutum, exercituum aeternorum, Cherubim ac Seraphim senis alis praediti, binis quidem velantes pedes suos, binis vero capita, et duabus alis volantes ac dicentes una cum mille millibus archangelorum et denis millibus denum millium angelorum indesinenter ac sine vocis intermissione clamantibus, et omnis populus simul dicat: Sanctus, sanctus, sanctus Dominus Sabaoth; pleni sunt caeli et terra gloria eius; benedictus in saecula, amen* . . . [The *Sanctus* in turn leads into a long post-sanctus devoted especially to a summary of the incarnation and Christ's life on earth, which culminates in the institution] . . . (36) *In qua enim nocte tradebatur, sumpsit panem sanctis ac immaculatis manibus suis et elevatis oculis ad te, Deum ac Patrem, fregit ac dedit discipulis dicens: Hoc est mysterium novi testamenti, accipite ex eo, manducate, hoc est corpus meum, quod pro multis frangitur in remissionem peccatorum.* (37) *Similiter calicem miscuit ex vino et aqua, sanctificavit ac dedit iis dicens: Bibite ex eo omnes, hic est sanguis meus, qui pro multis effunditur in remissionem peccatorum; hoc facite in meam commemorationem; quotiescumque enim manducabitis panem hunc et bibetis hunc calicem, mortem meam annuntiabitis, donec veniam.* (Anamnesis) (38) *Itaque memores passionis eius et mortis et a mortuis resurrectionis atque in caelos reditus nec non futuri eius secundi adventus . . . offerimus tibi, Regi ac Deo, secundum constitutionem eius, panem hunc et calicem hunc . . .* (Epiclesis) (39) *et poscimus te, ut . . . supra hoc sacrificium mittas sanctum tuum Spiritum . . . ut exhibeat panem hunc corpus Christi tui et calicem hunc sanguinem Christi tui* [the anaphora ends with a long series of petitions for all classes of the faithful terminating in the doxology] (50) . . . *quoniam tibi omnis gloria, veneratio, gratiarum actio, honor, adoratio, Patri et Filio et Spiritui Sancto, et nunc et semper et in infinita et sempiterna saecula saeculorum.*

The whole congregation answers: *Amen.*

Commentary

The anaphora, which is addressed to the Father, refers to each stage of the work of creation and sets out the blessings of providence with oriental prolixity, relating the history of the flood, Abraham and the patriarchs, the deliverance from Egyptian tyranny and settlement in the Promised Land, culminating in the *Sanctus*. With the *Sanctus* it returns to the Son and his excellence is then described, and thus is reached the institution of the eucharist. The anamnesis and epiclesis together form a unity. There follows a long prayer in litany form, ending with a short doxology.[1]

(j) THE LOUVAIN PAPYRUS (SIXTH CENTURY)

In 1936, Professor L. Th. Lefort of the University of Louvain acquired a most interesting Coptic manuscript from Berlin. It contains a fragment of the anaphora used in an unknown church, probably in Middle Egypt. The document dates from the sixth century. Fortunately, Professor Lefort published the manuscript in *Le Muséon*, for the original was irrecoverably lost in a fire in the University library in 1940. The translation given below was made from the Greek version prepared from the Coptic text by Professor Lefort:[2]

> (*Sanctus*) . . . the earth (is full) of thy glory. Heaven and earth are full of that glory with which thou hast enlightened us in thine only-begotten Son Jesus Christ, the First-born of all creation; who sitteth at the right hand of thy majesty in heaven; who shall come to judge the living and the dead.
>
> (*Anamnesis*) We commemorate his death by offering thee these thine own creatures, this bread and cup.
>
> (*Epiclesis*) We pray and invoke thee that thou wouldest send down upon these offerings thy Holy Ghost the Paraclete from heaven . . . to sanctify . . . this bread as the body of Christ and this cup as the blood of Christ's new covenant.

[1] Cf. Dom H. Leclercq, *Messe*, 25, loc. cit.
[2] L. Th. Lefort, *Coptica lovaniensia*, n. 27 (*Le Muséon*, vol. 53, 1940, p. 24, Louvain).

(*Institution*) Since the Lord himself, when he was about to deliver himself up, took bread, gave thanks over it, blessed it, broke it and gave it to his disciples and said to them: Take, eat, for this is my body which will be given for you.

Likewise, after they had eaten, he took also the cup, gave thanks over it and gave it to them saying: Take, drink, for this is my blood, which will be poured out for many for the remission (of sins) . . .

4. CONCLUSION

As is obvious from the evidence of the *Didache* (90), St Justin († 167), St Hippolytus († 235), etc., the eucharistic thanksgiving was improvised for a long time and developed with some freedom of style while yet expounding themes pre-determined by tradition. In this way there were produced fixed texts or models which were proposed rather than imposed for the use of celebrants, providing them with a pattern and main points for an improvisation on similar lines. Gradually, however, eucharistic thanksgiving crystallized into yet more rigid, permanent and official forms which were imposed on all and which could be altered only by competent ecclesiastical authority. In this way there arose the great flowering of diverse and closely related liturgical thanksgivings. The dangers inherent in such improvisation are obvious.

In this period of transition, some councils could not hide their concern: thus, for example, Canon 23 of that at Carthage (397) enjoins him who celebrates the liturgy not to use at the altar *preces, nisi prius eas cum structioribus fratribus contulerit*[1] and the Council of Milevium (412) decrees in Canon 12: *Placuit etiam et illud ut preces vel orationes seu missae quae probatae fuerint in concilio sive praefationes* (anaphoras) *sive commendationes . . . ab omnibus celebrentur. Nec aliae omnino dicantur in ecclesia, nisi a prudentioribus tractatae vel comprobatae in synodo fuerint, ne forte aliquid contra fidem, vel per ignorantiam vel per minus studium sit compositum.*[2] Comparison of these ancient sources gradually reveals the basic parts of the traditional eucharistic anaphora:

---

[1] Labbe and Cossart, 2, 170.
[2] J. A. Jungmann, *Gewordene Liturgie*, p. 70: *Praefatio und stiller Kanon.*

Preface
Sanctus
Words of Institution
Consecration
Anamnesis
Epiclesis
Intercession[1]
Final doxology.

We shall base our study (in Chapter 17) of the origins and history of the modern Roman canon on these sources.

[1] Not necessarily in this position.

15

THE PREFACE: THE PROLOGUE TO THE EUCHARISTIC THANKSGIVING

THE ceremonies of the offertory are ended: the preparation for the sacrifice has been made: " Bless these sacrificial gifts, prepared for the glory of thy holy name." Notice once again that, whatever their importance and no matter how much liturgical expressions anticipate coming events, the ceremonies of the offertory are not independent but entirely relative, being meaningful only through and because of the eucharistic act of sacrifice properly so called: far from constituting an act of oblation essential to the sacrifice, the ceremonies of the offertory merely herald it, prefigure it and, above all, prepare for it. They are subsidiary to the "thanksgiving ", the " eucharist ", that we are now about to consider.

We consider first the preface.

NAME AND CHARACTER OF THE PREFACE

Praefatio is derived from *praefari* and philology shows that the preposition *prae* (before) suggests an audience, a gathering of people, in the presence of whom, before whom, an utterance is made. The same shade of meaning is to be found in the expressions *praedicare, praelegere, praestare, praesentia,* etc. To the Romans, *praefari* meant to utter juridical or ritual formulas. Indeed, when speaking of the declaration of a vow by the *pontifex maximus,* Titus Livy wrote: *Pontifice maximo praefante carmen* and elsewhere he records the *solemne carmen precationis quod praefari solent magistratus.*[1] It is, therefore, not impossible that the liturgy is indebted for this term to the religious vocabulary of the Romans.

St Cyprian († 258) used the term *praefatio* to designate the dialogue which introduces the thanksgiving which he called *oratio: ante orationem praefatione praemissa.*[2]

---

[1] Batiffol, *Leçons sur la Messe*, p. 192.
[2] *De Domin. orat.*, 31, in Hartel, *C.S.E.L.*, 3, 289.

This expression is most suitable as the name of the solemn thanksgiving addressed to God before the congregation in the course of the holy sacrifice, and therefore *praefatio* was in ancient times the name given to the great eucharistic prayer, or canon of the Mass, from the *Vere dignum* of the introductory dialogue to the *Amen* of the final doxology. However, its meaning was later restricted to the designation of the beginning of this thanksgiving, the lyrical passage from the secret to the *Sanctus*. In the oldest Roman Sacramentaries—the Leonine (fifth–sixth century), Gelasian (*c.* 700) and the Gregorian at Padua (which dated from the time of Honorius I, 628–38)—this passage has no title. *Praefatio* appears for the first time as the title of this prayer in the Gregorian Sacramentary which Pope Hadrian sent to Charlemagne (790), in which it designates the " preface " for Christmas. In the Gallican liturgy, our preface was called *Contestatio* (" testimony ") and indeed this solemn prayer of thanksgiving provides an imposing witness to the faith: the Church prays as she believes. It is also called *Immolatio* because it introduces the sacramental immolation of the Eucharist.

In the Mozarabic (or Visigothic) liturgy of Spain, it bears the name *illatio* (*in-ferre*), " offering ", which is an exact equivalent of the term *anaphora* by which the Greeks designated it.

As we have seen, the preface is a prayer of thanksgiving of the most solemn kind, the majestic manner of which is in marked contrast with the style of the prayers of the offertory which precede it. It is intoned by the priest alone, as the spokesman of the whole congregation. It everywhere begins with a characteristic dialogue with which it is organically connected. " In the Roman liturgy, the preface," Batiffol writes, " has preserved its natural solemnity. It is sung or, more exactly, declaimed: aided by the silence and attention of the people, it fills the church. Its purpose is to speak before God, with dignified and noble joy, the thanks of the redeemed earth." [1]

THE PREFACE AS THE BEGINNING OF THE CANON

In origin and structure the preface and canon are a unity. Indeed, in former times, the canon began immediately after the introductory dialogue of the preface, as St Cyprian attests: " When we stand for the eucharistic thanksgiving (*oratio*), we must attend and apply

[1] *Leçons sur la Messe*, p. 203.

The Preface

ourselves to the prayers with all our hearts. Wherefore, the priest prepares the hearts of his brethren before this prayer (*oratio*) by means of a preface (the introductory dialogue, *praefatione praemissa*) saying *sursum corda*."[1] St Cyprian, then, considers our preface as an integral part of the canon.

Furthermore, the *Liber Pontificalis* (sixth century) attributes the following decree to Pope Sixtus I († 142): *ut intra actionem, sacerdos incipiens, populo (= populus) hymnum decantare: Sanctus . . .*

Actio refers to the group of prayers forming the eucharistic thanksgiving and the associated rites, especially that of consecration. If, then, the *Sanctus* is to be sung not before but during the eucharistic thanksgiving, it is clear that the preface belongs to the canon.

In the Gelasian[2] and other eighth-century Sacramentaries, the heading *Incipit canon actionis* (" Here begins the rule of the action ") is placed before *sursum corda* and thus includes the preface. According to *Ordo Romanus I* (eighth century), the canon begins with *Te igitur: dum incipiunt dicere hymnum angelicum id est sanctus, quem dum expleverint surgit Pontifex solus et intrat in canonem:*[3] and this has been the rule since that time, so that by the time of Amalarius the division between preface and canon was absolute. Yet even then sight had not been entirely lost of the organic unity between them, for he teaches with regard to the *Te igitur* that this phrase is found " in the middle of the canon ": *Subdiaconus medio canone, id est, cum dicitur Te igitur . . .*

Today the canon begins at the *Te igitur* under the title *Canon Missae*.

DIVISIONS OF THE PREFACE

The preface may be divided as follows:

The introductory dialogue.
A. The beginning of the preface.
B. The main section, or proper, of the preface.
C. Conclusion (or transition to the *Sanctus*), normally commencing *Per quem majestatem tuam . . .*

---

[1] *Liber Pont.* (Duchesne) I, 128.
[2] Ed. Wilson, p. 234.
[3] Mabillon, *Musaeum Italicum*, I, p. 12.

The introductory dialogue.—It is noteworthy that in all liturgies, both Eastern and Western, the eucharistic thanksgiving begins with this dialogue. But this thanksgiving itself is yet more venerable. In one bound, it takes us back through the centuries to the primitive synaxes to which St Justin bears witness in his Apology. The oldest text we have of the Roman thanksgiving dates from the time of St Hippolytus (218-35) and it is not without emotion that we here see the distant reflection of the opening dialogue which still arises in our own times from the lips of bishops and priests at the head of their congregations:

Dominus vobiscum.	The Lord be with you.
Et cum spiritu tuo.	And with you.
Sursum corda.	Lift up your hearts.
Habemus ad Dominum.	We lift our hearts to the Lord.
Gratias agamus Domino Deo nostro.	Let us give thanks to the Lord our God.
Dignum et justum est.[1]	That is right and just.

A few years later, *sursum corda* and its response are to be found in the writings of St Cyprian[2] at Carthage and later still, in those of St Augustine († 430) at Hippo,[3] and a verbal echo is found in Rome and Carthage from the Greek liturgies of Jerusalem and Antioch.[4] By about the year 390, St Augustine was able to assert that every day over the whole earth humanity with one voice proclaimed that its heart was uplifted towards God: *respondet sursum corda se habere ad Dominum.*[5] The universality of its employment incontestably witnesses to the great antiquity of this dialogue.

By his urgent exhortations, the priest desires: (a) to win the attention of the faithful; (b) to prepare them for the central rite of the eucharistic offering; (c) to make them active participants in his sacrifice, which is also their own.

Sursum corda! "Lift up your hearts"—above terrestrial conceptions and preoccupations, for the heavenly mystery, the divine miracle draws near: in a few moments the whole Christian body, in entire thanksgiving, will offer the eucharistic body and blood,

---

[1] The Verona Anaphora (Hippolytus), ed. Hauler.
[2] *De Dom. orat.*, 31.
[3] *Sermo* 68, 5.
[4] Batiffol, *Leçons sur la Messe*, p. 196.
[5] *De vera relig.*, 5.

through, with and in Christ to the infinite majesty of the Father. As one man, the whole congregation proclaims itself ready: *Habemus ad Dominum!*

And straightway the priest utters the decisive acclamation which is the inspiration of the whole of the canon: *Gratias agamus Domino Deo nostro!* Immediately, the people reply like the conscript fathers to the Roman Senate: *Dignum et justum est.*

Henceforward priest and faithful are closely bound together in a common uplifting of souls towards the Father. With complete awareness, hierarchically united to its shepherd, the Christian community proclaims its absolute unity with its head and ratifies the words of its sacred interpreter in every respect. The minister's thanksgiving is truly its own: let it lift itself up, therefore, officially, as a society: *Vere dignum et justum est, aequum et salutare, NOS tibi semper et ubique gratias agere . . .*

A. *The beginning of the preface.*—The beginning of the preface is always the same:

(i) *Vere dignum et justum est, aequum et salutare, nos tibi semper et ubique gratias agere:*

(ii) *Domine sancte, Pater omnipotens, aeterne Deus,*[1]

(iii) *per Christum Dominum nostrum.*

(i) Just it is indeed, fitting, right, and for our lasting good, that we should always and everywhere give thanks to thee,

(ii) Holy Lord, almighty father, eternal God,

(iii) through Christ our Lord.

This passage is a masterpiece of logical and doctrinal cohesion and concision in that it goes immediately to essentials, the thanksgiving (i); it is addressed directly to the Father (ii); and it rests upon the mediation of Christ, the sovereign high priest (iii).

Worship of the Father and the priestly mediation of Christ, which are so characteristic of liturgical prayer, we treated at length in connection with the collects; for the doctrinal significance of these matters reference should be made again to that section of this commentary.[2] It will have been noted how clearly our text bears the imprint of the Roman mind.[3]

[1] It should be noted that the new *Ordo* for Holy Week (1956) has changed the punctuation: *Domine, sancte Pater, omnipotens aeterne Deus.*
[2] Vol. I, Chap. 20, pp. 164–87.
[3] Cf. Vol. I, Chap. 19, pp. 153–55.

The three elements composing this beginning are to be found in the prefaces of the Ascension, the Holy Ghost and the Dead. Elements (i) and (ii) only open the prefaces for Christmas, the Epiphany, Lent, the Holy Cross, the Sacred Heart of Jesus, Christ the King, the Holy Trinity, the Blessed Virgin Mary and St Joseph. From this it may be understood why this traditional outline was written in an abridged form in manuscripts. Thus, for example, we read: *Vere dignum. Aeterne Deus, per Christum Dominum nostrum.*

B. *The main section, or "proper" of the preface.*—Because it is changed to suit the mystery or feast, the main part, or proper, of the preface enlarges upon the reason for thankfulness, and there were therefore a great variety of prefaces in the ancient Latin liturgy.

In former times, especially in Gaul, each Mass had its own proper preface, and even in the Roman rite (Leonine Sacramentary) there were almost as many prefaces as Masses (269 to 281).

The table on p. 169 renders commentary superfluous.

The ancient sacramentaries contain magnificent prefaces for Advent, St John the Baptist, every Sunday after Pentecost, the week-days of Lent, etc.

It may be asked how so deep-rooted a tradition came to be broken in about the tenth century. The further back we go, the more prefaces there are, as is natural in a prayer which was originally improvised. It seems clear that the number of prefaces in the Roman rite came to be reduced under the influence of the Gallican liturgy. Thus although the Leonine Sacramentary (ancient Roman, sixth century) had 269 prefaces, the Gelasian (*c.* 700) contained only fifty-eight and the revised Gregorian (ninth century) a mere fourteen (although the appendix contained more than one hundred). Wherever the Roman liturgy was firmly rooted, the tradition of numerous prefaces was maintained until the eleventh and twelfth centuries. Thus, the Missal of Leofric, Bishop of Exeter, preserved a proper preface for each Mass until the second half of the eleventh century.

At Rome, in the reign of St Gregory the Great († 604) the number of prefaces was reduced to nine: those for Christmas, Epiphany, Lent, the Holy Cross, Easter, the Ascension, the Holy Ghost, the Holy Trinity and the Apostles. These nine prefaces

The Preface

Liturgical Source	Masses	Proper Prefaces
MOZARABIC SACRAMENTARY (Spain)[1]	157	157
GALLICAN SACRAMENTARIES:		
Missale Gothicum ((seventh century)[2]	68	68
Missale Reichenau (fragment) (seventh century)[3]	11	15
Missale Gallicanum (seventh century)[4]	20	18
Missale Francorum (seventh century)[5]	13	10
The Bobbio Missal (eighth century)[6]	62	76
ROMAN SACRAMENTARIES:		
Sacramentarium Leonianum (sixth century)[7]	281	269
Sacramentarium Gelasianum (*c.* 700)[8]	270	58
Sacramentarium Gregorianum (Muratori, ninth century)[9]	259	87
Liber Sacramentorum (Menard, tenth century)[10]	291	214
THE AMBROSIAN MISSAL	336	263

occur in the Gelasian (*c.* 700) and Gregorian (ninth century) Sacramentaries, although the prefaces for Lent and the Holy Trinity are to be found only in the appendix of the latter. In the Leonine Sacramentary (sixth century) are to be found the prefaces for the Ascension, the Holy Ghost and the Apostles. As this sacramentary lacks the section from January to April, it is impossible to pronounce upon the antiquity of the other prefaces. It seems certain that the beautiful preface for Christmas was composed by St Gregory himself.

At the Synod of Placentia (Piacenza) (1095), Urban II introduced

---

[1] Dom Ferotin, *Liber M. Sacramentorum* (Paris, 1912).
[2] Muratori, *Liturgia Romana vetus*, vol. 2, p. 238 (Naples, 1760).
[3] *P.L.*, 138, 863.
[4] Muratori, *ibid.*, p. 371
[5] Muratori, *ibid.*, p. 315.
[6] Mabillon, *Iter Italicum*, 1, 2, 273.
[7] Ed. Feltoe (Cambridge, 1896).
[8] Ed. Wilson (Oxford, 1894).
[9] Muratori, *op. cit.*, p. 1.
[10] *P.L.*, 78, 26.

into the Missal a preface in honour of Mary to obtain her intercession on behalf of the Crusade.

The common preface, which was called *quotidiana* until the sixteenth century, immediately precedes the canon of the Mass in the Gelasian[1] and Gregorian[2] Sacramentaries and is a pattern rather than a proper form.

As late as 9 April 1919, Benedict XV introduced two new prefaces: one in honour of St Joseph and the other for the dead.[3] On 12 December 1925 Pope Pius XI added the preface for Christ the King,[4] and on 29 January 1929, that of the Sacred Heart of Jesus.[5]

Our present Missal thus contains fifteen prefaces. Each of the cycles of the liturgical year except Advent has its proper preface. But notice that, according to the liturgical order of precedence laid down by the litany of the saints, St John the Baptist takes precedence over St Joseph. But there is no longer a preface proper of Precursor. It is to be hoped that Advent and St John the Baptist will soon have restored to them one of their traditional prefaces.

Many dioceses and religious orders, etc., enjoy proper prefaces on certain specific festivals, such as that of the founder of an order.

In time with the rhythm of the liturgical seasons, the prefaces, with great magnificence, unfold the successive mysteries of our redemption as so many reasons for which it is "just . . . and fitting, right, and for our lasting good that we should always and everywhere give thanks to the Lord, holy Father, almighty and eternal God".

" For " (*quia*), preface after preface goes on to say:

". . . for, through the mystery of the Word made flesh, thy splendour has shone before our mind's eye with a new radiance, and through him [*the Word made flesh*] whom we recognize as God made visible, we are carried away in love of things invisible" (Christmas).

". . . for that restoration of our human nature which thy only-begotten Son accomplished when he put on mortality like ours and showed his immortality among us under a new light" (Epiphany).

---

[1] Ed. Wilson, p. 234.
[2] Ed. Lietzmann, 12.
[3] *Acta Apost. Sedis*, 1919 (XI), pp. 190-1.
[4] *Acta Apost. Sedis*, 1925, pp. 655-68.
[5] *Acta Apost. Sedis*, 1929, pp. 44-77.

"... by thy ordinance [Father] the salvation of mankind was accomplished on the wood of the cross, so that life might rise again there where death had its beginning, and that he who conquered through a tree should on a tree himself be conquered (The Holy Cross).

"... but more triumphantly than ever [to praise thee] on this day, when Christ our passover was sacrificed. For he is the true Lamb who has taken away the sins of the world: he who by dying has brought our death to naught, and by rising again has restored us to life " (Easter).

"... through Christ our Lord, who after his resurrection appeared openly to all his disciples and was lifted up to heaven before their eyes, so that he might grant us fellowship in his Godhead " (Ascension).

"... who ascended above all the heavens and, taking his seat at thy right hand, sent down the Holy Spirit as he had promised, upon his adopted children " (Pentecost—The Holy Ghost).

Space will not allow us to comment upon these venerable formulas here: analysis of the contents of the prefaces leaves us speechless at the loftiness and quantity of the doctrine contained in them in such concise terms.[1]

C. *Conclusion*.—In the common preface the conclusion is thus formulated:

Per quem [Christum] majestatem tuam laudant Angeli, adorant Dominationes, tremunt Potestates. Caeli caelorumque Virtutes ac beata Seraphim socia exsultatione concelebrant.	It is through him [Christ] that thy majesty is praised by Angels, adored by Dominations, feared by Powers; through him that the heavens and celestial Virtues join with the blessed Seraphim in one glad hymn of praise.
Cum quibus et nostras voces ut admitti jubeas, deprecamur, supplici confessione dicentes:	We pray thee let our voices blend with theirs, as we humbly praise thee, singing:

This passage acts as a link binding the main section (or proper) of the preface to the *Sanctus*. As it is normally invariable, it is abbreviated in the manuscripts of the sacramentaries to the initial

---

[1] On this point, refer back to the examination of the collects, Vol. 1, Chap. 19.

preposition *Per*. It is found not only in the common preface, but also in those of Lent, the Cross, the Blessed Virgin Mary and St Joseph. As *Per quem* refers to Christ the main section of the preface has to be so drafted that this relative pronoun refers to its true antecedent (see, for example, the prefaces of Lent and St Joseph). If, on the other hand, the proper of the preface commemorates a mystery, the transition to the *Sanctus* is effected with the formula . . . *et ideo cum Angelis et Archangelis* . . . *hymnum gloriae tuae canimus, sine fine dicentes* . . .: the prefaces of Christmas*, Epiphany,* Easter,* the Ascension, the Sacred Heart,* Christ the King,* the Apostles* and the Dead. In the prefaces marked *, the phrase *per Christum Dominum nostrum* does not occur at the beginning. It was only in exceptional cases that Christ's priestly mediation was not verbally expressed in the ancient Roman liturgy.[1] It may be that this lacuna results from the corruption in the manuscripts of an imperfectly understood abbreviated formula.

Finally, two prefaces offer special formulas of transition: that of the Holy Ghost (*Quapropter profusis gaudiis, totus in orbe terrarum mundus exsultat. Sed et supernae Virtutes* . . .) and that of the Holy Trinity (*Quam laudant Angeli atque Archangeli*, etc. . . .).

Christ is raised above the angels (*melior angelis effectus*),[2] not only as God but also as a man endowed with the fullness of sanctifying grace; he is the head of the angelic hosts: *Qui est caput omnis principatus et potestatis*, "He is the fountain head from which all dominion and power proceed".[3] He is the mediator both of angels and men. *Per quem majestatem tuam laudant Angeli*.

It is worthy of note that all the prefaces end by recalling the angelic choirs which glorify the divine majesty in heaven and with which the Church conjoins its praise.[4] Pseudo-Dionysius the Areopagite identifies nine choirs of angels, divided into three orders, arranged from the most to the least perfect thus:[5]

    I. Seraphim
       Cherubim
       Thrones (*Throni*)

---

[1] The preface of the Kingship of Christ refers explicitly to Christ's priesthood.
[2] Heb. 1. 4.
[3] Col. 2. 10.
[4] This reference is omitted only from the prefaces of the Holy Ghost and the Holy Trinity.
[5] See Prat, *Theologie de S. Paul*. 1. *La hierarchie des Anges*. Note R.

II. Dominations (*Dominationes*)
Principalities (*Principatus*)
Powers (*Potestates*)
III. Virtues (*Virtutes*)
Archangels (*Archangeli*)
Angels (*Angeli*).

Each of the angelic choirs (except the principalities) is mentioned somewhere in the prefaces. When the priest mentions only some of them by name he groups together all the others in the phrase *omnis militia caelestis exercitus*. *Caeli* refers to the thrones, and when this term is used of "heavens", the angels in general are designated by *virtues: Virtutes caelorum*.[1]

The preface for the Holy Ghost calls all the angels *supernae virtutes atque angelicae Potestates:* "the supraterrestrial virtues and angelic Powers."[2]

In the latest editions of the Missal, the unity of the preface and *Sanctus* is emphasized by the use of a colon (instead of a full stop) after *sine fine dicentes*.

THE DECORATION OF THE TEXT OF THE PREFACE IN MANUSCRIPTS AND MISSALS

It was natural that a prayer as venerable and important as the preface should be accentuated in the manuscripts by the use of suitable decoration. The ornamentation of the capital P of the *Per omnia saecula* . . . which concludes the secret (and is the immediate prelude to the preface) used to be especially favoured; the foot of this letter was often extended to the bottom of a page (see, for example, the Missal of the Abbey of Lesnes in Kent, twelfth–thirteenth century).

As all the prefaces, without exception, begin with the phrase *Vere dignum et justum est, aequum et salutare* these words were abbreviated, even in the oldest sacramentaries to the letters V D which, although at first distinct were later run together to form a monogram (Fig. 2) over which was written the sign of abbreviation

[1] Cf. Gihr, *Le Saint Sacrifice de la Messe*, 2, 273; Dom Capelle, *Mélanges;* Lebreton, II (*Rech. de sc. relig.*, 40, 1952, 139–52).
[2] The prayer *Proficiscere anima christiana* (*Rit. Rom.* VI, 7, 4) for the dying mentions all the nine choirs of angels.

(Fig. 3). This, at first separate, was later made to cross the central oblique stroke (Fig. 4) and thus the two letters were bound together

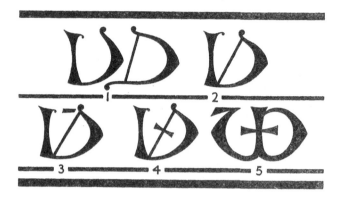

by a " cross " which was emphasized when the central stroke was written vertically (Fig. 5). This monogram survived until the fifteenth century but was suppressed in the first printed Missals.

From the middle of the ninth century onwards, the custom arose of illustrating the phrases *Domine, sancte Pater, omnipotens aeterne Deus* with a design representing the Father or the Son reigning in heaven, called the *Majestas Domini*. The Father (or Son) is usually depicted in an oval (*mandorla*) enthroned upon a sphere or arc in the midst of a starry sky, holding the world in one hand and a book (*codex*) in the other and surrounded by angels and the symbols of the four evangelists. Sometimes all three divine persons are shown in the midst of the angelic choirs (e.g. Missal of Tours, fifteenth century) and at others the *Majestas Domini* is combined with the monogram *Vere dignum*.

THE PREFACE, MODEL FOR THE FORMULARIES OF THE SACRAMENTS AND SACRAMENTALS

The preface, the solemn thanksgiving of the eucharistic sacrifice, has become the exemplar upon which many formularies in the liturgy of the sacraments and sacramentals have been modelled. The very characteristic preface of the Mass with its introductory dialogue is found in the liturgies of baptism (blessing of the font);

confirmation (consecration of chrism); penance (public reconciliation of penitents); ordination (diaconate, priesthood and consecration of bishops); extreme unction (in certain ancillary rites of the visiting of the sick); and matrimony (as in the ritual of Sanctorius for the nuptial blessing).[1]

The preface and its dialogue also exert some influence outside the sacraments, in the liturgy of the most important sacramentals of the blessing of candles, ashes and palms; the praeconium of the paschal candle; the dedication of churches and consecration of altars; the blessing and rehallowing of cemeteries; the consecration and coronation of emperors, kings and queens; the blessing of abbots and abbesses; and the consecration of virgins.[2]

In their turn, these sources constitute a valuable basis for the study of the preface of the Mass because their form has usually been preserved without alteration. Thus no secondary material interrupts the flow of thought and expression in the prefaces for the blessing of fonts, consecration of chrism, reconciliation of penitents and ordination:[3] they contain neither diptychs nor other interpolations.[4]

As regards the theme, there is a noticeable difference between the prefaces of the Missal and those of the Pontifical: in the Missal, the theme of the thanksgiving is drawn from the mystery or feast being celebrated, whereas in the Pontifical the thanksgiving is very short and quickly gives way to prayer, which almost entirely dominates some prefaces (see, for example, the consecration of virgins).

It is greatly to be desired that the faithful should join in this thanksgiving by making responses collectively to the priest during the introductory dialogue; by uniting themselves intimately with the priest by meditating upon the preface he is singing; and by all standing up together from the priest's signal, *Per omnia saecula*, until the end of the singing of the *Sanctus*.

---

[1] Dom Cagin, *Eucharistia*, p. 132.
[2] The preface does not always figure in the modern Roman rites.
[3] We have omitted the preface at the ordination to the diaconate: the interpolation here is obvious and, moreover, in no way influences the flow of the text.
[4] See below, Chapter 18: "From the beginning of the canon to the consecration."

16

THE SERAPHIC HYMN: THE "SANCTUS"

THE preface culminates in the *Sanctus* and reveals the fullness of its meaning: the angelic hierarchy now enters into the eucharistic sacrifice.

The priest and the sacred ministers bow down; the choir and the whole congregation unite their voices in the seraphic hymn—*hymnus seraphicus*—the trisagion:

Sanctus, sanctus, sanctus Dominus Deus Sabaoth.	Holy, holy, holy art thou, Lord God of hosts.
Pleni sunt caeli et terra gloria tua.	Thy glory fills all heaven and earth.
Hosanna in excelsis.	Hosanna in high heaven!
Benedictus qui venit in nomine Domini.	Blessed be he who is coming in the name of the Lord.
Hosanna in excelsis.	Hosanna in high heaven!

Commentary

The eucharistic sacrifice perpetuates from century to century the seraphic hymn which Isaias heard when he was called to the prophetic ministry:

"In the year of King Osias's death, I had a vision. I saw the Lord sitting on a throne that towered high above me, the skirts of his robe filled the temple. Above it rose the figures of the seraphim, each of them six-winged; with two wings they veiled God's face, with two his feet, and the other two kept them poised in flight. And ever the same cry passed between them, Holy, holy, holy is the Lord God of hosts; all the earth is full of his glory . . ."[1]

Sanctus, sanctus, sanctus Dominus Deus exercituum, plena est omnis terra gloria ejus. The Church has lengthened the text (*caeli et terra*) and addressed it directly to the Lord (*gloria tua*).

---

[1] Isaias 6. 1–3.

The Church rightly extols the holiness of the Trinity in this sacrifice, the source of all holiness: "so that this most holy sacramental rite ordained by thee to be the source of all holiness, may sanctify us in very truth . . ."[1] Indeed, our holiness originates in that of the soul of Christ which is full of grace and truth. Our participation in the very holiness of God—sanctifying grace—which spreads abroad in glory for the elect and is what constitutes the holiness of the righteous in this world—is primarily that glory of God which fills heaven and earth.

The hymn acclaims the Lord as the "God of Armies" (*Sabaoth*)— not the military forces of this world, but the angelic hosts to whom Daniel bears witness: "a thousand thousand they were that waited on his bidding, and for every one of these, a thousand others were standing there before him" (Daniel 7. 10).

Hosanna is a Hebraic exclamation taken from Psalm 117, verse 26, and meaning "Give aid *or* salvation". In practice, it corresponds to *Vivat*. The joy of the crowds on Palm Sunday throbs through this hymn. *Hosanna in excelsis* is taken from St Mark (11. 10); St Matthew writes *Hosanna in altissimis* (21. 9).

Soon the impressive, deep silence of the consecration will descend upon the congregation, but immediately after the elevation of the chalice, the whole body will rise and proclaim Christ's eucharistic entry into his temple with the same cry of joy that once greeted Jesus' triumphal entry into Jerusalem: *Benedictus qui venit in nomine Domini, hosanna in excelsis.* Granted the fact of the division of the *Sanctus* chant into two parts by the rite of consecration, the first hosanna may be regarded as an act of homage to the Holy Trinity and the second as an acclamation of Christ, hailing his eucharistic coming.

The text of the *Sanctus* was sometimes (though rarely) illuminated in the manuscripts: thus, for example, Codex 299 in the *Bibliotheca Riccardia*[2] shows the living Lamb of God surrounded by cherubim.

THE *SANCTUS* IN THE SETTING OF THE EUCHARISTIC THANKSGIVING

Does the *Sanctus* belong to the primitive structure of the canon of the Mass? It seems certain that this question, formerly so con-

---

[1] The secret for St Ignatius Loyola, 31 July.
[2] Ebner, *Quellen und Forschungen*, p. 443.

troversial, should be answered in the affirmative. The main points of the controversy are these:

1. It is certain that from time immemorial the *Sanctus* has formed part of the Latin eucharistic thanksgiving both in the Roman and in the Gallican, Ambrosian and Mozarabic liturgies.

2. However, the Ambrosian liturgy contains two canons (for Maundy Thursday and for the Vigil of Easter) which seem to date back to an earlier period and which enlarge upon the Christological theme which is unbroken from the preface to the words of institution and which contain no *Sanctus*.

3. Moreover, the well-known anaphora which was originally written by Hippolytus in Greek in the third century, the Latin version of which was recently discovered at Verona by Hauler, does not mention the *Sanctus*.

4. Dom Cagin has published a comparative study of this and four other anaphoras dating back to the fifth century and independent of one another: the *Statuta Apostolica* (Ethiopic) which was translated into Latin by Ludolf in 1699; the *Testamentum Domini* (Syriac) which was discovered and translated in 1899 by Mgr Rahmani; the Ethiopic liturgy of the Saviour and the Ethiopic liturgy of the Apostles. Of these only the last contains the *Sanctus* and then only in such a way that it rudely interrupts the flow of ideas.[1]

5. The question therefore arises: Is the simpler form of the canon primitive or does it represent a later abridged form of a longer thanksgiving dating back to apostolic times and including the *Sanctus*? Although Dom Cagin supports the former hypothesis, it is clear that the *Sanctus* belongs to the primitive structure of the eucharistic thanksgiving. In the second half of the fourth century the *Sanctus* was sung in the liturgy of the Apostolic Constitutions (composed by a Syrian), in the Egyptian anaphoras of Serapion and Der Balyzeh and, according to the evidence of St Cyril's Fifth *Catechesis*, at Jerusalem;[2] whilst in Spain the treatise *De Trinitate et de Spiritu Sancto* bears witness that "all Christ's churches from

[1] Cf. Dom P. Cagin, *L'Eucharistia: Synopsis*, p. 148 f.; pp. 184–5.

[2] Dr Schermann of Munich maintains on the basis of the papyrus discovered at Der Balyzeh that the ancient Egyptian liturgy contained a *eucharistia* with the *Sanctus* and that the Verona liturgy is a summary of this. *Aegypt. Abendmahlsliturgiën des 1 Jahrtausend* (Schöningh, Paderborn, 1912).

The "Sanctus"

East to West confess that the Father is worthily praised by the seraphim ".

From the fact of the universality of the use of the *Sanctus* in liturgies, Eisenhofer concluded that the Verona anaphora was an exceptional type.[1] In support of his thesis he quotes the letter from St Clement († 101) to the Corinthians, in which there is an obvious reference to the trisagion: " Consider with what zeal the whole multitude of his angels stands about him and fulfils his will. Indeed, the Scripture says, ' ten thousand thousands of angels stand before him and thousands of thousands serve him; and they cry " Holy, holy, holy is the Lord Sabaoth, all creation is full of his glory ".' And we too bound together in concord by community of sentiment, cry as one mouth earnestly to him in order to share in his great and marvellous promises." [2] Now, according to Baumstark, this epistle was inspired directly by the euchology of the primitive Christian services arranged on Sunday mornings to replace the Jewish Sabbath meetings at which the *Sanctus* was sung. So then, with no break in continuity, the primitive Church may have taken over from the liturgy of the synagogue not only the traditional theme of the thanksgiving (*Schema Berakha*) but also the *Sanctus* which formed part of it.

THE CHANT AND RITUAL ATTITUDE

It traditionally belongs to the congregation to sing the *Sanctus*, as the Apostolic Constitutions (fourth century) attest: " All the people together say, *Sanctus*." [3] The *Liber Pontificalis* records that Sixtus I († 125) decreed: *ut intra actionem, sacerdos incipiens, populo* (= *populum*) *hymnum decantare Sanctus*.[4]

According to the *Ordo* of John the Archcantor (seventh century) the *Sanctus* was then intoned by both people and clergy.[5] During the preface, the priest stood at the head of the clergy and congregation, but at *supplici confessione dicentes* all—priests, clergy and people —bowed their heads while singing the *Sanctus*.

---

[1] *Handbuch der Liturgik*, 2, p. 161.
[2] We do not maintain that St Clement is here referring explicitly to the eucharistic prayer in the form it took in his times. This is, however, possible.
[3] Funk, 8, 12.
[4] Duchesne, 1, 128.
[5] Silva Tarouca, *Memoriae Acad. Pont. Archeol.*, 1, pp. 198–9.

In this solemn hymn, the unity of the congregation and the heavenly hosts is positively demonstrated.

In *Ordo Romanus I* (eighth century) the district subdeacons have replaced the people in the singing of this chant.[1] The ceremony was imposing: whilst the trisagion was being sung, the pope, bishops, priests, deacons and subdeacons all bowed low; after the *Sanctus* only the pope stood upright to enter into the holy of holies of the canon, *intrat in canonem;* everyone else continued to bow low. The subdeacons stood upright again at *nobis quoque peccatoribus*. Traces of this ancient ceremonial have survived in the rubrics of our present Missal. The priest still bows while saying the *Sanctus* (" a moderate bow ").[2] The deacon and subdeacon adopt the same stance at high Mass.

Nowadays, the union between priest and faithful in the *Sanctus* can be achieved only at a dialogue (low) Mass. At high and sung Masses, the *Sanctus* is performed by the choir and people; the priest says it in an undertone. While the congregation continue the *Sanctus* chant, the priest, for his part, is isolated in the recitation of the canon. Furthermore, according to the provisions of the rubrics and the latest decrees, the *Sanctus* chant is divided into two clearly distinct parts by the rites of consecration and elevation. The first extends from the beginning to the first cry of *Hosanna in excelsis* inclusive; the second, from *Benedictus qui venit* to the end. According to the Instruction of the S. Congregation of Rites (9 September 1958) when the *Sanctus* and *Benedictus* are sung to a plainchant melody they are not to be divided and are therefore sung in full before the elevation. When a polyphonic setting is used, however, the *Sanctus* is first sung to " *in excelsis* ": then the elevation takes place, during which the choir remains silent and worships with the congregation. After the elevation, the choir continues the chant: *Benedictus* . . . When sung by the whole congregation, the *Sanctus* is organically connected to the end of the preface sung by the priest and is its natural complement. Again, nothing is as impressive as a Christian congregation united in heart and soul to its shepherd, following his solemn thanksgiving, embracing his thoughts and entering unfalteringly into the flow of his prayer by offering the holy acclamation required of it by the celebrant at exactly the right

---

[1] *Ordo I*, 16; cf. *Ordo II*, 10.   [2] *Rit. serv.*, 7, 8.

moment. In practice, however, in many places, the congregation, lost in its private devotions, remains silent and the seraphic hymn called for by the celebrant is unheard amid a noisy scraping of chairs and an indescribable shuffling of feet that can scarcely be drowned by mighty chords on the organ and tumultuous strokes on the bell. . . .

ASSOCIATED CEREMONIES

According to the prescriptions of the Missal, the acolyte must ring a small bell at the beginning of the *Sanctus*[1] to attract the attention of the faithful. This signal should be short and discreet and one stroke (*ictus*) is enough. A decree of the Sacred Congregation of Rites (25 October 1922) declares that it is obligatory also at sung or high Mass and defines it as (a) a signal of the approaching consecration; (b) a sign of joy; (c) a profession of faith in the coming eucharistic presence of Christ; and (d) a sign of union with the angelic choirs in praise and adoration.

The special importance attached by the faithful to seeing the host led, in former times, to the ringing of a special bell, called the *Sanctus*, immediately after the preface. The *Sanctus* bell was usually small in size and hung in a turret placed between the nave and the choir. Its ringing acted as a warning of the coming consecration and elevation to those who were prevented from being present at the whole Mass; when they heard it, they would hasten to the church. A small bell—also called the *Sanctus*—was also rung inside the church to warn the congregation—and sometimes, when it was hung before an open window, to call the absent instead of a *Sanctus* bell in a turret.

At high Mass, according to the rubrics of the Missal, from about the end of the preface the acolytes should light and hold two (or preferably four) candles in honour of the coming consecration. These are extinguished only after the elevation of the chalice or, if communion is given to the faithful, after that ceremony. At low Mass, immediately before the elevation, the acolyte lights a special candle placed on the epistle side of the altar.[2] He extinguishes it after the communion of the priest and faithful. This candle is also a signal announcing the approaching eucharistic coming of Christ. At low Masses celebrated more solemnly (for example,

[1] *Rit. serv.*, 8, 8.   [2] *Rubr. Gen.*, 20.

parochial Masses which are not sung), candles may be carried by two acolytes from the beginning of the canon until the communion.[1]

From the fifth century in the East and the ninth in the West, a special kind of fan—the *muscarium* or *muscifugium*—came to be used to keep flies from the sacrificial offerings. In the East, where they are still used, these are made from parchment and cloth bearing peacock's feathers and are called *rhipidia*. The two deacons who wave them were said to represent the cherubim and seraphim recalled by the *Sanctus*, and the peacock's eyes, the innumerable eyes seen by the prophet Ezechiel on the wings of the cherubim (Ezech. 10. 12). In the West, where it was called the *flabellum*, this fan disappeared at the end of the Middle Ages.

THE *VERE SANCTUS*: THE TRANSITION BETWEEN THE *SANCTUS* AND THE NARRATIVE OF THE INSTITUTION OF THE EUCHARIST, *QUI PRIDIE*

Dom Cagin maintains that there is today a sharp break between the *Te igitur* and the *Sanctus*. In former times, the *Sanctus* used to be linked directly with the *Qui pridie* by a formula of transition, the *Vere sanctus*, which led into the narrative of the institution. Thus in the Gallican liturgy, the *Missale Gothicum* on the feast of the Circumcision, we read: *Vere sanctus, vere benedictus Dominus noster Jesus Christus Filius tuus: qui venit quaerere et salvum facere quod perierat;* and in the Sunday Mass (*Missa Dominicalis*): *Vere sanctus, vere benedictus Dominus noster Jesus Christus Filius tuus: qui venit de caelis ut conversaretur in terris: homo factus ut habitaret in nobis: Hostia effectus ut nos faceret Sacerdotes, Ipse enim qui pridie* . . . The Ambrosian Rite, which in many respects has preserved the structure of the Roman Rite before the pontificate of St Gregory, still contains a *Vere sanctus* called the *Post sanctus*, which links the *Sanctus* to the *Qui pridie* and is used on Holy Saturday.[2]

CONCLUSIONS

1. It is important that the congregation should begin once again to sing the *Sanctus*, which is traditionally its prerogative. Melodies 18 in the Kyriale for ferial Masses (and *Requiems*) are simple, adapted to the preface and very easy to learn. Numbers 1, 11 and 12 are especially suitable on more solemn occasions.

[1] S.C.R., decr. 3059, 8.   [2] Dom Cagin, *L'Eucharistia*, pp. 92–3.

2. For this reason, the faithful should stand not only during the preface, but also during the *Sanctus* and should kneel altogether only after the first *Hosanna in excelsis*.

3. The warning stroke on the bell (like all other such warnings) should be discreet and should not be allowed to degenerate into noisy tinklings prejudicial to the solemn chant of the *Sanctus*.

4. It is desirable, too, that the *Benedictus* chant should not be overlong and so detract from the canon, for if it is, how can choristers and faithful associate themselves with the canon itself?

5. Wherever it has been customary, it is important to bring back the use of the *Sanctus* candle before the elevation at low Mass.

17

THE CANON

In looking through the manuscripts of tenth- and eleventh-century Missals, who would not be struck by the splendour of the pages devoted to the text of the canon of the Mass? In many manuscripts between the white pages with simply written characters are inserted a group of purple parchment sheets covered with the text of the canon in silver or gold uncials. These provide striking evidence of the paramount dignity of this venerable text which preserves for us the words of consecration, and by which the unique sacrifice of our redemption is made present upon our altars, is brought immediately within our grasp, with all its power to give glory, honouring the Holy Trinity, and all its outpourings of grace for us.

THE NAMES AND LIMITS OF THE CANON

After the *Sanctus* our present Missal says at the head of the following prayer: *Canon Missae*, "Canon of the Mass". What does this title mean? The expression canon is derived from Greek and means "rule". *Incipit canon actionis*, "Here begins the rule of the action", the Gelasian Sacramentary (*c.* 700) says.[1] What action? The act of oblation, the offering of the holy sacrifice. In the religious speech of the Romans, *actio* was used in this sense and it is clearly this meaning that the word has kept in the liturgical language of the Church concerning the Mass. So then, the canon is the rule for the offering of the eucharistic sacrifice properly so called, that is, the order to be followed in the formulation of the thanksgiving (*eucharistia*) and eucharistic rites. From this, the term came to be applied to the form of words and eucharistic rites themselves or to the eucharistic oblation (*actio*) so governed (*prex canonica canon actionis*). This expression is used for the first time in this sense in the sixth century by John of Syracuse in a letter to St Gregory the Great († 604): *Orationem dominicam mox post canonem dici statuistis.*[2]

[1] Ed. Wilson, p. 234.   [2] *Ep.* 12; *P.L.*, 77, 956.

The Canon

The canon is the embolism, the extended paraphrase, of the *gratias agens, benedixit* of the solemn thanksgiving or eucharist celebrated by the high priest of the Last Supper. In accordance with the customs of his ancestors, Christ, in the presence of the twelve, intoned the traditional thanksgiving prescribed by the Jewish ritual for the paschal celebration which, together with the commemoration of the creation, recalls that of the unending blessings with which God has surrounded the people of Israel. It was during the eucharistic hymn (*gratias agens*) that he instituted the holy Eucharist, and the first priests, faithful to their master's words, " Do this in commemoration of me ", took up and enlarged upon Christ's solemn thanksgiving.

Thus, with no break in continuity, the main theme of the thanksgiving of the Last Supper developed in the various Eastern and Western liturgies into a wonderful lyrical flowering of related anaphoras (Eastern liturgies), eucharists (Greek liturgies), *immolationes* or *contestationes* (Gallican liturgy), *illationes* (Mozarabic liturgy) and canons (Roman liturgy). All these eucharists unfold according to a traditional pattern and, like the ring for the stone, form the setting for the prayer of consecration.

As regards the limits of the canon, we have already explained above concerning the preface that in ancient times this latter formed a unity with the thanksgiving and that, faithful to tradition, the Gelasian Sacramentary has the words *Incipit canon actionis* before *Sursum corda*.

The solemn eucharistic thanksgiving used to be introduced by *Gratias agamus*. Later, changes began to be made. According to the first Roman *Ordo* (eighth century) the canon begins after the *Sanctus* and ends before the *Pater*. Remember, too, that in the time of Amalarius (ninth century) the division into preface and canon was complete. But even then the organic unity of the two parts had not entirely been forgotten for Amalarius teaches concerning the *Te igitur* that this prayer is found in the middle of the canon (*Subdiaconus medio canone, id est, cum dicitur Te igitur . . .*). Our printed Missals uphold the illusion of separation by emphasizing the division between the preface and canon unreasonably. The earliest printed examples (before 1530) put the title " Canon " before the *Te igitur* and at the top of the following pages. Today, the official title is *Canon Missae* and is placed at the beginning of the

Te igitur as is *Commemoratio pro vivis*, *Infra actionem* and *Commemoratio pro defunctis* before other parts. But there is no reason for printing *Canon Missae* in huge letters which emphasize the division even more strongly.

The end of the canon is not explicitly indicated today, but it ends before the *Pater*. Indeed St Gregory the Great teaches that the *Pater* follows immediately upon the canon: *Mox post precem*.[1] The official description of the rites of the Mass at the beginning of the Missal clearly suggests this in the title of section nine: *De Canone post consecrationem usque ad Orationem Dominicam*.[2]

THE NATURE, CHARACTER AND GENERAL PLAN OF THE CANON

The whole of the canon gravitates about the central rite of consecration upon which it depends. The rite of consecration is a sacramental rite signifying—and therefore making present—the sacrifice of the cross. The Mass is, therefore, a true sacrifice, but sacramental in nature. The canon, which is centred on the consecration, is, therefore, not merely prayer, or even *the* prayer (*oratio*, St Cyprian;[3] *prex*, Pope St Innocent,[4] and St Augustine;[5] *canonica prex*, Pope Vigilius [† 555]) but is also an action (*actio*), *canon actionis* as the Gelasian Sacramentary (*c.* 700) expresses it.

A sacrifice does not consist merely in a victim, which is the matter of the sacrifice, but is an act, the offering of the victim. Therefore, if the eucharistic rite is truly to bring us the sacrifice of Calvary, not only the victim once offered, but also Christ's act of oblation, must there be made present. This historical act of oblation was a preeminently holy act, endowed with all the religion, adoration and love of the Father of which Christ's priestly soul was capable.

Thus the Mass in very truth is the highest form of adoration possible. The secret for the ninth Sunday after Pentecost defines with admirable brevity what is effected by the canon: ". . . each and every offering of this memorial sacrifice carries on the work of our redemption . . ." By making present the very sacrifice of the cross, the eucharistic rite perpetuates its memory pragmatically; it is the

---

[1] *Ep.* 12; *P.L.*, 77, 956.
[2] *Rit. serv.*, 9.
[3] *De Dom. Orat.*, 31.
[4] *De nominibus recitandis antequam precem sacerdos faciat* (*Ep.* 2; *P.L.*, 69, 18).
[5] *Contra litt. Petilliani*, 2, 69; *P.L.*, 43, 281.

commemoration of the mystery of the redemption and is therefore also a celebration of the mystery.

Study of the historical evolution of the anaphora in general affords striking evidence of its truly Trinitarian character.

(a) In the first place thanksgiving ascends in solemn praise to the Father through Christ, the sovereign high priest (*tibi gratias agere, Domine sancte, Pater omnipotens . . . per Christum Dominum nostrum*);

(b) then the thanksgiving unfolds, extolling the themes of the creation of the world, which is attributed to the Father, and the redemption of mankind effected through the Son. From Isaias' *Sanctus* to the *Qui pridie* with the consecration which makes present upon the altar the living and glorified Christ, himself the priest and victim of the cross, there are set forth God's prefigurative acts under the old covenant and their realization under the new.

(c) After the consecration, the ritual commemoration of the Last Supper, the thanksgiving is continued, magnifying in turn the blessed passion, resurrection and ascension of Christ (*anamnesis*), beseeching the Father to accept our offering, invoking the Spirit of Pentecost (*epiclesis*) that by his divine power the bread and wine may be transubstantiated into the body and blood of Christ and that eucharistic communion may produce in the communicants abundant fruits of salvation.

(d) Lastly the thanksgiving culminates in a solemn trinitarian doxology in which, through Christ's priesthood, all is centred once more on the glory of the Father and the Son in the unity of the Holy Ghost.

When he died upon the cross, Christ triumphed over Satan and saved mankind. In making the sacrifice of Calvary really present, the Mass also makes present this great victory, and the anaphora therefore takes on the appearance of a liturgy of triumph. The eucharist is the sacrifice of thanksgiving for Christ's victory in all its many aspects. The anaphora is so truly a thanksgiving that it bears the name of its function, *eucharistia*.

THE ORIGINS OF THE TEXT OF THE ROMAN CANON

According to the Council of Trent, the canon is composed of the words of our Lord himself, the traditions of the Apostles and the pious institutions of the holy pontiffs.[1] History illustrates this statement in a most interesting way. The pivot around which the whole of the anaphora is arranged is undoubtedly the narrative of the Last Supper with the relevant and efficacious words of consecration. It is most remarkable that despite their immense variety of forms and tongues all the anaphoras are at one in the ceremonies and expression of the consecration. This is truly the definitive proof of their apostolic antiquity. But this rite is not an isolated one: like the stone set in the ring, it forms part of a series of closely related formulas: the preface (with or without the *Sanctus*) before it, the anamnesis and epiclesis after it, the whole being closely connected with the final doxology, the glorification of the Father through Christ the sovereign high priest in the unity of the Holy Ghost. The congregation's *Amen* ratifies this thanksgiving. Such, in their main outlines, are the basic, primitive elements composing the anaphora. This formula, however, underwent some expansion in the course of the following centuries.

We can now consider the Roman canon found in our Missal, though we cannot here enlarge upon the varying theories of Bickell, Bunsen, Probst, Dom Cagin, Drews, Funk, Bishop and others regarding the primitive content and arrangement of the Roman canon. In a study of this kind certain preliminary remarks are necessary:

(a) It must not be forgotten that primitively a fairly large part of the thanksgiving was left to personal improvisation.

(b) It is not *a priori* impossible that even in the time of Hippolytus (218–35) several anaphoras were in use in Rome.

(c) The documentary and historical evidence concerning the Roman canon is very small and our conclusions from it can only be tentative.

Without trying to attempt too much—to establish for example the text of the primitive or apostolic anaphora itself—but, in accordance with the requirements of historical method, if we are content to start from the firm foundation of the modern Roman canon, and by studying the formularies themselves, go back to their sources and to historical evidence concerning them, thus elucidating critically the precise meaning of their expressions, and comparing them with the corresponding formulas of non-Roman liturgies, we

[1] Sess. 22, 4; Denzinger, 942.

The Canon

are led to precise results like those already to the credit of such liturgists as P. Batiffol, Baumstark, Dom F. Cabrol, Dom B. Botte, C. Callewaert, Dom B. Capelle, or philologists like Mlle Christine Mohrmann.

FIRST TRACES OF A LATIN CANON IN ROME

There is no doubt that Greek was the principal liturgical language of the Roman Church in the first three centuries. After the conquest of Greece, Asia Minor and Egypt, Greek gradually became the universal language and was spoken by vast numbers even at Rome. Thus, St Paul wrote his Epistle to the Romans in Greek, and it was at the Romans' request that St Mark recorded in Greek his Gospel of St Peter's preaching; the Epistle of St Clement of Rome is in Greek; several of the earliest popes were Greeks as their names show: Anacletus or Cletus (88 or 90), Telesphorus († 136), Hyginus († 141), Anicetus († 166), Soter († 175), Callistus († 222), and their epitaphs, like all the oldest inscriptions in the Roman catacombs, are in Greek. Ecclesiastical writers who lived at Rome—such as Hermas (140), St Justin († 167), Tatian († 165)—composed their works in Greek. But Hippolytus' († 235) Ἀποστολικὴ παράδοσις is the principal piece of evidence for the use of Greek as a liturgical language in Rome at this period. It is probable that at this, as at other later periods, the lessons were also read in Latin. Moreover, a century later, the Latin author Rhetor Marius Victorinus († 363) supplies one last piece of evidence of the use of Greek as a liturgical language. Commenting on the text of Titus 2. 14 καθαρίσῃ ἑαυτῷ λαὸν περιούσιον (" [Christ] who gave himself for us, to ransom us from all our guilt, a people set apart for himself, ambitious of noble deeds ") he recalls a liturgical prayer used at Rome, an offertory prayer (*oratio oblationis*) which he quotes in Greek:[1] *Hinc oratio oblationis intellectu eodem precatur eum* σωσον περιούσιον λαον.

At about 375, on the other hand, a certain Isaac, a convert from Judaism, an apostate and the opponent of Pope St Damasus, reproaches the Romans for calling Melchisedech " high priest " (*summus sacerdos*), " as our people dare to call him " in the course of the eucharistic oblation, the canon (*sicut nostri in oblatione praesumunt*). Thus, the Latin canon was in use in Rome in the reign of Pope

---

[1] *Adv. Arium*, II, 8; *P.L.*, 8, 1094.

St Damasus (366-84). This was the earliest form of our Roman canon, and it does not appear to be a version from a Greek or Eastern original. To what degree some of its prayers depend—either by translation or by influence—upon such sources remains in the realm of hypothesis. If the present Roman canon shows itself to be so truly Roman in workmanship, it owes this to the mastery of those who fashioned it.

Furthermore, the ancient Roman (*Latin*) canon was used not only in Rome but also elsewhere, especially at Milan, where St Ambrose both used it and preserved important fragments of it in his treatise *De Sacramentis* (390). Although the Ambrosian authorship of this treatise has been denied or contested for many years, the exhaustive studies made by Dom G. Morin, O. Faller, Dom R. H. Connolly and others have definitively restored this work to St Ambrose († 397) and this attribution is today acknowledged by such eminent critics and liturgists as C. Callewaert, Dom B. Capelle, Dom O. Casel, F. J. Dölger, A. Manser—and even by Harnack—who consider the question settled.

This treatise is a series of catechetical instructions on the mysteries of Christian initiation, preached to the neophytes by St Ambrose in the year 390. In the fourth book the earliest text of our Roman canon is quoted literally. As Dom Capelle has said, all serious exegesis of liturgical prayer must begin from this work.[1]

St Ambrose, Bishop of Milan, recited this canon. He himself was of Roman origin and had been reared in Rome; he was greatly attached to the Roman Church and was a close friend of St Damasus. In 382 he had been present at a council called by this pope. He declares unequivocably that he makes every effort to follow the Roman Church in all things.[2] He had doubtless received the text of the canon from Pope Damasus. We are therefore entitled to assume with C. Callewaert that St Ambrose has preserved for us in *De Sacramentis* important fragments of the first Latin recension of the Roman canon.[3]

When treating of the words of consecration, St Ambrose wrote: " All the rest that is said above [that is, before the consecration] is spoken by the priest: praises are addressed to God (preface),

---

[1] *Le Canon Romain attesté en 359?* in *Rev. d'Hist. Eccl.* 51 (1946), pp. 417-21.
[2] *De Sacramentis*, Bk. 3, 1, 5; *P.L.*, 16, 43.
[3] *De Missalis romani liturgia*, pp. 87-90.

The Canon

prayer is uttered for the people, for kings and for others." [1] *Oratio* here doubtless means the *Te igitur* which occurs in the ninth-century Ambrosian liturgy (corresponding to the letter with the form in the Roman liturgy); in it prayers were offered for the universal Church, the bishop of Milan, the Emperor, kings, their wives and children and for all who profess the true Catholic and Apostolic faith. St Ambrose also quotes a prayer (*Fac nobis hanc oblationem*) which is equivalent to our *Quam oblationem*. When we add to these the liturgical formulas the texts of which he quotes later (after the consecration) it becomes apparent that the sections of the Roman canon for which there is fourth-century attestation are as follows:

Preface[2]; *Te igitur; Quam oblationem; Qui pridie* (with the consecration); *Unde et memores; Supra quae; Supplices*. It is also certain that there was a final doxology,[3] for St Ambrose quotes it several times in this same treatise, and it concludes the Ambrosian canon.

Here, then, is a starting point for our study. We shall compare these texts from *De Sacramentis* with the elements related to them in the Roman canon, especially in the form in which they occur in the text of the Gelasian Sacramentary (c. 700), the liturgy preserved in which dates back to the fifth and sixth centuries. We shall also quote and comment upon the earliest forms of the later parts of the canon.

THE UNITY OF THE ROMAN CANON

Scientific study confirms the soundness of the impression of the twofold structure; even a superficial reading of the canon of the Mass reveals it clearly:

(a) Some prayers follow one another in an order which is both impressive and natural, e.g. *Qui pridie* (institution), *Unde et memores* (anamnesis), *Supra quae, Supplices*.

(b) Others pose insoluble problems. What connection is there, for instance, between the *Memento* of the living and the *Communicantes* which follows it or between the *Supplices* and the *Memento* of the dead?

Some of the prayers are of a definite eucharistic character, that is, they offer up thanksgiving to the Father and are derived directly

---

[1] *De Sacramentis*, Bk. 4, 4, 14; *P.L.*, 16, 440.
[2] The *Sanctus* also dates back to the earliest period.
[3] He mentions it in this treatise at 4, 6, 29; 6, 5, 24 (*P.L.*, 16, 446; 460).

from the oblation or acceptance of the eucharistic sacrifice. Others, on the contrary, are clearly intercessory and secondary and evoke the memory of the living, the dead or the saints and beg graces for the faithful.

How may these differences be explained? The following points seem certainly to be established:

(a) At various times elements alien to the canon have been incorporated into its traditional framework (interpolations). Thus, the *Memento* of the living and of the dead, the *Nobis quoque peccatoribus* and diptychs in general are interpolations. In the Roman canon in its present form five prayers are concluded *Per Christum Dominum nostrum: Communicantes,* Hanc igitur,* Supplices,** the *Memento* of the dead* and *Nobis quoque peccatoribus*. Four of these five (marked *) even conclude with *Amen*. As the primitive canon was a single continuous prayer with no breaks of this kind, the question arises whether interpolation has occurred; this is subjected to scientific examination below.

The nature—whether primitive or secondary—of the various elements is revealed only by the light of history and a comparative study of Eastern and Western anaphoras. Many of them raise thorny problems. We shall consider the analytical study of these texts briefly:

(b) Some texts which formerly served to link together the various prayers of the canon have now disappeared. Thus, the *Sanctus* was once linked to the *Qui pridie* by the formula *Vere sanctus* . . . some examples of which we quoted above.[1]

(c) Lastly, notice that the order of parts has sometimes been reversed, with the result that the fundamental and primitive unity of the canon—although it is always discernible—has obviously been broken.

Despite these insertions, the canon yet remains the paramount eucharistic prayer of the kind spoken of by the earliest Christian documents. Its basic pattern is maintained from the preface to the final doxology preceding the *Pater*. At first sight, it is tempting to regret the insertion of alien elements into the theme of the thanksgiving; closer examination, however, reveals a deeper purpose, a guiding idea with a fruitful lesson. The Church not only offers, she is also offered. Anxious to associate her children as closely as

[1] Chap. 16, p. 182.

The Canon

possible in Christ's oblation, she does not hesitate to let them encroach upon the most sacred part of the Mass, her great thanksgiving, her eucharist, and so break the unity of the anaphora, intermingling her living, her dead and her saints—like the drop of water in the chalice of wine—in the unity of Christ's oblation.

THE LITERARY PECULIARITIES OF THE CANON

We cannot here enter upon a dissertation on the literary character of the very varied prayers of the canon of the Mass.

The solemn *prex* owes much to the style of the official petitions addressed to the emperors. We must be content to point out some of the peculiarities of its style:

(a) Parallelism in construction:
supplices *rogamus* ac *petimus;*
uti accepta *habeas* et *benedicas;*
orthodoxis atque *catholicae et apostolicae fidei cultoribus* (Te igitur);
in *sanctas* ac *venerabiles* manus suas (before the consecration);
de tuis *donis* ac *datis* (Unde et memores);
respicere et *accepta habere;*
sanctum sacrificium, immaculatam hostiam (Supra quae);
omni *benedictione caelesti* et *gratia* repleamur (Supplices);
partem aliquam et *societatem* (Nobis quoque), etc.

(b) Marked preference for expressions in threefold form:
haec dona, haec munera, haec sancta sacrificia illibata (Te igitur).
hostiam puram, hostiam sanctam, hostiam immaculatam (Unde et memores).
per ipsum et *cum ipso* et *in ipso,* etc.

(c) Combinations of terms containing five expressions:
benedictam, adscriptam, ratam, rationabilem acceptabilemque (Quam oblationem).
creas, sanctificas, vivificas, benedicis et praestas nobis (Per quem).

Quintuple series are sometimes formed by the combination of triple expressions with parallel words:
Hostiam puram, hostiam sanctam, hostiam immaculatam, panem sanctum vitae aeternae et calicem salutis perpetuae.
Munera pueri justi Abel et sacrificium patriarchae nostri Abrahae et quod tibi obtulit summus sacerdos tuus Melchisedech, sanctum sacrificium, immaculatam hostiam.

THE SILENT RECITATION OF THE CANON

The preface is sung by the priest, the *Sanctus* by the congregation, and in ancient times the canon was also sung aloud: according to the *Ordo* of John the Archcantor (seventh century) the pope at that time sang the canon *de simili voce et melodia* (as the preface). The pontiff sang the preface " in such a way as to be heard by all " (*ut ab omnibus audiatur*) and the canon less loudly, " in such a way as to be heard by those about the altar " (*ut a circumstantibus altare tantum audiatur*). Thus the canon was sung in a lower voice.

The *Ordo* of St Amandus (ninth century) says, *di(s)cit pontifex canon(em) ut audiatur ab eis:* the pope said the canon loudly enough to be heard by those about the altar. *Ordo I* (eighth century) provides indirect proof for the same practices, in that it prescribes that the subdeacons who have been bowing since the *Sanctus* should stand upright at *Nobis quoque peccatoribus* without mentioning the raising of the celebrant's voice. Nevertheless, the recitation of the canon in an undertone was universal by the ninth century, as is shown by the ancient Carolingian commentary on the Mass *Quotiens circa se* (800), which, after commenting upon the *Hosanna*, continues: *facto magno circumquaque silentio incipit jam sacerdos . . . hostiam consecrare;* and also by Amalarius' *De Ecclesiae Officiis* (823). The ninth-century *Ordo II* bears witness to the same custom in Frankish lands: *Pontifex tacite intrat in canonem:* " the pontiff begins the canon silently ". This tradition of silent recitation is upheld in the present rubrics of the Mass: *incipit canonem, secreto dicens*,[1] and at the *Nobis quoque peccatoribus: elata aliquantulum voce dicens . . .* What was the origin of this tradition?

The silent recitation of the canon is inspired by several factors:

(a) The canon is the celebration of the sacrosanct mystery of the eucharistic sacrament and we can therefore understand the desire to protect this *sacramentum* from all abuses on the part of the uninitiated. In early times this was easy but later, after the mass conversion of the barbarians, steps had to be taken to safeguard its inviolability and it was therefore enveloped in mystery and silence. Just as lay persons were not allowed to touch the sacred vessels, so they were forbidden to " touch " the canon of the Mass, that is,

---

[1] *Rit. serv.*, 8, 1.

to mingle their voices with that of the celebrant who recites the canon for them, for the canon is a thanksgiving which appertains not to the faithful but to the ministry of the priesthood, to the official mediator between God and Christian people. The consecration of the holy eucharistic mysteries, before which the angels tremble, ought to fill the faithful with holy fear. In the East, by the fifth century, a wall (*iconostasis*) separated the altar from the faithful and hid it from their sight and by the sixth century the recitation in an undertone of the canon was general there, though in 565 Justinian, in a new law, commanded that the anaphora was henceforward to be said in such a way as to be heard by the people, thus reversing the previous practice.

It should also be noticed that from Pope Innocent I's letter to Decentius (416) it appears that the canon was said silently at Rome in his reign. The same feeling of reverential dread gave rise in the custom current in Rome in the sixth and seventh centuries of hiding the eucharistic mysteries from the faithful by hanging four curtains (*tetravela*) from the ciborium.

(b) Moreover, preoccupations of a practical kind seem to have been involved in this discipline of silence. The singing of the whole of the thanksgiving would demand an even greater effort on the part of the celebrant as prayers unknown in the primitive text—such as the two mementos, *Nobis quoque peccatoribus* and the other diptychs—came to be incorporated in it.

Furthermore, the singing of the *Sanctus* by the congregation sometimes lasted some little time. This may explain how, so that the Mass might not take too long, it came about that many priests adopted a compromise, beginning the canon before the end of the chant; they would then be forced to recite it in an undertone.

The Council of Trent expressly refers to the legitimacy of the practice of reciting the canon silently: "If anyone says that the rite of the Roman Church in which part of the canon and the words of consecration are uttered in an undertone should be condemned . . . let him be anathema."[1] As a matter of fact, some heretical systems which denied the distinction between the priest and the faithful contended in favour of the recitation of the canon aloud. If the Church in the course of the centuries has changed her customs

---

[1] Sess. 22, 9; Denzinger, 956.

concerning the recitation of the Mass aloud, it must be recognized that this is a disciplinary measure which she has the right to impose by authority. If, for reasons of which she is the sole judge, she one day thinks it opportune to restore the ancient usage, the abuses of which the heretics stand condemned in this matter will constitute no objection in principle to such restoration.

18

FROM THE BEGINNING OF THE CANON TO THE CONSECRATION

THE *TE IGITUR* WITH THE COMMEMORATION OF THE UNIVERSAL CHURCH, THE POPE, THE BISHOP (THE PRINCE), AND OF ALL THE BISHOPS

GELASIAN SACRAMENTARY (Liturgy of fifth–sixth centuries)	ROMAN MISSAL	
Te igitur clementissime Pater, per Jesum Christum Filium tuum Dominum nostrum supplices rogamus et petimus uti accepta habeas ✠ ✠ et benedicas, haec dona, ✠ ✠ haec munera, haec sancta sacrificia illibata. Inprimis quae tibi offerimus pro Ecclesia tua sancta catholica, quam pacificare, custodire, adunare et regere digneris toto orbe terrarum, una cum famulo tuo papa nostro Illo et antistite nostro Illo episcopo.	A. Te igitur clementissime Pater, per Jesum Christum Filium tuum Dominum nostrum supplices rogamus, ac petimus, uti accepta habeas et benedicas, haec ✠ dona, haec ✠ munera, haec ✠ sancta sacrificia illibata, B. in primis, quae tibi offerimus pro Ecclesia tua sancta catholica: quam pacificare, custodire, adunare et regere digneris toto orbe terrarum: una cum famulo tuo Papa nostro N. et Antistite nostro N. et omnibus orthodoxis atque catholicae et apostolicae fidei cultoribus.	A. And so, through Jesus Christ, thy Son, our Lord, we humbly pray and beseech thee, most gracious Father, to accept and bless these offerings, these oblations, these holy, unblemished sacrificial gifts. B. We offer them to thee in the first place for thy holy Catholic Church: be pleased, throughout the whole world, to keep her in peace, to gather her in unity and to guide her, together with thy servant our Pope N., our Bishop N., and all who believe and preserve the catholic and apostolic faith.

(A) In the first part of this section of the canon (from the beginning to *sacrificia illibata*) we beseech the most merciful Father to deign to accept our offerings and in consequence to bless them by consecration. This is the "commendation of our offering" (*commendatio oblationis*) mentioned by Pope Innocent I in his letter to Decentius of Gubbio (416).

(B) We then set out in order the intentions for which we are offering the sacrifice; this is the intercession (*intercessio*) for the universal Church, the Pope, the Bishop (the Prince), and all the bishops. The whole prayer (A and B) forms an organic unity.

(A) *The "commendatio oblationis"*.—The priest "enters into the Holy of Holies of the canon of the Mass"; he is now more than ever conscious of his unworthiness. As a suppliant, he lifts up his eyes, his arms and his heart towards heaven, to God from whom alone help can come to him, only to bow low straightway in the knowledge of his unworthiness.

To what does the conjunction *igitur* (and so; therefore) refer? It links this prayer with the preface and even with the offering of bread and wine. In many prefaces, indeed, it is by means of this or some similar conjunction (*ergo, quapropter, idcirco*) that the text of the thanksgiving is made to give way to supplication, which is its logical and practical corollary, so making supplication an integral part of the preface itself. Thus, for example, the preface for the dedication of churches, after a finely phrased thanksgiving, continues: *Te igitur, Domine, proprio ore tuo hostias super eam impositas benedicito* . . . The preface for the blessing of a cemetery, although without a conjunction, is expressed in a style which recalls the canon: *Per quem te, Domine, suppliciter deprecamur* . . .

Commentary

Te igitur, clementissime Pater, per Jesum Christum . . . The petitions are addressed to the most merciful Father, extolled in the preface, and rely upon Christ's priestly mediation.

Supplices rogamus ac petimus.—*Supplex* is the name given to the humble attitude of one who suffers a punishment (*supplicium*)—and this term has called forth a corresponding ritual attitude, a low bow (*Ordo II*, Romano-Carolingian, ninth century).

The repetition of the synonyms *rogamus ac petimus* gives expression to the urgency with which the priest addresses his supplication to the Father. As the leader or the interpreter for the congregation of the faithful, who offer the oblation, he speaks in the plural; he appeals to the priestly mediation and merits of Christ himself represented by the altar.[1] In the Middle Ages the priest used to kiss the representation of the cross which decorated the first page of the canon, as a sign of unity with Christ, the supreme Mediator. It was only in about the twelfth century that this kiss was transferred to the altar; consequently, the Carthusians, Carmelites and Dominicans do not perform this rite.

[1] Cf. Vol. I, Chap. 3, pp. 164-87.

The Beginning of the Canon

Uti accepta habeas, et benedicas, haec ✠ dona, haec ✠ munera, haec ✠ sancta sacrificia illibata. We beseech the Father to accept, and therefore to bless, the bread and wine, that is the matter to be transubstantiated in the eucharistic sacrifice.

Dona, munera and *sacrificia* are synonymous in the literature of the prayers of oblation (*secretae*) and mean the material offerings of bread and wine. In liturgical language, *benedicere* used in connection with the offerings means " to consecrate ". *Dona* is somewhat rare, *munera* occurs frequently, and *sacrificia* is the exact synonym of *munera* in these prayers.

The word *illibata*, which is non-biblical and does not, it seems, occur elsewhere in the Roman liturgy, is excellent Latin: St Cyprian uses it freely and it forms part of the vocabulary of Pope Gelasius.

May God now accept and bless this bread and wine for they are soon to become the body and blood of Christ. There is nothing here to suggest that the consecration has already been effected. These material offerings of bread and wine are present upon the altar, however, only because of the holy Eucharist to which they will lend the clothing of their accidents, and therefore the burning faith of the Church anticipates events and, through the nature of the bread and wine, contemplates the coming holy and unblemished offering of the body and blood of Christ. The gesture is suited to the words: the expression *benedicas* has led to the threefold signing with the cross, or blessing, of the *oblata* in connection with the three words by which they are designated.

(B) "*Intercessio*" (*from* "*in primis*" *to the end*).—*In primis quae tibi offerimus pro Ecclesia tua sancta catholica: quam pacificare, custodire, adunare et regere digneris.* The holy eucharistic sacrifice which emanates from the holy universal Church is offered primarily for the holy universal Church herself. All the instigators of schism are condemned by this prayer, for how can schismatics pretend to pray " for the Church universally spread abroad " from which they have separated themselves? St Optatus of Milevis demonstrated to the Donatists in 370 that such prayer was a falsehood which sullied their sacrifice every day.[1] The term *catholica* which has been extended by the addition of *toto orbe terrarum* (*diffusa*) belongs to the ecclesiastical vocabulary of the time of the Peace of Constantine

---
[1] *De schismate donatistarum*, 2, 12.

and the foundation of the Christian Roman Empire. This prayer enlarges upon a theme which is particularly dear to Christians, the tradition of which dates back to the earliest times of the Church. Thus the *Didache* (90) prays for the unity of the Church and all later liturgies follow this early example.

Quam pacificare, custodire, adunare et regere digneris. These terms are to be found almost literally in Pope Vigilius' letter to Justinian: *ut catholicam fidem adunare, regere Dominus et custodire toto orbe dignetur.* The Gelasian Sacramentary, the collect for Holy Church on Good Friday, and the first prayer after the kiss of peace all use expressions similar to those at this point in the canon.

Pacificare—The priest asks the Father for external peace; that is that the Church may be delivered from persecution.

Custodire—He beseeches him to protect her from all who might disturb this peace.

Adunare—Christ's Church is one: unity is one of her distinctive marks. The Eucharist is the first cause of this unity and St Cyprian of Carthage teaches that this sacrament represents the unity of the Christian body.[1] This theme is well illustrated by many secrets, among which that for Corpus Christi, which was composed by St Thomas, is especially noteworthy, re-echoing as it does the teaching which the Angel of the Schools had set forth in his *Summa Theologica* regarding the effect produced by the Eucharist.[2] The Council of Trent confirmed this teaching: the Eucharist is not only the symbol, but also the sacrament, the effective sign of unity:

". . . he desired that this sacrament should be the symbol (*symbolum*) of the unity of this body of which he himself is the head and to which he has desired that we should be most closely united as members by the bonds of faith, hope and charity so that we might all profess the same doctrine and that there might not be schisms among us." [3]

This prayer for peace and unity for the holy catholic Church spread abroad throughout the world relates directly to pagans and heretics and *a fortiori* to our separated brethren. It is, indeed, by the support afforded by their conversions that the one, holy, catholic Church into which they are integrated, grows unceasingly.

---

[1] See, e.g., *Ep.* 63, 13 in *P.L.*, 4, 384; *Ep.* 76.6 in *P.L.*, 3, 1142.
[2] *Summa Theol.*, III, q. 74, a. 1; III, q. 79, a. 1.
[3] Sess. 13, 2; Denzinger, 875.

The Beginning of the Canon

Regere—May the Father deign to govern his Church through his Spirit which dwells in her and gives life to the whole body, both the priestly hierarchy and each of her baptized members. The priest's prayer therefore descends through the hierarchy: the pope, the head of the universal Church; the bishop, the head of his particular Church; and all the orthodox bishops who profess the Catholic and apostolic faith.

From a penetrating study devoted by Dom B. Capelle to the last section of this prayer, it appears (a) that St Gregory in his Sacramentary knew the whole text to the words *papa nostro illo;* (b) that the phrase *et antistite nostro N.* is a later Gallican addition; and (c) that the final *et omnibus orthodoxis . . . fidei cultoribus* has every appearance of belonging to the Roman text before the time of St Gregory and that it was, therefore, suppressed by this pope. However, it crept once again into the Gallican copies of the Gregorian Sacramentary as well as into the Gelasian Sacramentary of Gellonius (770–80), to reappear finally in the Roman Missal under Alcuin of York. By comparison with parallel texts in Eastern intercessory prayers, in which the order of intentions is always the holy Church, our Bishop, all other orthodox bishops, the learned author concludes that our phrase *et omnibus*, etc., means not the faithful but the bishops. *Orthodoxis* is not a noun, but an adjective, as is apparent in the parallels in Eastern liturgies, qualifying *episcopis* (here understood) as it does in them.[1]

Intercession for the pope: "*una cum famulo tuo Papa nostro N.*"—*Una cum:* this adverb and preposition do not relate (as some think) to the rather distant verb *offerimus,* but, quite naturally, link the reference to the Church to that of the hierarchy: "in communion with" (compare the similar phrase in the Praeconium of the Paschal candle).

Papa nostro N.—Originally, the word Pope was not reserved to the Bishop of Rome but was used for any bishop. Thus, for example, St Jerome uses it both for Anastasius and Damasus, the Bishops of Rome, and for Augustine of Carthage, Theophilus of Alexandria and others. It was only in the sixth century that there appeared the tendency to reserve this title to the Bishop of Rome, but even then St Gregory of Tours († 593–4) remained true to the

---

[1] Dom B. Capelle, *Et omnibus orthodoxis, atque catholicae et apostolicae fidei cultoribus* in *Miscellanea historica in honorem Alberti De Meyer,* Vol. 1 (1946), pp. 137–50.

ancient practice. Even at Rome, the word *Papa* only occasionally means Bishop of Rome when it occurs in the *Registrum* between the middle of the fifth and the eighth centuries and, in the *Liber Pontificalis*, *papa* finally replaces *episcopus* only with Anicetus (535–8). Thus, in the fourth–fifth century, the phrase *Papa nostro N.* meant "for our bishop". On the other hand, as in the time of St Gregory, the exclusive meaning of the term *papa* was fixed, this term must from thence forwards be interpreted as relating to the Bishop of Rome, the head of the universal Church. In sacramentaries intended for use in Rome, there was no other local bishop to be mentioned.

In his prayer for the Church, the priest first commemorates the Sovereign Pontiff, its visible head, Christ's vicar, Peter's successor, the living centre of ecumenical unity, the supreme shepherd of both bishops and faithful, with whom all churches must be in unity: *Ubi Petrus: ibi Ecclesia.*

The Pope's name is uttered in all Masses celebrated throughout the world. When he says the pope's name, the celebrant bows slightly towards the book.[1] The pope himself says: *una cum me indigno famulo tuo, quem gregi tuo praeesse voluisti.* When the apostolic throne is vacant, the reference is omitted.

To pray for the pope is to bear witness that one is living in communion with the head of the true Church. It is of little importance whether the Mass is celebrated in Latin, Greek, Syriac or Coptic: the universal Church is neither Latin, Greek, Syriac or Coptic. She is Roman—that is, she is united to the pope of Rome as her visible head, and prays for him. To erase the pope's name from the holy sacrifice is to separate oneself publicly from the Catholic Church. When Photius, the Patriarch of Constantinople, brought about the division of the Greek Church, the names of the popes were deleted from the schismatic liturgy and this has been the common practice of heretics.

Intercession for the Bishop: . . . "*et Antistite nostro N.*"—Ancient manuscripts mention only the pope, but once the meaning of the word pope became limited to the Roman bishop, a commemoration of the local bishop was made in Gaul. As the pope is the head of the universal Church, so is the bishop the head of his local Church: in these two commemorations there is summarized the whole of

---

[1] S.C.R., decr. 3767, 25.

the doctrine of the hierarchic constitution of the Church. *Antistes* means " he who is at the head ".

Mention of the names of the bishops in the diptychs used to be evidence of their communion with the Church and their orthodoxy. The name said here is not that of the celebrant's Ordinary (as in the Breviary) but that of the bishop of the diocese in which he is celebrating Mass. It is first mentioned on the day on which the bishop named canonically takes possession, either in person or by proxy, of his see,[1] and it is omitted on his death and at Rome, the bishop of which is the pope. The name of a vicar apostolic who has been consecrated bishop is not mentioned because he is not appointed to a diocese. The bishop himself prays: *et me indigno servo tuo*.

Intercession for the prince.—To pray for the prince is a Christian's duty[2] and from the tenth century until 1570 (Missal of St Pius V) the name of the prince (emperor or king) was included in the canon at this point in the form *et rege nostro N*. After the concordat of 1801 between Pius VII and Napoleon I, the prayer for the king was transferred to a point after Mass.

In the Middle Ages, the priest also prayed for himself at this point in the canon.

"*Et omnibus orthodoxis, atque catholicae, et apostolicae fidei cultoribus.*"—This text originally referred to " all the orthodox bishops who confess the catholic and apostolic faith ". The Roman canon was originally related to the Eastern anaphoras and was drawn up at the time of the great heretical offensives against the Church (fourth – fifth centuries), when the expression *sorthodoxi* and *fidei cultoribus* called to mind not so much the faithful as the valiant bishops, the appointed defenders of orthodoxy, who by their discourses, writings and labours never ceased from refuting errors, confessing, explaining and glorifying " the catholic and apostolic " faith—such men as Athanasius, Basil, Ambrose and Leo.

DECORATION AT THE BEGINNING OF THE CANON

From the eighth century onwards, the canon began to be decorated with illuminations, usually based on the initial T of *Te igitur*, which lends itself admirably to adaptation as a crucifix. In the period eighth–tenth centuries this representation was simple,

---

[1] S.C.R., decr. 3500 ad 2.   [2] See I Tim. 2. 1-2.

but in succeeding ages it grew ever more complex until finally the whole of the scene of the crucifixion was shown on a page by itself and *Te igitur* was given a new initial T—which, in its turn, began to be illuminated. Until the eleventh century, Christ was shown as alive upon the cross; thereafter he was shown either dying or in death. Sometimes, the *Majestas Domini* (which actually belongs to the *Sanctus*) replaced this scene of the crucifixion here. At the foot of the great illuminations of the *Majestas Domini* or the crucifixion, there often appeared a small golden cross, which marked the place where the priest was to kiss the book. St Pius V omitted this small cross from his Missal of 1570.

So then, from the capital T of *Te igitur*, there came three crosses: the great crucifixion, that represented on the initial itself, and finally the small cross which marked the beginning of the text.

THE *MEMENTO* OF NAMED LIVING PERSONS AND THE FAITHFUL PRESENT

GELASIAN SACRAMENTARY (Fifth–sixth centuries)	ROMAN MISSAL	
Memento, Domine, famulorum famularumque tuarum et omnium circumadstantium quorum tibi fides cognita est et nota devotio, qui tibi offerunt hoc sacrificium laudis, pro se suisque omnibus, pro redemptione	*Memento, Domine, famulorum famularumque tuarum N. et N. et omnium circumstantium, quorum tibi fides cognita est et nota devotio, pro quibus tibi offerimus: vel qui tibi offerunt hoc sacrificium laudis, pro se suisque omnibus, pro redemptione*	Remember, Lord, thy servants N. and N., and all those here present with us, whose faith has been proved and whose fidelity is known to thee. We offer for them, or they themselves offer, this sacrifice of praise for themselves and all their own, for the redemption
animarum suarum, pro spe salutis et incolumitatis suae, tibi reddunt vota sua aeterno Deo vero et vivo.	*animarum suarum, pro spe salutis et incolumitatis suae: tibique reddunt vota sua aeterno Deo, vivo et vero.*	of their souls, for the hope of safety and salvation, and they now send up their prayers to thee, the eternal, living and true God.

This prayer is a diptych. Etymologically, the word diptych means an object folded into two; more specifically, it refers to a kind of book or notebook, composed of two leaves hinged down one side, usually made of wood, ivory, base metals, silver or even gold. In accordance with established custom, consuls of the fifth and sixth centuries offered ivory diptychs, bearing their portraits, names and titles and other traditional decoration, to their friends and even to the Emperor to commemorate their appointment. When, in the fifth century, bishops became very influential, the public magistrates began to present them, too, with diptychs and these are often preserved in cathedral treasuries and chapter libraries. Sometimes the portrait of a long-forgotten consul was later transformed into the image of a saint and his other inscriptions adapted accordingly. Very often the reverse of the diptych was inscribed with the names of the bishops and faithful whom it was especially desired to commemorate at the holy sacrifice of the Mass. Distinction was made between the diptychs of the living and the diptychs of the dead and sometimes special diptychs were reserved for bishops. On them, there were inscribed the names of those who were distinguished for their sanctity. As the diptychs were read during the canon of the Mass, this insertion of the names was expressed by the word *canonizare*, " to canonize ".

Among the Greeks, the deacon proclaims the names aloud; among the Latins, a subdeacon used to read them in an undertone, and at the end of the list the celebrant said " a prayer over the names " (*oratio super nomina* or *diptycha*). The number of names thus mentioned later became so great that supplementary sheets of parchment had to be used to contain them all, and thus gradually the diptychs were transformed into books placed upon the altar. Gradually, the recitation of these lists was replaced by general prayers embracing all those named and, by extension, the prayer came to be called a diptych. The present examples are the *Memento* of the living, *Communicantes* (with the names of saints), the *Memento* of the dead, and *Nobis quoque peccatoribus* (with the names of saints). In the reign of Pope Innocent I the Roman canon already contained a list of the names of those who offered—which corresponds exactly to our *Memento* of the living—which was preceded by a commendation of the offerings (which is the purpose of the modern *Te igitur*), as is shown by that pope's reply to Decentius, the Bishop of Gubbio, who had consulted the pope on this subject.[1]

Commentary.—At the *Memento*, the deacon used to go to the ambo and read the list of names. Immediately afterwards, the priest would go on: *quorum tibi fides cognita est*, etc. When the ceremony disappeared, the prayer survived. Instead of the names being read, the diptychs were now placed on the altar and, in an

[1] *Ep.* 25: *ad Decent*, 2, P.L., 20, 553.

undertone, the priest then mentioned the names of those whom he especially wished to commend at the holy sacrifice. From this practice are derived the letters N. and N. in the Missal. As the *Memento* is a prayer which forms part of the external, public worship of the Church, the excommunicated, heretics, schismatics and unbelievers cannot be mentioned in it expressly, but there is nothing to forbid interior commendation of them to God's goodness at this time. Pope St Pius X especially adjured priests to remember the dying in each of their Masses, and this commemoration is proper here.

That this diptych refers especially to those present is apparent from the phrase *et omnium circumstantium* (those who stand about the altar). In former times, the altar was placed at the intersection of the nave and transept and those present at Mass stood; chairs were not found in churches before the thirteenth century.

Quorum tibi fides cognita est et nota devotio.—*Fides cognita* in Titus Livy and among the Africans means "proven faithfulness".

Pro quibus tibi offerimus: vel qui tibi offerunt.—In former times, "to hear Mass" and "to bring an offering" meant the same thing and in the ancient sacramentaries the text contains only *qui tibi offerunt* (who offer to thee). *Pro quibus tibi offerimus vel* (for whom we offer unto thee: or) was added in about the year 1000, when the faithful no longer brought their oblations to the altar and Masses for the dead were more numerous.

Incolumis means "intact, whole and safe, in good condition, complete, in good health, prosperous".

Tibique reddunt vota sua is a biblical phrase meaning "who bring their gifts to the altar": under the old covenant many sacrifices were offered in fulfilment of a vow (*votum*) and the word vow thus came to mean the offering of the sacrifice itself. In the fourth century *vota* signified prayers.

UNION WITH THE VICTORIOUS MEMBERS TO GAIN THEIR INTERCESSION

Communicantes, et memoriam venerantes, in primis gloriosae semper Virginis Mariae, Genitricis Dei et Domini nostri Jesu Christi: sed et beatorum Apostolorum ac

United in the same holy communion we reverence the memory, first, of the glorious ever-virgin Mary, Mother of our God and Lord Jesus Christ,

| *Martyrum tuorum, Petri et Pauli, Andreae, Jacobi, Joannis, Thomae, Jacobi, Philippi, Bartholomaei, Matthaei, Simonis, et Thaddaei: Lini, Cleti, Clementis, Xysti, Cornelii, Cypriani, Laurentii, Chrysogoni, Joannis et Pauli, Cosmae et Damiani: et omnium Sanctorum tuorum: quorum meritis precibusque concedas, ut in omnibus protectionis tuae muniamur auxilio. Per eundem Christum Dominum nostrum. Amen.* | and likewise that of thy blessed Apostles and Martyrs Peter and Paul, Andrew, James, John, Thomas, James, Philip, Bartholomew, Matthew, Simon, and Thaddaeus: of Linus, Cletus, Clement, Sixtus, Cornelius, Cyprian, Lawrence, Chrysogonus, John and Paul, Cosmas and Damian; and of all thy Saints. Grant for the sake of their merits and prayers that in all things we may be guarded and helped by thy protection: through the same Christ our Lord. Amen. |

This diptych bears the name *infra actionem* (during the canon). In the Gelasian Sacramentary, *Communicantes* was a variable prayer, proper to some Masses, included with the collect, secret and preface.

The Roman Missal still contains six variants of this diptych: for the octave of Christmas, the Epiphany, Maundy Thursday, the Easter Vigil, the Saturday after Easter, the Ascension, and from the Vigil of Pentecost until the Saturday after Pentecost. The fundamental concept which has inspired the *Communicantes* and *Nobis quoque peccatoribus* is that of faith and trust in the communion of saints. Comparison of *Communicantes* and its variants with the works of St Leo convinced Mgr Callewaert that he should be considered its author.

It is curious that the first part of *Communicantes* contains no finite verb, but depends upon two participles: *communicantes* and *venerantes*.

Communicantes signifies in the communion of the Church, the communion of the saints.

This prayer bears the clear imprint of its origins: born on Roman soil, it expresses the local liturgical worship of the city of Rome: all its martyrs are Roman martyrs, either born at Rome or popular in Rome because their relics rest and are venerated in Rome's basilicas. The only exception is St Cyprian of Carthage; he, however, was a famous champion of the unity of the Church and his cultus was very popular there.

In primis gloriosae semper virginis Mariae, Genitricis Dei et Domini nostri Jesu Christi.—The list opens with Mary, giving her the glorious title *Theotokos* (Mother of God) which was bestowed upon her by the ecumenical Council of Ephesus (431). She is honoured in Rome at the basilica of St Mary Major which was built and consecrated after that Council by Sixtus II (432–40), to perpetuate the memory of Mary's triumph over Nestorius.[1] The Queen of Martyrs, she leads a blood-stained procession of twelve Apostles and twelve Roman witnesses (martyrs).

The Apostles.—Scripture gives four lists of Apostles all beginning with Peter and ending with Judas. In the canon, Peter and Paul are named first. They are followed by Andrew, Peter's brother, the first chosen, then follow the two sons of Zebedee, James the Great and John, his younger brother. The others follow in the order of the liturgical year, from Thomas to Thaddaeus. This simple and practical order has also been followed in the Litany of the Saints.

SS. Peter and Paul, Patrons of the city of Rome.—By their preaching and labours, Peter and Paul founded the Church of Rome; in their blood, they baptized and hallowed it: they are both rightly accounted patrons of the city. Between 64 and 68—probably in 67—Peter underwent martyrdom in the Vatican Gardens near Nero's Circus and Paul was beheaded near the second military milestone on the Ostian Way. The bodies of the Prince of the Apostles and the Doctor of the Gentiles were buried in underground crypts not far from the places of their martyrdoms. According to the *Liber Pontificalis*, Pope Anacletus († 88) caused an oratory (*memoria*) to be built over each of the Apostles' tombs; in the persecutions of 258, the remains of the two Apostles were translated *ad catacumbas* near the second milestone on the Appian Way. The Philocalian Calendar for 336 shows that this translation was commemorated on 29 June. Greek and Latin *graffiti* discovered there recently take the form of pilgrims' invocations of the Apostles.[2] Constantine marked the new tombs with massive bronze tablets (one of which, reading *Paulo Apostolo Mart*, still survives today) and erected basilicas over them. Despite works of restoration undertaken by many popes, the Constantinian basilica of St Peter was threatened

---

[1] The earliest reference to Mary in the Roman anaphora is that in the Anaphora of St Hippolytus (175–235), quoted in Chap. 14, above, p. 149.

[2] J. Lebreton, *La venue de S. Pierre à Rome* in *Histoire de l'Eglise*, vol. I, pp. 227–32 (Fliche et Martin); Card. Schuster, *Liber Sacramentorum*, vol. 7, pp. 348–57.

by ruin by the fifteenth century and Pope Nicholas V (1447–55) drew up a grandiose plan for its complete rebuilding. The work was set in hand by Julian II (1503–13) and the new basilica was finally consecrated by Urban VIII on 18 November 1626.

At the very beginning of his pontificate Pius XII ordered excavations to be undertaken beneath the basilica in order to discover the tomb of the first pope. In his radio message of 23 December 1950 he was able to announce to the world the sensational news that " the tomb of the Prince of the Apostles has been found. . . . The great dome [of St Peter's] rises over the exact spot where the first Bishop of Rome, the first pope, lies . . ."

Constantine's basilica of St Paul-without-the-walls soon seemed too small and Valentinian II († 387), Theodosius († 395) and Honorius († 423) all worked on the construction of another, larger shrine which was completed by Galla Placidia († 450) and St Leo I († 461) and destroyed by a fire in 1823. Through the beneficence of Leo XII († 1829) and his successors it rose again from its ashes and was solemnly dedicated by Pius IX on 10 December 1854. The dedication feast is, however, kept on 18 November, with that of St Peter's. In the seventh century, at the time of the Saracen invasions, the heads—but not the bodies—of Peter and Paul were transferred to the archbasilica of the Lateran.

The fervour of the cultus that the Apostolic Church devotes to her venerable apostolic founders is more readily understood when their sanctity—unparalleled in the college of the Apostles—is recalled. " God," St Thomas says, " bestows on every man grace proportionate for the mission for which he has been chosen "; and again, " Among the other saints [i.e. other than our Lady and St Joseph] it is the Apostles who have been raised to the highest dignity . . . for they have received the Holy Ghost yet more abundantly." [1] St Thomas further points out that they gave back what they had received in their lives as " friends of God ", as founders and sustainers of and intercessors for the Church. Writing on the holiness of the Apostles and their companions, Journet says, " The first beatings of the heart of the Church determined the rhythm of the whole of Christian life to come ".[2]

The Twelve Martyrs.—The fact that there is no saint in this list who was not martyred is a sign of its antiquity.

[1] *Comm. in Rom.*, 8, 23, lect. 5.   [2] *Destinées d' Israël*, p. 112 (Paris, 1944).

The names are in hierarchical order: popes (Linus, Cletus, Clement, Sixtus II, Cornelius); bishop (Cyprian); deacon (Lawrence); laymen (Chrysogonus, John, Paul, Cosmas, Damian).

St Linus († ? 79) was St Peter's first successor; his name is not, however, mentioned in the oldest lists of bishops of Rome. When in the pontificate of Urban VIII, the foundations were dug for the ciborium of the high altar in the basilica of St Peter, there was found near the altar a sarcophagus bearing the inscription LINUS: according to the *Liber Pontificalis*, St Linus was buried near St Peter. Almost nothing is known of this saint's biography. He ruled the Church during the violent persecution of Nero. The Church celebrates his feast on 23 September.

St Cletus († ? 89): the successor of Linus. His feast is celebrated on 26 April.

St Clement († ? 97): The *Titulus Clementis*, well-known throughout Christendom, shows archeological strata comprising (a) a first-century dwelling where, doubtless, St Clement and other Christians met together, (b) the *Dominicum Clementis* (a fourth-century church built over this house), and (c) the present basilica. According to an inscription on the base of the altar, St Clement's relics are preserved here. His feast is celebrated on 23 November.

St Sixtus II († 258): Despite Valerian's edict, St Sixtus (Xystus) celebrated the holy mysteries in the catacombs of Callistus and was surprised there and beheaded upon his throne. His body is buried in the crypt of the popes. His deacon (Lawrence) was beheaded three days later. His feast is kept on 6 August.

Cornelius († 253) died in exile at Centumcellae (Civitavecchia) on 14 September 253 after a troubled reign of two years (Novatian Schism). His body was translated to Rome and buried in the crypt of Lucinus in the catacombs of Callistus. His epitaph has been preserved. Others of his relics are venerated at St Mary in Trastevere. His feast is kept with that of St Cyprian on 14 September.

Cyprian († 258): According to St Augustine, he was pre-eminently the *catholicus episcopus, catholicus martyr*. As Bishop of Carthage, he fought for the unity of the Church: his good relations with Pope Stephen are beyond doubt. He suffered martyrdom in the Valerian Persecution (258) and Carthage built three basilicas in his honour. By 336, the feast of this great African bishop was already celebrated at Rome where his cultus was closely linked with that of Pope Cornelius: his portrait was painted close to that pontiff's in the crypt of Cornelius. He was so popular at Rome that, according to the *Comes* of Wurzburg (seventh century), the Sundays after his feast (14 September) were named in relation to it (*Ebdomada I, II, etc., post natale Sancti Cypriani*).

Lawrence († 258): After SS. Peter and Paul, St Lawrence is the third patron of the Eternal City: Lawrence is to Rome what Stephen is to Jerusalem. His relics were placed in the catacomb of Cyriacus in the *Ager Veranus*, and Constantine built a splendid basilica over his tomb. This by successive additions and modifications has grown into the present St Lawrence-without-the-walls, completed under Honorius III († 638) and magnificently restored by Pius IX. Within the city, many churches and chapels have been dedicated to him, among them the stational church *S. Laurentius in formoso ubi assatus est*, known as St Lawrence in Paneperna in the Missal. The memory of this illustrious martyr is recalled every day in the third prayer of thanksgiving after the Mass. The feast of St Lawrence is celebrated on 10 August, and according to the *Comes* of Wurzburg, the following Sundays were, in the seventh century, named according to their relationship to this day: *Ebdomada I, II, etc., post S. Laurentium*.

St Chrysogonus († 304): St Chrysogonus, martyred at Aquileia, occupies a place among the Roman saints, not because of his origins, but because of the cultus paid to him in the fourth-century basilica in Trastevere which bears his name. His portrait is reproduced in the glittering procession of martyrs in the basilica of St Apollinaris Nuovo at Ravenna. His feast is celebrated on 24 November.

SS. John and Paul († 362): These martyrs are generally considered to be two Roman officers of the imperial palace, who were put to death and buried in their house on the Coelian Hill in the persecution of Julian the Apostate. But this opinion must be received with caution, for (a) Julian persecuted the Church in the East, but not the West, (b) Romans were never buried within the city, (c) Eastern law permitted the removal of portions from relics, Roman law did not, (d) its ancient name points to this house as having belonged to Pammachius. It is therefore highly probable that these were two Eastern martyrs. A church had been built over the house of Pammachius and dedicated to SS. John and Paul before the pontificate of Pope Symmachus (498–514), for he restored its apse. Their feast is celebrated on 26 June.

SS. Cosmas and Damian († 362): Famous physicians, natives of Syria, Cosmas and Damian cared for the sick without accepting payment, and were therefore called *Anargyres*. They died as martyrs in 362 at Cyros in the land of their birth. Justinian built a beautiful basilica over their tomb. During the fourth century their cultus spread to Constantinople and from there to Rome: Pope Symmachus built their oldest shrine at Rome on the Esquiline Hill.[1] Felix IV (526–30) dedicated the basilica of Romulus Augustulus to their honour, together with the *templum sacrae Urbis* in the forum; five other shrines were dedicated to them in other quarters of the city. Their feast is celebrated on 27 September.

In Gaul and Germany, the names of local saints were added to this list.

The conclusion *Per . . . Amen* shows conclusively that *Communicantes* is an interpolation into the canon. In the liturgies of other churches—for example, the Ambrosian Liturgy of Milan—the named saints are proper to that church.

HANC IGITUR

The imposition of hands over the oblations.—Before saying the prayer, the celebrant stretches out his hands over the host and chalice. Imposition of hands in the eucharistic rite is shown on a fresco in the catacomb of Callistus (third century) and mentioned in the canons of Hippolytus (fourth century), but its introduction at the *Hanc igitur* is of later date: in former times a low bow was made during this prayer. The imposition of hands was suggested by the marked emphasis upon propitiation and expiation: in Leviticus, this gesture accompanies sacrifices of expiation (Lev. 1. 4; 16. 20–21). It appeared here in the fourteenth century: by anticipation, the priest heaps upon the divine Lamb the sins and suffrages of all who are present.

Hanc igitur oblationem servitutis nostrae, sed et cunctae familiae tuae, quaesumus, Domine, ut placatus accipias: diesque nostros

And so, Lord, we pray thee graciously to accept this offering of our priestly ministry and of thy whole household.

---
[1] *Lib. Pont.*, I, 262.

in tua pace disponas, atque ab aeterna damnatione nos eripi, et in electorum tuorum jubeas grege numerari. Per Christum Dominum nostrum. Amen.[1]

Order our days in thy peace, and command that we be rescued from eternal damnation and numbered with the flock of thy elect: through Christ our Lord. Amen.

This prayer certainly existed in the sixth century, for it occurs in the Leonine Sacramentary. It originally served to commend to God the intentions of those who had offered oblations and is an authentic prayer *post nomina* which was once variable according to circumstances. Most of the old variants have now disappeared, however, although there are special forms for the octaves of Easter and Pentecost (referring especially to the neophytes), on Maundy Thursday (in thanksgiving for the institution of the Eucharist) and at the consecration of bishops (*quam tibi offerimus etiam pro hoc famulo tuo quem ad Episcopatus ordinem promovere dignatus es*). The interpolation of this prayer into the canon seems to have taken place before the pontificate of Pope Vigilius († 555).

According to the *Liber Pontificalis* (I, 312), St Gregory added the petition for peace and those which follow it to this prayer: in his pontificate, Italy was ravaged by plague, war and famine and Rome besieged by the Lombards.

Servitutis nostrae sed et cunctae familiae tuae.—This clause is paralleled in the anamnesis: *Unde et memores, Domine, nos servi tui sed et plebs tua sancta.* In the liturgy, *servus* and *servitus* mean priest and priestly ministry, as against the faithful (*familiae tuae* and *plebs tua sancta*). To the Roman, the first meaning of *familia*, was a master's staff of servants (*famuli*) and its later extended meaning "family" in the modern sense; in Christian usage, it designates the congregation of the children of God. The double conjunction *sed et* ("but also") emphasizes once more the role of the faithful as offerers: not only the priests, "but also" the Christian congregation offer the holy sacrifice. Cardinal Schuster believed this prayer to be an important part of the "commendation of the oblations" spoken of by Pope Innocent I in his letter to Decentius, and he explains its relationship to the preceding one thus: the priest begins the canon by reciting the preface, which the people complete with the *Sanctus*.

---

[1] *Amen* is omitted in the Gelasian Sacramentary (liturgy of the fifth and sixth centuries).

Meanwhile, the priest commends the oblations in *Te igitur* and begins the *Communicantes;* after the *Sanctus,* the deacon said the diptych *Memento* for the living. The priest and the deacon thus prayed together. The *Memento* ends: *qui tibi offerunt hoc sacrificium laudis pro se suisque . . . tibi reddunt vota sua . . .* At this point the priest terminated his commendation of the oblation in the prayer *Hanc igitur oblationem.* The prayer is then, properly, a prayer *super diptycha,* the natural conclusion of the deacon's prayers over the diptychs.

According to a decree of the Sacred Congregation of Rites dated 25 October 1922 (n. 4377) it is most fitting (*maxime expedit*) that a warning stroke should be given on the sanctuary bell a little before the consecration (as is the universal practice) for the benefit of the faithful furthest from the altar. The ending of the stretching out of hands over the oblation or the beginning of the next prayer, *Quam oblationem,* is the suggested time for this warning.

QUAM OBLATIONEM: THE PRECONSECRATORY EPICLESIS

The text of this section dates back to the fourth century and is to be found in the treatise *De Sacramentis:*

DE SACRAMENTIS (Fourth century)	ROMAN MISSAL	
Fac nobis hanc oblationem	*Quam oblationem tu, Deus, in omnibus, quaesumus, bene✠dictam,*	Be pleased, O God, to bless this offering, to accept
ascriptam,	*adscri✠ptam,*	and approve it fully,
ratam,	*rat✠am,*	to make it perfect
rationabilem,	*rationabilem,*	and worthy
acceptabilem	*acceptabilemque*	to please thee,
quod figura est	*facere digneris:*	so that it may become
Corporis	*ut nobis Cor✠pus*	for us the Body
et Sanguinis	*et San✠guis*	and Blood
	fiat dilectissimi Filii tui,	of thy dearly beloved Son,
Domini nostri	*Domini nostri*	our Lord
Jesu Christi.[1]	*Jesu Christi.*[2]	Jesus Christ.

The fourth-century *quod figura,* etc., must not be interpreted according to the canons of later scholastic terminology. The relative pronoun *quod* is here equivalent to *quae;* indeed, the *Liber Ordinum*[3] contains the version *quae est imago et similitudo. Figura,* then, is synonymous with "sacramental sign", under which the

---
[1] *De Sac.,* 4, 5, 21; *P.L.,* 16, 443.
[2] The prayer is identical in the Gelasian Sacramentary, but without crosses.
[3] Ed. Férotin.

The Beginning of the Canon

body and blood of Christ are really present. The alteration of *est* to *fiat* is very characteristic: it makes the prayer one addressed to the Father for the transubstantiation of bread and wine into the body and blood of Christ.

Commentary.—We beseech God to deign to bless this offering of bread and wine fully and in every way (*in omnibus*); *benedicere* is synonymous with *sanctificare*, and means to consecrate, and is so used often in the liturgy.

The two words *adscriptam* and *ratam* are taken from Roman juridical language and both mean basically the same thing: *adscriptam* that something is transferred to someone, and *ratam* that that transfer is confirmed and ratified: the word *legitima* is often used similarly in the Gallican liturgy.

Rationabilis is here a synonym of *spiritualis*, "spiritual" (cf. Rom. 12. 1 and I Peter 2. 5): we ask that the Lord will make our material offerings spiritual through the operation of the Holy Ghost; Dom Casel interprets *rationabilis* as "as a true oblation should be": "make it a true oblation". The sense is, perhaps: "valid", "in accordance with the rules".

Acceptabilem means acceptable, worthy of acceptance and, therefore, pleasing.

The blessing asked of the Father is clearly consecration itself and it follows from this that the conjunction *ut* does not indicate purpose ("in order that," "so that") but consequence ("with the result that"). Notice that we ask for consecration not for its own sake, but for ourselves: *ut nobis corpus et sanguis fiat*. In making present the sacrifice of the cross in the eucharistic rite, the high priest applies its infinite merits to us.

Prayers which, like this, pray for transubstantiation are to be found in all liturgies; by the Greeks, they are called *epicleses*. They usually invoke the Father (but sometimes the Son) to send down the Holy Ghost upon the bread and wine that he may change them, by divine power, into the body and blood of Christ. In many cases, the epiclesis follows the consecration.[1] Here, however, as in the anaphoras of Serapion, Der Balyzeh and the Louvain papyrus (see chapter 14), it is placed before the consecration and presents no difficulties.

[1] See, e.g., Hippolytus, *Trad. Apol.* quoted in Chap. 14, pp. 149–50; The Apostolic Constitutions, Chap. 14, pp. 158–60. This usage is discussed in Chap. 21, pp. 238–40.

19

THE CONSECRATION AND ELEVATION

THE CONSECRATION

DESPITE their astonishing diversity, all Latin, Greek and Eastern anaphoras are at one in the words of consecration formerly spoken by Christ. In his study *L'Eucharistia*, Dom Cagin systematically compared seventy-six ancient consecratory formulas from various liturgies and concluded that they are all fundamentally alike and, in large measure, agree literally with the texts of the synoptic Gospels and the first Epistle to the Corinthians. This unity is easily explained by the fact that the consecratory formula formed part of the tradition of the Apostles and was part of the orally transmitted Gospel before ever this was permanently fixed by being committed to writing. The formulas of consecration in different liturgies all show tendencies: (a) towards symmetry in the two consecrations of bread and wine; (b) towards ever more literal agreement with the words of Scripture; and (c) towards greater fullness of expression and solemnity (as, for example: *in sanctas ac venerabiles manus suas, et elevatis oculis in caelum ad te Deum Patrem suum omnipotentem* and *mysterium fidei*). If we compare the words of consecration in *De Sacramentis* with the formula in the Gelasian Sacramentary (700) and the modern Missal, it quickly becomes apparent that in the present text (a) there is a tendency to greater fullness and solemnity (as in the examples under (c) above), (b) there is a marked attempt to quote Scripture more closely (for example *elevatis oculis* is found in Luke 6. 20; 18. 13; John 6. 6; 11. 41; *dedit*—from Matt. 26. 26; Mark 14. 22; Luke 22. 19—replaces *tradidit* and *edite* had become *manducate* as in I Cor. 11. 24). In addition, expressions not found in Scripture are omitted (for example, *fractumque, apostolis suis* (used twice), *pridie quam pateretur* (in the second formula), etc.

Notice particularly the omission of *quod pro multis confringetur*

The Consecration and Elevation

in the consecration of the bread and the expansion of the consecration formula for the wine.[1]

DE SACRAMENTIS (Fourth century)	MISSALE ROMANUM[2]	ROMAN MISSAL
Qui pridie, quam pateretur,	*Qui pridie quam pateretur,*	He, on the day before he suffered death,
	accepit panem in sanctas ac venerabiles manus suas,	took bread into his holy and worshipful hands,
respexit in caelum ad te, sancte Pater omnipotens, aeterne Deus,	*et elevatis oculis in caelum ad te Deum Patrem suum omnipotentem,*	and lifting up his eyes to thee, God, his almighty Father in heaven,
gratias agens benedixit, fregit, fractumque apostolis suis et discipulis tradidit dicens:	*tibi gratias agens, bene ✠ dixit, fregit, deditque discipulis suis, dicens:*	and giving thanks to thee, he blessed it, broke it, and gave it to his disciples, saying:
Accipite et edite ex hoc omnes.	*Accipite, et manducate ex hoc omnes:*	Take, all of you, and eat of this,
Hoc est enim Corpus meum quod pro multis confringetur.	*Hoc est enim Corpus meum.*	For this is my Body.
Similiter etiam calicem postquam coenatum est, pridie quam pateretur, accepit	*Simili modo postquam coenatum est, accipiens et hunc praeclarum Calicem in sanctas ac venerabiles manus suas:*	In like manner, when he had supped, taking also this goodly cup into his holy and worshipful hands,
respexit in caelum ad te, Sancte Pater omnipotens aeterne Deus,		
gratias agens benedixit apostolis suis et discipulis suis tradidit dicens:	*item tibi gratias agens, benedixit, deditque discipulis suis, dicens:*	and again giving thanks to thee, he blessed it, and gave it to his disciples, saying:
Accipite, et bibite ex hoc omnes.	*Accipite, et bibite ex eo omnes.*	Take, all of you, and drink of this,
Hic est enim Sanguis meus.	*Hic est enim Calix Sanguinis mei, novi et aeterni testamenti: mysterium fidei: qui pro vobis et pro multis effundetur in remissionem peccatorum.*	For this is the Chalice of my Blood, of the new and everlasting covenant, a mystery of faith. It shall be shed for you and many others, so that sins may be forgiven.
Quotiescumque hoc feceritis, toties commemorationem mei facietis donec iterum adveniam.	*Haec quotiescumque feceritis, in mei memoriam facietis.*	Whenever you shall do these things, you shall do them in memory of me.

The interpolation *mysterium fidei* in the formula for the consecration of the wine first appeared in the liturgy in the Bobbio Missal and the Gelasian and Gregorian Sacramentaries: it seems, therefore, to have originated in Gaul. It is taken from St Paul, who teaches:

---

[1] With the table below, compare that in Chap. 2, pp. 16-17 above, where the Scripture texts are to be found.

[2] The text in The *Sacramentarium Gelasianum* (liturgy of the fifth–sixth centuries) is very similar, the only, non-important, variant readings being: (a) There is no *et* before *elevatis oculis*, (b) *posteaquam* replaces *postquam*, (c) *dedit* replaces *deditque*.

diaconos habentes mysterium fidei in conscientia pura (I Tim. 3. 9). Many exegetes interpret this phrase as relating to the holy Eucharist; it is well known that in the primitive Church the ministry of the eucharistic blood was proper to the deacons.[1] *Mysterium fidei* would thus appear to be either an exclamation made by the deacons or a declaratory interjection referring to the transubstantiation brought about by the words of consecration. The Eucharist is certainly the paramount "mystery of faith", as St Thomas has declared so simply yet completely in his hymn *Adoro*.

THE MYSTERY OF THE CONSECRATION

Nowhere is the priest's personality more fully effaced, nowhere is his oneness with Christ more clearly affirmed than in the rite of consecration: the priest does not say, "This is the body of Christ", but, in Christ's person, "This is my body". "The priest," St Thomas teaches, "bears the image of Christ, in whose person and power he utters the words of consecration."[2] "The same (Christ) now offers through the ministry of priests who then offered himself on the cross."[3]

We have already shown above (chapters 3 ff.) that the rite of consecration lies at the heart of the eucharistic sacrifice and we would refer the reader once again to that important section of our study, in which we concluded that the rite of consecration makes the sacrifice of the cross sacramentally present in the liturgy of the Mass, which is therefore a true sacrifice, albeit a sacramental sacrifice in relation to that of the cross. "If anyone says that a true and proper sacrifice is not offered to God in the Mass, let him be anathema."[4] "The Eucharist is the perfect sacrament of the Lord's Passion."[5] "This sacrament is both sacrifice and sacrament (communion): it is a sacrifice in as much as it is offered (given to God); it is a sacrament (communion) in as much as it is taken as food (given to men)."[6] We further concluded that, as a sacrifice is, above all, an action, an act which consists in the oblation of the victim, and as the eucharistic rite truly brings us the sacrifice of

---

[1] See Chap. 11, p. 100.
[2] *Summa Theol.*, III, q. 93, a. 1 ad 3.
[3] *Conc. Trid.*, Sess. 22, 1; see further Chap. 3 above, p. 22.
[4] *Conc. Trid.*, Sess. 22, Can. 1; Denzinger, 948.
[5] *Summa Theol.*, III, q. 73, a. 5 ad 2.
[6] *Summa Theol.*, III, q. 79, a. 5.

The Consecration and Elevation

Calvary, not only the victim once offered, but also the act of oblation by which Christ delivered himself up as a victim to his Father on Good Friday must be made present. The historical act of oblation made by the high priest of the new covenant was superlatively holy, laden with all the religion, adoration and love of the Father of which Christ's priestly soul was capable. This priestly and oblatory act—which redeemed the world—is made present in the Mass which is therefore the highest of all forms of worship. The primarily sacrificial, oblatory orientation of the Mass has, however, all too often been forgotten: we reverse it absolutely, applying it entirely to ourselves, relating it to our own ends, " our spiritual profit ". Voided of the element of offering, the Mass appears to be merely a pious " exercise " in which the priest exercises his power to change bread into the body and wine into the blood of Christ—a ceremony which is productive of communions, assuring us of a supply of consecrated hosts. The holy sacrifice of the Mass then becomes merely a preparatory or introductory pre-eucharistic rite, which brings us the object of true eucharistic devotion, by which our souls are fed, the divine " Prisoner of the tabernacle " whom we visit! Public devotions to the Blessed Sacrament are not of divine institution (as are the sacrifice and communion) but are of ecclesiastical origin: it was in reaction against the heresies which, in various ways, denied the real presence that in and after the eleventh century the Latin Church inaugurated a public cultus of the worship of the consecrated Host. The most recent forms of this cultus of the Eucharist are most venerable and of great importance, but, in comparison with Christ's institution, they are secondary forms. There can, indeed, be no true comparison between a brief low Mass, in which the very sacrifice of our Redeemer is made present with all its power to give glory to the Father, and exposition or a procession of the Blessed Sacrament, however solemn, in which we, poor sinners, pour out upon the sacred Host our humble and always-deficient human worship, however fervent it may be.

THE CONSECRATION OCCUPIES A CENTRAL PLACE IN THE LITURGICAL ECONOMY OF THE MASS

It is not, therefore, surprising that the rite of consecration occupies a central place in the liturgical economy of the sacrifice—

indeed there is an obvious equilibrium between the pre- and post-consecratory rites in the canon of the Mass: the separation of the *Sanctus* and *Benedictus*, the placing of the *Memento* of the living before and that of the dead after the consecration; the two lists of saints, the signs of the cross (3 + 5 before, 5 + 3 after), etc. Furthermore, the whole of the offertory liturgy is subordinate to the consecration, because it is its preparation, and the whole of the liturgy of the communion is subordinate, because it constitutes the fullness of the participation of both priest and faithful in the offering of the eucharistic sacrifice in the consecration.

THE ELEVATION

The elevations of the sacred Host and chalice are indubitably the most impressive ceremonies of the Mass as far as the faithful present are concerned. The rubrics of the Missal make this appear quite natural and might give the impression that the ceremony is as old as the consecration itself:

"The celebrant ... standing upright, elevates the Host as high as he conveniently can, and fixing his eyes upon it (as he does at the elevation of the chalice also) shows it reverently to the people for their adoration."[1] "Taking the chalice with the Blood in both hands, he elevates it as before (i.e. as he did the Host) and, raised as high as he conveniently can, he shows it to the people for their adoration."[2] Yet this ceremony appeared in the Mass for the first time only in the thirteenth century at Notre-Dame in Paris. Furthermore, before the eleventh century, no signal announced the moment of consecration.

The eleventh century was disturbed by a new, anti-eucharistic heresy. Berengarius of Tours († 1088) denied transubstantiation and possibly even the real presence of Christ in the eucharistic species. This, like all other dogmatic errors, provoked a twofold reaction, the one, on the part of theologians, probing the doctrine ever more deeply to refute the objections made to it, the other, religious and practical on the part of the people, who witnessed to their faith in suitable devotional practices. Although Berengarius' errors had no direct influence upon the institution of the rite of elevation, indirectly they contributed a great deal to the drawing of the attention of the faithful to the consecrated Host: the new trend

[1] *Rit. serv.*, 8, 5.   [2] *Rit. serv.*, 8, 7.

in medieval devotion became particularly noticeable in the increasingly obvious desire of the faithful to see the sacred Host.

What was the custom at the consecration at that time? If he is to grasp the Host at the words *accepit panem* the priest must of necessity lift it up and, in the twelfth century, the celebrant commonly raised it chest-high, or even higher, as Archbishop Hildebert's poem on the holy sacrifice shows. This practice was not without danger: the priest visibly elevated the Host throughout the prayer *Qui pridie*, yet the words of consecration were said in an undertone: the faithful might easily fall into the error of adoring that which was as yet only bread.

This then was the situation when, at the beginning of the thirteenth century, Eudes de Sully, Bishop of Paris, published a decree forbidding the raising of the Host above chest-height before the words of consecration and ordering its elevation *ita quod possit ab omnibus videri* after the words *Hoc est corpus*.[1] It cannot be denied that this decree instituted a new ceremony, a new elevation of the Host, which must henceforward be raised high enough to be seen by all after the consecration.

The genuflexions, too, date from about this time. The Carthusian Missal, which has preserved ancient traditions, does not mention them, and ritual genuflexion was prescribed for the priest before and after the consecration only in the eleventh century. According to *Ordo XIV* (1311), the priest used to bow his head in adoration of the precious blood. Having appeared in Burchard's *Ordo* (1502), the genuflexions passed naturally into the Roman Missal of 1570.

The new ceremony of elevation suited the mind of the times very well, and mystics and theologians soon began to discuss it. Thus St Gertrude, the Abbess of Helfta (1256–1301), teaches in her *Insinuationes divinae pietatis* that those who lovingly perform this devotion will be granted especial joys in the beatific vision. William of Auxerre (*c.* 1150–1232) was the first theologian to discuss the point authoritatively. In his *Summa aurea* he poses the strange question, " Whether they sin mortally who, when in mortal sin, gaze upon the sacred Host "; he replies in the negative because this exercise may in itself bring them to great love and he adds that God

[1] *Statuta Eccl. Parisiensis*, p. 11 (Paris, 1777).

is especially inclined to grant petitions made by the faithful as they contemplate the sacred Host. St Albert the Great († 1280) approved of elevation on the principle *ostensio boni provocat ad bonum* and later theologians have supported his view.

But even the best customs may give grounds for abuses and that of elevation gave rise to many in the Middle Ages, mostly based on the people's great desire to see the consecrated Host: soon it was regarded as the highest form of devotion to be present at as many elevations as possible, and in some churches the congregation would leave immediately after the elevation. Such abuses were not restricted to the faithful alone: in Germany, for example, many priests began to display the Host in every direction, so that all might see.

The Church, of course, reacted strongly against such abuses as may still be seen in the Ritual with regard to the Viaticum: *(Viaticum) . . . alicui ad adorandum solum, vel devotionis seu cuiusvis rei praetextu, ad ostendum non deferatur.*[1]

Henry of Hesse († 1397) declared unambiguously that for some of the faithful it would be better not to gaze on the sacred Host and attacks on the abuses were maintained until the longing to gaze on the Host began to fade towards the end of the Middle Ages. The Councils of Cologne (1536), Augsburg (1548) and Rheims (1583) insist that the faithful remain bowing low throughout the elevation and this was the universal custom by the eighteenth century.

Yet, according to the rubrics of the Missal, the priest elevates the Host and chalice in order to show them to the people: they then ought to adore, raising their heads and looking at both Host and chalice; and therefore, on 12 June 1907, St Pius X granted an indulgence of seven years to all who at the elevation (and during solemn exposition) look upon the sacred Host with faith, devotion and love and say " My Lord and my God! " Those who perform this devotion daily can gain a plenary indulgence once a week.

The faithful should kneel and should bow their heads low when the priest genuflects before and after each elevation; they should raise their heads and adore the sacred Host and the chalice during each elevation.

[1] *Rit. Rom.* V, 4, 5.

The Consecration and Elevation 223

Elevation of the chalice dates only from the fourteenth century and was ordered only by the Roman Missal of 1570: interest here was not so great as the customary use of metal chalices made it impossible for the faithful to see the consecrated wine.

RELATED CEREMONIES

The lifting of the chasuble.—At the moment at which the celebrant elevates the Host and chalice, the deacon at high Mass (the acolyte at low Mass) lifts up the hem of the chasuble from the right side.[1] In the twelfth century, when the priest was vested in a chasuble of circular cut, it was necessary to lift its hem to free his arms at the elevation.

Censing of the host at the elevation dates from the thirteenth century.

The tower bell.—Its ringing at the elevation is a signal to draw the attention of the faithful to the consecration: its introduction is usually attributed to Gregory XI (1371-7) but it seems that he merely extended a local French practice to the universal Church, for it was ordered by William of Paris in 1208.

The sanctuary bell.—The custom of ringing a bell inside the church began in 1215: the present regulations require three strokes (*ictus*) on the bell at each elevation at all Masses except low Masses at an altar of solemn exposition (or other altars during such exposition) or during choral office or processions in church, and on Maundy Thursday and Good Friday.

Silence.—Singing should be silenced during the elevation, but a low-pitched and soft chord on the organ is permitted.

CONCLUSION

1. The faithful must be instructed with regard to the importance of the mystery of the consecration by which is made present not only Christ's body and blood but also his act of oblation through which he gives glory to the Father; their attention must be concentrated upon the sacrifice as the highest form of adoration. The faithful should not only acclaim Christ's real presence on the

[1] *Rit. serv. in celeb. Miss.*, 8, 6.

altar but should also unite themselves actively to his sacrifice, offering it to the Father with him.

2. It is important that the practice of ringing the tower bell during the elevation at high and sung Masses should be restored in accordance with the prescriptions of the *Ceremonial of Bishops* (1, 6, 3) so that the sick and absent, being suitably instructed, may join from afar in the offering of Christ's body and blood.

AT THE HEART OF THE EUCHARISTIC SACRIFICE: THE ANAMNESIS

THE rite of consecration is the central mystery of the holy sacrifice of the Mass; it brings us not only what is offered—the eucharistic body and blood of Christ—but also the act of oblation, by which Christ offers them up to the Father. The Church gives further expression to this in the prayer following the consecration, which is called the *anamnesis*, the " commemoration ". Together, the consecration and anamnesis constitute the Church's ritual response to the Master's command; " Do this in commemoration of me ". We examined the consecration in the last chapter: we must now consider the Lord's command itself and the Church's response, the anamnesis.

THE LORD'S COMMAND: "DO THIS IN COMMEMORATION OF ME"

At the end of the Last Supper Christ said to the Apostles: " Do (ποιεῖτε) this in commemoration of me " (Luke 22. 19). " Do this ": the Apostles are to repeat all that Christ has just done and said, both ceremonies and prayers. We translate τοῦτο ποιεῖτε as " do this ", but notice that the verb which commonly means " to do ", " to perform an act ", can also often mean " to perform a sacred act ", that is " to offer ": it may therefore relate here to a ritual act of oblation.

Expression of the anamnesis in liturgy often echoes the Lord's command. Thus, Serapion's anaphora, after the consecration of the bread, reads: " Wherefore we also making the likeness of his death (το ὁμοίωα τοῦ θανάτον ποιοῦντες), offer bread ", and again, after the consecration of the chalice: " Wherefore we, too, offer this chalice, fulfilling the likeness of blood." In our Latin liturgy, in a similar way, *agere*, *facere*, and *operari* are used of offering the eucharistic sacrifice. Christ not only commanded " do this ": he also explained, " in commemoration of me ".

The Mass is thus a commemorative celebration: if we place the institution of this rite in its true setting—on the eve of his passion (Latin liturgy), the night on which he was betrayed (Eastern liturgies)—it is obvious that Christ was referring to the commemoration of his death. St Paul rightly declared: "So it is the Lord's death that you are heralding, whenever you eat this bread and drink this cup, until he comes" (I Cor. 11. 26): the holy Eucharist, the Apostle is saying, is the commemoration of the death of Christ. Just as the annual immolation of the paschal lamb commemorated the deliverance from Egypt, so also the eucharistic rite is the commemoration of Christ's redeeming sacrifice.[1]

Christ's words, however, were more than a command: they also conferred upon the Apostles that priestly power without which Christ's command would have been valueless.[2]

Thus in a single utterance Christ instituted the priesthood and initiated the holy sacrifice of the Mass: priesthood and sacrifice are indissolubly bound to one another. Christ ordained his first priests so that they might offer the holy sacrifice. The Council of Trent stresses the unity between priesthood and sacrifice once again in its declaration that "Sacrifice and priesthood are, by God's ordinance, united . . . wherefore as under the New Testament the Catholic Church has received the holy and visible sacrifice of the Eucharist by the Lord's institution, it must also be declared that there is in her a new and external priesthood into which the old has been changed."[3]

Celebration of Mass—the "liturgy"—is the fundamental means by which this priesthood is exercised: in the mind of Christ, the life of the priest is basically and from its outset, liturgical.

THE ANAMNESIS: THE CHURCH'S RESPONSE TO CHRIST'S COMMAND

The primary role of the anamnesis is to give expression to the act of oblation performed in the consecration: following Christ's example, by his command and in his power, the Church celebrates

---

[1] This is the teaching of the Council of Trent: Sess. 22, 1.
[2] See chap. 4, pp. 29 ff., and especially the decree of the Council of Trent, p. 9, and the canon, p. 32.
[3] Sess. 22, 1; Denzinger, 949.

the Eucharist, thus making sacramentally present Christ's redeeming sacrifice (both the victim and the act of offering) at the consecration itself. But such is the profundity of the mystery of consecration that the Church feels bound to give expression to and enlarge upon the act of oblation she has just performed, and this she does in this first prayer after the consecration.

To his command "Do this", Christ added the explanation, "in commemoration of me": the Church therefore prays *Unde et memores* in the anamnesis, the commemoration.

It must be remembered that if, when we offer the holy sacrifice, we commemorate the passion and death of our Saviour, we do not do so in a subjective manner—in an act which originates or exists only in our mental faculty of memory—but that the eucharistic rite is itself the sacramental and objective commemoration of the death of Christ. When we consecrate bread and wine, we commemorate the redeeming passion and death of our Saviour in a real, objective manner. The unity between the consecration and the anamnesis is so perfect that in the *Liber Ordinem* (Mozarabic) the latter is called *Collatio post pridie* or, more briefly, *Post pridie*, and in the Gallican liturgy *Post mysterium* and *Post secreta*. In his treatise *De Missa et Orationibus*, St Isidore of Seville († 636) includes them both under the single title *Confirmatio Sacramenti*.[1] In both the liturgy of the Apostolic Constitutions and the Anaphora of Serapion, the anamnesis and the consecration are bound together in one.

THE TEXT (see next page)

Calling therefore to mind: the mysteries commemorated.—As it is the objective commemoration of Christ's redemption, this rite must commemorate, first, the mysteries of death and triumph (the passion, resurrection and ascension), and secondly, the preparatory and complementary mysteries (the incarnation, nativity and *parousia*).

Originally, the anamnesis commemorated the Lord's *passio* in the primitive Christian meaning of that word—that is, not only the passion but rather the whole of the mystery of the redemption, the saving death and glorious resurrection-ascension together, for the resurrection is an integral part of the mystery of the redemption:

[1] *De Ecclesiasticis Officiis*, 1, 15.

The Mass

DE SACRAMENTIS (fourth century)	MISSALE ROMANUM [1]	ROMAN MISSAL
Ergo memores	Unde et memores (a) Domine, nos servi tui (b) sed et plebs tua sancta, ejusdem Christi Filii tui Domini nostri (c)	CALLING therefore TO MIND the blessed Passion of this same Christ, thy Son, our Lord,
gloriosissimae ejus passionis et ab inferis resurrectionis, et in caelum adscensionis, offerimus tibi	tam beatae passionis, nec non et ab inferis resurrectionis, sed et in caelos (d) gloriosae ascensionis:	and also his resurrection from the grave, and glorious ascension into heaven, we thy servants, Lord, and with us all thy holy people,
	offerimus praeclarae majestati tuae de tuis donis, ac datis, hostiam ✠ puram, hostiam ✠ sanctam, hostiam ✠ immaculatam Panem ✠ sanctum vitae aeternae, et Calicem ✠ salutis perpetuae.	OFFER to thy sovereign majesty, out of the gifts thou hast bestowed upon us, the pure Victim, the holy Victim, the spotless Victim, the sacred Bread of everlasting life, and the Cup of eternal salvation.

for just as Christ died for us, so also is he risen for us (cf. Romans 4. 25). The Mass is therefore the commemoration of Christ's resurrection, and this mystery has been commemorated in the anamnesis since the earliest times. In Hippolytus' *Traditio Apostolica*, for example, we read: " Wherefore, remembering his death and resurrection, we offer bread and the chalice to thee . . ."; and in the Der-Balyzeh papyrus: " We proclaim thy death and confess thy resurrection and beseech . . . ".

The ascension, too, is part of the economy of redemption for, by his sacrificial suffering and passion, Christ subjected to himself the empire of souls and became king by right of conquest:[2] he won the right to be the father (the new Adam) of a restored humanity, to transmit to it once again life divine. By his blood, he has won to himself the Church. Before passing on to us the " spiritual life ", that is, the " life of the Holy Spirit " which he had won for us on the cross, Jesus had to obtain the recognition of his conquest. As a conqueror he went up to heaven and displayed the evidence of his victory, his sacred wounds: at once the Father's bounty gave

---

[1] In the Gelasian Sacramentary the prayer is the same except at the following points: (a) *memores sumus;* (b) *tui servi;* (c) *Christi filii tui Domini Dei nostri;* (d) *in caelis.* The crosses are not marked (Wilson, p. 235).

[2] Cf. Leo XIII, Encycl. *Annum sacrum*, 25 May 1899.

his supreme sanction to Christ's triumph by the sending of the Holy Spirit. St John writes: " The Spirit ... had not yet been given to men [Pentecost], because Jesus had not yet been raised to glory [Ascension] " (John 7. 39). This mystery of ascension is therefore also commemorated in the majority of anamneses. Thus, for example, in the liturgy of the Apostolic Constitutions: " Wherefore we, remembering his passion and death, his resurrection from among the dead and his ascension into heaven . . . offer unto thee . . ."

The resurrection and ascension of Christ, then, are both part of the mystery of redemption. Both have a liturgical significance for they are the manifestation of the Father's acceptance of the victim offered on the cross, where the words of consecration assumed their fullest significance: " This is my body, given for you ". . . " This is my blood which is to be shed for you ". But external, visible giving and offering calls for external and visible acceptance. In the Old Testament this was frequently signified by the outpouring of fire from heaven upon the victims;[1] the Father likewise bestowed on Christ's sacrifice visible ratification: he raised the holy victim from the dead and assumed him into his glory.

When Jesus gave up his soul to his Father intrinsically his sacrifice was perfect and complete. But a sacrifice is offered in order to be accepted and without this acceptance it is useless. As the offering of the sacrifice is an external, visible rite so its acceptance must be also. Under the old Covenant God often showed his acceptance by sending down fire from heaven to consume the victim offered in his honour; this he did, for example, with the sacrifices of David, Solomon, Elias, etc. These figures could not be without their fulfilment in reality and to Christ's offering with the shedding of blood corresponds the Father's public acceptance, exalting the sacred Victim by causing him to rise in glory from the tomb and by assuming him into heaven.

> In Jewish sacrifices [wrote Pope Benedict XIV († 1758) in his commentary *De sacrosancto Sacrificio Missae*] the victim was burned upon the altar of holocausts so that all that was imperfect in it was consumed by the flames and the smoke went up as a sweet-smelling savour, as the Scripture says. Under the new Law, the victim was consumed in the resurrection and

[1] See, e.g., Gen. 15. 17; Judges 6. 19–20; I Par. 21. 26; II Par. 7. 1–2; I Kings 18. 38.

ascension of Christ. For in the resurrection, what was mortal in Christ was absorbed by life, as the Apostle says in the second Epistle to the Corinthians, and what was corruptible in him was taken away; and in the ascension, the victim was accepted by God as an odour of sweetness and placed at his right hand.

The Resurrection.—Notice that it was the victim of the sacrifice who was raised up: the uncreated flame of the Father's glory was poured out upon him and raised up his flesh, henceforward incorruptible and clothed in immortality. By so glorifying the victim offered in his honour, the Father openly manifested his acceptance of him into his glory. Far from weakening Christ's position as victim, the resurrection strengthens it, for it is the Father's act of acceptance of his offering upon the cross.

Furthermore, in raising Christ from the tomb, the Father confirmed him in his high priesthood. " He did not raise himself to the dignity of the high priesthood," St Paul wrote; " it was God that raised him to it, when he said, Thou art my son, I have begotten thee [by raising thee from the dead] this day " (Heb. 5. 5): in his resurrection, he was shown to be the *Pontifex futurorum bonorum* (Heb. 9. 11).

The Ascension.—By assuming the victorious Lamb into his glory, the Father set the seal of his ultimate ratification upon Christ's sacrificial work. The ascension is thus the fulfilment of all the mysteries of Christ, who descended into this world as the high priest of the new covenant and re-ascended to the Father as its glorified victim. Offered and immolated in bloodshed upon the cross, glorified in his resurrection, raised to the heavens in his ascension, the immortal Lamb now abides forever in his condition as glorified and accepted victim upon the altar on high. The holy sacrifice of the Mass, which commemorates the sacrifice of the cross in the only way declared acceptable by the Father, also commemorates, therefore, this sign of the divine acceptance and ratification of that sacrifice.

The preparatory and complementary mysteries: the Incarnation, the Nativity and the Parousia.—In many anamneses, commemoration of the preparatory and complementary mysteries of the redemption

—and especially the incarnation and manifestation (epiphany) or the nativity and the triumphal return, the parousia at the end of time—has been added to the central nucleus of the redemptive mysteries.

The Incarnation and Nativity.—The incarnation of the Word is intimately connected with the redemption of the world through the sacrifice of the cross. When the Word, the second Person of the Holy Trinity, took on human nature, there came into being Jesus Christ, the God-man, the priestly mediator, standing between God and men, and it was the divine nature of the Word which consecrated him, anointed him, made him " Christ " for ever. It was by virtue of this anointing and the priestly power it bestowed that Christ was enabled to offer sacrifice for the redemption of the world. It was in his incarnation that he received from Mary the body and blood that he was to offer upon the cross. This fact was clearly recognized and plainly stated in early liturgies, such as that of the *Traditio Apostolica* of St Hippolytus, but in our Roman anamnesis it seems to be a ninth-century innovation, probably of Gallican origin, for it is first expressed in Latin in a ninth-century manuscript known as Reims 213.

The Parousia.—St Paul wrote: " So it is the Lord's death that you are heralding, whenever you eat this bread and drink this cup, until he comes . . . " (I Cor. 11. 25–6). The Eucharist is a sacramental rite which will come to an end only with the world; in instituting it, the Council of Trent teaches, Christ desired that it should be the commemoration of his death until the end of time: *in finem usque saeculi*,[1] when all sacramental signs, having become superfluous, will come to an end and the glorious reality will be revealed unveiled. Eastern anamneses commemorate this revelation of the parousia especially vividly and in the Ambrosian liturgy it is linked directly with the Lord's command, " Do this ": " Each time that you do this, you will do it as my memorial; you will profess my death, proclaim my resurrection and hope for my coming until I come again to you from heaven." [2]

As it celebrates all these mysteries, the anamnesis is a profession of faith, and this is particularly obvious in the Eastern liturgies and in the Mozarabic liturgies which were so strongly influenced by

---

[1] Sess. 22, 1; Denzinger, 938.
[2] The Stowe Missal contains an almost identical passage.

them; indeed, Visigothic anamneses frequently begin *Credimus* (we believe), *Annuntiamus* (we proclaim) or *Confitemur* (we confess).

WE OFFER: "OFFERIMUS"

(a) "*We, thy priests*" (*nos servi tui*).—Christ offered himself once for all, in bloodshed, upon the cross. Likewise, he once offered himself personally without bloodshed, sacramentally, at the Last Supper. He left his eucharistic sacrifice to his beloved Bride, the Church, whom he charged to offer it again in every place until the end of time, and, in accordance with their Master's command, this his priests do.

Servus, in liturgical usage, means "priest" (as opposed to the congregation—*plebs tua*) and *servitus*, "priestly ministry" (as, for instance, in the prayer *Hanc igitur oblationem servitutis nostrae*). Expressions equivalent to the phrase *nos servi tui* occur in many ancient anamneses: as, for example, in the anaphora of Hippolytus: "Wherefore we remembering . . . offer bread and the chalice unto thee, giving thanks to thee that thou hast found us worthy to stand before thee and minister"; and in the Apostolic Constitutions: "In accordance with his command, we offer unto thee, King and God, this bread and chalice, giving thee thanks through him that thou hast found us worthy to stand before thee and exercise the priesthood for thee."

The use of the plural form *nos servi tui* recalls the ancient custom of concelebration (joint celebration by several priests) which is still practised in the East, and survived in the West in certain circumstances until the thirteenth century, since when it has disappeared except in the ceremonies of ordination to the priesthood and the consecration of bishops.

(b) "*And with us all thy holy people*" (*sed et plebs tua sancta*).—By virtue of their baptism, the Christian "people" (*plebs*) also share effectively in the offering of the sacrifice. The faithful are not, of course, mediators between God and the people; but there is offered to the Lord by the hands of the priest a sacrifice which originates in material gifts of bread and wine, created by God (*de tuis donis ac datis*) and presented by the people (in the offertory rite). As we have already noted,[1] by virtue of their baptismal character, Christian people share in a mysterious but very real way

---

[1] Chap. 5 above, pp. 42, ff.

in Christ's priesthood. The whole Church, as it is the mystical body of the high priest, is a priestly body: *gens sancta, regale sacerdotium* (I Peter 2. 9). Because the Priest offers the sacrifice on behalf of the faithful, they offer through him.[1]

Tua: Both priests and people are marked with the indelible seal of Christ: they bear the mark which shows that they belong to him. *Vos estis Christi*, St Paul wrote to the baptized of Corinth: "You are Christ's".

Sancta: As well as impressing the indelible character upon the soul, baptism infuses into it sanctifying grace for the holy fulfilment of our participation in Christ's priesthood.

Offerimus: Our active participation in our high priest's offering is expressed in its fullness in this word, which constantly recurs in all ancient anaphoras.

De tuis donis ac datis: Despite the wondrous transubstantiation effected by the priest's consecration, the eucharistic offering, the gift (*dona*), yet remains theirs in its origin: they supplied the bread and wine, the accidents of which are essential to Christ's eucharistic presence. It is, then, from created things, from the Lord's terrestrial gifts (*de tuis donis ac datis*), that we take in order to make a heavenly offering to him.

The sign of the cross: According to the Missal, the priest must make the sign of the cross three times over the chalice and host *hostiam ✠ puram, hostiam ✠ sanctam, hostiam ✠ immaculatam*), once over the Host alone (*Panem ✠ sanctum*) and once over the chalice alone (*calicem ✠ salutis petpetuae*). All five of these signs of the cross appear in the Sacramentary of Angoulême (eighth–ninth century), but in later Sacramentaries that over the Host alone is sometimes omitted as the first three were, in early times, made over the Host alone; for symmetry, both final signings were omitted in some Missals.

---

[1] Chap. 7 above, pp. 56 ff.

21

THE CANON FROM THE ANAMNESIS TO THE FINAL DOXOLOGY

THE PRAYERS FOR THE ACCEPTANCE OF THE EUCHARISTIC SACRIFICE: *SUPRA QUAE* AND *SUPPLICES*

Our offering of the holy sacrifice must be matched by the Father's acceptance of it into his glory. This is the purpose of the two following prayers. The texts date back to St Ambrose's treatise *De Sacramentis*. Comparison of our prayers *Supra quae* and *Supplices* with this archetypal text reveals that (a) they are closely related to the anamnesis and, in fact, continue it, and (b) that in *De Sacramentis* the order of the parts is reversed: the elements now forming *Supplices* precede those now forming *Supra quae*.

"SUPRA QUAE"

The relative pronoun refers to our oblations, which have been substantially transformed into the body and blood of Christ under the persisting accidents of bread and wine. *Respicere digneris* is taken from Genesis 4. 4: *respexit Deus ad Abel et ad munera ejus.*

As in the anamnesis we offer (*offerimus*) the body and blood of Christ to the Father, so here, in *Supra quae*, we beseech the Father to be pleased to accept our offering (*et accepta habere*). In the light of the distinction established above[1] between the thing offered (*res oblata*) and the act by which we offer that thing (*oblatio rei*), the meaning of this prayer is obvious. We ask the Father to look benevolently upon and to accept, not the thing offered in itself (that is, the eucharistic body and blood of Christ which are infinitely acceptable as such), but the act of oblation by which we, who are sinners, offer this infinitely worthy oblation. In other words, we ask the Father to accept the body and blood of Christ as offered by our sinful hands. It is for this reason that the Church now

[1] Vol. 1, Chap. 1, pp. 2f; Chap. 3 above, p. 28; Chap. 5, p. 48; Chap. 19, pp. 218-9.

De Sacramentis[1] (fourth century)	Roman Missal[2]	
(a) . . . et petimus et precamur ut hanc oblationem suscipias (b) in sublimi altari tuo (c) per manus angelorum tuorum, sicut suscipere dignatus es munera pueri tui justi Abel, et sacrificium patriarchae nostri Abrahae et quod tibi obulit summus sacerdos Melchisedech.	Supra quae propitio ac sereno vultu respicere digneris: et accepta habere sicuti accepta habere dignatus es munera pueri tui justi Abel, et sacrificium Patriarchae nostri Abrahae: et quod tibi obtulit summus sacerdos tuus Melchisedech, sanctum sacrificium, immaculatam hostiam. Supplices te rogamus, omnipotens Deus: jube haec perferri per manus sancti Angeli tui in sublime altare tuum, in conspectu divinae majestatis tuae: ut quotquot ex hac altaris participatione sacrosanctum Filii tui Cor✠pus et san✠guinem sumpserimus, omni benedictione caelesti et gratia repleamur. Per eundem Christum Dominum nostrum. Amen.	On these offerings be pleased to look with a favourable and gracious countenance, and accept them as it pleased thee to accept the offerings of thy servant Abel the just, and the sacrifice of our Patriarch Abraham and that which thy great priest Melchisedech offered to thee, a holy offering, a victim without blemish. (A) Humbly we ask it of thee, God almighty: bid these things be carried by the hands of thy holy angel up to thy altar on high, before the face of thy divine majesty, (B) so that those of us who by taking part in the sacrifice of this altar shall have received the sacred body and blood of thy Son, may be filled with every grace and heavenly blessing: through the same Christ our Lord. Amen.

commemorates three men of pre-eminent sanctity: Abel the Just, Abraham our father, the forefather of all the faithful because of his great faith (cf. Gal. 3. 7), and Melchisedech, the great high priest whose name means King of Justice, who was King of Salem, the King of Peace (Heb. 7. 2). What they offered is not here important —the point is that their act of oblation was holy because they were holy, and therefore their offering was holy. We pray that our act of oblation of the body and blood of Christ may be as holy as theirs, that is, pleasing to God and therefore accepted by him.

According to the *Liber Pontificalis*, the phrase *sanctum sacrificium, immaculatam hostiam* was added to the text by St Leo I († 461) against the Manichees who maintained that the use of wine—and therefore the eucharistic rite—is evil. It was to combat this error

---

[1] *De Sacramentis*, 4, 4, 27; P.L., 16, 445.

[2] The text in the Gelasian Sacramentary is identical except that the crosses are omitted.

that Pope St Gelasius († 496) temporarily forbade the distribution of communion under the accidents of bread alone.

Anti-semitism and Liturgy.—At the height of anti-semitic demonstrations in 1938, Pope Pius XI spoke of this prayer thus: "*Sacrificium patriarchae nostri Abrahae:* notice that Abraham is called our forefather, our ancestor. Anti-semitism is not compatible with the sublime thought and reality expressed in this text. . . . The promise was made to Abraham and his issue. The text, St Paul points out, does not say *in seminibus tamquam in pluribus, sed in semine tamquam in uno, qui est Christus* (Gal. 3. 16). The promise is fulfilled in Christ and, through Christ, in us who are the members of his mystical body. Through Christ and in Christ, we are the spiritual issue of Abraham. . . . Spiritually, we are Semites."

" SUPPLICES "

This prayer is orientated in two directions: (a) from earth to heaven, praying that our offering may be carried from our terrestrial altar to the *sublime altare* in heaven by the hands of an angel, (b) from heaven to earth, asking that from this " carrying up " abundant outpourings of " grace and heavenly blessing " may fill the souls of the communicants.

(a) *From earth to heaven* (from the beginning to *in conspectu divinae majestatis tuae*).—Comparison of this prayer with that in *De Sacramentis* shows it to be a prayer for the acceptance of our sacrifice. *Supplices* has suggested the low bow which now accompanies it; in the Middle Ages the priest sometimes crossed his arms over his chest (*cancellatis manibus*) as the Carthusians and Dominicans do today. The construction *rogamus-jube* appears somewhat strained, but in former times the priest could insert a particular intention here: *hic orat apud se quod voluerit, deinde dicat: Jube* is read in some manuscripts.

Jube haec perferri: " bid these things be carried (to heaven) ".—The demonstrative pronoun *haec* here corresponds to the relative (*Supra quae*) and comparison with *De Sacramentis* shows that it refers to " this offering " (*hanc oblationem*)—not, that is, to the body and blood of Christ, the object offered, but our poor, wretched act of offering of this divine victim. St Thomas notes that we ask that the angel may bear to the sublime altar of heaven not the body of Christ, which abides there continually, but the act of oblation, the offering which we make of it in our prayer upon our earthly altar.[1]

Per manus sancti Angeli tui in sublime altare tuum, in conspectu divinae majestatis tuae.—The identification of this angel has aroused a great deal of controversy. Some see him as the Holy Ghost, others as the Word.

But the underlying text preserved in *De Sacramentis* obviously speaks of the created angels: *per manus angelorum tuorum*, and this interpretation is confirmed by the passage in the Apocalypse which inspired this text: " There was another angel which came and took his stand at the altar, with a censer of gold; and incense was given him in plenty, so that he could make an offering on the golden altar before the throne, out of the prayers said by all the saints " (Apoc. 8. 3). The same conclusion, moreover, is suggested by comparison of *Supplices* with Eastern prayers of oblation, and many liturgists therefore, rightly, see this as an angel, a celestial spirit, in the usual sense of the word.

It is not possible to determine which angel is referred to here: some identify him with the angel who guards the church or altar, others with the priest's guardian angel. The reference is, however, probably to St Michael, the Defender of the Church, or perhaps to a personification of the angelic hosts who attend the celebration of the holy sacrifice. As he does our prayers, the angel bears our act of oblation to the heavenly altar.

Sublime altare is explained by the phrase later set in apposition to it *in conspectu divinae majestatis*:[2] it means the Godhead itself. The altar, in fact, receives the oblation in God's stead: it is the throne of the Godhead. " Blind fools, which is greater, the gift, or the altar that consecrates the gift? " (Matt. 23. 19).

(b) *From heaven to earth* (from *ut quotquot* to the end).—This second part (lacking in *De Sacramentis*), which prays for an abundant outpouring of " every grace and heavenly blessing " on behalf of the communicants, is to some degree similar to—without actually being an example of—Eastern and Western epicleses. It is first found in the Gelasian Sacramentary (liturgy of the fifth–sixth centuries). Some learned liturgists (such as Duchesne, Dom

---

[1] *Summa Theol.*, III, q. 83, a. 4 ad 9.
[2] This phrase does not occur in *De Sacramentis;* in the oldest manuscripts in which it is found, it is expressed in the accusative *in conspectum*.

Cabrol and Salaville) believe that these two parts of the canon—*Supra quae* and *Supplices*—together constitute a true (Roman) epiclesis of an intentionally subdued and mysterious kind. Others (including Batiffol, Bishop, Callewaert, Dom de Puniet, Varraine, Dom Botte), on the other hand, express serious reservations or even deny its possibility. The importance of the problem posed by these sections is such that we shall discuss it and the epiclesis below.

At the words *ex hac altaris participatione*, the priest kisses the altar on which the eucharistic body and blood of Christ are lying: the altar is the image of Christ, the living altar.[1] At the sacred words *Corpus* and *Sanguinem*, the priest makes the sign of the cross over the Host and chalice. The Eucharist is the source of all grace: when saying the words *omni benedictione caelesti et gratia repleamur*, he makes the sign of the cross upon himself.

Finally, notice that the conclusion *Per eundem Christum Dominum nostrum* is not primitive.

ADDITIONAL NOTE: THE EPICLESIS

In all Eastern and many Western anaphoras there are prayers called epicleses (ἐπίκλησις means invocation) which are placed after the consecration and in which the Father is invoked to send down the Holy Ghost upon the bread and wine that, by his divine power, they may be transubstantiated, becoming the body and blood of Christ, and that the holy Eucharist may produce abundant fruits of salvation in the communicants. Occasionally the epiclesis prays for the descent of the Word to produce the same effects.

Thus, the Latin version of Hippolytus' *Traditio Apostolica* asks the Father to " send down thy Holy Spirit upon the oblation of thy holy Church " and grant that " the saints who communicate may be filled with the Holy Spirit to be strengthened in faith and truth ". The anaphora of Serapion of Thmuis contains an original epiclesis which asks for the descent not of the Holy Ghost but of the Word: " O God of truth, let thy holy Word come down upon this bread, that the bread may become the body of the Word, and upon this cup, that this cup may become the blood of the truth. And grant that all those who participate therein may receive a life-giving remedy." The epiclesis of the fourth-century *Apostolic Constitutions* asks for the sending of the " Holy Ghost, the witness

---

[1] Vol. 1, Chap. 3, pp. 31 ff.

of Christ's sufferings that he may make this bread into the body of thy Christ and this chalice into the blood of thy Christ, and that those who share therein may be confirmed in piety, receive the remission of sins, be delivered from the devil and his lures, be filled with the Holy Ghost, and being made worthy of thy Christ, may obtain eternal life."

These epicleses raise two problems: Why is there this close intimate connection between the Holy Ghost and the eucharistic sacrifice? And how may we explain the placing of this invocation for consecration after the consecration itself?

The consecration is effected by the divine power which, as such, is an attribute of the three divine Persons: it is the greatest miracle wrought by the divine love. Now the Holy Ghost proceeds from the love of the Father and the Son and this work of love is therefore attributed especially to the Holy Ghost. "The power of the Holy Ghost," Leo XIII wrote, "has brought about not only Christ's conception, but also the sanctification of his soul, which is called anointing by the sacred books; all his deeds, and especially his sacrifice, were accomplished under the influence of the Holy Ghost. It is through the Holy Ghost that he offers himself, an unblemished victim, to God."[1]

With regard to the second problem, it must first be noted that eucharistic transubstantiation is the effect of the words of consecration alone and cannot be attributed to the epiclesis: schismatic Greeks, especially since the seventeenth century, have denied that the words *Hoc est enim corpus meum* are sufficient for consecration and maintain that an epiclesis is also necessary.

But against this we must set the teaching of the Church. The Council of Florence and the decree regarding the Armenians declared that the form of this sacrament consists in the words of our Saviour, and the Council of Trent[2] that "it has ever been believed in the Church of God that immediately upon the consecration the true body and blood of our Lord together with his soul and divinity are present under the species of bread and wine." In their letters to the peoples of the East, the popes have several times declared that an epiclesis is not necessary for consecration.[3]

[1] Encyclical, *Divinum illud*, 9 May 1897.
[2] Sess. 13, 3.
[3] E.g. Benedict XII (1341); Clement VI (1351); Benedict XIII (1729); Benedict XIV (1741); Pius VII (1822) and St Pius X (1910).

With regard to the position of the epiclesis, notice that, in general, the thanksgiving in the canon is set out according to a definite pattern: (a) thanksgiving for the creation and government of the world by the Father, who has sent his only Son (preface); (b) thanksgiving for the incarnation and redemption of the world by the Son (from the *Sanctus* to the epiclesis); and (c) thanksgiving for the Holy Ghost's mission of sanctification, by which the Son's mission is completed (epiclesis). The effect of the words of consecration is, of course, instantaneous, but so devoid of understanding are we before this transcendent mystery, that we are reduced to thinking successively and separately about its several aspects and to expressing them in a series of paragraphs although they are not in fact separable, and the pattern of our thinking follows that of the creeds and is inspired by the order of the three divine Persons. A similar order of events is to be found in Scripture itself: thus, the woman with the issue of blood was healed instantaneously when she touched the fringe of Christ's robe: Christ said " Be healed " to her only after the miracle had already occurred.

There still remains the question: is *Supplices* an epiclesis? As Callewaert has rightly pointed out, there is one most important difference between *Supplices* and a normal epiclesis: we ask that our offering be carried by an angel from our terrestrial altar to the heavenly altar and we beseech God to deign to accept it, whereas an epiclesis asks the Holy Ghost to come down from heaven on to our terrestrial altar to sanctify and consecrate our oblation there. As Batiffol has pointed out, there seems no reason why the entirely Roman *Supplices* should be compared with later and completely alien Greek, Gallican and Visigothic prayers. *Supplices* is not, strictly speaking, an epiclesis.

THE DIPTYCH *MEMENTO ETIAM* OF THE DEAD

(a) *Memento etiam, Domine, famulorum famularumque tuarum N. et N. qui nos praecesserunt cum signo fidei, et dormiunt in somno pacis.*

Remember also, Lord, thy servants N. and N. who have gone before us with the sign of faith and sleep the sleep of peace.

(b) *Ipsis, Domine, et omnibus in Christo quiescentibus, locum refrigerii, lucis et pacis, ut indulgeas, deprecamur.*

To them, Lord, and to all who rest in Christ, grant, we entreat thee, a place of cool repose, of light and peace:

| *Per eumdem Christum Dominum nostrum. Amen.* | through the same Christ, our Lord. Amen. |

This diptych is to be found neither in the Gregorian (seventh century) nor the Gelasian (*c.* 700) Sacramentaries and is lacking in various manuscripts dating from the seventh to the ninth centuries. One Mass in the Bobbio Missal, however, contains the Roman canon including this prayer. From the *Ordo* of John the Archcantor (seventh century), it appears that it was permitted to read the names of the dead on weekdays but not on Sundays; our *Memento* of the dead was only inserted into the canon after *Supplices* on ferial days and is therefore missing from many manuscripts of that period which contain only Masses for Sundays and feasts.

The prayer itself is composed of two clearly separate sections:

(a) from the beginning to *somno pacis*. This section is written in the style of the *Memento* for the living. Moreover, the names of the dead are mentioned, not after the letters N. and N., but at the end of this section, and a somewhat lengthy rubric divides this section from the next in the Missal.

(b) From *Ipsis, Domine* to the end.

Commentary.—According to Durandus of Mende († 1296), the priest used to say a private prayer for himself at this point; this, too, began *Memento*. This explains the conjunction *etiam* (also): the priest makes commemoration not only of himself, but also of the dead.

Qui nos praecesserunt cum signo fidei: The sign of faith is the indispensable baptismal character (cf. Eph. 1. 3; Apoc. 7. 3).

Et dormiunt in somno pacis; in Christo quiescentibus; locum refrigerii, lucis et pacis: A Christian cemetery (*cæmeterium*) is, as the root-meaning of the word itself suggests, the "dormitory" of the Christian community. While commemorating the names, the priest keeps his eyes fixed on the sacred Host (*intentis oculis ad sacramentum super altare*) whereas in the *Memento* for the living before the consecration he keeps them closed.

Locum refrigerii: The suffering souls in purgatory, thirsting for the beatific vision, long for the refreshment of beatitude where "the Lamb who dwells where the throne is, will be their shepherd, leading them out to the springs whose water is life; and God will wipe away every tear from their eyes" (Apoc. 7. 17). Primitive Christian art represented heavenly blessedness as a garden full of flowers, made fruitful by springs of water, where birds sang and flocks grazed.

Lucis: Heaven is the dwelling-place of light (cf. Apoc. 21. 23–5). Souls in purgatory groan in the darkness of that mysterious night in which "there is no working any more" (John 9. 4). In the catacombs the soul was often shown between two lights and inscriptions beseeching light for the dead are very numerous.

Et Pacis: Heaven is the abode of unbroken peace, that peace beyond all understanding. Such peace will soon be the lot of those of the suffering souls who were of good will.

Per eumdem Christum Dominum nostrum: During this conclusion, the priest bows his head. When he died upon the cross, Christ bowed his head and then, straightway, went down into limbo to deliver the righteous: the priest therefore bows his head and prays that the merits of the blood of Christ may be applied to the souls in purgatory and that they may be delivered from their sufferings: so those given to symbolism interpret this action, but their explanation has no historical basis. Brinktrine sees it as a practical signal, dating from the Middle Ages, by which the priest warns the clergy of the coming *Nobis quoque peccatoribus.*

THE DIPTYCH *NOBIS QUOQUE PECCATORIBUS*

Nobis quoque peccatoribus famulis tuis, de multitudine miserationum tuarum sperantibus, partem aliquam, et societatem donare digneris cum tuis sanctis Apostolis et Martyribus: cum Joanne, Stephano, Matthia, Barnaba, Ignatio, Alexandro, Marcellino, Petro, Felicitate, Perpetua, Agatha, Lucia, Agnete, Caecilia, Anastasia, et omnibus Sanctis tuis intra quorum nos consortium, non aestimator meriti, sed veniae, quaesumus, largitor admitte.
Per Christum Dominum nostrum.[1]

To us also, thy sinful servants, who put our trust in thy countless acts of mercy, deign to grant some share and fellowship with thy holy apostles and martyrs: with John, Stephen, Matthias, Barnabas, Ignatius, Alexander, Marcellinus, Peter, Felicity, Perpetua, Agatha, Lucy, Agnes, Cecily, Anastasia, and all thy saints. Into their company we pray thee to admit us, not weighing our deserts, but freely granting us forgiveness:
through Christ our Lord.

[1] The text in the Gelasian Sacramentary is identical, except that it lacks *partem aliquam societatem; Agathe; Agne; et cum omnibus sanctis.*

The Canon from the Anamnesis

According to the rubrics of the canon, the celebrant is to say the first words of this diptych *elata aliquantulum voce*[1]: this rubric perpetuates the memory of the ceremonial of the papal Mass at the time of Constantine, when the district subdeacons bowed low from the *Sanctus* to *Nobis quoque peccatoribus*.[2] When the canon was said in an audible voice (eighth century) no indication was needed to inform these ministers when to stand up straight again; in the ninth century it came to be recited in a low voice and thus some such signal became necessary. As a result a direction was inserted for the celebrant (originally the pope) to raise his voice at the beginning of this diptych. When saying these words, the priest strikes his breast: the gesture is in keeping with the words.

Famulis tuis means primarily the priests themselves; the *Sacramentarium Rossianum* extend the meaning of the word to cover both men and women: *famulis et famulabus tuis*.

This diptych and the *Communicantes* are closely related. The *Communicantes* refers to Mary, the Mother of God, the twelve Apostles and twelve martyrs. This diptych commemorates St John the Baptist, seven male and seven female martyrs. There are, however, striking differences between these two diptychs: (a) in *Communicantes*, the list of saints forms a natural part of the text, but in this prayer the style is forced as the repetition of the preposition *cum* shows: the list of saints is probably a late interpolation; (b) the list of martyrs named here is not of so markedly a Roman character as that of the *Communicantes*; (c) in *Communicantes*, we commend ourselves to the intercession of the saints here below, in *Nobis quoque peccatoribus* we ask that, cleansed from all sin, we may be admitted into their company above.

St John the Baptist.—This *Joannes* was always identified with St John the Baptist in the Middle Ages. There should be nothing surprising in the great devotion of the Roman Church to St John the Baptist. Scripture reveals him as a very great saint: "He is to be high in the Lord's favour" (Luke 1. 15), the angel said to Zachary, high in favour by reason of his mission and his holiness; "when he is yet a child in his mother's womb he shall be filled with the Holy Ghost": he was conceived in original sin, but born without stain of sin; he was, moreover, a great prophet, "something

---

[1] *Ritus servandus* says *vocem aliquantulum elevat* (Tit. IX, 3).
[2] Chap. 16, pp. 179–181.

more . . . than a prophet" (Matt. 1. 9). "There is no greater than John the Baptist among all the sons of women (Luke 7. 28); cf. Matt. 11. 11). St Thomas explains this passage by placing it in the context of the Old Testament: there is no greater as *a prophet* than John the Baptist; among all the forerunners of Christ he is the forerunner in the highest sense of the word. All the prophets were precursors, but only St John was *the* Precursor; his mission was unique. Furthermore, he was the witness to the light, he baptized Christ, and named him "the Lamb that takes away the world's sins"; he was a great penitent (Luke 1. 80); he remained unmarried and died a martyr. In the liturgy, the hierarchy of the saints is determined not according to their degree of sanctity—which must be unknown to us—but according to the closeness of their relationship with the Redeemer as such during his public ministry and thus John, the Precursor, stands at the head of this list. The whole Church was dedicated to him by Sergius III († 911), and the pope's cathedral—the Archbasilica of the Lateran—is dedicated to him as are five other shrines in Rome. Both his birth (24 June) and his beheading (29 August) are commemorated in the general calendar of the Church. Twenty-three popes have borne his name.

St Stephen.—In the fifth century, shortly after the discovery of his relics, several basilicas were built in Rome in honour of Stephen, the deacon of Jerusalem, the first martyr, and in the Middle Ages there were thirty-five churches and chapels dedicated to him in Rome alone. His feast is celebrated on 26 December.

St Matthias.—He was one of the seventy-two disciples and after our Saviour's ascension was elected to the Apostolic College to replace Judas. His feast is celebrated on 24 February (leap-year, 25 February).

St Barnabas.—St Paul honoured him with the title of Apostle, and the Church follows his lead, for the Holy Ghost named him with St Paul for the evangelization of pagans. After his apostolic journeyings with St Paul, he lived in Cyprus. His feast is celebrated on 11 June.

St Ignatius.—Christian antiquity venerated St Ignatius as a personal disciple of St Peter; he was consecrated bishop by the Prince of the Apostles and was his second successor in the see of Antioch. He was arrested in Trajan's reign and carried to Rome. On the

The Canon from the Anamnesis 245

journey, he wrote seven epistles. He died a martyr in one of Rome's amphitheatres in 110 or 118, and his relics were taken to Antioch. His feast is celebrated on 1 February.

St Alexander.—According to Batiffol, this martyr was not the first pope of that name, but one of the seven sons of St Felicity buried in the *Coemeterium Jordanorum*. Cardinal Schuster, on the other hand, believed that this was the martyr whose tomb lies some six miles from Rome on the *via Nomentana*, who is commemorated, with two companions, on 3 May.

SS. Marcellinus and Peter.—Marcellinus was a priest, Peter an exorcist: they were beheaded near to the *Silva nigra* on the *Via Cornelia* under Diocletian. Their feast is celebrated on 2 June.

SS. Felicity and Perpetua.—Many believe that Felicity is the Carthaginian martyr of that name who suffered with Perpetua in 336. Others maintain that she was the Roman mother of seven sons who were martyred with her (23 November). In former times the list at this point read *Perpetua, Agnes, Caecilia, Felicitas,* and the reference to the Carthaginian Perpetua may have attracted the name of the Roman *Felicitas* which was also the name of her companion in martyrdom in Africa. The African martyrs were thrown to wild beasts together on 7 March 202 or 203, but as 7 March is the *natale* of St Thomas Aquinas, Pope St Pius X ordered the anticipation of their feast by one day.

St Agatha.—This famous Sicilian martyr died at Catania in 251 under the Emperor Decius. Her feast is celebrated on 5 February.

St Lucy.—She was born at Syracuse and underwent martyrdom under Diocletian in 304. Her feast is celebrated on 13 December.

St Agnes.—Despite her extreme youth—she was aged between eleven and thirteen years—St Agnes gathered the palm of martyrdom under Diocletian (or Decius). Pope Honorius I († 638) translated the martyr's head from her first resting-place in *agello suo* to the *Sancta Sanctorum* in the Lateran and a scientific examination of the relics in 1902 revealed the saint's age at death. Her feast is celebrated on 21 January.

St Cecily.—A Roman virgin and martyr who died, probably, in the third century. Her feast is celebrated on 22 November.

St Anastasia.—A native of Sirmium whose relics were translated to the church of the Resurrection (*Anastasis*) at Constantinople and, later, to Zara in Dalmatia. Her cultus grew popular at Rome in the Byzantine period where her *dies natalis* was celebrated on 25 December.

THE END OF THE CANON

Per quem haec omnia, Domine, semper bona creas, sancti✠ficas, vivi✠ficas, bene✠dicis, et praestas nobis.

Through him, Lord, thou dost ever create these things that are good, thou dost hallow, quicken, bless and give them to us.

Per ip✠sum, et cum ip✠so, et in ip✠so, est tibi Deo Patri ✠ omnipotenti, in unitate Spiritus✠Sancti, omnis honor et gloria.

Through him, and with him, and in him, is to thee, God the Father almighty, in the unity of the Holy Spirit, all honour and glory,

Per omnia saecula saeculorum.
℞ *Amen.*

for ever and ever.
℞ Amen.

Notice, first, that the three sentences which form the end of the canon are clearly separated from one another by rubrics.

"PER QUEM . . . PRAESTAS NOBIS"

Many liturgists believe that this is a fragment of a prayer said over the offerings of the fruits of the earth which used to be made, together with bread and wine, by the faithful and which were blessed in the course of the holy sacrifice. Mgr Callewaert's studies led him, however, to an entirely different conclusion.[1] He suggests that comparison with the usage in the rest of the canon makes it certain that the demonstrative *haec* here signifies the eucharistic oblations present upon the altar. The use of *omnia* although there is but one Host and a small quantity of wine actually present today was fully justified of the eucharistic oblations in, say, the fifth century when large numbers of loaves and huge chalices of wine were consecrated for the communion of the faithful in both kinds.[2]

Bona, it is suggested, should be translated as an adjective, as though the sentence read . . . *haec omnia semper creas bona*: in other words, "all that thou hast created, that thou hast preserved in being, is good." The text then stands revealed as based firmly

---

[1] See *La Finale du Canon de la Messe* in *Rev. d'Hist. éccl.*, vol. 39 (1943), pp. 5–21.
[2] Cf. the secrets for 24 June, "We heap up gifts upon thine altars", and the Mass of Abbots, "May the offerings we lay upon thy sacred altars . . ."

on Genesis 1 and a counter to the errors of the Manichees who, in the fifth century, maintained that matter was created by an evil principle and therefore rejected bread and wine and the Eucharist.

The end of the canon, then, certainly relates to the sacrificial offerings and it is to them that the verbs (a) *creas*, (b) *sanctificas, vivificas, benedicis*, and (c) *praestas*, refer.

(a) *Creas:* Although what God receives as the result of the offering of the holy sacrifice is the body and blood of his divine Son, our offering begins with bread and wine, whose accidents persist, and thus, as in the anamnesis, we can here speak of our offering as created (*offerimus . . . de tuis donis ac datis*). Indeed, what else can we offer except God's own gifts as symbols of our homage?

(b) *sanctificas, vivificas, benedicis:* Fundamentally, these three words are synonymous and refer to the consecration.

(c) *et praestas nobis:* There is an obvious reference here to the communion.

Thus, in these five verbs, there is revealed the outline of the whole of the holy sacrifice:

1. The offering to God of created, terrestrial gifts (*creas*).
2. The consecration of our offerings, by which they are sanctified (*sanctificas*) and changed into the living body and blood of Christ (*vivificas*) and so are most fully blessed (*benedicis*).
3. Holy Communion in the sacrifice, in which God returns our gifts to us now made divine (*praestas*).

Blessing of the fruits of the earth.—In former times blessings of the fruits of the earth were inserted at this point on certain days. In the Leonine Sacramentary, the blessing was of water, milk and honey; in the Gregorian, of grapes (6 August, St Sixtus). The *Sacerdotale Romanum* (1580) prescribes the blessing of wine and fruits (3 February, St Blaise), bread (5 February, St Agatha) and of the paschal candle. The oil of the sick is still blessed at this point in the pontifical Mass on Maundy Thursday.

THE DOXOLOGY: " PER IPSUM, ET CUM IPSO, ET IN IPSO "

The Christian doxology is, as we have seen,[1] firmly rooted in Scripture; during the early centuries it was gradually enlarged until it named all three divine Persons explicitly. The oldest

[1] Vol. 1, Chap. 18, pp. 133–5.

doxologies are addressed to the Father or the Son, or (especially from the second century onwards) to the Father through the Son. The Trinitarian form, rare in the second century, became standard in the third. In the West, the normal form is *Gloria Patri et Filio et Spiritui Sancto* and in the East, *Gloria Patri per Filium in Spiritu Sancto*.

The doxology in the anaphora of St Hippolytus is closely related to that of our canon: *ut te laudemus et glorificemus per Puerum tuum Jesum Christum, per quem tibi gloria et honor, Patri et Filio cum Sancto Spiritu, in sancta Ecclesia tua, et nunc et in saecula saeculorum. Amen.* The present form is more concise, dignified and solemn: in it we give all honour and glory to the almighty Father, through Christ, the God-man, the priestly mediator between God and men, in the unity of the Holy Ghost. We give this glory to the Father not only through Christ (*per ipsum*) but also to the Son with the Father (*cum ipso*), for he, too, is God, co-equal with the Father and with him the recipient of his own priestly glorification, and in Christ (*in ipso*), for the Son is in the Father, as the Father is in the Son, and both Father and Son are in the Holy Ghost, as the Holy Ghost is in them.[1]

In the realm of ideas, there is a close connection between *Per quem* and *Per ipsum*, for it is through Christ (*per quem*) that the Father bestows the saving gift of the holy eucharistic sacrifice upon us and it is through him (*per ipsum*), Christ, that we give all honour and glory to the Father.

CEREMONIES

After the *Per quem*, the priest uncovers the chalice, genuflects, takes the Host between his right thumb and index finger and the chalice in his left hand and traces three crosses over the chalice with the Host saying: *Per ip✠sum, et cum ip✠so, et in ip✠so*; then, with the same Host, he makes the sign of the cross twice between the chalice and himself, saying: *est tibi Deo Patri ✠ omnipotenti, in unitate Spiritus ✠ Sancti*; then he elevates the chalice and Host a little whilst saying: *omnis honor et gloria*. The elevation is the only primitive ceremony at this point.

[1] Another view, which accords with Hippolytus' *in sancta Ecclesia tua*, explains the doxology of Christ and his Church, his mystical body, which glorifies the Father through him, as through its head, with him, being united with his offering, and in him, because, by the grace of the Holy Ghost, she lives in and offers in Christ.

The Canon from the Anamnesis

According to *Ordo I* (eighth century), when the pope has said *Per quem* the archdeacon is to raise the chalice, the two handles of which were covered with a cloth (*offertorium*). The pope raises the host at the same time and touches the edge of the raised chalice with it, saying: *Per ipsum . . . honor et gloria*. This rite would seem to have signified that Christ's eucharistic body and blood constitute *one* sacrificial offering. There is no mention of signs of the cross. Immediately afterwards the chalice and *oblatae* were placed on the altar again. The two last signs of the cross are to be found in *Ordo II* (ninth century). According to this document the bishop *touches* the chalice at the side (*e latere*) with the Host with which he makes (but outside the cup) two signs of the cross. At this period, in fact, the Host was placed on the corporal not in front but to the right of the chalice.

When the Host came to be placed in front of the chalice the two signs of the cross were made between the chalice and the celebrant. These two signs of the cross appear to have been derived from the fact that there were two *oblatae*, that is, two large hosts at the papal Mass. These signs of the cross are frequently wanting in many of the manuscripts, even of the thirteenth century.

In the tenth century three signs of the cross make their appearance at *per ipsum* (1st), *cum ipso* (2nd) and *in ipso* (3rd). Since by this time only one large host was consecrated these three signs in conjunction with the three pronouns of the divine name of the Son are thereby explained.

According to Innocent III († 1216)[1] these three signs are to be made above the chalice. The practice is justified by the fact that the chalice contains the blood of Christ, the divine Person mentioned by the text. The two other signs made outside the chalice refer to the two other divine Persons.

Finally there follow the Little Elevation (*elevatio minor*), the only one in the Mass until the twelfth century and the only one to be found even nowadays in the eastern liturgies. The imposing ceremony of this elevation, which forms the solemn conclusion of the thanksgiving of the canon, is a final expression of the intuitive and striking nature of the oblation of the eucharistic sacrifice which goes up from our hands to the honour and glory of the Blessed Trinity. In addition, this elevation forms a part of the ceremonies

---

[1] *De sacro altaris mysterio*, 5, 7.

preparatory to the communion. The priest raises the Host and shows it to the faithful to inform them that communion is about to be given.[1] In the same way he holds up the Host at the communion of the faithful or of the sick outside Mass, saying: *Ecce Agnus Dei, ecce qui tollit peccata mundi.*

"PER OMNIA SAECULA SAECULORUM. AMEN"

Today, this conclusion is separated from the doxology by a rubric; the priest sings or says *Per omnia saecula saeculorum* only after replacing the Host upon the corporal, covering the chalice with the pall and genuflecting. Until the twelfth century, the conclusion followed the doxology without a break and was said during the elevation. The division was first mentioned by Stephen of Beauge, Bishop of Autun († 1136), but was still not universal in the fifteenth century. It passed into the Roman Missal of 1570 through Burchard's *Ordo*.

Amen: This Amen is the Christian community's ratification of the whole of the eucharistic thanksgiving (notice that this is the only Amen in the canon marked ℞). The repeated Amens in the canon first appeared in ninth- and tenth-century manuscripts, but were confirmed only in the Missal of 1570. This final Amen is, however, unique among them, for " when we respond to the doxology with the triumphal Amen, we make ourselves one with Christ and his Church in confessing the eternal glory of God, together with the triumphant success of his merciful plans for the world ".[2]

---

[1] See below, Chap. 24.
[2] Dom J. de Puniet, *La Liturgie de la Messe*, p. 191.

22

THE LORD'S PRAYER

THE Lord's Prayer is the most typical of all Christian prayers in that (a) it was composed and taught by Jesus Christ himself (Matt. 6. 9); (b) it is the prayer proper to the Children of God, the baptized; (c) it is, as Tertullian says, a summary of the whole Gospel.[1] It is, therefore, not surprising that it occupies a prominent place in the holy sacrifice. On the one hand, it constitutes, as it were, an extension of the thanksgiving and offering of the canon (in its first three petitions, which give glory to the Father); on the other, it is a most fitting preparation for holy communion (in its petitions, especially the fourth and fifth, which implore graces for us): "Give us this day our daily bread. And forgive us our trespasses, as we forgive them that trespass against us." Indeed, many of the Fathers believed that the fourth petition related to the Eucharist.

The saying of the fifth petition with contrition was considered a sacramental of purification; St Augustine said, "Having cleansed our countenances with these words, we approach the altar".[2]

The *Pater* is used universally as a preparation for communion: with the embolism *Libera* it is said on Good Friday (although there is no Mass), and until the eleventh century was said before communicating the sick.

THE INVITATORY: WHY WE DARE SAY THE LORD'S PRAYER

This is a most presumptuous prayer: what pagan would ever have dared to call Jupiter or Apollo "My Father?" But what pagans would not dare we Christians, made partakers of the divine life, of the Word's own sonship, made children of God, by grace, not only in name but also in fact, and relying on Christ's express teaching, say not "Our God and Master" but "Our Father . . ."

---

[1] *Breviarium totius Evangelii* (*De Oratione* 1).
[2] *Sermo* 17, 5; *P.L.*, 38, 127.

Oremus: Praeceptis salutaribus moniti, et divina institutione formati, audemus dicere:	Let us pray. Urged by our Father's bidding, and schooled by his divine ordinance, we make bold to say:

St Jerome († 420) emphasized the presumption necessary to say this prayer: *Sic docuit (Christus) Apostolos suos, ut cotidie in corporis illius sacrificio credentes audeant loqui: Pater noster.*[1] Likewise, St Augustine said: *Audemus quotidie dicere: Adveniat regnum tuum.*[2] Theodoret († 458) wrote: "We teach this prayer to none of the uninitiated, but only to the faithful. No uninitiated person would dare to say: Our Father who art in heaven . . . before receiving the grace of adoption,"[3] and his teaching was generally accepted at that time, as early liturgies show. Thus, in the Roman rite, the words of the *Pater* were solemnly revealed to instructed catechumens as a sacred trust at the well-known ceremony *Aperitio aurium* on the fourth Wednesday in Lent. In the commentary—preserved in the Gelasian Sacramentary—which accompanied the tradition of the words, the attention of the catechumens is drawn to the temerity of those who, in prayer, dare to call God their Father.

THE LORD'S PRAYER

Pater noster, qui es in caelis: Sanctificetur nomen tuum: Adveniat regnum tuum: Fiat voluntas tua, sicut in caelo, et in terra.	Our Father, who art in heaven, hallowed be thy name. Thy kingdom come. Thy will be done, on earth as it is in heaven.
Panem nostrum quotidianum da nobis hodie: Et dimitte nobis debita nostra, sicut et nos dimittimus debitoribus nostris. Et ne nos inducas in tentationem.	Give us this day our daily bread. And forgive us our trespasses, as we forgive them that trespass against us. And lead us not into temptation:
℟. *Sed libera nos a malo.* Amen.	℟. But deliver us from evil. Amen.

THE LORD'S PRAYER IN THE MASS

Before St Gregory († 604).—The Lord's Prayer according to St Matthew (6. 15) is quoted in the *Didache* (90) with the doxology:

---
[1] *Adv. Pelag.*, 3, 15.
[2] *Sermo* 110, 5.
[3] *Haereticarum Jablarum compendium*, 5, P.G. 83,399.

The Lord's Prayer

" For to thee is the power and the glory for ever "—a doxology which seems to prove that the *Pater* was then said at the celebration of the Eucharist. But there is no clear evidence of its use at Mass until the fourth century—although it cannot be concluded from this that it was never used, particularly when its origins and especial value for this purpose are taken into consideration.

According to the commentary devoted to the holy sacrifice by St Cyril of Jerusalem († 386), the Lord's Prayer was then closely connected with the eucharistic thanksgiving in the canon and both were concluded by the same *Amen*.[1]

The *Pater* is linked with the canon in St Ambrose's treatise *De Sacramentis*, and St Augustine said: *ubi peracta est sanctificatio dicimus orationem dominicam*.[2] It would seem that so universal a usage must date back to the earliest times, but the liturgies of the Apostolic Constitutions (fourth century) and Serapion of Thmuis (*c*. 358) and the Constitutions of Hippolytus do not mention the *Pater*.

St Gregory.—St Gregory, who reformed the Roman liturgy at so many points on the pattern of the Greek liturgy, placed the *Pater* after the canon. To John, the Bishop of Syracuse, he wrote, " We say the Lord's Prayer immediately after the canon (*mox post precem*), for the Apostles were wont to consecrate the victim of the oblation (*oblationis hostiam*) only in connection with this prayer. It seemed most inconvenient to me that we should say over the oblation a prayer framed by a *scholasticus* and not recite the traditional prayer, which was composed by our Redeemer, over the body and blood of Christ. Among the Greeks, the Lord's prayer is also said by all the people, but among us by the priest alone." [3]

Some liturgists—including Batiffol[4]—infer from this text that, in St Gregory's time, the *Pater* was not said (or was no longer said) in the Mass, and that he introduced it. Others[5] conclude that the *Pater* until this time stood after the fraction, and that St Gregory moved it to its position after the canon and before the fraction, where it occurs in the Eastern liturgies of St James, St Mark, St Basil and St John Chrysostom. It would seem that this latter is

---
[1] *Catecheses mystagogica*, 5, 11–8; P.G., 33, 1118–23.
[2] *Sermo* 227 (P.L., 38, 1099); cf. *Ep*. 149, 16 (P.L., 33, 636).
[3] *Ep*. 9, 12 (26); P.L., 77, 956–8.
[4] *Leçons sur la Messe*, pp. 276–8.
[5] E.g. Duschesne, *Origines du culte chrétien* (1920), p. 195.

the most likely explanation for St Augustine testifies to the recitation of the *Pater* in the holy sacrifice by " almost the whole Church " (*fere omnis Ecclesia*): that Rome itself should provide an exception to this rule would be very strange if not inexplicable.

Why, then, did St Gregory move the *Pater* from after to before the fraction? It must be remembered that the fraction is a ceremony performed in preparation for communion and belongs to the fullness, but not to the essence of the eucharistic rite. Only the canon is essential to the liturgical sacrifice which is completed before the fraction. Now, the fraction used to be begun at the altar but completed away from it, at the throne and in the *presbyterium* and the pope used to say the Lord's Prayer before communicating at the throne after the fraction. But the whole trend of the first three petitions, which give glory to the Father, are scarcely suitable to this position and moment: St Gregory saw it as the natural complement of the thanksgiving and eucharistic oblation of the canon and he therefore judged it more logical and fitting that, following the example of the Greeks, it should be said in close relation to the canon.

COMMENTARY

Our Father, who art in heaven.—This fundamentally Christian prayer is addressed directly to the Father of our Lord Jesus Christ and of us. " Father " implies " child ": Christ is the Son by nature, we are sons, children, by participation, through grace, in the sonship of the Word. Christ, the only-begotten Son, always made this distinction: when speaking of himself and us, he said not " our Father " but " my Father and your Father " (John 20. 17); although, when speaking to us, he said " This, then, is to be your prayer, Our Father, who art in heaven " (Matt. 6. 9). Christians must pray in a Christian manner, to worship in spirit and truth not the God of the philosophers, but the Father of our Lord Jesus Christ, " our Father ". Furthermore, we say not " My Father " but " our Father " because the Christian is not an isolated individual but a member of a living body, the Church, which is a society, the prayer of which is collective. The prayer of the Christian is, in the first place, a universal prayer, a catholic prayer which makes no distinction of race, tribe or language.

Hallowed be thy name.—The Father is, of course, holy: the seraphim before the throne sing " Holy, holy, holy "; heaven and earth are full of his glory. But the Father's holiness must be recognized and acknowledged by men who see our good works (cf. Matt. 5. 16). This first petition, as St Thomas observes, is an act of faith.

Thy kingdom come.—May the Father's name be so hallowed that his rule may be acknowledged by all. The kingdom of God is both internal and external; internal, through sanctifying grace; external, in the hierarchical and social constitution of the Church. Although Christ's kingdom is not of this world (it is come down from heaven), it is, however, in this world. We ask, therefore, that the rule of God may grow in depth in souls and increase in extent by the incorporation into it of pagans. This earthly kingdom will one day be consummated in glory at Christ's triumphal return in the parousia; this second coming (*adventus*) is also envisaged in this petition, which, St Thomas remarks, is an act of hope.

Thy will be done on earth as it is in heaven.—This petition defines the previous one: the whole of Christian morality consists in fulfilling the will of the Father, and this will is love. May we, following Christ's example, fulfil it wholeheartedly, as sons, especially in times of trial: " My Father, if it is possible, let this chalice pass me by; only as thy will is, not as mine is " (Matt. 26. 39). This third petition, St Thomas notes, is an act of charity.

Give us this day our daily bread.—In this petition we solicit the food which sustains our natural lives. But here, just before the communion, we are asking for the bread of life which comes down from heaven and which will soon be distributed to the faithful, that they may participate fully in the holy sacrifice.

Moreover, many of the Fathers of the Church have understood the phrase ἄρτος ἐπιούσιος, *Panis supersubstantialis* (Matt. 6. 11), as referring to the heavenly bread, the holy Eucharist[1] and this is the exegesis made by the two oldest commentaries on the Mass: the fifth Catechetical Lecture of St Cyril of Jerusalem († 386) and *De Sacramentis* by St Ambrose.

And forgive us our trespasses, as we forgive them that trespass against us.—When said with true contrition, this petition contributes to the worthy preparation of the communicants: if we forgive others with all our hearts, the mercy of God will be poured out upon us.

---

[1] On this point see J. Lebreton, *La vie et enseignement de J.C.N.S.* vol. 2, pp. 78–80 (Beauschesne, Paris).

Christ attached so much importance to this petition that he returned to it immediately after saying the prayer: " Your heavenly Father will forgive you your transgressions, if you forgive your fellow men theirs; if you do not forgive them, your heavenly Father will not forgive your transgressions either " (Matt. 6. 14–5).

And lead us not into temptation.—God tempts no one, but he allows us to be tempted (cf. I Cor. 10. 13). The Greek word πειρασμός means not only temptation, but also all kinds of trials, persecution and suffering. We ask not that we shall be kept free from them (for trials may exert a purifying influence and be a source of great merits), but for the grace of God, that we be not overwhelmed by them.

But deliver us from evil.—The Greek Fathers interpret " evil " as " the evil one ", the devil, the Latin Fathers as evil in general.

WHY THE LORD'S PRAYER IS SUNG OR SAID ALOUD AT MASS

The rubrics concerning the recitation of the *Pater* might, at first sight, seem strange. At the Office, and other liturgical services, the *Pater* is said silently; except at the ferial *preces* of Vespers and Lauds when the officiant says it aloud. At Mass, on the other hand, it is always said or sung aloud. How did this difference arise?

As we have said, the *Pater* is a prayer proper to those who are baptized, to Christians. In former times neither the text of the creed nor that of the *Pater* might be written down; for fear of profanation, they were transmitted orally. St Ambrose once said: *Cave, ne incaute symboli vel dominicae orationis divulges mysteria . . . Dominica oratio quam vulgare non opus est.*[1] Only Christians, the baptized, were allowed to attend the eucharistic sacrifice and there this most Christian of prayers could safely be said or sung aloud. At the Offices, on the other hand, which the non-baptized might attend, the discipline of silence was rigidly enforced. The only exception to this rule—the recitation of the Lord's Prayer aloud at Lauds and Vespers—was first made by St Benedict († 543), and is justified in the monastic enclosure. When, later, the Benedictines were entrusted with the choral offices in the Roman basilicas, their monastic practice passed into the Roman rite.

It should be noted that according to the new *Ordo* for Holy Week (1956) on Good Friday the celebrant, his hands joined, and

[1] *De Cain*, II, 35, 37.

The Lord's Prayer 257

with him the whole congregation, recite the Lord's Prayer together (*recto tono*) wholly in Latin, concluding it with *Amen*. The restored Good Friday office is, in fact, a congregational communion service to which the Lord's Prayer forms the preparation (particularly on account of the petition "Forgive us our trespasses as we forgive them that trespass against us"). According to the Instruction of the S. Congregation of Rites (1958) at low Masses the congregation may say the Lord's Prayer (wholly in Latin with *Amen* at the end) with the celebrant.

THE EMBOLISM UPON THE SEVENTH PETITION:
"*LIBERA NOS, QUAESUMUS, DOMINE*"

At high Mass, at the end of the *Pater*, the subdeacon moves to the Epistle side of the altar and gives the paten to the deacon, who uncovers it, wipes it with the purificator and proffers it to the celebrant. The subdeacon then takes off the humeral veil and returns to the foot of the altar.

At low Mass, before the *Libera*, the priest takes the paten from beneath the corporal and purificator, wipes it with the latter and, with his right hand, holds it upright on the altar while he says the prayer *Libera*. The beginnings of our ceremony are to be discerned in those of *Ordo I*.[1]

Libera nos, quaesumus, Domine, ab omnibus malis, praeteritis, praesentibus, et futuris: et intercedente beata et gloriosa semper Virgine Dei Genitrice Maria, cum beatis Apostolis tuis Petro et Paulo, atque Andrea, et omnibus Sanctis, da propitius pacem in diebus nostris: ut ope misericordiae tuae adjuti, et a peccato simus semper liberi, et ab omni perturbatione securi. Per eumdem Dominum nostrum Jesum

Deliver us, we pray thee, Lord, from every evil, past, present, and to come, and at the intercession of the blessed and glorious ever-virgin Mary, Mother of God, of thy blessed apostles Peter and Paul, of Andrew, and of all the saints, be pleased to grant peace in our time, so that with the help of thy compassion we may be ever free from sin and safe from all disquiet. Through the same

[1] Cf. Chap. 9 above, pp. 76–7; Chap. 11, p. 95.

Christum Filium tuum, qui tecum vivit et regnat in unitate Spiritus Sancti Deus.	Jesus Christ, thy Son, our Lord, who is God, living and reigning with thee in the unity of the Holy Spirit:
Per omnia saecula saeculorum R̷. *Amen.*	World without end R̷. Amen.

Commentary

This prayer is an embolism of the last petition of the *Pater* and is found in the Gelasian and Gregorian Sacramentaries. The prayer is invariable in the Roman liturgy, but in the Gallican and Mozarabic it changed at each Mass. Formerly the *Libera* was sung like the *Pater*. This practice survived only on Good Friday. According to the new Holy Week *Ordo* the *Libera* is said aloud by the celebrant *alone* after the collective recitation of the *Pater*.

This prayer reveals the incompatibility of evil and peace. We ask to be delivered from all evil, whether past, present or to come. Sin and its results are the greatest evils and against them the Church invokes the mighty intercession of Mary, of its guardians, SS. Peter and Paul, and of St Andrew.[1] In the Middle Ages, celebrants mentioned other names—such as St Michael, St John the Baptist, St Stephen, or the patron of the diocese or monastery—after these.

. . . *da propitius pacem in diebus nostris*. The whole prayer turns upon this petition, which is paralleled by *diesque nostros in tua pace disponas* which St Gregory caused to be inserted into the *Hanc igitur* when Italy was ravaged by plague and famine and Rome was besieged by the Lombards.

At these words, the priest makes the sign of the cross upon himself with the paten, kisses its edge, slides it under the host and finally sets it down, with the host, a little to the right of the centre of the corporal. In former times, the sign of the cross was made together with the conclusion (*Per D.n.J.C.*) and the fraction was performed after the prayer; later, when the fraction came to take place during this conclusion, the sign of the cross was anticipated and connected to the principal petition of the prayer.

---

[1] Invocation of St Andrew here is usually attributed to St Gregory the Great, but this cannot be proved, especially as the Apostle's name occurs in some Gelasian Sacramentaries.

ADDITIONAL NOTE: THE NUPTIAL BLESSING AND EPISCOPAL BLESSINGS

In nuptial Masses (*pro Sponso et Sponsa*) the nuptial blessing is placed between the *Pater* and *Libera* in our Missal. The priest turns to the bride and groom and says a twofold blessing. This is the only trace in the Roman rite of the ancient *Benedictiones episcopales* that the bishops of France and Germany used to bestow upon the people at pontifical Masses. They had passed from Eastern into Visigothic and Gallican liturgies, even into the Masses celebrated by a simple priest; these blessings were probably intended for those of the faithful who were not going to communicate. After the *Amen* of the *Libera*, the deacon turned to the congregation and cried *Humiliate vos ad benedictionem;* the bishop then pronounced the words. The bishop then took the crozier and blessed the congregation with a triple sign of the cross: *Benedictio Dei omnipotentis Patris et Filii et Spiritus Sancti descendat super vos et maneat semper.* Rome was opposed to this insertion; but the use of these *Benedictiones* was so firmly implanted in Gallican countries that neither the decrees of Pope Zachary (751) nor of Charlemagne succeeded in abolishing them. These *Benedictiones* are still in use today in the Church of Autun, where they are permitted because of their immemorial antiquity.

23

PREPARATION FOR HOLY COMMUNION

The greater the soul's capacity by charity to receive grace, the more abundantly will that grace be poured into it in holy communion. That is why preparation for communion is so important—even more important than thanksgiving. We must prepare for communion by being sorry for our sins (in acts of contrition, the prayers at the foot of the altar), by confessing our faith (in the Mass of the Catechumens), by accepting sufferings and sacrifices, mingling them, like the drop of water in the chalice of wine, and offering them in Christ's great sacrifice (in the offertory and consecration). We must long to be united as closely as possible in victimhood with Christ himself that we may be offered with him to the glory of the Father (communion). By active participation in the various phases of the holy sacrifice of the Mass, the soul is gradually prepared to be abundantly filled with the graces poured out in holy communion: such intelligent, devout and active participation in the Mass itself is the best—and natural—preparation for communion. As this great rite draws near, the Church supports this preparation by suitable ceremonies and prayers which in the Mass extend from the lesser elevation to the *Domine, non sum dignus*. These ceremonies and prayers fall into two groups.

1. FROM THE LESSER ELEVATION TO THE KISS OF PEACE

The primitive substratum consists in the three ceremonies:

(a) THE LESSER ELEVATION: the priest elevates the sacred host to warn the faithful that communion is about to be distributed;

(b) THE FRACTION; the eucharistic bread is broken for distribution to the faithful;

(c) THE COMMIXTURE: the eucharistic bread is mingled with the

The ceremonies in their present order	Antiquity	St Gregory († 604)	Eleventh Century
1. LESSER ELEVATION (in the doxology of the canon)	×		
2. Pater and Libera		×	
3. FRACTION (during the conclusion of Libera)	×		
4. Pax Domini		×	
5. COMMIXTURE (with Haec commixtio) and the singing of the Agnus Dei	×		
6. Domine J. C., qui dixisti			×
7. Kiss of Peace		×	

Precious Blood so that the faithful may receive the two species, not as separate entities, but as united in one.

In the present rite (a) the elevation[1] has been separated from this other ceremony and has lost much of its primitive significance; (b) the fraction[2] is no longer linked with the communion of the faithful, as only the priest's host is broken.

We summarize here a very penetrating study by Dom B. Capelle:[3]

THE FRACTION AND COMMIXTURE IN THE CEREMONIAL OF PONTIFICAL MASS (*Ordo Romanus I*, eighth century)

(A) *When the Pope himself celebrated*

The paten was held before the pope by the second deacon. The pontiff, after saying *Pax Domini sit semper vobiscum*, blessed the chalice three times. The longer recension of *Ordo I* here adds *mittit in calicem de sancta* (the commixture), but Dom Capelle has conclusively proved that this clause is an interpolation;[3] the natural sequence to *Pax Domini* is the kiss of peace.

The first Fraction: The pope then broke one of his two *oblata* and placed one half of it on the altar and the other (with the unbroken *oblata*) on the paten; he then returned to his *cathedra*, preceded by the deacon with the paten. Dom Capelle believes that the fragment left upon the altar was the *fermentum* which the pope

---
[1] See Chap. 21, pp. 248–49.
[2] See Chap. 22, p. 258.
[3] *Le rite de la Fraction dans la Messe romaine* in Rev. Bénéd., 53 (1941), pp. 16–26.

sent to the city churches (*tituli*). There then followed the real fraction.

The second Fraction: The archdeacon elevated the consecrated chalice. The acolytes approached the altar with their *saccula* slung about their necks. The archdeacon filled the *saccula* with the consecrated *oblata* from the altar and the acolytes took them to the bishops and priests in the *presbyterium* for the fraction. The pope himself took no part in this, the true fraction which is a direct preparation for communion: his one-and-a-half oblata were broken by his two deacon-escorts. Under the Greek Pope Sergius I (687–701) the *Agnus Dei* was sung, in accordance with Byzantine custom, during this general fraction by the bishops and presbyters.

The third Fraction: After the fraction, the deacons proffered the paten to the pope. He took one fragment, detached a particle and consumed the rest. The archdeacon then carried the chalice from the altar to the throne.

The Commixture: The pope placed the detached particle of the *oblata* in the chalice, saying: *Fiat commixtio et consecratio, etc.*, and communicated in the Precious Blood.

(B) *When the Pope himself did not celebrate*

In this case, the ceremonial was somewhat different.

(a) If the *fermentum* (a fragment of *oblata* consecrated by the pope) was brought to the bishop before the *Pax Domini*, he made the sign of the cross three times and placed it in the chalice, saying *Pax Domini*, etc. (*Ordo I*, supp. 1): this commixture was performed not after, but during the *Pax Domini*. The *fermentum* was a bond, joining all Masses in space: the pope sent it to the bishops and priests of the *tituli;* in their turn, bishops would send a fragment of their Eucharist to their priests, and (in giving communion) priests gave their Eucharist to the faithful.

(b) If the *fermentum* was not brought to the bishop: In this case, commixture as in (a) was still performed at the altar during the *Pax Domini* (*Ordo I*, supp. 2), the bishop breaking one of his own hosts. This was a new ceremony which corresponded to the first fraction at papal Masses.

Thus, at a pontifical Mass when the pope himself did not celebrate, there were performed (a) the fraction of the *oblata*, (b) the threefold sign of the cross and (c) the commixture during *Pax Domini*.

The modern ceremonies

The fraction before the *Pax Domini* has been preserved, and now takes place during the conclusion of *Libera;* the triple sign of the cross is still made, but now during the *Pax Domini;* the commixture has also survived. The true fraction—that at the throne when the pope celebrated—has now disappeared as small, unleavened hosts are now used for the communion of the people, but the *Agnus Dei* is still sung in its ancient position. The kiss of peace which was once introduced by *Pax Domini* has now been displaced and the tenth-century prayer *D. J. C. qui dixisti* interpolated into the rite.

THE FRACTION AND COMMIXTURE TODAY

(A) *The Fraction* ("*fractio*")

Whilst saying the conclusion of *Libera: per eumdem* . . . the priest breaks the sacred Host over the chalice into two parts and places the right-hand half on the paten. Then, over the chalice, he breaks a particle from the left half whilst saying *Qui tecum vivit*, etc., and places the remainder on the paten. One part of the Host is used for the priest's communion, another for the commixture and the third for the viaticum for the dying.

(B) *The Commixture* ("*commixtio*")

(1) The *Consignatio*: With the particle held between the thumb and index finger of his right hand, the priest makes the sign of the cross three times over the chalice, holding the knob of the chalice in his other hand and saying:

Pax ✠ *Domini sit* ✠ *semper vobis* ✠ *cum*. The peace of the Lord be always with you.

This custom became universal only in the thirteenth–fourteenth centuries. As soon as the people has answered *Et cum spiritu tuo*, the priest proceeds to the commixture.

(2) The Commixture (*commixtio*): Allowing the particle to fall into the Precious Blood, the celebrant says:

Haec commixtio, et consecratio Corporis et Sanguinis Domini nostri Jesu Christi, fiat accipientibus nobis in vitam aeternam. Amen.	May this sacramental mingling of the Body and Blood of our Lord Jesus Christ be for us who receive it a source of eternal life. Amen

Consecratio must here be understood in its oldest and most general sense, as "sanctification". It does not mean consecration in the narrower modern sense of that word.

The commixture was first practised because, when leavened bread was used in the Mass, the Eucharist—called *sancta* or *fermentum*—which was reserved from one Mass to the next, became hard and it was necessary to soften it before using it for communion. When the use of the *sancta* was discontinued, this ceremony was transferred to the Host of the Mass at which it was consecrated.

(C) *The Chant: "Agnus Dei"*

Having recovered the chalice with the pall, the priest genuflects; then joins his hands and bowing low, strikes his breast three times saying:

Agnus Dei, qui tollis peccata mundi: miserere nobis.	Lamb of God, who takest away the sins of the world, have mercy on us.
Agnus Dei, qui tollis peccata mundi: miserere nobis.	Lamb of God, who takest away the sins of the world, have mercy on us.
Agnus Dei, qui tollis peccata mundi: dona nobis pacem.	Lamb of God, who takest away the sins of the world, give us peace.

Christ is the Lamb of God, prophesied by Isaias, who by the shedding of his blood has merited the taking away of the sins of the world, and by the application of whose eucharistic blood they are indeed taken away from each communicant.

The *Agnus Dei* is today sung after the fraction: in former times it accompanied that ceremony. Actually, before the eighth century, the fraction took place in silence at Rome and it was the Greek Pope Sergius I who introduced this Byzantine custom there. It seems probable that the *Agnus Dei* was at first repeated as often as necessary until the fraction was completed and it was only in the twelfth century that the number of repetitions was fixed at three, all of which were everywhere concluded *miserere nobis* (as they still are today in the Archbasilica of the Lateran and on Maundy Thursday) until about the eleventh century when *dona nobis pacem* and *dona eis requiem (sempiternam)* (at Masses of the Dead) first appeared.

The new *Ordo* for Holy Week (1956) has restored the triple *miserere nobis*, as in the eighth century. In reality, as the kiss of peace is omitted, there is no reason to say *dona nobis pacem*.

THE PEACE

The Prayer for Peace

According to the rubrics of the canon, the priest should remain bowed low (*inclinatus*), keeping his hands joined and resting them on the near edge of the altar (*junctis manibus super altare*). The *Ritus servandus* (10. 3) adds that his gaze should be fixed on the sacred Host (*oculisque ad sacramentum intentis*).

Commentary

Domine Jesu Christe, qui dixisti Apostolis tuis: Pacem relinquo vobis, pacem meam do vobis: ne respicias peccata mea, sed fidem Ecclesiae tuae: eamque secundum voluntatem tuam pacificare et coadunare digneris: Qui vivis et regnas Deus per omnia saecula saeculorum. Amen.

Lord Jesus Christ, who didst say to thy apostles: I leave peace with you; it is my own peace that I give you: look not upon my sins but upon thy Church's faith, and deign to give her peace and unity in accordance with thy will: thou who art God, living and reigning for ever and ever. Amen.

Peace is the fruit of order: peace—with God, through sanctifying grace, divine charity, and with our neighbour through fraternal charity—is an absolute necessity for holy communion, the sacrament of charity.

Ne respicias peccata mea, sed fidem Ecclesiae tuae: It is the Church who is Christ's primary co-offerer of the holy sacrifice; the priest is her minister. The Eucharist originates rather from her hands than from his (*ab Ecclesia per sacerdotes immolandum*); the unworthiness of the minister can never lessen the worthiness of the offering made by the ever-holy Church.

Eamque pacificare: Deign to give peace to thy Church; that is, to her members: let peace reign among them.

Et coadunare digneris: May all the baptized (*co*) be gathered into (*ad*) the unity (*unum*) of the Church. May this unity grow ever stronger by growth in charity of all her members!

The Kiss of Peace

After the prayer for peace, the priest kisses the altar, and gives the kiss to the deacon, embracing him: he places both his hands on the deacon's arms and proffers him his left cheek, saying *Pax tecum*. The deacon, who has knelt through the prayer for peace and kissed the altar with the celebrant, bows his head, receives the peace and says *Et cum spiritu tuo*. They then both join hands and salute one another. The deacon gives the kiss to the subdeacon and he to the choir and to the acolyte who accompanies him. In the primitive Church the faithful used to exchange the kiss of peace in their everyday lives as well as at liturgical services, as a sign of charity and unity.[1]

This ceremony used to be performed before the offertory in the time of St Justin (and probably, therefore, at Rome) and in Eastern, Gallican and Visigothic liturgies always came before the preface. In the Roman rite—as at baptism and ordination—the *pax* usually concludes a ceremony; it occurs almost at the end of Mass today.

The peace which is passed from person to person originates directly from the eucharistic sacrifice: it is the peace itself, not the minister who passes it on, that is important and therefore he is not saluted with a bow before he gives the peace.[2] The kiss of peace is omitted on Maundy Thursday (from revulsion from Judas' betrayal), on Holy Saturday and at Masses of the dead, which were formerly part of a private liturgy.

According to the Missal and the Ceremonial of Bishops the kiss of peace is to be given at low Mass with what is called a *pax*, or *pax-brede* (*instrumentum pacis, osculatorium, paciferum* or *pacificale*, etc.); this is an instrument which came into use in the twelfth and

---

[1] See I Cor. 16. 20; II Cor. 13. 12; I Thess. 5. 26; Rom. 16. 16 and I Peter 5. 14.
[2] Cf. *Caer. Ep.*, I, 29, 8.

thirteenth centuries when it ceased to be the invariable custom to separate the sexes in church. The *pax-brede* is in the form of a flat plate, variable in shape, framed and fitted with a handle. It might be of almost any material, and was often richly decorated. According to the Missal and Ceremonial of Bishops, it is to be used at Masses when there is no deacon or subdeacon in giving the pax to all present, and at high Mass, in giving it to the faithful.

2. THE IMMEDIATE PREPARATION: THE PRAYERS BEFORE COMMUNION

In Christian antiquity, those who assisted at the holy sacrifice usually participated in it fully, by receiving holy communion, the earlier part of the Mass serving as their ideal and only preparation. Gradually, however, altars increased in number and low Mass at which only the celebrant communicated became more common, the offertory procession of the faithful disappeared and communion came to be distributed outside Mass on feast-days so that the concept of communion as the fullness of participation in the eucharistic sacrifice was forgotten by the faithful and communion came to be regarded as a private act of devotion, requiring private preparation. Before the tenth century neither Sacramentaries, Roman *Ordines* nor the commentaries of liturgists contained the slightest hint of any prayer of preparation for holy communion, although such prayers had begun to appear in books of private devotion in the ninth century. Gradually, however, such prayers crept first into the margins, then into the texts of copies of the *Ordo Missae;* by the thirteenth century, there were seventeen and four of these have been preserved by the Roman liturgy: *Domine Jesu Christe, Fili; Perceptio; Panem caelestem;* and *Domine, non sum dignus.* The fact that these were formerly private prayers is obvious for they are all formulated in the singular.

COMMENTARY

The first two of these prayers date from the ninth and tenth centuries; in his *Micrologus*, Bernard of Constance († 1100) affirms that they were both of monastic origin. They used to be said either before or after communion. Both are addressed to Christ and therefore during them the priest now keeps his eyes fixed on the sacred host.

(a) *Domine Jesu Christe, Fili*

This is the only prayer said formerly by the Cistercians, and today by the Carthusians and Dominicans, before communion.

Domine Jesu Christe, Fili Dei vivi, qui ex voluntate Patris, cooperante Spiritu Sancto, per mortem tuam mundum vivificasti: libera me per hoc sacrosanctum Corpus et Sanguinem tuum ab omnibus iniquitatibus meis, et universis malis: et fac me tuis semper inhaerere mandatis, et a te nunquam separari permittas: Qui cum eodem Deo Patre, et Spiritu Sancto vivis et regnas Deus in saecula saeculorum. Amen.

Lord Jesus Christ, Son of the living God, who, by the Father's will and the co-operation of the Holy Spirit, didst by thy death bring life to the world, deliver me by this most holy Body and Blood of thine from all my sins and from every evil. Make me always cling to thy commandments, and never allow me to be parted from thee: who with the self-same God the Father and the Holy Spirit art God, living and reigning for ever and ever. Amen.

Fili Dei vivi: With the faith that was Peter's at Caesarea and Mary's at Bethany, we greet the sacred Host as Christ himself, the Son of the living God.

Qui ex voluntate . . . vivificasti: Before requesting graces, we recall the mystery of redemption, the giving of life to the world through the merits of the Saviour Jesus. Redemption was the Father's will (cf. John 3. 16) and was contributed to by the Holy Ghost (cf. Hebrews 9. 14).

Libera me . . . meis: According to the doctrine of the Council of Trent, holy communion is "like an antidote by which we are delivered from our daily faults and preserved from mortal sins." [1] Venial sins may be remitted by fervent acts of charity—which themselves are produced by holy communion.

Et a te numquam separari permittas: Separation from Christ, which is brought about by mortal sin, is the greatest of evils; holy

---

[1] Sess. 13, 2; Denzinger, 875.

communion, according to the Council of Trent, preserves us from mortal sin.

(b) *Perceptio*

Perceptio Corporis tui, Domine Jesu Christe, quod ego indignus sumere praesumo, non mihi proveniat in judicium et condemnationem: sed pro tua pietate prosit mihi ad tutamentum mentis et corporis, et ad medelam percipiendam: Qui vivis et regnas cum Deo Patre in unitate Spiritus Sancti Deus, per omnia saecula saeculorum. Amen.	Let not the partaking of thy Body, Lord Jesus Christ, which I, unworthy as I am, make bold to receive, turn against me unto judgement and damnation, but through thy loving-kindness let it be for me a safeguard of mind and body, and in it let me find healing: thou who art God, living and reigning with God the Father in the unity of the Holy Spirit, world without end. Amen.

This prayer does not mention communion in the Precious Blood and is, therefore, used on Good Friday.

Prosit mihi . . . corporis: Notice that in this last prayer we ask that communion may exert its effect upon our bodies. The increase of sanctifying grace, charity and infused virtues which communion pours into the soul also indirectly benefits the body and weakens fleshly lusts.

(c) *Panem caelestem*

The solemn moment draws near: both priest and faithful by charity must expand their capacity to receive the grace which will be poured out so abundantly by holy communion. The priest therefore confesses his lively faith in the holy Eucharist in the words of Psalm 115, verse 4:

Panem caelestem, accipiam et nomen Domini invocabo.	I will take the bread of heaven, and will call upon the name of the Lord.

(d) *Domine, non sum dignus*

The priest cleanses his soul from every last stain of venial sin, making three times the declaration by which the centurion contritely confessed his utter unworthiness, expressed his unquenchable trust and gave moving witness of his love:

Domine, non sum dignus, ut intres sub tectum meum: sed tantum dic verbo et sanabitur anima mea.

Lord, I am not worthy that thou shouldst enter beneath my roof, but say only the word, and my soul will be healed.

Repeated three times.

This prayer was already being said by some priests and laymen before communion in the eleventh century and its use was widespread by the thirteenth.

24

HOLY COMMUNION

THE PLACE OF COMMUNION IN THE ECONOMY OF SACRIFICE: THE EATING OF THE DIVINE VICTIM

MANY authors appear to consider communion as an act of devotion independent of the holy sacrifice; but it is, in fact, the last " act " in the sacred " drama " of the Mass as the Gospel narratives clearly show: *Accepit panem . . . gratias agens benedixit, fregit, deditque discipulis suis.* . . . The last act of a stage-play is not something separate, unconnected with the rest, and so it is with communion. Of course, whenever we receive holy communion, we receive the Body and Blood of Christ; but we must realize what these sacred elements in fact are: they are the Body and Blood of Christ which were offered to the Father for us, the Lamb of God, the sacred Victim of our true sacrifice as they were offered. Communion ought, therefore, to symbolize and to be an act of the fullest participation in the sacrifice and of active and passive co-oblation with the divine victim. Throughout the Mass, the general trend is upwards, towards the Father, and so it should be with communion. Yet innumerable books of piety ask only such questions as " What profit shall I draw from this exercise? " and " What are the fruits of communion? " As we have seen, if we void the Mass of the essential element of oblation, consecration becomes no more than a ceremony of transubstantiation, " productive " of sacred Hosts for communion and devotion. But the perfect communion is that received at Mass, from the priest who celebrates it and, if possible, in a Host consecrated at that Mass.[1]

The true meaning of communion—fullness of participation in sacrifice—may be clearly seen by comparison with the prefigurative sacrifices of the old covenant: the Israelite who wished to worship God, who wished to consecrate and offer himself to his creator,

---

[1] See the quotation from the encyclical *Mediator Dei*, pp. 300–301.

expressed his interior offering in an external oblation of the most precious of his belongings, the immolation of which would represent the immolation of himself. He laid his hands upon it to transfer his personality to it, then offered it upon the altar. But the immolation and offering of the victim was valueless in God's sight unless the adoration that the victim symbolized exteriorly was interiorly present in the offerer (Ps. 50. 18-9). The better to express unity of his interior oblation with their exterior expression in his sacrifice, the Israelite then made himself one with the victim, his offering, by eating it, "communicating", so showing himself to be the true victim and principal offerer of the sacrifice.

We, the true Israelites, also owe God the homage of our adoration, and we too must translate our interior adoration into a tangible symbol, a sacrifice, but one ordained not by our own feelings, but instituted in accordance with a pre-arranged pattern, by the sovereign high priest of the new covenant—the holy eucharistic sacrifice. We, too, must place a lamb upon our altar, the Lamb of God who now offers himself eucharistically in our stead under the continuing accidents of our bread and wine. In his sacramental, tangible, eucharistic offering and immolation, the divine Lamb represents our homage, adoration and interior self-offering and sacrifice. The Christian must, therefore, offer and immolate himself with the divine victim—*hostia pro hostia*—to the glory of the Father, and he gives the supreme expression of this self-offering and immolation by entering into the sacrifice of the Lamb, uniting himself as closely as possible to, making himself one with, the divine victim by eating him. Why else did the Lord choose bread and wine except so that we might participate as closely as possible in his sacrifice? Ideally, therefore, the faithful should consummate their participation in their sacrifice at the proper, ritually determined time, by communicating with their priest in their own victim, offered in their name and on their behalf. The Israelite would never have been able to imagine the practice of communicating in the victim, before the victim had been offered and sacrificed. The Christian should communicate normally when the (his) Lamb of God has been offered and immolated—at the time indicated by Christ's institution: *accepit panem, gratias agens, benedixit, fregit, deditque.*

THE PLACE OF COMMUNION IN THE ECONOMY OF THE EUCHARISTIC SACRIFICE AND ITS EFFECTS IN US

It might seem strange that, throughout the religious history of humanity, men have first given their sacrifices to God, making them things consecrated to God, holy things, and then, hardly having offered them, these same offerers sit down to eat them. But, in truth, the eating of the sacrificial victim is the confirmation and consummation of the oblation, for in God is man's perfection and end, and man expresses his longing to reach that end in offering a sacrifice which represents himself. Then, the lamb having become the " Lamb of God ", a " holy " lamb, in its turn becomes a sign of the sanctification of those who communicate in it, and those who sit down to eat of it, become God's guests, admitted to his banquet that they may eat not their lamb, their offering, but God's. The sacrificial meal is thus a symbol of oneness and intimacy with the divine, and of future participation in God's gifts and blessings. Furthermore, communion in the sacrificial victim is an expression of the sanctification of him who has offered it, and of unity between God and the offerers, and between the offerers themselves.

So, then, far from weakening or profaning the sacrifice, communion strengthens and hallows the oblation, and is a clear symbol of (a) future communion with God in the enjoyment of eternal blessings, (b) the present sanctification, union with God of each of the offerers, and (c) the sanctification or union in God of each offerer with all the others.

THE DEEP SIGNIFICANCE OF JESUS CHRIST'S " FIRST SOLEMN COMMUNION " AT THE LAST SUPPER

In the first twelve centuries no one maintained that Christ did not communicate at the Last Supper: many Latin, Greek and Syriac Fathers, several Eastern Liturgies, such theologians as St Albert the Great, St Thomas and St Bonaventure state categorically that he did communicate there. The first to deny it was Peter of Poitiers, a twelfth-century chancellor of the University of Paris, and the second, Luther in the sixteenth century.

With regard to this point, notice first that Christ instituted the holy Eucharist within the framework of the Jewish Paschal feast. By ancient custom, the head of the family drank first from each of the prescribed four cups before circulating them among the assembled guests. The cup Jesus consecrated was, in all probability, the third, that " of blessing ". According to both St Matthew and St Mark, Jesus, immediately after proffering the consecrated cup, said: " I tell you this, I shall not drink of this fruit of the vine again, until I drink it with you, new wine, in the kingdom of my Father " (Matt. 26. 29; cf. Mark 14. 25). The words " I shall not drink . . . again " suggest that Jesus had just drunk, and the words " this fruit of the vine " that he was speaking of a cup still in his hand. So then, Jesus declared that he would not drink again of the eucharistic wine until it had become a " new " drink: the cup of heavenly beatitude and glory which he would share with his elect in his Father's kingdom, at the heavenly banquet (cf. Luke 22. 29–30). The pledge and sacrament of this banquet is, of course, the Eucharist; thus it seems certain that Christ communicated at the Last Supper.

St Thomas dedicated a whole article to this point: *Utrum Christus sumpserit suum corpus et sanguinem.* Christ, he taught, instituted the sacrament of his Body and not only gave it to his disciples, but also partook of it himself.[1]

But why did Christ communicate? Was he not himself both priest and victim of the holy sacrifice? Holy communion, like the other sacraments, is a visible sign which produces what it signifies. It is self-evident, however, that holy communion did not, and could not, produce its effects, grace, in Christ, for he himself has the fullness of grace. In his communion, our Lord, the Head, showed forth what it would effect sacramentally in us, his members. In the rite of consecration, Christ sanctified bread. The eucharistic Bread, which has been given to God for us, is become the Bread of God. Therefore, in participating ritually in this eucharistic Bread, Christ symbolized and manifested ritually his " communion " with the Father and his approaching glorification. Christ is the head of the Church, the head of the mystical body, and it is through him that we come to the communion of glory with him and the Father: glorification is brought to us, his members, through him, our head, and therefore, when he symbolized his own approaching glorifica-

[1] *Summa Theol.* IIIa, q. 91, a. 1. Cf. IIIa, q. 84, a. 7, ad 4.

tion, the First Communicant also symbolized our " communion " with him and with the Father in glory. Thus it is in the light of Christ's eucharistic communion that their communion is revealed to his members as the pledge of their future glorification. Christ, " the eldest-born among many brethren " (Rom. 8. 29), invites us to sit, as his guests, at his Father's table; it is his banquet, and ours only through him. He is the first to eat the eucharistic Bread, to drink the sacred Cup. In himself partaking with his Apostles of his sacred banquet at the Last Supper, Christ signified and manifested the fact that he was introducing them into his family-relationship with the Father, into vital union with himself and with one another through him.

HOLY COMMUNION AT THE PAPAL MASS ACCORDING TO *ORDO ROMANUS I*[1]

(a) THE COMMUNION OF THE CLERGY

In the previous chapter, we saw that the pope communicated seated upon his throne. After his communion, the archdeacon carried the chalice back to the altar and announced the place of the next station. He then poured a little of the Precious Blood from the pope's chalice into a *scyphus* of unconsecrated wine held by an acolyte. Meanwhile, the clergy in order approached the throne and the pope placed a fragment of the eucharistic Bread in the hand of each of them. They then returned to the altar, placed the hand containing the Eucharist upon it, then ate the sacred Bread. The leading bishop then took the pope's—the only consecrated—chalice from the archdeacon and proffered it to the other bishops, the priests and the deacons in turn. When all the clergy had communicated, the archdeacon poured what remained in the chalice into the *scyphus* for the communion of the people.

(b) THE COMMUNION OF THE FAITHFUL

In early times, all those present communicated at Mass. When the numbers grew too great for it to be possible for them all to communicate from the same chalice, there arose the practice called *immixtio*, by which the Precious Blood was mingled with unconsecrated wine which, as Pope Innocent III emphasized, was not there-

[1] Eighth century.

after regarded as itself consecrated by contact with the Precious Blood.

The pope then came down from the throne to give the eucharistic Bread to the nobility (*senatorium*). He was followed by the archdeacon who proffered to each of them the cup of wine mixed with the Precious Blood, from which each of them drank a few drops through a golden (or silver) tube (*pugillaris*). The eucharistic Bread was given to the other men by the bishops, to the women by priests; the chalice to both sexes by the deacons.

The *schola* began to sing the antiphon *ad communionem* as the pope began to communicate the *senatorium* and it was continued until the end of the communion.

On returning to the throne, the pope communicated the district subdeacon and acolytes and the *schola*.

THE COMMUNION TODAY

(a) THE PRIEST'S COMMUNION

The priest takes the two parts of the sacred Host between the fingers of his right hand and with them makes the sign of the cross over himself:

Corpus Domini nostri Jesu Christi custodiat animam meam in vitam aeternam. Amen.	The Body of our Lord Jesus Christ preserve my soul for everlasting life. Amen.

Bowing low, the priest communicates reverently in the eucharistic Body. He then puts the paten aside, joins his hands and rests for a few seconds in recollection and meditation upon the divine mysteries. He then removes every particle from the paten and corporal, placing them in the chalice, while saying verse 3 of Psalm 115:

Quid retribuam Domino pro omnibus quae retribuit mihi? Calicem salutaris accipiam, et nomen Domini invocabo. Laudans invocabo Dominum, et ab inimicis meis salvus ero.	What return shall I make to the Lord for all that he has given me? I will take the chalice of salvation and invoke the name of the Lord. Praised be the Lord! When I invoke his name I shall be secure from my enemies.

At the word *calicem*, he takes the chalice and, having ended the verse, makes the sign of the cross, saying:

Sanguis Domini nostri Jesu Christi custodiat animam meam in vitam aeternam. Amen.	The Blood of our Lord Jesus Christ preserve my soul for everlasting life. Amen.

Then, holding the paten under his chin in his left hand, he reverently communicates in the Precious Blood and the particle of the Host contained in it.

The priest does not communicate only as a personal act of devotion: even in communicating, he is the representative of Christ and his Church. He communicates first *in persona Christi*, the representative of Christ, the first of all communicants, and in his communion extends our Lord's communion into every Mass. The priest communicates secondly in *persona totius Ecclesiae cujus sacerdos est minister*, " in the person of the whole Church whose minister he is: "[1] he represents the Church; thus he represents in his communion (a) the Church's communion in the Father's glory through Christ; (b) the ritual sanctification of the Church though eating the divine victim, and (c) the unity of Christ and the communicating Church. Finally, the priest communicates as the leader of his congregation and presides at the eucharistic banquet.

(b) THE COMMUNION OF THE CONGREGATION OF THE FAITHFUL

The communion of the faithful is an extension of the priest's communion and should ideally be arranged in close connection with his. Communion when the priest does not communicate impairs not only the true concept of communion but also the ritual union (*cum unio*) which should embrace all the communicants.

In former times, the faithful went in procession twice to the altar: the first, to offer their material oblations, bread and wine; the second, to receive their consecrated oblations. The faithful should be able to communicate in their own sacrifice; in the Eucharist which originated from their own hands and was offered on their behalf. Until the thirteenth century it was the universal liturgical rule that holy communion should not be distributed except at Mass after the communion of the priest.

[1] *Summa Theol.*, III, q. 82, a. 6.

Ceremonies

By local custom, a bell is rung three times at *Domine, non sum dignus* as a signal to the faithful of the imminence of the moment of sacramental (or spiritual) communion: in former times the same result was effected by a cry of *Sancta Sanctis!* ("Holy things for the holy!") by the deacon.

The Confiteor: The Roman Missal directs that an acolyte shall say the *Confiteor* in the name of the congregation; the priest then says *Misereatur* and *Indulgentiam*. At high and pontifical Masses, the *Confiteor* is sung by the deacon, who stands bowed on the epistle side.

Confiteor, Misereatur and *Indulgentiam* first passed from the beginning of Mass to the rite of *Viaticum* in the eleventh century (Constitutions of Cluny), and from that rite back to communion at Mass by the twelfth century (among the Cistercians), and through other religious orders to the parish churches by the thirteenth. According to the new Holy Week *Ordo* (1956) the *Confiteor* and the absolution before the people's communion are omitted on Maundy Thursday because they have already been said at the beginning of Mass. On Good Friday and Easter night, on the other hand, they are said because they are omitted at the beginning. It is desirable that all should say the *Confiteor* and the *Domine, non sum dignus*, the latter with the celebrant.

Domine, non sum dignus: The faithful have been exhorted to use the centurion's confession as a private preparation for communion, to be said silently and contritely, since the eleventh century, but the custom gradually arose of the communicants repeating it aloud and together. The Roman Missal now prescribes (*Rit. serv.* 10. 6) that the priest shall say it three times aloud.

The order of communicants: According to the Apostolic Constitutions, the Bishop should communicate first, then priests, deacons, subdeacons, lectors, cantors, ascetics, deaconesses, virgins, widows, children and finally the congregation. An order of precedence is still observed today, in that at high Mass the deacon and subdeacon, and at low Mass the acolyte are communicated first in their respective orders,[1] while at ordination Masses the ordinands, and at nuptial Masses the bridegroom and bride are given precedence.

---

[1] S.C.R. Decree 1074; cf. *Caer. Ep.*, 2, 23, 6; 2, 30, 4.

Place of Communion: The deacon and subdeacon are communicated on the footpace of the altar, the clergy on the step within the chancel (*cancelli*) and the faithful at the rail.[1]

Position: In Christian antiquity and the early Middle Ages, the faithful communicated standing: moreover, the usual communion days were Sundays and the great feasts, when kneeling was forbidden. According to *Ordo V* (tenth century) the pope then communicated standing, but according to *Ordo X* (twelfth century), he did so sitting. Today, except for the celebrant, the bishop at his consecration Mass and the deacon and subdeacon at the papal Mass, all are communicated kneeling—a custom which arose only in the late Middle Ages.

The Communion Rite: The faithful used to receive communion of the Bread in their right hands, the left being crossed under it.[2] They covered their hands with a white cloth called *dominicale*. *Ordo VI* (tenth–eleventh century) mentions two ways of communicating: priests and deacons received the holy Eucharist in their hands, subdeacons, in their mouths. By the ninth century it was almost universally customary for the faithful to receive communion on their tongues.

In early times the faithful used to drink directly from the chalice, but quite soon began to use a golden or silver tube (*fistula, pugillaris, calamus,* etc.). This was the established practice before *Ordo Romanus I* was written, and remained so as long as communion was given in both species (that is, until the twelfth–thirteenth centuries).

A decree of the Sacred Congregation for Sacraments, dated 26 March 1929, in addition to a communion cloth makes the use of a plate (*patina*) compulsory. It must be gilded and have a smooth surface.

The Communion Formula: In Christian antiquity the communion formula was concise: *Corpus Christi*. The communicant replied, confessing his faith, *Amen* ("Thus it is"). The deacon likewise said: *Sanguis Christi, calix vitae* and the communicant again replied *Amen*. In the Middle Ages many formulas were current. Our present formula appeared almost literally in a tenth-century French

---

[1] *Rit. Rom.* V, 2, 4.
[2] Tertullian, *De Idol.*, 7; S. Cyrillus Hiersol., *Cat. Myst.*, 5, 21-2; Joan. Damascenus, *De Fide Orth.*, 4, 13.

Sacramentary: *Corpus et sanguis Domini nostri Jesu Christi custodiat animam tuam in vitam aeternam. Amen* (today: *Corpus Domini* . . .). The dialogue form, in which the communicant replies *Amen*, is still used at ordination Masses (except those of priests).

The Pax at Communion: In accordance with a modified form of ancient tradition, the communicant should, according to the Ceremonial of Bishops, kiss the bishop's hand (in practice his ring) before receiving the sacred host.[1] After receiving holy communion, prelates and *canonici parati* give the kiss of peace to the bishop himself (*osculari faciem*).[2]

THE COMMUNION CHANT (*COMMUNIO*)

It was natural that the two processions of the faithful to the altar, to offer their ordinary bread, and to receive their consecrated Bread, should be accompanied by singing. At the offertory it is called the *Offertorium*, and at the communion, the *Antiphona ad communionem* or simply *Communio*, the communion.

The *communio* consisted of a psalm preceded by an antiphon (*antiphona*)—usually taken from the psalm itself—which was begun at the beginning of the communion of the faithful. After every verse of the psalm (which was sung by the *schola*), the antiphon was repeated as a refrain. When the communion of the faithful ended, the pope gave a signal, the *Gloria Patri* was sung and the *communio* completed by the singing of the antiphon.[3] The length of the chant was gradually reduced until only the antiphon survived. The *communio* has, however, preserved its ancient form at Masses of the Dead when, after the antiphon *Cum sanctis tuis* . . . there follows the verse *Requiem aeternam*, after which the antiphon is repeated. The new *Ordo* for Holy Week (1956) has restored the ancient practice on Maundy Thursday. The *schola* can sing the antiphon while the celebrant distributes communion. And psalms (22, 71, 103, 150) are suggested for singing (with the antiphon, which is repeated after each psalm) if the communion is lengthy. On Good Friday Psalm 21 may be sung, but without an antiphon.

---

[1] *Caer. Ep.*, 2, 29, 5.
[2] *Ibid.*
[3] Cf. the introit: Vol. 1, Chap. 14, pp. 100–1.

Holy Communion

The oldest known communion chant is Psalm 33, mentioned in the Apostolic Constitutions. It is still used as a *communio* in the Roman liturgy on the eighth Sunday after Pentecost. Some *communiones* are not taken from psalms: some are drawn from the Gospels (especially during Lent; on the Feast of the Sacred Heart of Jesus) and other Scriptural books (e.g. on the Feast of Pentecost) or some other work (feast of St Ignatius, 1 February; St Agatha, 6 February). The *communio* of the Mass of the dead is taken from an apocryphal work (IV Esdras 2. 35. 32).

The Instruction of the S. Congregation of Rites (3 September 1958) has restored the former practice whereby, according to circumstances, several verses of the psalm may be sung with repetition of the antiphon after each verse or pair of verses until the time comes for concluding the psalm with *Gloria Patri*, which is followed by the final repetition of the antiphon.[1]

That the *communio* is truly the chant accompanying the communion of the faithful is obvious from the *Graduale*, a rubric of which directs the singers to begin it after the priest has communicated in the Precious Blood.[2] Like the introit and offertory, the communion often relates to the feast being celebrated.

A glance at the list of the *Antiphonae ad Communionem* for Lent reveals that Psalms 1–26 follow one another in strict numerical order in the stational Masses celebrated at the *tituli* between the pontificates of St Leo and St Gregory the Great; in our present Missal, however, this series is no longer complete, at differing times and for various reasons, Psalms 3, 12, 16, 17, 20 and 21 have now been replaced by texts from the Gospels: Ps. 3 (first week, Monday) by Matthew 25; Ps. 12 (second week, Saturday) by Luke 15; Ps. 16 (third week, Friday) by John 4; Ps. 17 (third week, Saturday) by John 8; Ps. 20 (fourth week, Wednesday) by John 9; and Ps. 21 (fourth week, Friday) by John 11. (Thursdays were aliturgical.)

According to the Instruction of the S. Congregation of Rites (3 September 1958) in Masses without communion of the congregation the communion antiphon is to be sung, not after the celebrant's communion, but while he communicates. If the congregation communicates, the antiphon is begun during the distribution of communion.

---

[1] The same arrangement holds good in future for the introit and offertory.
[2] *Graduale Romanum: De Rit. serv. in cantu Miss.*, 9.

THE ABLUTIONS

Neither the Roman *Ordines* nor liturgists before the eleventh century mention ablutions after the communion. *Ordo XIV* (fourteenth century) speaks of the preliminary ablution with wine.

Immediately after the communion of the faithful, the priest begins the cleansing of the chalice. While the acolyte is pouring the wine into it, the priest says this ancient postcommunion, which is to be found in the Leonine, Gelasian and Gregorian Sacramentaries:

Quod ore sumpsimus, Domine, pura mente capiamus: et de munere temporali fiat nobis remedium sempiternum.	That which our mouths have taken, Lord, may we possess in purity of heart; and may the gift of the moment become for us an everlasting remedy.

The washing of the celebrant's fingers and hands was certainly already customary in the eleventh century, but the form it took varied. Ives of Chartres, Alexander of Hales, Innocent III and Durandus of Mende mention a special place, the *lavatorium*. As well as washing their fingers over the chalice, celebrants washed their hands in some churches in a special *piscina* in the wall on the epistle side. The washing of hands has today disappeared from Masses celebrated by a priest, but the Ceremonial of Bishops prescribes it at pontifical Mass[1] before the reading of the *Communio* and also at low Masses celebrated by a bishop.[2]

Having consumed the wine, the priest goes to the epistle side where he cleanses his thumbs and index fingers over the chalice with wine and water, while saying this Gallican prayer:

Corpus tuum, Domine, quod sumpsi, et Sanguis, quem potavi, adhaereat visceribus meis: et praesta; ut in me non remaneat scelerum macula, quem pura et sancta refecerunt sacramenta: Qui vivis et regnas in saecula saeculorum. Amen.	May thy Body, Lord, which I have taken, and thy Blood which I have drunk, cleave to every fibre of my being. Grant that no stain of sin may be left in me, now that I am renewed by this pure and holy sacrament; who livest and reignest world without end. Amen.

[1] *Caer. Ep.*, 2, 8, 76.   [2] *Ibid.*, 78.

Our liturgical books still provide for an ablution by the faithful, which has, however, fallen into disuse: thus, according to the Missal, the faithful, when they communicate at Mass, should be proffered wine mixed with water in a cup (*vasculum*) and a linen towel, by an acolyte.[1]

[1] *Rit. serv. in celbr. Miss.*, 10, 6.

25

THANKSGIVING AFTER COMMUNION: THE POSTCOMMUNION

THE postcommunion is the Church's principal act of thanksgiving, and concerns both celebrant and faithful . . . *cum Orationes, quae in Missa post communionem dicuntur, non solum ad sacerdotem, sed etiam ad alios communicantes spectent:*[1] it is therefore formulated in the plural. But a considerable number of postcommunions do not mention communion at all—their primary purpose is expressed by their alternative title in some Sacramentaries, *ad complendum*: they perfect the eucharistic sacrifice in which communion is the fullness of participation. The postcommunion must usually be considered in relation to the sacrifice rather than to the communion—and certainly never to the communion alone. May the sacrifice of the cross, which is made present in the eucharistic rite, bring into active being in us the fullness of its sanctifying effects: such is the Church's petition in these prayers: *ejusdem redemptionis fructum percipere mereamur* (The Seven Holy Founders, 12 February; cf. the First Sunday in Lent). The principal effect of the sacrifice of the cross made present in the Mass is the remission of sins: *percipientes hoc munere veniam peccatorum* (*Missa pro remissione peccatorum;* cf. third Tuesday in Lent): this remission is the cleansing of the soul: *mysteria nos . . . sumpta purificent et suo munere tueantur* (Fourth Sunday after Pentecost); *purificent nos . . . sacramenta quae sumpsimus* (Commemoration of St Nicomedes, 15 September); this is expressed in many ways: *caelestis . . . participatio sacramenti . . . fideles tuos mundet et muniat* (St John Baptist de Rossi, 23 May); *per hoc sacrificium . . . ab omnibus tentationibus emundemur* (for the grace of continence); *a cunctis nos . . . reatibus et periculis propitiatus absolve* (Third Sunday in Lent; cf. For a man deceased, 9).

Remission of sins in its multitudinous aspects is not, however, the only subject matter for these prayers: divine help, restoration,

[1] *Rit. Rom.*, V, 2, 11.

sanctification, vivification of the soul: all these, and other topics, feature each in several prayers.

Nevertheless, many postcommunions—especially those of medieval or later date—are concerned especially with the wonderful effects of holy communion. These effects are, broadly speaking, (a) our incorporation individually into Christ, that is, the union of each of us separately with Christ; (b) our incorporation into Christ, the Head of the Church, that is into the unity in Christ of all his members so making them one with another; and (c) participation in future divine blessing: the glorious resurrection and beatitude in glory.

(a) *Individual incorporation into Christ.*—" As I live because of the Father, the living Father who has sent me, so he who eats me will live, in his turn, because of me " (John 6. 58). In the ineffable mystery of the life of the Trinity, the Father communicates his divine life and all his attributes to his Son, the only-begotten from the bosom of the Father. All that the Word has is the Father's gift. The divine nature of the Word was united to human nature that he took from the virginal womb of Mary: Christ's soul and body are united with his divine nature in the unity of his person (cf. I John 1. 1–3). At the moment of the Incarnation (the Annunciation), the Father poured into the soul of the Word the fullness of grace, participation in the divine life. Now, Christ was made man that he might redeem us, might win supernatural life for us through the sacrifice of the cross. In his resurrection, he has become a " life-giving spirit "—he has been made able to give of his fullness, to communicate the life of grace to those who are made living members of him (by baptism). Through the renewal of the sacrifice of the cross in the eucharistic sacrifice, Christ applies to us the merits of his sacrifice with bloodshed, communicates divine life to us; we participate most fully in the sacrifice in eucharistic communion. So then, for love of us, Christ is become the channel of the divine life, the living and divine sacrament, so that we may receive of his fullness. We receive the eucharistic Body of Christ really present under the continuing accidents of bread corporeally, but the mode of Christ's eucharistic presence is such that there is no immediate contact between his body and ours, but through this corporeal reception, the Body of Christ sanctifies our souls—or, rather, through his eucharistic Body, the soul of Christ, full of grace and truth, pours grace into our souls and gives them of its fullness.

Christ instituted this sacrament under the guise of food as the discourse in which the Eucharist was promised shows most clearly (John 6. 53–8): and at the Last Supper itself, he said: " Take, eat ", " Drink . . . of this " (Matt. 26. 26, 27). The Council of Florence (1438–45) declared that " the effect of this sacrament is the uniting of man to Christ ". " And because through grace man is incorporated into Christ and united to his members, therefore through this sacrament grace is increased in those who receive it worthily: and all the results that material food and drink bring about in the life of the body—sustenance, growth, restoration and delectation—this sacrament effects in the spiritual life . . ." [1]

Clothed under sacramental appearances, as food, the eucharistic and invisible Body of Christ symbolizes the nutrition of the communicants, their incorporation into Christ, and therefore effects it. The real presence must not be seen so much as an end in itself, as in connection with life, that spiritual growth which it brings about as an efficient cause. Christ instituted holy communion primarily to feed and give life sacramentally to our souls. The mere presence of Christ in the tabernacle, as such, is not to be compared with the vivification that Jesus sacramentally effects in those who communicate. The holy Eucharist, the Bread of heaven, the Wine of God, feeds, strengthens and increases supernatural life. Together with sanctifying grace, it increases the infused theological and moral virtues (especially charity), the gifts of the Holy Ghost, his fruits and blessing—in short, the spiritual life (the life of the Holy Spirit) in all its manifestations.

The sacrament of charity: "He who eats my flesh, and drinks my blood, lives continually in me, and I in him " (John 6. 57) . . . " God is love; he who dwells in love, dwells in God, and God in him " (I John 4. 17). The mutual and permanent indwelling of the communicant in Christ and Christ in the communicant implies his transformation in Christ, his beloved, through the charity which pours into him in communion (*transformatio hominis in Christum per amorem*).[2] Indeed, charity is inseparable from and grows

---

[1] *Decret. pro Armenis* (Denzinger, 698); cf. *Conc. Trid.*, Sess. 23, 2 (Denzinger, 875).
[2] St Thomas, IV, dist. 12, q. 2, a. 2, sol. 1.

together with the state of grace; it is the most excellent of all virtues, the soul of our spiritual life, perfection itself.[1] The effect proper to communion is increase in charity. In the furnace of the love of Christ, the communicant is strongly urged to acts of charity by the sacrament of the Eucharist.[2] The increase of charity is the special effect of communion. It increases charity not only as an infused virtue but also in a bursting forth of acts. Indeed, the Eucharist not only derives from the charity of Christ who loves us *in finem*, but also movingly represents the charity of the Lord who sacrificed his body and blood for our salvation and has given them to us as food and drink; and above all, through its sacramental efficacy it infuses ever-increasing charity into us and moves us to perform works of charity.

Christ's eucharistic presence in us is, of course, ephemeral: when the accidents of bread or wine are changed, it comes to an end. But the spiritual effect wrought by this transitory sacramental "passing" are abiding. Indeed, the administration of all sacraments lasts only a few moments: baptism "passes", but once the rite is performed, the baptized person is left in a lasting, permanent state: the "state of grace" infused by it. So, too, eucharistic communion passes, but its effect endures: each communion leaves us more firmly incorporated in Christ in a mutual, permanent and vital immanence and indwelling of Christ in us and of us in Christ. Whether we are in the least aware of it or not, this effect is produced, abides and, day by day, is reinforced: "He who eats my flesh and drinks my blood, lives continually in me, and I in him" (John 6. 57).

In giving life to charity, holy communion indirectly weakens concupiscence: some theologians, including Suarez, maintain that its effect in this respect is direct. In fact, communion communicates to sinful flesh some affinity to the sacred Body of Christ; our flesh is purified and hallowed, we acquire a right to the especial graces by which those temptations which threaten this likeness may be resisted.

These wondrous effects, the enlargement of the spiritual life in all its manifestations, are implored continually by the post-

---

[1] *Summa Theol.*, II–IIae, q. 184, 1.
[2] See *Summa Theol.*, III, q. 79, a. 1 ad 2, and compare *In Lib. IV Sent.*, d. 12, q. 2, a. 2; *Summa Theol.*, II, q. 78, a. 3 ad 6; IV, d. 7, q. 2, sol. 3 ad 5.

communions in a multitude of ways. Thus, as an especial effect, the Church asks sometimes for the increase of faith: " Grant, we pray thee, almighty God, that we may ever more steadfastly emulate the faith of those whom we commemorate by partaking of thy sacrament " (feast of the Twelve Holy Brothers, 1 September; cf. Votive Mass for the Propagation of the Faith), and sometimes for the increase of charity: " Lord, we pray that the grace of the Holy Spirit may enlighten our hearts and fill them with . . . perfect charity " (Mass for Charity); ". . . may this heavenly sacrament kindle in us the same fire of love which moved . . . Teresa . . ." (October 3); and again, sometimes, for the growth of the gifts of the Holy Ghost: wisdom (the feast of the Sacred Heart of Jesus), strength (St Josaphat, 14 November) and understanding (the Epiphany).

In other postcommunions, the Church asks for the fruits of the Holy Ghost (for example, patience: Occasional Prayers, 28) and chastity (Occasional Prayers, 26) and meekness (St Margaret Mary Alacoque, 17 October)—in short, for eternal life: " May his blood, we pray thee, become a spring of water within us bringing everlasting life . . ." (The Precious Blood, 1 July).

The persistence with which the Church begs the effects of the Eucharist upon the body itself is striking: " May the sacrament we have taken . . . comfort us with bodily support " (Third Sunday after Easter); " . . . may we advance in bodily and spiritual health by receiving this sacrament " (Trinity Sunday; compare seventh, fifteenth and sixteenth Sundays after Pentecost).

(b) *Incorporation into Christ, the Head of the Church.*—As each communicant is vitally one with Christ, so, through this same Christ, all the communicants are vitally one with one another. We cannot be incorporated into Christ without forming a body living a single life in the oneness of a single Spirit. So then, the Eucharist is the sacrament of the unity of the Church. It is the property of a sacrament to produce what it signifies. The words of consecration said over the bread signify the physical body of Christ, and thereby make it present. But Christ's human body made present under the continuing accidents of bread is, in its turn, a sign: the efficacious and sacramental sign of a new and most noble reality. The physical and eucharistic Body of Christ is the efficacious sacramental sign of his other body which fills time and space: his noble, real, living mystical body: his Church. As it signifies his mystical body, his eucharistic Body is also its cause: the Eucharist makes the Church; that is, in the one Christ it incorporates the communicants vitally into one another and effects the vital unity between them. It is because the bread is one that we are all one body who eat of the one bread (I Cor. 10. 17). "The only Son," wrote St Cyril of Jerusalem, "the Wisdom and Counsellor of the Father invented a marvellous means by which it became possible for Christians to become one among themselves and with God . . . When he gives Christians his Body to eat in the Eucharist, he makes them 'concorporeal' with him and with one another. They are physically united because they are bound together in the unity of Christ through participation in his sacred Body. All we who partake of one bread form a single body, for Christ cannot be divided."[1] "Christ himself," St Hilary teaches, "is the Church, for, through the sacrament of his Body, it is universally contained in him."[2] The same teaching is found in the later Fathers. St Thomas teaches, "the effect (*res*) of this sacrament is the unity of the Mystical Body".[3]

The Council of Trent proclaimed: "Christ desired, moreover, that (this sacrament) should be a pledge (*pignus*) of our future glory and eternal blessedness and also a symbol (*symbolum*) of that body of which he is the head and to which he has willed that we should be united in the closest bonds of faith, hope and charity, that all may speak the same way and that there may be no schisms among us."[4]

Thus, the Eucharist is the sacrament of our "communion" in the Church—not only of our external or social communion in a visible community, but also of our oneness of life in the Mystical Body of Christ. St Pius X called the communion table "the symbol, root and main cause of catholic unity" (*mensae quae symbolum, radix atque principium est catholicae unitatis*).[5]

The Head and his members share the same indivisible charity. The Eucharist which incorporates us vitally into Christ, infuses

[1] *In Joan. Ev.*, I, II; *P.G.*, 74, 556–60.
[2] *In Psalm* 125, n. 6; *P.L.*, 9, 688.
[3] *Summa Theol.*, III, q. 73, a. 3; cf. *ibid.*, q. 82, a. 9 ad 2.
[4] Sess. 13, 2 (Denzinger, 875); cf. 22, 8 (Denzinger, 882).
[5] *Constitutio apostolica de SS. Eucharistia promiscuo ritu sumenda* in *A.A.S.* (1912), p. 615.

supernatural charity into us. He who does not love his brother sins against the holy Eucharist. So, in the first Easter Mass and the Masses of Easter Sunday and Monday, the Church prays: " Pour into us the Spirit of thy love, O Lord, so that we whose hunger thou hast satisfied with thy Easter sacrament may, by thy loving-kindness, be made one in heart." [1] It is given emphasis by being repeated throughout Eastertide at the rite of communion outside Mass.

But the Mystical Body of Christ to which we are united by eucharistic communion has a visible, social and external structure and therefore such communion is the visible, sacramental and efficacious sign which draws us together in the external and visible society of the one Church of Christ and, contrariwise, exclusion from communion, " excommunication ", is the supreme form of ecclesiastical censure.

As the Mystical Body extends to the Church militant, suffering, and triumphant, union with the eucharistic Christ implies union with his universal Church, entering through him into vital unity with his militant, suffering and triumphant members. So, then, every communion strengthens the intimacy, the vital spiritual unity, between the communicant and our Lady, or the saints in Paradise, and brings the communicant into a vital intimacy incomparably closer than simple proximity in space with his beloved dead in purgatory. And finally, it makes yet closer that vital cohesion by which the faithful are living members of one another in the one Christ.

It is therefore obvious that holy communion is a collective act relating to the whole community present at Mass as such. Communicants must be re-educated with great care in their understanding of collective participation in the life of the eucharistic Christ, of their deep-rooted vital oneness and fundamental unity in Christ. And nothing can contribute so much to this as the collective communion of the congregation with the priest in the holy sacrifice which it offers with him.

(c) *Participation in future divine blessing.*—Glory is, indeed, the natural condition of divine life. " The man who eats my flesh

---

[1] Cf. the postcommunions for the Saturday of the third week in Lent, and the ninth Sunday after Pentecost, and the Secret for Corpus Christi.

and drinks my blood enjoys eternal life, and I will raise him up at the last day " (John 6. 55). Such is Christ's formal promise. Through eucharistic contact, some degree of affinity is set up between Christ's glorious body and our weak and mortal flesh. By bringing to us his glorified flesh in holy communion, Christ so exerts his supernatural entry into our bodies as, in some degree, to mould them to his and make us concorporeal with him. In his encyclical *Mirae Caritatis* (28 May 1902), Pope Leo XIII taught that " the august sacrament of the Eucharist is both the cause and the pledge of bliss and glory, not for the soul alone, but also for the body ". Final blessedness implies the glorious resurrection of the body, and this is one of the fruits of eucharistic communion.

" And I tell you this, I shall not drink of this fruit of the vine again, until I drink it with you, new wine, in the kingdom of my Father " (Matt. 26. 29): " as my Father has allotted a kingdom to me, so I allot to you a place to eat and drink at my table in my kingdom" (Luke 22. 29–30): notice the close connection Christ made between the eucharistic and the heavenly banquets: the former is not merely a sign, an image or figure, of the latter; it is more: " that which is drunk now will be drunk new in the Father's kingdom ", the cup of the eucharistic sacrifice pours out the germ of glory, heavenly blessedness, into the communicants. St Paul teaches that anyone who drinks the Lord's chalice unworthily, drinks condemnation to himself; so therefore, whoever drinks in holiness, drinks to his own glorification. Look once again at the postcommunions: " grant that the Saviour of the world . . . may also bestow upon us eternal life " (Christmas, Mass of the day); " we pray thee, Lord our God, that the rite we accomplish in this mortal life may win us everlasting life with thee " (Maundy Thursday); " Lord, we have eaten the bread of eternal life; and we . . . pray that it may be our lot to reign with him for ever in his heavenly kingdom " (The Kingship of Christ).

The eucharistic banquet is the sacrament of our companionship with Christ in glory and therefore is also its efficacious cause. Moreover, the eucharistic banquet is the pledge, the foretaste of that heavenly and mystical banquet at which divinity itself, without any sacramental veils whatever, will be revealed to us. Eucharistic communion is the prelude to this enjoyment of the godhead in the beatific vision: " Grant us, Lord, we beseech thee, through all eternity that enjoyment of thy godhead which is foreshadowed in this life by our partaking of thy precious body and blood" (Corpus Christi).

SYNTHESIS

Ecce Agnus Dei, the rite of communion begins: "Behold the Lamb of God", prefigured under the old covenant, immolated with bloodshed upon the cross, made present in the Eucharist: given to the Father in sacrifice, given to men in communion; perfected for ever in glory.

O sacrum convivium in quo Christus sumitur; recolitur memoria passionis ejus in which we celebrate the memorial of the passion in the past; *mens impletur gratia* in which the soul is filled with grace, in the present; *et futurae gloriae nobis pignus datur*, in which there is given to us a pledge of future glory. St Thomas found his inspiration for this wonderful antiphon in the tripartite structure of his article in the *Summa* which treats of the threefold significance of this sacrament for the present, the past and the future. He enlarged upon these same three points in the collect, secret and postcommunion for Corpus Christi.

26

CONCLUDING PRAYERS AND CEREMONIES

In all the weekday Masses of Lent, the postcommunion is followed by a prayer *super populum* (over the people), which is an ancient blessing, once found in all Masses, to be said over the congregation as a conclusion to the holy sacrifice. Mass nowadays is concluded with a somewhat ill-assorted group of rites the occurrence of which in representative sources from *Ordo I* (eighth century) to the decrees of Leo XIII (1884; 1886) is shown in the table[1] on the next page.

THE PRAYER OVER THE PEOPLE (*ORATIO SUPER POPULUM*)

After the postcommunion at ferial Masses in Lent, the priest says the invitatory *Oremus;* the deacon immediately turns to the congregation and cries: *Humiliate capita vestra Deo!* ("Bow down your heads before God!"). The celebrant then chants the appointed prayer and the congregation replies *Amen*.

The nature of this prayer has been the subject of a great deal of discussion. Comparative liturgy shows that it is very ancient: an equivalent form is preserved on a fragment of papyrus from Cairo dating from the reign of Justinian (527–65); the liturgy here preserved may date back to the time of the *Didache* (90).

In the oldest Sacramentary—the Leonine—the prayer *super populum* appears at the end of more than 160 Masses. In the Gelasian Sacramentary there are sixty-eight in the Masses and fifteen in the appendix, whereas in the Gregorian it occurs only on 2 February and the week-days of Lent.

In the Leonine Sacramentary this prayer—like the collect, secret and postcommunion—bears no title. Yet it is immediately

---

[1] Dom L. Beauduin, *Les additions successives à la Messe* (*Quest. lit.*, 1920, pp. 158–66, Louvain).

294   The Mass

Source	Ite, Missa Est	Placeat	Blessing	Last Gospel	Prayers after Mass
Ordo Romanus I (eighth century)	+				
Micrologus (eleventh century)	+				
Mitrale of Sicard (twelfth century)	+				
De Mysteriis (Innocent III)	+				
Sarum Ordinary (thirteenth century)	+	+	+		
Durandus, Rationale (thirteenth century)	+	+	+		
Ordo Romanus XIV (fourteenth century)	+	+	+		
De Canonum observantia, Ralph of Tongres († 1409)	+	+	+		
Alphabeticum sacerdotum (1499)	+	+	+	+++	
Burchard's Ordo Missae (1502)					
Ordinarium Constanc. (1557)	+	+	+		
St Pius V's Missal (1570)	++	++	++	++ After taking off the chasuble	
Leo XIII (1884; 1886)					+

distinguishable from them, for whereas they are collective prayers of the whole congregation including the priest (and are therefore normally formulated in the first person plural), this is a prayer for the congregation between whom and God the priest mediates; it is formulated in the second person (*Benedicat vos* . . . etc.), or, when addressed to God, in the third (*Protege, Domine, famulos tuos* . . . etc.). In the Gregorian Sacramentaries, this distinction was already being lost, and in thirty-seven prayers *super populum* in the present Missal, seventeen are exactly similar to the collects in structure.

Amalarius (ninth century) called this prayer *ulterior benedictio*, (as opposed to the postcommunion which he called *ultima benedictio*); a suitable name, because in all its forms the priest implores divine blessing and protection.

By contrast with the collects, secrets and postcommunions, these prayers stress permanence and continuance of the blessings they beseech: *semper, jugiter, indesinenter, custodire, conservare, perpetua defensione conserva, beneficiis attolle continuis, perpetua protectione*, etc.: the congregation needs the permanent protection of heaven; and they express the humility with which the congregation awaits the blessing: *supplices, supplicantes, populus supplex, suppliciter deprecantes, inclinantes se*, etc.

The restriction of these prayers to the weekdays of Lent was probably the outcome of the deacon's command *Humiliate*, and the kneeling which came to accompany it in certain places: bowing the head and kneeling were penitential gestures in the early Church.

THE DISMISSAL OF THE FAITHFUL

The present ceremony: After the priest's salutation *Dominus vobiscum*, the deacon turns to the faithful to pronounce the official dismissal: *Ite, missa est*. The tone is always joyful, as is that of the reply of the faithful: *Deo gratias*. Mass is not a mere public meeting: it is a sacred and hierarchical gathering, presided over by the bishop (or priest), begun by him and closed by his authority, as *Ordo I* shows: " At the end of the prayer, the deacon, being so bidden by the archdeacon, looks towards the pontiff until he gives the signal, and then says to the people, *Ite, missa est*. And the faithful reply, *Deo gratias*."

Origin and meaning: The deacon's dismissal seems to have been taken from the juridical language of the Romans: *Senatum mittere* or *dimittere*. *Missa* is a Low Latin noun, synonymous with *missio*, dismissal (cf. *collecta* for *collectio*, etc.). Thus, St Augustine wrote, *Post sermonem fit missa catechumenorum*.[1] So, then, the deacon's cry means " Go, it is the dismissal ! " It was from this by metonymy that the whole ceremony, by the eleventh century, had come to be called *Missa*, the Mass.

The connection " Gloria in excelsis—Ite, missa est": The rubrics of the Missal link *Ite, missa est* with the *Gloria in excelsis*. Masses in which the *Gloria* is not said are concluded *Benedicamus Domino*.[2] The author of the *Micrologus*, Bernold of Constance, noted this usage and argued that *Ite, missa est* is necessary on feast-days because of the congregation present in church: on other days, when religious (who would be reciting the Office immediately afterwards) formed almost the whole congregation, the dismissal was superfluous. The *Gloria in excelsis* is also omitted on these days and hence the connection arose. Durandus of Mende offers a similar solution: *Benedicamus Domino* was related to private Masses.

Batiffol offers another, very plausible, solution:[3] the Greater Doxology was for many years reserved to the bishop.[4] A simple priest was not allowed to chant the *Gloria;* it is probable that he was not allowed to pronounce the bishop's authoritative dismissal, *Ite, missa est*, and he therefore replaced it with *Benedicamus Domino*.

At Requiem Masses, the deacon, facing the altar, intones *Requiescant in pace*—a custom which was universal by the thirteenth century.

According to the new Ordo for Holy Week (1956) *Ite, missa est* is not sung on Maundy Thursday in spite of the fact that the *Gloria* figures in the Mass. This is because the office does not end at this point.

THE BLESSING

The priest then bows and says:

---

[1] *Sermo* 49. 8.
[2] Cf. *Rubr. Gen. Miss.*, 13, 1.
[3] *Leçons sur la Messe*, p. 303.
[4] Vol. 1, Chap. 18, p. 136.

Concluding Prayers and Ceremonies

Placeat tibi, sancta Trinitas, obsequium servitutis meae: et praesta; ut sacrificium, quod oculis tuae majestatis indignus obtuli, tibi sit acceptabile, mihique, et omnibus pro quibus illud obtuli, sit, te miserante, propitiabile. Per Christum Dominum nostrum. Amen.

May the tribute of my humble ministry be pleasing to thee, Holy Trinity. Grant that the sacrifice which I, unworthy as I am, have offered in the presence of thy majesty, may be acceptable to thee. Through thy mercy may it bring forgiveness to me and to all for whom I have offered it: through Christ our Lord. Amen.

Placeat dates back to the ninth century (being found, e.g., in the Amiens Sacramentary) and was formerly held to be a private prayer unconnected with the liturgy of the Mass. It used to be headed *Oratio post Missam* and was commonly said after the blessing (until *Ordo XIV*, fourteenth century).

After saying *Placeat*, the priest kisses the altar, looks up to the cross, turns to the faithful and blesses them saying:

Benedicat vos omnipotens Deus, Pater, et Filiaus, et. Spiritus Sanctus.
℟. *Amen.*

Almighty God bless you: the Father, the Son, and the Holy Ghost.
℟. Amen.

The beginnings of our present rite are to be found in *Ordo I*. Immediately after the deacon had dismissed the people, the procession reformed to lead the pontiff back to the *secretarium*, headed by the seven acolytes with candles and a subdeacon with a censer. As the pope passed the *presbyterium*, the bishops asked a blessing, *Jube, Domne, benedicere;* the pope blessed them, saying, *Benedicat vos Dominus,* and they replied *Amen.* The priests then asked and were granted a blessing in similar terms, and as he made his way to the sacristy the pope blessed the monks, *schola*, military standard-bearers, acolytes, district crucifers, the *mansionarii* and the faithful.

To a large degree, the ceremony of blessing at the end of Mass originated in and was spread by erroneous interpretation of the Councils of Agde (506) and Orleans (511) in Gaul, which decreed that the people were not to leave until after the blessing of the *sacerdos:* these are Gallican decrees and must be interpreted in connection with the Gallican rite; they relate not to a final blessing, but to the characteristic Gallican *Benedictiones episcopales* after the *Libera* (see chapter 22). When, in the later Middle Ages, these decrees were incorporated into collections of canon law, *sacerdos* had lost the meaning "bishop", and they came to be interpreted as referring to a general blessing given by the priest at the end of Mass. Bernold of Constance mentions that it was so usual that priests could only omit it at the risk of scandal.

At pontifical Mass, the bishop intones the blessing preceded by two versicles, *Sit nomen Domini* and *Adjutorium*, and makes the sign of the cross in blessing in three (sometimes four) directions.

THE LAST GOSPEL

After the blessing, the priest moves to the Gospel side and says:

| ℣. *Dominus vobiscum* | ℣. The Lord be with you |
| ℟. *Et cum spiritu tuo* | ℟. And with you. |

Then he makes the sign of the cross first upon the altar or the book and then upon his forehead, lips, and breast, saying:

| *Initium sancti Evangelii secundum Joannem.* | The beginning of the holy Gospel according to John. |
| ℟. *Gloria tibi, Domine.* | ℟. Glory to thee, Lord. |

Then he reads the beginning of the Gospel according to St John: John 1. 1–14, at the end of which the response *Deo gratias* is made.

In the Middle Ages, the beginning of St John's Gospel was held in such veneration that it was read as a sacramental at many ceremonies, e.g. over the newly-baptized and newly-married, etc., as a protection against the snares of the devil. It seems probable that its incorporation into the end of Mass should be considered as a final act of faith and thanksgiving to the incarnate Word. Durandus is the earliest witness that this Gospel was sometimes read at the end of Mass and in the fifteenth century it was included in several Missals, though many priests said it after taking off the chasuble and it is unknown to *Ordo XIV*. According to the Ceremonial of Bishops (1600), the bishop is still to say it in procession to the place where he vested.[1] According to the new *Ordo*

---

[1] *Caer. Ep.* 2. 8. 80.

for Holy Week (1956) the last Gospel is omitted on Palm Sunday and at all the solemn functions of Holy Week.

THE PRAYERS AFTER MASS

Before 1859, Pius IX had decreed that special prayers should be said in the Papal States after low Mass during Lent. These included three *Aves*, the anthem *Salve Regina* and four prayers: one from a votive Mass of our Lady, a prayer for the remission of sins, the collect from the Mass for Peace and a prayer for enemies. In his encyclical *Cum sancta Mater Ecclesia* (27 April 1859) on the outbreak of war between Austria and Sardinia, Pius IX recalled the attention of the faithful to these prayers for peace and asked that prayers for this intention should be ordered elsewhere.

Twenty-five years later, Leo XIII in a decree dated 6 January 1884, ordered that after private Masses, the priest, kneeling before the altar, should say three *Aves*, the *Salve Regina* with a versicle and the prayer *Deus refugium* for the needs of the Church. According to a decree of the Sacred Congregation of Rites (20 August 1884), these prayers must be said kneeling and alternately with the faithful.

On 20 April 1884, Leo XIII published his encyclical *Humanum genus* against freemasonry, in which he named our Lady, St Joseph, St Michael, St Peter and St Paul as powerful intercessors and champions of the faith in this struggle. In 1886, *Deus refugium* was changed to include references to our Lady, SS. Joseph, Peter and Paul and another prayer—that to St Michael—was added.

In his consistorial allocution on 30 June 1930, Pius XI commanded that these prayers should henceforward be said for Russia.

THE THANKSGIVING: *TRIUM PUERORUM*

While returning to the sacristy, the priest says the antiphon *Trium Puerorum* and the *Benedicite*,[1] which was said by the three young Hebrews who were thrown into a furnace by King Nabuchodonosor. In her thanksgiving, the Church calls upon all creation to bless the Lord; in turn she addresses herself (a) to the supra-terrestrial creation: the angels and those created things above the earth (vv. 1–8); (b) to the earth itself and all that is in it (vv.

[1] *Rit. serv. in celebr. Miss.*, 12, 6.

9-13); (c) to Israel, the chosen people of God (vv. 14-17). To these, the fourth-century Church added a doxology, blessing the Holy Trinity. Then follows Psalm 150, in which the word *Laudate* occurs eleven times. The priest then says the *Kyrie* and a series of versicles and responses concluded by three collects. The last of these (*Da nobis, quaesumus*) is the most recent (fourteenth-fifteenth century): it commemorates the patron of the palatine chapel (St Lawrence) in which, before their departure to Avignon, the popes used to celebrate Mass.[1]

PRIVATE THANKSGIVING: AN ADDITIONAL NOTE

The highest significance of communion does not lie in our Lord's " visit " to the soul so much as in the sacramental efficacy by which it infuses divine life, and quickens supernatural charity. This is why Christians apply themselves diligently to sustaining interior recollection by excluding all earthly preoccupations from their hearts and minds and to adhering as closely as possible to the eucharistic Christ, dwelling in him in silence and adoration, in order to receive of his fullness. The more the soul acknowledges its thirst, the more abundantly that thirst will be assuaged, and this is the purpose of prayers which the Church suggests to us after communion; they include St Thomas's prayer *Gratias tibi ago* and St Bonaventure's *Transfige*. Meditation on the Lord's Prayer (included among the official prayers of thanksgiving) is also very suitable. Through these and similar prayers the Church seeks to intensify the ardour of our charity, increasing our souls' capacity to receive what God so abundantly offers. In his encyclical on the liturgy, *Mediator Dei*, His Holiness Pope Pius XII wrote:

" Far from discouraging the interior sentiments of individual Christians, the liturgy fosters and stimulates them in order to increase their likeness to Christ and through him to guide them to the heavenly Father. And this is why it requires those who have communicated at the altar to render due thanks to God. . . . Indeed, these acts of private devotion are quite necessary, if we are to receive in abundance the supernatural treasures in which the Eucharist is so rich, and to pour them out upon others according to our powers, in order that Christ our Lord may reach the fullness of his power in the souls of all. . . . Certainly the author of that

[1] The text of all these prayers of thanksgiving is to be found in the Missal.

golden book, *The Imitation of Christ*, is in tune with the precepts and the spirit of the liturgy when he urges those who have received Holy Communion: 'Remain in secret and enjoy thy God; thou possessest him whom the whole world cannot take away from thee.' Through the sacrament of the Eucharist Christ is in us and we abide in Christ; and as Christ, abiding in us, lives and works, so we too, abiding in Christ, must live and work through him." [1]

[1] Trans. Canon G. D. Smith, sect. 132–6, *passim*.

INDEX

Aaron, II: 10
Ablutions, II: 104-5, 282-3
Abraham, II: 11-12, 235-6
Absolution, I: 122
Acolyte, I: 24, 56, 100; II: 41-2, 52, 123; censing by, II: 116; in preparation for Mass, II: 76; *Sanctus*, II: 181; training of, II: 54-5
Ad catholici sacerdotii fastigium, II: 38
Adam of St Victor, I: 210
Adoration, I: 169
Adrian I, Pope (772-95), I: 107
Advent, I: 105, 198; II: 81; collects, I: 185; Gospels, I: 233; introit (1st Sun.), I: 99; II: 68; preface, II: 170
Agape, II: 137n, 138
Agatha, St, II: 245, 247
Agnes, St, II: 245
Agnus Dei, I: 183; II: 264
Ahib, II: 1
Alae, I: 71
Alb, I: 63
Albert the Great, St (d. 1280); Christ's communion, II: 273; elevation, II: 222; offerings, II: 69
Alcuin (d. 804); *Comes*, I: 108, 128, 150, 196, 200; II: 88, 201
Alexander, St, II: 245
All Saints; *Alleluia*, II: 208
Alleluia, I: 82, 206-8
Aloysius Gonzaga, St (1568-91); collect of Feast, I: 154
Alphabetum sacerdotum (1495), I: 116n, 123
Alphonsus Liguori, St (1696-1787), II: 68, 127
Altar; asylum, I: 37; candles, I: 56; cards, I: 14; consecration of, I: 4, 16; construction, I: 7; crosses, I: 27, 35, 39; crucifix, I: 43-6; front, I: 28; kinds, I: 7, 9, 41; lighting, I: 5; mensa, I: 8; ornaments, I: 43; parchment, I: 25; position, I: 5, 11-14; relics, 1: 9, 23-5; sepulchre, I: 9; sprinkling of, I: 21; stripping, I: 44
Amalarius (d. 850); bread, II: 84; canon, II: 185; concluding prayer, II: 295; Gregorian chant, I: 108; secret, II: 127
Ambo, : 191-3; Gospel, I: 216-17; requiem, I: 224
Ambrose, St (c. 340-397); altar, I: 34, 37; antiphonal singing, I: 103; basilica (Milan), I: 6, 36; chrism, II: 45; creed,

I: 241; Doctor, I: 248; Gospel-book, I: 231; Lord's Prayer, II: 253-6; *paenula*, I: 65; prayer of, I: 49, 51; priest at Mass, II: 22; canon, II: 190-1; Theodosius, II: 52, 56
Ambrosian Missal, I: 49; II: 12; lessons, I: 189; *Sanctus*, II: 178
Amen, I: 161-2; II: 250
Amice, 1: 61-3
Amiens Sacramentary, I: 124
Amula, II: 75
Anamnesis, *see* Commemoration
Anastasia, St, II: 245
Andrew, St, II: 258; Feast, II: 49
Angels, orders of, II: 172-3
Anglo-Saxon Pontifical, I: 20
Angoulême Sacramentary, I: 149; signs of the cross, II: 233
Annunciation, Feast of the, I: 166-7; II: 82, 103, 285
Antependium, I: 11, 40
Antiphon, I: 101-8; II: 81
Antiphonarium Gregorianum, II: 81
Antiphonary, I: 25; II: 91, 103, 107
Anti-semitism, II: 236
Antony of Padua, St (1195-1231), II: 126
Apostolic Constitutions, II: 134n; antiquity, II: 134; bread, II: 67; deacon, I: 215; II: 100; *Gloria*, I: 135, 137; kiss of peace, II: 78; offerer, II: 45; *Offerimus*, II: 232; *Sanctus*, II: 179; thanksgiving, II: 139, 158-160
Archdeacon, I: 88; II: 101
Archisynagogus, I: 79
Arianism, I: 141-2, 181-2, 184, 242-6
Armenians, II: 96, 100
Ars, Curé of, II: 38
Ascension, the, I: 175; II: 207, 228, 230; antiphon, I: 104; lessons, I: 198; preface, II: 168, 170
Ash Wednesday, II: 62
Asperges, I: 96-8; II: 62
Assumption, I: 106; vigil, I: 186
Asylum, right of, I: 37
Athanasius, St, I: 136; II: 153
Athos, Mt., II: 154
Atrium, I: 71-2, 100
Augustine, St (354-430), I: 106, 155, 159, 204; II: 56, 60, 166, 186; " altars ", I: 33; *Amen*, I: 161; *confiteor*, I: 122; creed, I: 241; Doctor, I: 248; hymns,

302

II: 80; immolation, II: 26; *jubilus*, I: 207; Lord's Prayer, II: 251-4; mystical body, II: 66-7; *sacerdotes*, II: 44
Augustine of Canterbury, St (d. 605), I: 107
Aurelian (d. 585), I: 136

Baldaquin; notable examples, I: 6-7
Baptism, I: 111-12, 162; character of, II: 42, 62
Baptistery, I: 15
Barnabas, St, II: 244; Epistle of, II: 136
Basil the Great, St (329-79), I: 103; *Gloria*, I: 136; Last Supper, II: 96
Bede the Venerable, St (673-735), II: 85
Bells, I: 52-5; hallowing, I: 52-3; named, I: 53; use of, I: 54; sanctuary, II: 223; Sanctus, II: 181; tower, II: 223, 278
Benedict, St (c. 480-547), I: 13, 39, 52, 121; scapular, I: 62; Lauds and Vespers, I: 129; Lord's Prayer, II: 256
Benedict VIII, Pope (1012-24), I: 246-7
Benedict IX, Pope (1032-45, *res.*), I: 79
Benedict XIII, Pope (1724-30), I: 211
Benedict XIV, Pope (1740-58), I: 35, 43, 194; *De sacrosancto Sacrificio Missae*, II: 229
Benedict XV, Pope (1914-22); Missal, I: 194; prefaces, II: 170
Benedictines, I: 115-16
Benedictus, I: 38
Berengarius of Tours (d. 1088), II: 220
Bernard of Constance (d. 1100), II: 267
Bernardinus a Piconio; *Epistolarum Sancti Pauli*, I: 49
Berno, Abbot of Reichenau (d. 1048), I: 247
Biretta, I: 67
Bishops; ablutions, I: 282; altar, I: 41; blessing of bells, I: 52-4; *cappa magna*, I: 116; communion, II: 278; consecration of altar, I: 19-30; crozier, I: 223; final blessing, II: 298; Gospel, I: 223; intercession for, II: 202; pontifical Mass, II: 259, 262; position at Mass, I: 69
Blaise, St (c. 316), II: 247
Blessing; bells, I: 52-4; candles, I: 57; episcopal, II: 259; fruits of the earth, II: 247; final (Mass), II: 296-8; font, I: 95; II: 175; Jewish Pasch, II: 137
Bonaventure, St (1221-74), II: 273; *Stabat Mater*, I: 211; *Transfige*, II: 300
Boniface II, Pope (530-32), I: 107
Bread; blessed, I: 75n; eucharistic, I: 74-7; II: 78, 84-6; offering of, II: 92-5; *panis supersubstantialis*, II: 255
Breviarium ecclesiastici ordinis, II: 93
Breviary, I: 34, 106
Bridget, St (1304-73), II: 79
Burchard, John, of Strasbourg; *Ordo servandus*, I: 47; II: 101, 221

Caesarius, St, of Arles (d. 543), I: 129, 136
Calix benedictionis, II: 6; *major*, II: 75
Callistus, St, Pope (m. c. 222), II: 148
Cambrai Pontifical, I: 24
Cambrai, Synod of (1374), II: 86
Candles, I: 56-60; blessing of, I: 184, 217; Mass, II: 181; number, I: 58; Paschal, I: 216-17
Candlesticks, I: 43; Paschal, notable examples, I: 217
Canon of the Mass, II: 184-96
Canon; (801), II: 23; (810), I: 48; (813), II: 41; (816), II: 85; (1169), I: 52; (1197), I: 7; (1198), I: 7, 8, 9; (1201), I: 29; (1268), I: 14; (1269), I: 13, 14; (1296), II: 90; (1305), II: 87
Canones Hippolyti, I: 180
Canonization, II: 79
Cantors, I: 25
Cardinals, titles of, I: 10
Carissime (lessons), I: 197
Carmelite *Ordinale*, I: 210; II: 198
Carthusians, I: 116, 160; II: 96, 198, 236, 268
Cassian (d. 435), I: 62, 119
Catafalque, position of, II: 53
Cataracta, I: 10
Catechumens, Mass of, I: 69 and *passim*
Cathedra, I: 69; II: 75
Cathedral, Dedication of, I: 42
Cecily, St (3rd cent.), II: 245
Celestine, St, Pope (422-32), I: 61, 103-5
Celtic liturgy, I: 141
Cement, blessing of, I: 21, 24
Censer, I: 100, 221
Censing, I: 16-18, 125; Gospel, I: 229; host, II: 223
Ceremonial of Bishops, II: 77, 105, 224
Chalice, II: 88-90; institution of Eucharist, II: 6; offering of, II: 100-1; veil, II: 77; *see* Calix
Charlemagne (742-814), I: 16, 89, 107, 149, 246; II: 164
Charles the Bald, Emperor (875-7); *Horae*, I: 124
Charles IV, Emperor (1316-78), I: 216
Charles V, Emperor (1500-58), I: 216
Charoseth, II: 5
Chasuble, I: 65; lifting of, II: 223

Chrism; consecration of altar, I: 26–33, 42; of Christ, I: 164
Christ; Anointed One, I: 31; body and blood of, II: 18; communion, II: 273; High Priest, I: 1, 164–87; II: 10–12; mystical body, I: 32; perfect sacrifice, II: 12–14; representation, I: 45; sole mediator, II: 30, 108; synagogue, I: 80–1; *see* Last Supper
Christ the King, Feast of, II: 82; preface, II: 168–72
Christmas, Masses of, I: 167; *communicantes*, II: 207; preface, II: 168, 170, 172; secret, II: 125
Chrysogonus, St, II: 211
Ciborium, *see* Baldaquin
Cippi, I: 11
Circumcision, I: 208
Cistercians, II: 268
Clavi, I: 63
Clement, St, Pope (d. *c.* 99), II: 210; great prayer, I: 178; II: 132, 142–5; letter to Corinthians, II: 139, 179
Clement of Alexandria (*c.* 150–215), I: 61, 232
Clement V, Pope (1305–14); Avignon, I: 90
Clement VIII, Pope (1592–1605), I: 105
Cletus, St, Pope (d. *c.* 91), II: 210
Clovis (*c.* 465–511), I: 201
Codex Alexandrinus, I: 136, 141
Collect, I: 144–63, 185–7; characteristics, I: 153–5; *clausula*, I: 157, 183; *cursus*, I: 156–7; " solemn ", II: 74
Comes, *see* Alcuin, Murbach, Wurzburg
Commemoration, II: 225–33
Commixture, II: 261–5
Communicantes, II: 206
Communion, I: 76–7; II: 271–83; chant, 280–1; rail, I: 3
Confession, I: 73; confessional, I: 15, 115
Confiteor, I: 116, 119–22; II: 278
Conrad II, Emperor (1024–39), I: 210
Consecration; bishops, II: 78; church, I: 4; cross, I: 8; Eucharist, II: 18–19, 216–20
Consignatio, II: 263
Constantine, Emperor (306–37), I: 12, 41, 45–6, 102, 221; basilicas, I: 85, 146; peace of, I: 160; II: 199; St Peter's, II: 209
Constitutiones Apostolorum, I: 180
Contrition, I: 76, 125
Cornelius, St, Pope (251–3), I: 84; II: 210
Coronation of kings, II: 79
Corporal, II: 72–3
Corpus Christi, II: 8, 90, 103; creed, I: 247; *Lauda Sion*, I: 211; secret, II: 200; thanksgiving, 152

Cosmas and Damian, SS., II: 212
Councils; Augsburg (1548), II: 222; Carthage (397, 407, 418), I: 155, 179; II: 58, 96, 161; Chalcedon (451), I: 242–3; Cologne (1536), II: 86, 222; Constance (1414), I: 216; Constantinople (381), I: 242; Ephesus (431), I: 219, 242; Florence (1438), I: 219; II: 36, 85, 96, 239, 286; Frankfurt (794), I: 246; Hippo (393), I: 179; II: 58; Laodicea (4th cent.), I: 65; Lateran (1059), I: 219; London (1268), II: 59; Mâcon, II: 58; Milevium (412), II: 161; Nicaea (325), II: 58; Orange (441), I: 215; Rheims (1583), II: 222; Trent (1545), I: 2, 19, 153, 171; II: 9, 21–2, 29, 32, 35, 39, 46, 63, 65, 67, 94, 96, 107, 195, 200, 226, 239, 269, 289; Trullo (691), II: 100; Vatican (1869), I: 219
Covenant, new, I: 19–20
Credo, I: 69, 73
Creed, Apostles', I: 241–2; Athanasian, I: 242; Nicene, I: 59, 242; when sung, I: 247
Cross; altar, I: 43, 46; processional, I: 46, 89; sign of, I: 20, 109, 227–9; II: 233, 249
Crozier, I: 223
Crucifix; origin, I: 46
Cushions (Missal), I: 194
Cyprian, St (*c.* 210–58), I: 85, 156, 215; II: 96, 100, 207; account of, II: 210; anointing, II: 45; canon, II: 186; *illibata*, II: 199; preface, II: 163–5; *symbolum*, I: 241; *turificati*, II: 115
Cyril of Alexandria, St (*c.* 376–444), I: 219
Cyril of Jerusalem, St. (*c.* 315–87); bread of Eucharist, II: 45; " concorporeal ", II: 289; Lord's Prayer, II: 253–5

Damasus, St, Pope (366–84), I: 207; II: 190, 201
Daniel; angelic hosts, II: 177
Deacon; catechumens, I: 73; dismissal, II: 295–6; *Flectamus*, I: 147, 163; Gospel, I: 215, 218–32; *Libera nos*, II: 257; *Memento*, II: 205, 214; offertory, II: 92–9; preparation, II: 72–7; relics, I: 25; *Sanctus*, II: 180; stational Masses, I: 100–2; *super populum*, I: 293
Dead, Masses of, II: 77, 81, 98, 296; *communio*, II: 280–1; gradual, 206; *Judica*, I: 119; preface, II: 170, 172
Dedication (churches), I: 4; Mass, I: 29
Deprecatio, II: 74
Der Balyzeh fragments, II: 151–3

De Sacramentis, II: 216-17, 228, 234-7
De Virginitate, I: 136
Didache; Lord's Prayer, II: 142, 252; *super populum*, II: 293; thanksgivings, I: 178; II: 132, 138-142, 158, 161; unity, II: 200
Didascalia, II: 158
Dies irae, I: 211
Divini cultus, I: 107
Doctors of the Church, I: 248
Dominic, St (1170-1221), I: 121
Dominicans, I: 116, 160, 219, 222; II: 198, 236, 268
Domine, non sum dignus, II: 270, 278
Dominus vobiscum, I: 38, 144; II: 69, 73-4
Donatists, II: 199
Door-keeper, II: 52
Doxology, II: 247-8; see *Gloria in Excelsis*
Drogo of Metz (826-55); sacramentary, I: 36
Dunstan, St (d. 988); Pontifical, I: 24, 36
Durandus of Mende (d. 1296), I: 35, 38; II: 101, 128, 241; Pontifical, I: 16, 19; II: 63

Easter; *Alleluia*, I: 208; collects, I: 154, 158; *Gloria*, I: 136, 139; gradual, I: 206; lessons, I: 198; offertory, II: 81-2; preface, II: 8, 171-2; secret, I: 44
Eastern liturgies, I: 15
Eastward position, I: 145-6
Ecclesiastical Ordinances, I: 179
Egbert of York, St (d. 729); Pontificals, I: 36
Elevation, The, II: 220-3; lesser, II: 249, 260
Ember lessons, I: 197
Epiclesis, II: 238-41
Epiphany; collect, I: 157; *communicantes*, II: 207; introit, I: 103; lessons, I: 198; offertory chant, II: 82; preface, II: 168, 170, 172; secret, II: 40, 125
Epiphanius, St (d. 403), I: 242-3; II: 60
Eucharist, Holy; institution, II: 5; reasons for, II: 14; parallel accounts, II: 16-17
Euchologia of Serapion, I: 181
Eugene (Eugenius) IV, Pope (1431-47), II: 79
Eusebius (d. 340), I: 32, 214
Eutyches (5th cent.), I: 242
Exsultet, II: 7
Eyes, raising of, II: 93-4

Faithful, Mass of, I: 69, 74
Faldstool, I: 109, 115
Fan, II: 182
Felicity and Perpetua, SS. (3rd cent.), II: 245
Felix II, St, Pope (483-92), I: 131
Fenestella, I: 10
Fire, symbolism of, I: 59
Fish, eucharistic, I: 40
Five Wounds, I: 35, 39; Mass, I: 44
Flabellum, II: 182
Flectamus genua!, I: 147, 163
Flacius Illyricus (9th cent.), Missal of, II: 84, 101, 106
Font, blessing of, I: 95; II: 175
Footpace, I: 7
Fraction, II: 76, 261-5
Francis of Assisi, St (1181-1226), I: 121
Francis Caracciolo, St (1563-1608), II: 127
Fratres (lessons), I: 197
Frontal, I: 11
Fulda Sacramentary, I: 149

Gabriel of the Sorrowing Virgin, St (1828-62), II: 127
Gall, Sacramentary of St (780-810), I: 149
Galla Placidia, Empress (d. 450), II: 209
Gelasian Sacramentary (c. 700), I: 50, 130, 155; II: 41, 191; blessing of corporal, II: 73; blessing of font, I: 95; canon, II: 199-201; collects, I: 185; *communicantes*, II: 207; consecration, II: 216-17; consecration of altar, I: 20-30; consecration of chalice and paten, II: 88; history of, I: 149; secret, II: 125-6; preface, II: 128, 164, 168-9; *supplices*, II: 240; Lord's Prayer, II: 252, 258; *super populum*, II: 293
Gelasius I, St, Pope (d. 496), I: 107; II: 74, 199, 236; collects, I: 148; *Kyrie*, I: 128, 131-2
Gellonian Sacramentary (770-80), I: 149
Gerbert's Sacramentary, I: 51
Gertrude, St (d. 1302), II: 221
Girdle, I: 64
Gloria in Excelsis, I: 133-43, 144, 169, 250
Gloria Patri, I: 90, 102-4, 115, 125; II: 81
Good Friday, I: 189; II: 7, 200, 269; *Confitemini Domino*, I: 209; *Flectamus*, I: 147-8; Solemn Prayers, I: 130-1
Gospel at Mass, II: 214-32; proper of the season, II: 233-8
Gospel Book, I: 43, 100, 218-19
Glossolalia, I: 133

Index

Gradual, I: 82, 204–6
Graduale Romanum, I: 106, 205, 207, 209, 210
Gratiarum actio, I: 152
Great Scrutiny, I: 241, 245
Greek in Early Church, II: 189
Greek usages, I: 127–9, 148, 218, 222
Gregorian Chant, I: 106–8
Gregorian Sacramentary (8th cent.); Annunciation, II: 103; *Gloria*, I: 137; Lord's Prayer, II: 258; origin, I: 149; prayers to Christ, I: 185; preface, II: 164, 168–9; secret, II: 125; *super populum*, II: 293
Gregorian water, I: 17, 20, 24, 25
Gregory the Great, St (d. 604), I: 94, 103, 150, 201, 207; II: 84, 184, 201, 217; Doctor, I: 248; *Gaudeamus omnes*, I: 105; *Gloria*, I: 137; gradual, I: 205; Lord's Prayer, II: 186, 253; prayer for peace, II: 213; Roman Sacramentary, I: 129
Gregory II, St, Pope (715–31), I: 86
Gregory of Tours, St (d. 594), I: 231; II: 201

Hadrian I, Pope (772–95), I: 149; II: 88, 164
Hagadah, II: 5
Hagios o Theos, I: 182
Halinard of Lyons (d. 1052), I: 49
Hanc igitur, II: 40–1, 58, 212–14
Hallel, II: 4–6, 134
Hands (ritual attitudes), I: 159
Hats in church, I: 223
Helena, St (c. 250–330), I: 45
Henry II, St, Emperor (1002–24), I: 36, 246–7
Henry of Hesse (d. 1397), II: 222
Hilary, St (c. 367), II: 289
Hincmar of Rheims (d. 882), I: 97
Hippolytus, St (d. c. 235), II: 40, 178; doxology, II: 248; preface, II: 166; thanksgiving, II: 161; *see Traditio Apostolica*
Holy Cross, Feast of; preface, II: 171
Holy Ghost, I: 50
Holy Innocents, Feast of; gradual, I: 206; II: 49
Holy of Holies, I: 124; of the Mass, II: 198
Holy Thursday, *see* Maundy Thursday
Holy Saturday, I: 54, 60, 119, 148; II: 58
Holy Trinity; preface, II: 168
Holy Water, I: 95, 98
Holy Week; new *Ordo*, II: 256–8, 278, 280, 296, 299

Honorius of Autun (12th cent.), I: 33, 230–1; oblation, II: 61
Hosanna, II: 177
Hostia, II: 84
House-churches, I: 70–3
Humeral veil, II: 47

Ignatius of Antioch, St (d. c. 107), II: 96, 244
Ildephonsus of Toledo, St (d. 667), II: 45
Immolation, II: 4, 25–6
Impluvium, I: 71
Incarnation, The, II: 231, 285
Incense, I: 25; Gospel, I: 218–22; Jewish and Roman use, II: 114–5; offertory, II: 116–20; symbolism, II: 120–2
Indulgentiam, I: 122
Infula, I: 67
Innocent I, Pope (d. 417), II: 78, 195, 197, 213
Innocent II, Pope (1198–1216), I: 110, 229; II: 249; *Judica me*, I: 119; *hostia*, II: 84; offerers, II: 58–9
Interpolation, I: 27
Introit, I: 99–102; chant, I: 102–6
Invocation, II: 102–4
Irenaeus of Lyons, St (c. 125–202), II: 96
Isidore of Pelusium, St (d. c. 450), I: 232
Isidore of Seville, St (d. 636), II: 45, 51; *De Missa*, II: 227
Ite, missa est, II: 295–6

James, St; "light", I: 59; Feast, II: 49
Jean, Abbot of Fécamps (d. 1078), I: 51; II: 103
Jerome, St (d. 420), I: 156, 232; *Alleluia*, I: 207; *Amen*, I: 161; baptism, I: 44; deacon, I: 215; Doctor, I: 248; Lord's Prayer, II: 252; "Pope", II: 201; Psalms, I: 105; vestments, I: 61
Jews; diaspora, I: liturgy, I: 78; Pasch, II: 1–9; Pasch and Mass, II: 134–9
John, St; altar, I: 35; angels, II: 237; Ascension, II: 229; candlesticks, I: 56; Christ and the Father, I: 170–1; Christ on the Cross, I: 173; II: 7; Christ our Advocate, I: 175; grace, I: 143; incense, II: 121; incorporation into Christ, II: 285, 287; *In principio*, II: 298; light, I: 59; Pilate, II: 13; prayer, I: 177; redemption, II: 268; sons of God, II: 113
John I, St, Pope (523–6), I: 107
John XXIII, Pope (1410–15, *deposed*), I: 216
John and Paul, SS., II: 211

Index

John Chrysostom, St (c. 344–407), I: 37, 45, 223, 232
John of Avranche (d. 1079); *hostia*, II: 84
John the Archcantor (7th cent.), II: 194, 240
John the Baptist, St, I: 121, 133, 186; II: 108, 125, 170, 243
Joseph, St, II: 127, 168, 170
Jube, domne, I: 192, 220
Jubilus, I: 207
Judas, II: 6, 15, 18
Julian (Julius) II, Pope (1503–13), II: 209
Julian the Apostate (c. 331–63), II: 211
Justin, St (d. c. 167); *Apology*, I: 131, 188, 215; II: 56, 95, 142, 146–8, 161, 166
Justinian, Emperor (c. 482–565), II: 195, 200, 293

Kiddush, II: 4
Kiss; altar, I: 37–8, 125; Gospels, I: 230; offering dish, II: 78; peace, I: 109; II: 266–7, 280
Kyriake, I: 70
Kyrie, I: 49–50, 90, 125, 126–32, 182, 250; II: 74

Laetare, I: 238
Laity, II: 52
Lauds, I: 47, 129
Langton, Stephen (c. 1150–1228); *Veni, Sancte Spiritus*, I: 210
Last Supper, The, I: 2, 44, 70, 171, 173–4; II: 84, 273; liturgy of, II: 9–20; parallel accounts, II: 16–17
Lateran Basilica, I: 41, 85, 90, 100; II: 108, 209
Lauda Sion, I: 211
Law and Prophets, I: 80
Lawrence, St (d. 258), II: 211
Lectern, I: 193
Lectionary, I: 83, 91; Epistles, I: 198–200; Gospels, I: 233–7; principal, I: 196
Lector, I: 190, 215, 226; II: 51–2
Lectorium, I: 193
Lent; *Antiphonae ad Communionem*, II: 281; cycle, I: 91; Ember Saturday, II: 125; 5th week, II: 95; 1st Sun., I: 41; II: 284; 4th week, I: 241; preface, I: 168; 2nd Sun., I: 209; sequences, I: 210; 3rd Sun., II: 284; Thursday Gospels, I: 233
Leo the Great, St, Pope (440–61), I: 92, 107, 156, 204–5, 215; II: 45, 207, 209, 235
Leo III, St, Pope (795–816), I: 246

Leo IV, St, Pope (847–55), I: 219
Leo VII, St, Pope (936–39), I: 144
Leo XII, Pope (1878–1903), I: 67, 113; *Mirae Caritatis*, II: 291; prayers after Mass, II: 299
Leonine Sacramentary (6th cent.), I: 124, 148–9; collects, I: 155–7; offertory, II: 99; preface, II: 164, 168, 169; secret, II: 126; *super populum*, II: 293
Lessons, I: 188–203, 214–38; St John and St Paul, I: 238
Levate!, I: 147
Liber Pontificalis, I: 35, 64; II: 87, 210, 213, 235
Liber Sacramentorum, I: 149
Libera nos, II: 257–8
Light, I: 59
Linea, I: 63
Linus, St, Pope (d. c. 79), II: 210
Litanies, I: 17, 90, 126–30
Liturgy, I: 42; purpose of, I: 112; rhythmic prose of, I: 155
Lord's Prayer, I: 49–50, 169–71; II: 251–7; commentary on, II: 254–7
Louis XIV (1638–1715), I: 223, 231
Louvain papyrus, II: 160
Lucian of Antioch, St (d. 312), I: 33
Lucy, St (d. 304), II: 245
Luke, St; chalice, II: 13; future blessing, II: 291; Christ and the Father, I: 170; Christ's last words, I: 173; Gospel lessons, I: 238; Last Supper, II: 16–17; new covenant, II: 19–20; Pentecost, I: 59
Lustration, I: 16, 20–2
Luther; Christ's communion, II: 273

Magnificat, I: 38
Malachias, II: 49
Maniple, I: 64
Mappula, I: 64
Marcellinus and Peter, SS. (d. 304), II: 245
Mark, St; Gospel, I: 189, 238; Last Supper, II: 6, 16–17; new covenant, II: 19–20
Martyrs' tombs, I: 10–11, 33; *titulus*, I: 10
Mary, The Blessed Virgin, II: 107; Annunciation, I: 31, 166–7; candles (bees), I: 57; Seven Sorrows, I: 206; II: 127; *Stabat Mater*, I: 211
Mary of Jesus, Mother (d. 1884), II: 49
Mass; Catechumens, I: 78 to end; Faithful, I: 74–6, and II; High and Low, II: 41
Matins, I: 19, 47

308   Index

Matthew, St; baptism, I: 241; future blessing, II: 291; Gethsemani, I: 172; gift and altar, II: 237; good works, II: 255; Gospel lessons, I: 238; Last Supper, II: 6, 16-17, 286; law and prophets, II: 131; Lord's Prayer, I: 170; II: 251; new covenant, II: 19-20
Matthias, St, II: 244
Maundy Thursday, I: 38, 44; II: 18, 90, 178, 207, 213, 280; bells, I: 54; holy oils, II: 45, 247; introit, II: 102; Last Supper, I: 171; II: 84; Stational Mass, I: 41
Maximus of Ravenna (6th cent.), I: 65
Maximus of Turin, St (d. *c.* 467), II: 45
Mediator Dei, I: 107, 122; II: 23, 30, 59, 64, 71, 300
Meditation, I: 48, 203
Melchisedech, II: 9-11; 189, 235
Memento, II: 204
Memento etiam, II: 241-2
Men and women in church, I: 226-7
Mensa; consecration of, I: 17, 18, 20-1, 26
Menti nostrae, II: 38n
Mercier, Cardinal (1851-1926), II: 98
Michael, St, I: 30, 120-1; II: 118, 237
Michael Cerularius (11th cent.), II: 85
Micrologus, I: 49; II: 267
Midrash, I: 80
Miltiades, Pope (310-14), I: 41
Mirae Caritatis, II: 291
Misereatur, I: 122
Miserentissimus, II: 46, 66, 68
Miserere, I: 49, 126
Missa catechumenorum, I: 71
Missal, I: 48, 91, 106; Augsburg, I: 210; Cologne, I: 210; Francorum, I: 20; II: 73, 88; Gallican, I: 154; Gothicum, II: 41; Monte Cassino, I: 196; Roman, I: 128, 200, 233-7; Stowe, I: 127
Missal stand, I: 14, 194
Monstrance, I: 43
Moses, I: 31; II: 13, 19; Pasch, II, 1-2
Mozarabic liturgy, I: 189, 246; II: 15, 103, 128, 185; commemoration, II: 226; preface, II: 164; *sanctus*, II: 178
Munda cor meum, II: 220
Murbach *Comes*, I: 196-200
Muscarium, II: 182
Mystici Corporis Christi, I: 183; II: 39, 47, 58, 66

Nativity, The, I: 149; II: 231
Nestorius (d. *c.* 451), I: 184, 242
Nicholas II, Pope (1058-61), I: 219

Nicholas V, Pope (1447-55), II: 209
Nicholas of Tolentino, St (1243-1305), II: 79
Nisan, II: 1
Nobis quoque, II: 242-6
Northward position, I: 223
Notker of St Gall (d. *c.* 912), I: 209
Noyon Pontificals, I: 36
Nuptial Mass, II: 259

Oath, I: 37, 232
Oblatio, see Offering
Offering, I: 75; II: 34, 38; the faithful, II: 56-9, 232-3; money, II: 78; prayers, II: 106-9, 123-9; priest, II: 102, 232-3; site, II: 75-6
Offertory; bread, II: 92-5; chant, II: 79-83; Gallican liturgy, II: 91-2; meaning, II: 110-13; procession, II: 74-9; wine, II: 95-101
Obsecratio, I: 153
Office, Divine, I: 15, 114
Oils, Holy; catechumens, I: 18, 27, 42; chrism, I: 18, 42; II: 45; sick, I: 53
Optatus of Milevis (4th cent.), II: 199
Opus Dei, I: 14
Orarium, I: 65
Oratio, I: 151
Orate Fratres, II: 123
Ordination, I: 41; II: 35, 47, 54, 78
Ordines Romani, I: 24, 47, 56, 89, 204
Ordo; (I), I: 109-10, 115, 125, 136, 145, 218, 224, 230-1; II: 75-6, 81, 88, 93, 95, 101, 105, 185, 249; (II), I: 125, 224, 230; II: 116, 124, 194, 249; (III), I: 115, 125; (IV), I: 125; (V), I: 125; II: 116, 279; (VI), I: 115; II: 73, 105, 117, 124, 279; (VII), II: 104; (X), II: 279; (XII), I: 222; (XIV), II: 104, 105, 107, 117, 221; (XV), II: 104; (XVI), II: 104; of Amandus, I: 221; II: 76; of Burckard, I: 121
Oremus, I: 147-8; II: 69, 73
Orientation (churches), I: 146, 226
Origen (186-253), I: 179
Orphrey, I: 68
Ostiarii, I: 73
Otto, St (d. 1139), II: 86
Our Lady of Mount Carmel, II: 49
Our Lady of the Snows, I: 30

Palm Sunday, I: 41
Paenula, I: 65
Pammachius, House of, II: 211
Pange lingua, I: 45n
Papa nostro, II: 201

Index

Papal Mass, I: 83, 100–2, 109, 115; II: 75, 249, 261–2, 275–6
Paradosia, II: 40
Paris, Stational liturgy, I: 94
Parish church, Feast of Dedication, I: 42
Parousia, II: 231
Parurae, I: 63
Pasch, Jewish, II: 1–9; and Mass, II: 134–9
Paschal candle, I: 96, 216–17; II: 7
Paschal cup, II: 4
Paschal lamb, II: 1–4; as antitype, II: 70
Paschaltide; *Alleluia*, I: 208
Passiontide, I: 45, 119, 155; secret, II: 125
Paten, II: 77–8, 86–9
Pater, see Lord's Prayer
Patina, II: 279
Patrick, St (*c.* 389–461), I: 52
Paul, St; Abraham, II; 235; *Amen*, I: 161; *Apostolus*, I: 196; " at the right hand ", I: 176; bread, II: 76; Christ, the eldest born, II: 275; Christ's servants, II: 110 commemoration, II: 226; *cum spiritu tuo*, I: 144; doxologies, I: 133; Epistles, I: 49, 188; Feast, II: 49; High Priest, I: 175; II: 230; in Rome, I: 121; II: 208; in synagogues, I: 81; kiss, I: 37; Last Supper, II: 16–17; lessons, predominance, I: 201; light, I: 59; Melchisedech, II: 235; New Adam, I: 166; new covenant, II: 19–20; *parousia*, II: 231; paschal victim, II; 65, 71; prayer, I: 177; priesthood, II: 37; redemption, II: 268; Romans, to the, II: 189; " Saints ", II: 62; temptation, II: 256; to the baptized, II: 112
Paul I, St, Pope (757–67), I: 107
Paul III, Pope (1464–71), I: 116
Paul V, Pope (1605–21), I: 13; *Ritus servandus*, I: 47, 61, 62
Pax-brede, II: 266–7
Pax Domini, II: 262–3
Pax vobis, I: 144
Pelagius II, Pope (579–90), I: 107
Penitential seasons, I: 89
Penitents, I: 73; II: 63
Pentateuch, I: 188
Pentecost, I: 139, 150, 208; after, I: 44, 105, 153, 154, 157, 158; II: 57; Gospels, I: 233; preface, II: 171; secret, II: 125
Pepin I (d. 838), I: 107
Peristylium, I: 71
Perpetua, St (d. 203), I: 135
Peter, St; holy priesthood, I: 178; immolation, II: 71; in Rome, I: 121;
II: 208–9; lessons, I: 201; royal priesthood, II: 44, 233; saints, II: 62; tomb, II: 209
Peter and Paul, SS.; Feast, I: 105; II: 49; inseparable, I: 121
Peter's St, Rome, I: 7, 35, 116; building of, II: 208–9
Peter's Chair at Rome, Feast of St, I: 186; II: 40
Peter's Chains, Feast of St, I: 30
Philip IV of Spain (1605–65), I: 231
Photius (*c.* 820–91), II: 85, 202
Pileus, I: 67
Pionius (d. 250), II: 48
Piscina, II: 282
Pius II, Pope (1458–64), I: 67
Pius V, St, Pope (1566–72), I: 248; Missal, I: 116, 158; II: 106; Psalms, I: 105; *Ritus servandus*, I: 47
Pius VII, Pope (1800–23), II: 203
Pius IX, Pope (1847–78), I: 41; II: 209, 211
Pius IX, Pope (1847–78), I: 41; II: 209, 211
Pius X, St, Pope (1903–14); elevation, II: 222; *Graduale*, I: 205–10; *mensa*, II: 289; Gregorian chant, I: 106, 108
Pius XI, Pope (1922–39); anti-semitism, II: 236; prayers after Mass, II: 299; prefaces, II: 170; *see* " Ad catholici sacerdotii fastigium ", " Divini cultus ", " Miserentissimus "
Pius XII, Pope (1939–59); *see* " Mediator Dei ", " Mystici Corporis Christi "
Placentia, Synod of (1095), II: 169
Planeta, I: 100
Pliny (the Younger, *c.* 61–113) & Letter to Trajan, I: 134, 182; II: 145–6
Pneumatomachoi, I: 245
Polycarp (d. *c.* 156), I: 33, 134, 138–9
Pontificals; *see* Anglo-Saxon, Cambrai, Dunstan (St), Durandus of Mende, Egbert of York, Noyon, Prudentius, Roman, Romano-Germanic
Pope; at Stational Churches, I: 83, 88–90, 100–2; kiss of peace, I: 115; sign of the cross, I: 110; prayers for, II: 202
Portulatio, I: 152
Postcommunion, II: 284–92
Prayers; after Mass, II: 299; at foot of altar, I: 115–25; concluding, II: 293–9; Jewish, II: 131–3; secret, I: 44; of the faithful, I: 130
Preaching, I: 203, 239–40
Precentor, I: 101–2
Prefaces, II: 128, 163–75
Premonstratensians, I: 219, 230
Presbyterium, I: 100

Priest; ablutions, II: 282; canon, II: 194; censing, II: 118–22; communion, II: 267–82; concluding prayers, II: 293–300; consecration of altar, I: 19–22; elevation, II: 220–3; fraction, II: 263; *Hanc igitur*, II: 212; *Kyrie*, I: 132; lesser elevation, II: 249, 260; lessons, I: 195, 232; *nobis quoque*, II: 243, 248; nuptial blessing, II: 259; oblation, II: 123–7; offertory, II: 91–110; ordination, I: 41; II: 35, 47, 54, 78; *Oremus*, I: 147, 159–61; peace, prayer and kiss, II: 265–6; *per sacerdotes*, II: 46–7; preface, II: 166–8; preparations for celebration, I: 47–51; II: 73–84; *Sanctus*, II: 176–81; Stational Churches, I: 100–4; vestments, I: 61–8; water, blessing of, I: 95–7
Prime, I: 48
Primus and Felicianus, SS. (d. *c.* 297), I: 23
Prince, prayers for, II: 203
Profuturus of Braga (6th cent.), I: 26
Proper of the Saints, II: 126; of the Season, I: 233–7; II: 126
Prudentius (d. 405), II: 115
Prudentius of Troyes (d. 861); Pontifical, I: 49
Psalms; basis of hymns, I: 133; *Hallel*, II: 4–6, 134; penitential, I: 17; text of, I: 105; (21), I: 38; II: 280; (22), II: 280; (25), II: 104; (28), I: 53; (33), II: 281; (37), II: 105; (42), I: 73, 115–18; (44), I: 27; (45), I: 27; (49), I: 250; 50), I: 21, 126; (62), I: 29; (67), I: 29; II: 82; (68), II: 82; (69), I: 119; (71), I: 104; II: 82, 280; (75), II: 81; (76), I: 54; (77), II: 82; (83), I: 49; (84), I: 49–50; (85), I: 49–50; (86), I: 27; (90), I: 209; (94), I: 103; (99), I: 165, 174; (103), II: 280; (115), I: 49–50; II: 269, 276; (117), I: 98, 206; (118), II: 83; (129), I: 49–50; II: 81; (135), II: 135; (145–50), I: 53; (150), II: 280, 300; (159), I: 25
Pulcheria, Empress (5th cent.), I: 36
Pyx, I: 43

Quam oblationem, II: 214–15

Ratherius of Verona (d. 974), I: 97
Readings at Mass, I: 188–203, 214–39
Relics, I: 9, 22–6
Reliquaries, I: 43
Requiem, *see* Dead, Masses of
Responsorial, I: 107

Resurrection, II: 228, 230
Responsum, I: 205
Rhabanus Maurus (d. 856), II: 85, 97
Rhipidia, II: 182
Ritus servandus, I: 47, 61, 62
Roman Pontifical, I: 16, 19, 55, 108; II: 78
Romano-Gallican *Ordines*, I: 20; II: 81
Rome; basilicas, I: 87–8; Stational Churches, I: 85–6; *see* Lateran, Peter's, St, Vatican
Rood, I: 46

Sacrament, Blessed; reservation, I: 3–4, 7
Sacramentary, I: 47, 91; history, I: 148–50; list, II: 169; *see* Amiens, Angoulème, Drogo of Metz, Fulda, Gelasian, Gellonian, Gerbert, Gregorian, Hadrian, Leonine, Roman
Sacred Heart, Feast of, I: 247; II: 82; preface, II: 168, 170, 172
Sacred Heart of Jesus, Daughters of, II: 49
Sacrifice, nature of, I: 2; perfect, II: 12–15
Sacristy, I: 56, 89
Salt, I: 96–7
Sanctoral cycle (lessons), I: 197
Sanctus, II: 176–83
Scapular, I: 62
Schola cantorum, I: 100–4; II: 76, 83; St Gregory and, I: 107
Scillitan martyrs (180), I: 135
Scyphus, II: 75, 275
Secret (prayers), I: 44; II: 40, 72, 110, 125–9
Sella gestatoria, I: 89
Senatorium, II: 75
Septuagesima, I: 198, 210
Sepulchre (relics), I: 26
Sequences, I: 209–13
Serapion, St (d. *c.* 370), II: 67, 154–8, 215, 225, 238
Servers, *see* Acolyte
Sicard of Cremona (1215), I: 34–5, 230; II: 58
Sigismund, Emperor (1368–1437), I: 216
Silvester I, St, Pope (314–35), I: 41, 64; II: 87
Simplicius, St, Pope (468–83), I: 92
Sindon, II: 75
Sixtus II, St, Pope (257–8), II: 210, 247
Sixtus IV, Pope (1471–84), I: 246
Sixtus V, Pope (1585–90), I: 90, 105, 248; II: 126
Spanish ceremonial, I: 25
Stabat Mater, I: 211

Index

Statio, I: 84
Stational Churches, I: 46, 85–8; Lent, I: 93; liturgy, I: 90, 88–94
Staves in church, I: 223
Stephen, St; gradual, I: 206; II: 244
Stephen of Beauge (d. 1136), II: 250
Steps to altar, 1: 5
Stipendium, I: 60, 79
Stole, I: 65
Strabo, Walafrid (d. 849), I: 52; oblations, II: 57
Strasburg papyrus, II: 153–4
Subdeacon; deposition of relics, I: 25; duties, II: 52; lessons, I: 191, 194–5, 221–4, 230–2; *Levate*, I: 147, 163; *Libera nos*, II: 257; mensa, I: 29; mixing, II: 95; papal Mass, I: 75; preparation for Mass, II: 75–6; *Sanctus*, II: 176, 180; Stational Churches, I: 83, 89, 100–2
Sudarium, I: 64
Supplices, I: 290; II: 236–8, 240
Supra quae, II: 234–6
Symmachus, Pope (498–514), I: 107, 136
Synagogue, I: 69, 79–80, 130, 188, 204, 250; Christ in, I: 80; St Paul in, I: 81

Tabernacles, I: 14, 43
Tablinum, I: 71
Te igitur, II: 197, 203
Temple (Jerusalem), I: 78–81; II: 3
Temporal cycle (lessons), I: 197
Tertullian (c. 155–225), I: 135, 204; attitude at prayer, I: 159; chrism, II: 45; Lord's Prayer, II: 251; statio, I: 84; vestments, I: 61
Thanksgiving, Eucharistic, I: 75; after communion, II: 284–92; after Mass, 299–300; in Mass, II: 131–61; Jewish, II: 30–1
Theodoret (d. 458), I: 33; Lord's Prayer, II: 252
Theodosius, Emperor (c. 345–95), I: 37; II: 209; St Ambrose, II: 52, 56
Theophilus of Antioch (d. 186), II: 44
Thomas Aquinas, St (c. 1226–74); *Adoro*, II: 218; altar, I: 34; Apostles, II: 209; catechumens, I: 250; Christ's communion, II: 273–4; collects, I: 150–1; Corpus Christi, II: 200; *Gratias tibi ago*, II: 300; Latin style, I: 158; *Laude Sion*, I: 211; Lord's Prayer, II: 255; mediation, I: 168–9; mystical body, II: 67; *Omnipotens*, I: 51; *O sacrum convivium*, II: 292; Passion, II: 13; prayer, II: 121; priests, II: 22, 33, 36–7, 53; sacramental teaching, II: 23–7, 40, 43–4; wine in water, II: 97; Word, the, I: 166
Thomas a Celano (1200–60), *Dies irae*, I: 211
Thurifer, I: 221
Thymiamaterium, I: 100
Tituli, I: 85–6
Tobias, hymn of, I: 29
Tract, I: 82, 209
Traditio Apostolica, II: 142, 148–51, 228, 238
Trajan, Emperor (98–117); Pliny's letter to, I: 134, 182; II: 145–6
Tribune (Gospel), I: 216
Trinitarian formula, I: 112
Trinity, the Holy, I: 14, 112–14, 165, 168, 183
Tunica, I: 63
Turibulum, II: 116

Umbraculum, I: 44
Unde et memores, II: 58, 62
Urban I, St, Pope (222–30), II: 87
Urban II, Bd, Pope (1088–99), II: 169
Urban VIII, Pope (1623–44), II: 209

Valentinian II, Emperor (375–92), II: 209
Vatican, I: 41; II: 208
Veil; chalice, II: 77; humeral, II: 77; *velum quadragesimale*, II: 63
Veni, Creator, I: 50
Veni, Sancte Spiritus, II: 210
Veni, Sanctificator, II: 103
Vere dignum, II: 173–4
Versum, I: 205
Vespers, I: 47, 129
Vestments, I: 61–8
Vexilla regis, I: 45n
Viaticum, II: 222
Victim, Paschal, II: 64–9
Victimae paschali laudes, II: 210
Vienna, stational liturgy, I: 94
Vigilius, Pope (537–55), I: 26; 186, 200, 213
Vitus, Modestus and Crescentia, SS. (300?), I: 155
Vulgate, The, I: 105, 197, 203

Wenceslas, St (d. 923), II: 85–6
William of Auxerre (c. 1150–1232), II: 221
Wine, Eucharistic, II: 86, 95–101
Wipo (11th cent.), I: 210
Word, The, I: 139–41, 165–8
Wurzburg *Comes*, I: 83, 196–200; II: 211

Zephyrinus, Pope (d. 217), II: 87, 148
Zozimus, Pope (417–18), I; 64, 207

Made in the USA
Las Vegas, NV
11 January 2023